CW01674612

ONLY TREES NEED ROOTS

ONLY TREES NEED ROOTS

As told by J.H.Jessen
&
Written by Jennifer M. Jessen

Eloquent Books
New York, New York

© 2009 by J.H. Jessen & Jennifer M. Jessen
All rights reserved. First edition 2009.

No part of this book may be reproduced or transmitted in any form or by any means, graphic, electronic, or mechanical, including photocopying, recording, taping, or by any information storage retrieval system, without the permission, in writing, from the publisher.

Eloquent Books
An imprint of Writers Literary & Publishing Services, Inc.
845 Third Avenue, 6th Floor–6016
New York, NY 10022
http://www.eloquentbooks.com

ISBN: 978-1-60860-282-7

Book Design by Julius Kiskis

Printed in the United States of America
17 16 15 14 13 12 11 10 09   1 2 3 4 5

Dedication

For our sons
John Nick and Mark
and
dedicated to Hans Michael Jebsen
without whose advice and encouragement this book would
never have been written.

"Quels livres valent la peine d'etre écrits hormis les Mémoires?"
Andre Malraux

Timeline by Date and Chapter

1995 Nick Married Silvana in London

1997 Nick Died

1999 John Married Karen in New York

2000 Sophie Born Oct. 20th

2002 Mark Married Gitte in Denmark

2002 Oliver Born Nov. 22nd.

Prologue

Nov. 24, 1931, was another beautiful morning in the British Crown Colony of Hong Kong. A gentle easterly breeze from the South China Sea swept the last few clouds from the islands of Victoria, Lantau, and the Kowloon Peninsula, herding them over the green hills of the New Territories towards the high mountains of Mainland China.

High up on the peak, Hong Kong's most prominent landmark, on the terrace of the villa Kik-Ud, stood a blond, blue-eyed man in a cotton kimono. He gazed down to the piers of Kowloon, where large, white liners were docked. In the harbour itself, freighters from all over the world were moored, British and American warships were anchored, and ferries criss-crossed the bay between Hong Kong island and Kowloon. A confusion of junks, motor boats and private yachts together with dozens of the noisy little walla-walla water taxis added colour to the scene.

Johan H. Jessen reached for his field glasses and adjusted the sights. Far in the distance a plume of smoke rose from a black-and-white China coastal freighter followed, a few seconds later by the blast of the ship's horn. It was the *Gustav Diederichsen*, one of his family's company ships, carrying almost 3,000 tons of tea, silks, hogbellies, human hair, dried eggs, and spices from the ports of Shanghai and Foochow to be transhipped from Hong Kong to the insatiable markets of Europe.

Down below in the middle of the harbour lay the *Grete Maersk* of the Danish Maersk Line for which his company acted as general agents. She was discharging electrical goods, locomotives and pharmaceuticals from Denmark and other European ports. Later in the day she would load the Chinese produce from the *Diederichsen* and take it to Europe.

Jessen turned to focus on Lei Yu Mun, the northern entrance to the harbour, where he could see a bright green freighter steaming in. She was the *Sophie Rickmers*, then the biggest ship of the Rickmers Line, arriving heavily laden with industrial goods from Europe to be discharged first in Hong Kong and then Shanghai. The *Sophie Rickmers* was one of the many ships of his father-in-law, Paul Rickmers. Earlier in the day, a pilot had reported from Shek-O the arrival of the *Peter Maersk* from San Francisco. This was starting out to be an excellent day.

The day, however, was to bring him even greater joy. His wife Etha was in the Victoria Hospital waiting to give birth to their first child. He checked his watch, then called for his Boy, Ah Chan, to prepare a white linen suit, a beige silk shirt, a blue tie, and to run his bath. "Tell Man Fat to bring the car around in half an hour. *Feidyah, feidyah,* Missy waiting!" he said, urging haste.

On the drive up to the hospital, as he sat behind Man Fat's broad back, his mind went back to his first meeting with Etha in the Cathay Hotel in Shanghai. She was travelling with her father, Paul Rickmers, on one of his ships, and Johan, stationed in Shanghai for his family's company, was summoned to show Etha the sights. From this first encounter, a brief intercontinental courtship had followed, culminating in a grand wedding in Hamburg before the two planned to set up house in Hong Kong.

The voyage out was their honeymoon, with a planned stop in Singapore at the Raffles Hotel. There the newlyweds found a telegram waiting for them. Johan's father, Heinrich Jessen, the co-founder of Jebsen & Jessen as well as Jebsen & Company, had died. After his customary morning ride, Jessen senior had dismounted, then suffered a massive heart attack—in a way a perfect death, but a disastrous shock to his family. To soothe her new husband's sorrow, Etha suggested having a child as soon as possible. It was this child that he was impatient to see. He hoped for a son to whom he could pass on his love of the East and the sea.

The child certainly had sea-faring ancestors on both sides. The Rickmers family came originally from the wind-swept island of Heligoland in the North Sea. The island was Danish until seized by the British in 1807, and was formally ceded to Britain in 1814. The British swapped this island for Zanzibar in 1890, at that time a German possession. Thus Heligoland became part of the German Empire, and within seventy-six years the inhabitants of this small island changed from being Danish to British to German.

The Heligoland Rickmers came from a long line of mariners, sea captains, and shipbuilders. In 1834 they established themselves in Bremerhaven, and within a few years owned a sizeable shipping company. Their shipyard built some of the world's fastest sailing ships and clippers. They built training ships for several major foreign navies and, by the beginning of the twentieth century, the Rickmers Line was one of the largest privately owned shipping companies in Europe, with services to most parts of the globe. They owned rice mills in Bremen and Hamburg, where hundreds of thousands of tons of rice arrived from Indonesia in Rickmers' ships.

From 1848 until 1914, about eighty-nine Rickmers' vessels had been launched, but during W.W.I the fleet was decimated. At the time Etha married Johan, the shipyard in Bremerhaven was expanding again as Paul Rickmers rebuilt his fleet.

On the Jessen side the new-born's heritage was also maritime. From the small town of Aabenraa in southern Denmark, the destinies of two local families—the Jebsens and the Jessens—had merged. The men of both families had long been sea captains, ship owners, and traders to the Far East.

In 1895, Jacob Jebsen and Heinrich Jessen decided to form a partnership. They opened offices in Shanghai and Hong Kong, and acted as traders and agents for major global industries and shipping companies. This also included the agency for the Jebsen fleet of Jacob's father, Michael Jebsen, which greatly advanced the growth of this budding company.

This commercial union was strengthened in 1899, when Johan's father Heinrich married Johanne Jebsen, his partner's sister. From this marriage two children were born: Christa, in 1900, and then Johan himself in 1903. Both children were born in Hong Kong and lived happily there in the villa Lysholt until the tragic death of their mother in 1907, when Christa was seven and Johan four. These idyllic early years in Hong Kong were what Johan hoped to recreate for children of his own.

Now, as Man Fat drew up in front of the Victoria Hospital, Johan jumped out of the car, then raced up the steps and through the corridors to Etha's room. As he cautiously popped his head around the door he saw Etha proudly holding a baby out to him.

"I knew it was you running like that," she said. "Look—it's a boy! The son you have been waiting for."

This son was to be christened Johan Heinrich after his father and all first born Jessens for generations. This is his story.

Acknowledgments

First of all my sincerest thanks go to **Michael Jebsen** who read endless drafts with great patience. The very **first idea** for this memoir came from my cousin **Bertram Rickmers** as we sat together with my son **Mark** in the bar of the Palace Hotel in Montreux, Switzerland. We had just attended a family reunion. It appeared that I was the last to have vivid memories of the grandfather he was never to meet.

As the book developed, many people read the first drafts and I thank them for their patience! My son **John** even had several copies of the first part bound with the express purpose of not allowing me to give up.

Ultimately, it has been the IT wizards who have brought the manuscript to a form I could send off to publishers. In Brussels my thanks go to **Detlef Grosse;** in Spain to **René Martens** and particularly to my daughter-in-law **Silvana** whose grasp of the intricacies of my computer never cease to amaze me, and last but not least to **Cindi Pietrzyk, Robert Rufa, Helen Holzer, Kim Pascarelli**, **Julius Kiskis**, Wendy Arakawa, and Mark Bredt of the AEG Publishing Group, New York, N.Y. To all of them heart felt thanks.

Michael Jebsen, my great-grandfather

Jacob Jebsen & Family

My grandparents J.H. Jessen & Johanne, née Jebsen

J.H.Jessen, Johanne, JHJjr.Christa at Villa Lysholt Villa Lysholt

Villa Lysholt Servants 1905

My Parents
Wedding 1931

Villa Lysholt, Hong Kong, where my father and his sister were born

Above: My Grandfather, Heinrich Jessen on his yacht *Below: Sailing with father in HK Harbour*

1

HONG KONG

Even as a boy they told me I had almost total recall, but I cannot remember my Chinese wet nurse. My first memories are of my amah, to whom I was devoted. She was called Baby Amah and wore black silk baggy trousers, little black silk slippers on her bound feet, and a long-sleeved white cotton jacket with frogged button holes. Her hair was always pulled back into a tight bun and she was an essential part of my life for my first six years.

Our house, called "Kik-Ud," which means "Lookout" in Danish, was high up on the peak with wonderful views of Hong Kong Harbour. In one direction you could see the islands and the mountains of China, and on the other you looked down to Happy Valley with its famous race course. My father was a member of the Hong Kong Jockey Club, the only non-British member at that time, and he owned a black stallion called Pumpernickel. I was about five when I saw Pumpernickel win first prize in a big race, to our great excitement. My mother, dressed as always in the height of fashion, wore a hat which my father and I thought looked quite silly, but still we were proud of her as she led Pumpernickel past the Tribune to receive a silver cup.

Kik-Ud had a sweeping lawn and manicured flower beds but, at the back, behind the vegetable gardens and the servants' quarters, it was jungle in those days. One afternoon a gardener, barefoot in black trousers and jacket, clutching his conical straw hat, came racing across the lawn to where my parents were taking tea.

"Masta, masta, big snake, come chop, chop!"

My father followed the gardener, and I tagged along behind. There was a path cut into the bushes, and under a tree we saw a ten-metre-long python, sleeping peacefully. It had an enormous swelling in the middle of its body. The gardener was terrified, so my father grabbed the machete from him and with one tremendous, clear swing, slashed the python's head off. The snake went into writhing convulsions, lashing out at the gardener's bare ankles and bringing him to his knees. At his cries, Cook and other servants came running. Someone sliced open the python's belly and, to my astonishment, extracted an entire pig; not very large but completely undigested. Father dragged me unwillingly back to the tea table, where Mother sat under a parasol, quietly reading her letters, undisturbed by the noise as well as by my excited chatter. I never did get to know what they did with the pig or the python.

The servants were my earliest companions. Most important was Ah Chan, our Number One Boy, with the company logo on his white, gold-buttoned jacket. The logo was three mackerel on a dark blue background, encircled with a laurel wreath. Two of the fish swam west and the other east. This was an adaptation of the Aabenraa town shield, where all three mackerel swim in the same direction. I thought this was brilliantly clever. Next came Cook, dressed in a white jacket, black trousers, and black silk slippers. Number Two Boy, who served at table also, wore a white jacket and black pants. Coolie Boy wore black trousers with a dark blue jacket, whilst the lowest coolie, who did all the dirty work, was entirely in black. We had three amahs. Number One Amah, who did the laundry, wore the same uniform as my Baby Amah, whilst Number Two Amah, who helped clean, wore blue pants and jacket. Everyone knew who was who in the house by these uniforms, and as it was important to them it became important to me.

Parents in front of Kik Ud 1932

Below: My father with Alf in front garden 1932

Above:
Launching of the M/S "Heinrich Jessen" in Kowloon

Partners Jacob Jebsen and J.H.Jessen on company ship

2

Karuizawa - Japan

It was the custom for European families to escape the heat and humidity of Hong Kong in July and August and sail to Japan. We always took one of the white Empress ships of the Canadian Pacific line from Hong Kong to Yokohama. All the ships had names like *Empress of Russia* or *Empress of Japan*, and I loved them all.

Once on shore, we would drive to Karuizawa, a mountain resort with lush woods all around. We stayed in one of the comfortable wooden bungalows with terraces, little gardens, and a *Neysan* maid to clean, make breakfast, and do the laundry. Baby Amah came with us, of course. Meals were taken in the Club House, and it was a special treat for me to have lunch with my mother every day. She and I usually went ahead in the middle of June, and my father would join us later for three or four weeks, depending upon how busy he was.

A modern child might have been bored, but for me it was enough to have a donkey to ride and a fishing net in which raw eggs could be lowered into the hot water of the sulphur springs to cook. They had a rather strange taste, and nobody would eat them except my amah and me.

In those days, all the local people wore simple grey-and-black cotton kimonos with wood and straw sandals held between their split-toed white socks. My mother and I could only communicate by sign language or the odd word of English. One day we thought a large grey rat had sneaked into my mother's bedroom and was perched on top of the curtain rail. Neysan rushed in with a big stick and killed it with a mighty blow. Only then did we see, to our distress, that it was not a rat but a squirrel that had come in from the woods. *Neysan* could not understand why we would want a rat to be killed but not a squirrel.

One summer Father arranged an excursion to the top of the volcanic Mount Asamayama. We drove around the mountain in a taxi, which deposited us at the top and promptly disappeared back to the valley for another fare. We admired the views and then sat in a pavilion eating my amah's favourite "icekleem." Suddenly sirens wailed and urgent voices shouted through loud speakers. We understood nothing, but all the other visitors began to rush madly about, and somehow my father gathered that a volcanic eruption was imminent.

There was pandemonium around the taxi stand. Astronomical prices were being asked, which my father was prepared to pay, but to no avail. Finally he shoved us onto the last overloaded bus, which proceeded to skid and swerve down the mountainside at breakneck speed. That night we stood under the door frame of our fragile bungalow, the safest place we could find, and watched both fascinated and appalled as Mount Asamayama spewed out molten lava and lit the sky a violent red.

We all loved these Japanese holidays in the cool forests where the local people were so gentle and friendly. Nobody had any idea of the storm clouds which were gathering.

Above:
Rickmer Rickmers in Hong Kong Harbour 1856

Sophie Rickmers in the South China Sea - 1931

3

SWITZERLAND

Soon after this, I took my first trip to Europe. My mother, Baby Amah, and I sailed on an Italian passenger liner to Venice. It took four or five weeks, with stops in Singapore, Colombo, Aden, and Port Said. My mother complained endlessly about the heat, but my amah and I loved every minute of the voyage.

In Venice we were fetched by Mother's sister, my Aunt Ursula, who drove us to Clarens, on Lake Geneva, where Grandfather and Grandmother Rickmers lived in the Villa l'Empereur. This house I was to love above all others. It sat in a park overlooking the lake and, its name derived from the time when Napoleon Bonaparte, on his travels to Italy, had stayed there.

Mother told me that my grandfather had decided to leave Hamburg for Switzerland in 1931. He found the situation under the Nazi regime ever more distasteful, and he wanted to take his family to the sanity of a neutral country.

Finally Grandfather chose the eastern shores of Lake Geneva, where the river Rhone flows into the lake. He considered this to be the most beautiful spot in Europe, with the Alps climbing up steeply on the French side of the lake whilst the gentle slopes on the Swiss side were covered with vineyards before rising up to more mountains.

When Paul Rickmers and family arrived in Switzerland, they took over an entire floor in the Hotel Trois Couronnes in Vevey—which was just as well because it took my grandfather a whole year to find the right house.

Mother and I stayed with my grandparents in Clarens for a few weeks, and it was very jolly after the quiet life I'd led in Hong Kong. My three uncles and two aunts came and went, but when we were all present we were nine at table. I had never been in a house with so many family members, and I would have liked to stay there forever.

The whole house was covered in ivy, and high on the roof was a weather vane, which my grandfather told me had been cast in copper in the shape of the sailing ship *Peter Rickmers*. She had been the fastest ship afloat in her day, but in 1908 on a voyage from New York to Rangoon she became stranded and then sank off Fire Island. The last thing that was saved as she went down was the ship's bell, which now hung at the front door, to be rung by the cook to call us in for meals.

My grandfather also had two reddish-copper hunting horns, one about two-and-a-half feet long and the other smaller. He kept them in the loggia outside his study, and if we did not respond quickly enough to the cook's bell, he would blow these horns to call us back. The sound of two short and one long blasts floating down to the farthest corner of the grounds led me to call him *Papi Lololo*, a name that stuck for years.

My grandfather Paul Rickmers 1937

Great-grandmotherDorothea Melchers (Original in Focke Museum Bremen)

Grandmother Mai Rickmers

M\S ETHA RICKMERS,
baptized by mother

Laimun on
Aabenraa Fjord - Denmark

4

DENMARK

After a few weeks revelling in the cool of Switzerland, Mother and I—and, of course my faithful amah—took a train from Basel to southern Denmark. This was the first time amah and I had slept in a wagon-lits, and we were thrilled by the whole experience. Mother was not.

My grandfather Jessen's house in Aabenraa was called "Laimun," after the harbour entrance to Hong Kong. Built originally as a summer house, it stood on lawns sloping down to the fjord with forests stretching behind. Unfortunately, I was never to know my father's parents. After Grandmother Johanne died in Hong Kong, my grandfather Jessen moved back to Europe for his children's sake. He remarried and had four more children, dying whilst still in his prime of a heart attack whilst out riding, leaving my step-grandmother to live alone with her children in the big house. My mother saw the difficulty I was having with all these grandmothers, so she suggested that I call one "Clarens Omi" and the other "Laimun Omi," which made life much easier.

The most vivid memory I have of this first Laimun visit is of walking from the house along the fjord to Aabenraa—accompanied, of course, by my amah. This walk of about thirty minutes took us nearly an hour as amah could not walk very fast on her tiny feet. She shuffled along, lagging farther and farther behind me until I began to get quite cross. The good burghers of Aabenraa were rightly outraged to see a small child imperiously urging this poor creature to get a move on. It didn't help when she kept calling back, "Yes, young master, so sollee!" In my defence, I had no idea that behaviour commonplace then in colonial Hong Kong was considered outrageous in democratic Denmark.

Villa Lensnack on Aabenraa Fjord - Denmark

5

Hong Kong

My first taste of Danish life was brief, and soon we were back in Kik-Ud with my father. I was enrolled in the Peak School almost immediately, kitted out in a uniform of grey shorts, brown blazer with gold buttons, and a brown cap with the gold school badge. I loved the Peak School, except for the compulsory school outings to Shek-O or Repulse Bay beaches. As soon as they saw us, the Hong Kong police would chase all the Chinese children away, waving batons at them to hurry and leave the beach just for us. I had always been close to our Chinese servants and would have loved to play with these children. but it was against the rules.

The Hong Kong years were idyllic. As was customary in that day and age I did not accompany my parents as much as modern children do. Indeed they were a glamorous couple, always dashing off to do exciting things—or so it seemed to me. Years later I would pore over Mother's photo albums and finally see what they had been up to. There were tennis afternoons and golf tournaments; jaunts on the company launch to surrounding islands where they had picnics with their friends; days spent sailing on my father's yacht; fancy dress and cocktail parties, dances, dinners, horse races, and loads of houseguests from Europe—such as my father's friend A. P. Møller. Why could I have not gone to those picnics and sailings, I wondered morosely. I also found heaps of press cuttings, including the launch of the *SS Heinrich Jessen* by my mother at the Kowloon Docks in February 1940. But I had been in Clarens then, of course.

Mother was feted for her style and beauty, and the gossip columns of the local press covered her comings and goings, sometimes to her annoyance. Whenever she sailed to Europe there would be articles in the society pages, which she would cut out and paste into albums. But she hated not looking her best and would cut any offending, unflattering pictures into little pieces. My father looked relaxed and happy in all the photographs. Business was expanding and there was not a cloud on their horizon.

As I grew a little older, my greatest joy was to leave my amah behind for a few hours and accompany my mother. I remember sitting beside her in her red Studebaker convertible, passing through Wanchai, the bustling market area of Hong Kong. A rotten tomato fell from a tenement onto Mother's immaculate, white sharkskin suit, bang into her lap. She scooped up the mess and threw it out of the window in disgust, but her skirt was ruined and she was devastated.

"Thank heavens we're going home!" she kept repeating as she tried to drive and scrub at her skirt with her handkerchief at the same time. She was practically in tears. Suddenly she braked violently and swerved into a narrow street.

"Here's my tailor," she said. "Come on—I'll tell him to make me another skirt. This one's ruined."

I followed her into the small, dark shop where we were greeted with, "Good mornin', Missy. Good mornin', young masta," and much bowing and clasping of hands. The tailor immediately noticed the state of Mother's skirt and looked up at her in amazement. "So elegan', Missy. Wha' happen?"

Mother started to tell him the whole story but it was too complicated for both of them. She cut herself short and just said, "Please make same, chop-chop, for lunch party next week."

The tailor said, "Velly good, Missy. How much meat Missy—wanchee makee looksee?"

From many visits here with Mother I knew this meant how much décolletage there was to be, but Mother insisted. "Same skirt. Same, same. No top piecee."

About a week later she came storming into the nursery, where father and I were lying on the floor, fixing my train. Not knowing whether to laugh or cry, she held up the new skirt which had been faithfully copied, down to the red splash exactly where the tomato had stained the original. This sent Father and me into gales of laughter until, finally, Mother forgot to be cross and joined in.

When she became pregnant in 1937, Mother decided to take me with her to

Europe, where she wanted to have this baby. We sailed alone, just the two of us, on one of the newest ships of the East Asiatic. This company had the first passenger ships in the world to run on diesel instead of coal. Built by the famous Burmester and Wain shipyards in Copenhagen, the vessels were smokeless and faster then than all other ships. They looked like giant yachts, with three masts and no funnels, so the Chinese called them, "Big white ship three piecee bamboo no smoke."

Once we arrived in Europe, things started to go wrong. The baby, who was to have been called Jes—after a Jessen ancestor from the 1700s who was a famous painter—was stillborn in a Hamburg hospital. Mother returned to Hong Kong as soon as she was able to travel. She left me in the care of my step-grandmother in Denmark.

6

LAIMUN

My step-grandmother was extremely good to me, but I found it very hard to say goodbye to my mother, especially since no reason was ever given for leaving me behind. Naturally I felt I was being punished, but what had I done? I also spoke hardly any Danish, and I knew I was to go to the Aabenraa school. I mostly spoke Cantonese and Pidgin English from my amah, real English from my parents and the Peak School and, at that time, not very good German.

The only young people still living in Laimun were my father's stepsister Evchen and his stepbrother Arwed, who were in their teens. My step-grandmother had to take on the task of training yet another child, and she spent at least two hours a day with me, helping me with my homework after school. Every evening she read me stories from the Old Testament in German, which obviously improved my language skills. Between this and the local school, I was almost fluent in both Danish and German after a couple of months.

In the summer of 1938, my Rickmers grandparents suddenly arrived from Switzerland. I was playing down by the fjord when a green car swept in through the gates, with two people in the back and a uniformed chauffeur at the wheel. I raced up over the lawn, heart pounding, for I had recognised the Maybach.

My grandfather in his plus fours and bow tie got out of the car and held his arms wide, calling out, "Yes, it's me, your Papi Lololo!" I was crushed in a bear hug, breathing in his wonderful tweedy, cigar smell. The chauffeur helped my grandmother out of the other door, and I ran to receive her embraces. She smelt as always of lavender. I was enchanted to see them both. My step-grandmother stood at

Evchen, teaching me to row on the fjord in front of Laimun

the front door, and my grandfather stepped up to kiss her hand.

My grandparents stayed in Laimun for three or four days, driving around from Løjt Kirkeby to Gråsten and then back around the west coast of Jutland. They bought three large farms and an estate, all of which had been earmarked for their consideration by an agent. I went with them to look at Grøngrift, the biggest estate, which they liked best of all, with its lake, rolling meadows, and woods leading down to a fjord. I thought it all looked pretty much like Laimun, and was more interested in the Maybach, with its cocktail bar and little walnut tables.

Before he left, my grandfather told me that, as I was Danish, all these properties would one day be left to me. In hindsight it was a pity that he had not put them in my name then and there, as in 1945, after the war, all Japanese and German-held land was seized by the Danish Government as war reparations, and so he lost them.

Left to right: Uwe, my father and Arwed, Laimun 1930

Above:]
Left to right: Kiki, me and Lori von Eckartsberg 1938 in Laimun

Right:
Father sailing to Finland

7

War Breaks Out

A year later, Mother was back in Europe, pregnant for the third time. It was a very difficult birth, and after my little brother was born in July, 1939, the doctors advised her to go to the mountains to recuperate. The baby stayed in the care of a nurse, and I was sent to join my mother at Mittelberg in the Alps.

For a month we walked and picnicked in the high meadows, and I was in seventh heaven—not only to be reunited with my mother, but also to have her all to myself. This idyll, however, was soon to be shattered by fears of war in that September of 1939.

One morning Mother received a frantic call from her father in Switzerland. Paul Rickmers ordered her to get out of Germany by the fastest means possible and to come to him in Clarens. We threw our things into our bags, got a taxi, and told the driver to race hell for leather to Lindau, on the shores of Lake Constance.

On the way we passed convoys of trucks loaded with soldiers. At the railway crossings, military trains roared past toward the north. Some of these trains were so long, carrying heavy artillery and tanks, that they had eight locomotives pulling them. As a small boy I was fascinated. It was as if my toy soldier games had come to life, but for my mother it was all terrifying.

When we finally reached Lindau, we scrambled and pushed our way onto a Swiss lake steamer heading for Rorschach on the other side of the lake. As we drew close to Rorschach, Mother pointed to a large red flag with a white cross flying on the quay and I could see the relief on her face. "Look, that's Switzerland!" she said.

Just before we docked, the captain announced over the tannoy that German troops had invaded Poland and war had been declared on Germany by Britain and France.

On the quay stood the stocky, reassuring figure of my grandfather, arms stretched in welcome and tears running down his cheeks. We stuffed our bags in the boot, piled into his car, and then he drove us himself back to Clarens.

On the steps of the l'Empereur stood grandmother, Uncle Claus, and Aunt Moni, all anxiously awaiting us. We sat down to a festive dinner, but most of the talk was of war.

Two days later, Claus, at just 18, received a telegram ordering him to enlist. He had just finished his final exams at the famous Salem school run by Professor Dr. Hahn, who was himself about to leave for England. Later, in Scotland, he founded the renowned boys' school, Gordonstoun.

Moni, Claus's twin, was also at the end of her studies at the English St. George's School, which was only a hundred yards down the lane from the Empereur. Uncle Peter had made his First Mate's Ticket and had been first officer on one of his father's ships until he was drafted into the German Navy and, at twenty-seven, became a commander of a minesweeper. Uncle Bertram was also called up and became a dispatch rider in Russia. Claus eventually became a "sparks." Neither Claus nor Bertram ever wanted to become officers.

Thus my poor grandmother had three sons in uniform and passed endless sleepless nights over many years. By some miracle all three survived unharmed. We were to learn later that Claus had the toughest time as he was a POW in Russia, and when he was finally able to return to Clarens, he was seriously emaciated and took months to recover.

Now in 1939, Mother asked the nurse in charge of my little brother, Peter Nicolai, to bring him to us in Switzerland. I remember vividly the three-month-old baby who was so happy, fat, and chuckling. We called him Nicky, and he rapidly became the darling of the whole house. Only he could divert the grown-ups from talk of war.

A few weeks later, to my intense distress, Mother, Nicky, and the nurse left for Genoa where they boarded the *Conte Verde*, an Italian passenger liner bound for Hong Kong. Once more I was left behind, this time in Switzerland.

We were not afraid that the ship would come under attack, as Italy was still neutral at this time. But worse was to happen. Even all these years later I still go cold when I recall the morning my grandparents called me into the study and, with breaking voices, told me that they had just received a telegram from the Conte Verde with the frightful news that my brother had died in the Red Sea.

It was years before I was told the entire story. Before leaving, Mother had stocked up on powdered milk supplied by the Hamburg Eppendorf hospital. Once the ship sailed, Nicky started to have diarrhoea, which became steadily worse as they sailed through the Suez Canal in intense heat. My mother and the nurse took turns at the baby's bed in the stifling cabin. One exceptionally hot night, when Mother was dining at the captain's table, the nurse left the sleeping baby and went up on deck for a breath of fresh air. When she returned, she found Nicky had turned onto his stomach and suffocated, too weak to turn back. The ship's doctor who had tried to cure Nicky's diarrhoea later said that the milk powder must have gone bad.

And so my mother arrived in Hong Kong with a small zinc coffin carrying the body of my brother to my father who waited, devastated, on the quay. Peter Nicolai was buried in a small grave in the Happy Valley cemetery, which today is taken care of by Hans Michael Jebsen—to whom I shall always be grateful.

Evchen, Uwe, step-grandmother, father, Heinrich Jessen, Arwed, Elke

8

Grandfather Rickmers

After this tragedy, my grandfather became like a father to me and we were practically inseparable. We went on long walks in the hills over Clarens with Biddy, the bull terrier bitch, and Grizzle, the Scotch terrier, as our constant companions.

At this time he must have been in his sixties—and if he seemed a stern man to the world, to me he was a jovial giant. We shared an early morning bath ritual. After our showers, hair lotion was freshly concocted daily. Bay rum, oil, and Dr. Dralle's patented hair lotion were mixed to make a sticky, oily mess to combat the curls we both detested. Then we would dress and descend to the breakfast table where, every morning without fail, my grandmother would exclaim in horror at our greased-down, slick hair, with its overpoweringly pungent smell.

Grandfather's breakfast was always the same—a huge French cup of strong black coffee and ten raw, spring onions. He was convinced this was extremely healthy. Breakfast was always followed by a fat cigar, and with this held firmly between his teeth he would retire to his study and begin to telephone his offices and agents.

Outside his study doors were two lights, one red, one green. When the green light was on one could enter after knocking, but when red it was categorically forbidden to even knock. This included his wife and children, as he could be conducting business by phone with Osaka, Bombay, or Rio. I was the only exception to this rule as I was his "assistant." He bought me a little red typewriter, and together we concocted letters of trade agreements, invoices, and orders to his agents. Of course these letters were never mailed, but in this simple way I learnt, at age eight, the difference between an open-shelter decker, a tanker, and a passenger ship. I knew the difference between long ton, short ton, and metric ton, the difference between dead weight and gross weight, and the significance of CIF, C&F, FAS, FOB, and a letter of credit. One never forgets such early lessons.

There was a large world map on one wall with a magnet behind it so that small iron Rickmers' ships could be moved into position daily. This, of course, was complicated by the fact that the Second World War was raging. I remember the sadness on his face as he had to remove ship after ship from the map, as they were either confiscated or sunk.

Now word came from my parents that they were to move to Shanghai. The fact that I could no longer picture the daily life of my parents made the distance between us seem even greater, and I was quite upset. Seeing this, my grandfather did his best to give me a mental picture of their new home. He took me over to the large globe which stood on a table in the middle of his study. "Now, show me Hong Kong," he said.

This was easy. I put my finger on it every time I was in the room—as if to feel closer to Kik-Ud.

"Good—now go up the coast of Mainland China until you find Shanghai."

I was appalled at how far away it was, and probably looked gloomier than ever. Grandfather took no notice because he said, "Right you are. Not so far now, is it?"

As I did not trust myself to answer, he went to his shelves and took down a heavy book. "Sit down, young man. This will be your geography lesson for today."

I thought this was pretty unfair, as it was Saturday and my tutor never came on weekends.

"Listen to this," he began. "Until 1842 China was almost a closed country. Very few non-Chinese were allowed in and very few Chinese were allowed out, but the rest of the world wanted to trade with China. There was a war and Shanghai had to allow foreign traders in. Are you following?"

I nodded.

"They still did not want the Chinese to mix with foreigners, so International Settlements were created, where all non-Chinese had to live in what are known as 'concessions.' The French have the nicest, so your parents will probably find a house there."

I stared at my feet. I couldn't picture any of this. My grandfather flipped through pages until he found some black-and-white photographs of large buildings along a port. It all looked very gloomy compared to the green hills and islands of Hong Kong. He put the book on my knees.

"Keep it. You can find out much more by yourself."

I took the book out to the garden and sat under the big cedar tree. The French Concession was the prime residential sector, where most foreigners lived in large, pleasant houses surrounded by walled gardens along tree-lined avenues. It was policed by the Indo-Chinese, led by French officers from French Indo-China. All this was very interesting but where would my parents live? How would I find them?

Finally a letter arrived from Father. He wrote that they had arrived in Shanghai with only Man Fat of the Hong Kong servants, together with Alf and Didi, the Alsatian and little bull terrier. In Cantonese, Didi means "little brother," which made no sense at all because she was a bitch. As she was somewhat jittery, my father called her "Jitty," which the Chinese servants could not pronounce, and the nearest they could get was "Didi."

Upon arrival in Shanghai, Father had taken an apartment in the Cathay Mansions, a smart residential hotel on Rue Bourgeat and Rue Cardinal Mercier. It had a good restaurant called the Sky Room at the top of the building, and he wrote that it would be ideal until they could move into a permanent home.

The news that interested me the most was that Father had bought a piece of land on which stood a dilapidated house, most of which he intended to have demolished. The land was on the corner of Avenue Petain and Route Francis Garnier, two of Shanghai's nicest avenues. The Chinese called these roads Petain-lu and Gani-lu, which was all rather confusing. A well-known architect named Antoine Bush from Alsace designed the new house, which would take about six months to build. There were three-and-a-half acres of land, which would be turned into a formal garden, and there was to be a greenhouse and a vegetable garden. How I longed to see it all.

Sooner than I had dared hope, this wish was about to be granted. Early in 1941 my grandfather received a telegram from Father, asking him to arrange for me to travel from Switzerland to Shanghai. I was a little over nine years old at the time.

First I had to be vaccinated against typhoid, paratyphoid, cholera, yellow fever, and smallpox. When I had recovered from this onslaught, my bags were packed and my grandfather and Aunt Moni took me by train from Lausanne to Zurich. I loved the red-velvet first-class compartment, but I did not then realise how much time I was about to spend on a train.

In Zurich we stopped at the Glockenhof Hotel, where my grandfather always stayed because it was close to his banks in the Bahnhofstrasse. The following afternoon, Grandfather took me to the railway station to board a train to Stuttgart. I was very well equipped with a red money-bag around my neck. It had a zip and a lock. In it were my tickets, hotel vouchers, money, passport, and step-by-step instructions worked out by the Wagons-Lits Travel Agency and the Soviet Tourist Bureau. My grandfather had taken me through the whole journey several times, using his globe to help me understand where I was to go and what I was to do, and I was not at all afraid.

At the station we met a Mr. and Mrs. Kiepert, acquaintances from Montreux, who were also travelling to Berlin via Stuttgart. They promised to keep an eye on me. Now it was time to say goodbye, and I hugged my grandfather with all my strength, crushed against the cigar fragrance of his tweeds. I think we were both close to tears.

Paul Rickmers, Moni, Ursula,
Mai Rickmers and me (age 8) in Clarens 1939

Me, ready to go !

9

EN ROUTE TO MOSCOW

The Kieperts and I travelled in the same compartment. We arrived in Stuttgart that evening and changed trains for Berlin. The station was milling with black-uniformed SS troops. We were all frisked and our papers checked, especially mine as I was a Danish citizen. The steam engines rolling in and out of Stuttgart Central Station were draped with huge swastikas, and the atmosphere throbbed with military excitement—especially frightening after peaceful Switzerland.

We boarded the night train to Berlin and, although we had first-class tickets, which entitled us to sit in a private compartment, we were thrown out by the SS, who ordered us to move back to the third-class compartments. Both first and second classes were now exclusively for German officers.

Our documents were checked at least three times during the journey. The Kieperts, being German nationals, did not attract much attention. I, on the other hand, seemed to intrigue both the police and the SS. My bags were opened twice, as if nine-year-old Danes were particularly untrustworthy.

Huddled in a corner on a wooden bench, I slept fitfully, as the train rolled slowly through the night. We passed smoke-filled industrial areas and, as dawn came, all I could see under the dirty grey skies was a chaos of trains and military personnel. I was quite upset and wondered what on earth was happening. Clarens already seemed like a dream.

When we finally arrived in Berlin on that dull, April day, the Kieperts and I piled into a taxi and drove to the Adlon Hotel. We were so hungry that even before

From Moscow to China

going up to our rooms we went straight to the dining room where breakfast was being served. We each ordered two boiled eggs, but the waiter sternly informed us that, for German Nationals, eggs were off. Mrs. Kiepert told him that I was Danish. I had to show my passport to the head waiter, after which two boiled eggs arrived with due ceremony. I slipped one of them to Mrs. Kiepert, which she didn't eat quickly enough. The headwaiter had seen her, and he strode over to reprimand her in a loud voice for unpatriotic behaviour. All the other guests in the dining room stared disapprovingly, and we fled to our bedrooms.

My train to Warsaw only left the following day, so I had hoped to get a good night's sleep as I was very tired. But that night the RAF made a serious raid on Berlin. Not carpet bombing—more of a statement to prove that Berlin was not out of reach, the adults assured me. We all had to rush down to the cellars in our dressing gowns! We heard a few bombs and a lot of anti-aircraft fire, but soon all was quiet and, after a couple of hours, we were allowed back to our rooms.

Sleep, however, was now impossible. I tossed and turned in bed until it was light, and then went down to the little hotel garden which was littered with shrapnel. As I had never seen this before, I had no idea what it was, but when a man told me, I put a piece in my pocket to show my parents.

Around lunchtime a slim, fair-haired man showed up and introduced himself to the Kieperts as Dieter von Hansemann. He was a junior employee in my father's company in Shanghai and was travelling through Siberia to Shanghai too. He must have been about twenty-five, and I looked forward to having a companion. But he told me that, although he would be on the same trains, we would not be in the same compartments. If I were in doubt about anything, I was to ask him—but otherwise he didn't seem to think we would see much of each other.

We shared a taxi to his father's house, where he picked up his bags and I was offered a piece of cake. After writing in Mr. von Hansemann Senior's guest book, at his request, we left for the station, which was teeming with pushing crowds of anxious people. Mr. von Hansemann Junior shoved me into my compartment and went off to find his. As the train drew out of Berlin, I found myself packed in with a crowd of civilians and lots of troops on board for the next stretch to Warsaw.

Warsaw was a depressing sight. Everything was grey, miserable, and dirty, with ruined buildings everywhere and German soldiers yelling at Polish POW labour gangs to hurry as they shovelled and cleaned up the rubble.

In the confusion I couldn't find Mr. von Hansemann, but I followed my grandfather's written instructions and boarded the Polish train bound for the Soviet border. Whenever I asked the Polish railway officials or train conductors where to go—in English, as my grandfather had advised—they were immediately kind and helpful, going out of their way to assist me.

Some time after the train left Warsaw, we stopped so that Soviet Military Police could get on board to check all documents and belongings—Eastern Poland was occupied by the Soviet Union. They were jolly and friendly, and one of the Russian officers in my compartment offered to help me find the right train for Moscow when we reached the border. I was grateful, as things were not turning out to be quite as simple as my grandfather and I had supposed.

We had to change trains at Bialystok because the Russian tracks were much wider and European trains could not continue into Russia. The new train's carriages were considerably more spacious and comfortable, the ride smoother. Here we had the strictest control yet, and all civilians were again frisked and interrogated.

Although at that time Russia was still a "semi-ally" of the German Reich, for some reason the German passengers were singled out and treated rather roughly. Again all the Russian officials were extremely kind to me, usually speaking in Russian—which I failed to understand—but often in broken English. It overwhelmed me how friendly and helpful they were.

The journey from Warsaw to Moscow took roughly twenty hours, with long stops in Minsk and Smolensk. The Intourist agent at Warsaw had promised to advise

Intourist in Moscow that I was on the train so that someone would be there to help me with my hotel reservations. I was greatly relieved by this as I had to stay a day and a night in Moscow before the Trans-Siberian train left.

On the way to Moscow, a general and a colonel—both Russian—came and shared the compartment. They spoke English, some German, and a little French. They were astonished that I was travelling alone, but delighted that I was discovering their beloved Motherland at such an early age. They took the ammunition out of their pistols and taught me how to hold an army pistol correctly and how to take aim.

Hotel Metropole

They were both officers in tank divisions and insisted that a) I should visit them sometime in the future so that they could teach me how to drive a tank, and b) I too would join a tank unit as soon as I was able. I agreed enthusiastically to both of these suggestions.

It was a long haul to Moscow. The train was slow and stopped often. Troops got off and on in an endless reshuffle. I told the general that an Intourist man had promised to send someone to help me in Moscow, so when we pulled into the station he jumped down onto the platform with me as an officer threw down my bags. The general stood there, holding me by the hand, yelling at the top of his voice for an Intourist agent to appear. One popped up as if by magic. I thanked my military companions, said goodbye rather reluctantly, and followed the Intourist man to his car.

He drove me to the Hotel Metropole, where he showed all my vouchers to the reception clerk. I was led to a huge, high-ceilinged room with a cavernous bathroom, where the plumbing seemed pretty bad even to me. I dumped my belongings and went out into the crisp, spring morning. When the doorman asked me if I needed a taxi and where would I like to go, I said I had no idea. I was just planning to walk around. He suggested that I should go to the circus and he told me which bus to take. I was to count six stops and then get off at a large square, where I would see a huge circus tent.

I had already seen the Circus Knie in Lausanne, but this Russian one was incredible. Acrobats, bears, tigers, elephants, high-trapeze artists—everything dazzled me. I sat squashed between jolly Russian families, who kept offering me nuts and sweets in the most friendly of manners. We could not converse, but we nodded and grinned at one another in appreciation of their circus, of which they were justly proud.

After the performance, I figured I could walk back to the hotel but I got totally lost. Finally I approached a policeman and tried him out in all the languages I could muster but he only spoke Russian. At last the word "Metropole" sank in. He pointed to my leather pouch and asked, "Roubles? Kopeks?" and when I nodded he took me to a taxi stand about three blocks away, chatting all the time and laughing—but what it was all about I was never to learn. Anyhow I joined him in his infectious laughter and we roared our way along in the jolliest fashion. At the taxi stand I uttered the only Russian words I had learnt from my Russian Officer friends—"Spassiba, Dosvedanje"—thank you and goodbye, at which he laughed even more and went off slapping his thigh with glee. The driver took me quickly back to the hotel where the doorman greeted me like an old friend, and I decided that I had never met nicer people than the Russian—an opinion I have not changed to this day.

Back at the hotel I had a hot bath. The tub took about two hours to fill, the water was a bit brownish, and the soap useless but I did my best to clean up. I gave my hair a good scrub as my grandfather's farewell gift of a bottle of his hair lotion had been perhaps over-enthusiastically applied and was now empty. Afterwards, for the first time in my life, I ordered room service.

There was a card in many languages with a long menu by the telephone. I found it hard to believe that all this could be delivered to my room. I ordered various fruit juices, a chocolate cake, a piece of apple pie, soup, stroganoff and rice, plus several sweet sodas. Some time later, when I had nearly fallen asleep, a couple of waiters arrived and pushed two laden tables into my room. They had a good laugh when they realised this feast was just for me and kept asking in broken English, "Where mother? Where father?" And when I said, "Shanghai," they shook their heads in disbelief.

As I ploughed through as much of this abundance as I could manage, I finally began to understand how lucky I was to have been given both hotel vouchers and an ample supply of cash in various currencies. Before falling asleep I listened to Russian music on the radio, and this was another treat because I had never had a radio in my bedroom before.

The next morning I was still pretty full so I decided to skip breakfast. I wandered down to the concierge and showed him my Trans-Siberian train voucher. He threw his hands up in dismay and started shouting orders to the pages. He asked me where my luggage was, and when I said I hadn't packed yet he sent a couple of bellhops up to my room with me. They threw my scattered belongings into my bags and rushed me back downstairs where a taxi was waiting with engine running. Apparently I had overslept and was about to miss the train. The concierge himself bundled me into the taxi whilst the bellhops threw my bags in after me, and off we dashed through the streets of Moscow.

At the station an Intourist man was anxiously pacing up and down. When he saw me, he grabbed my bags with one hand and me with the other and off we sprinted to the waiting train. We scrambled on board and walked through the carriages. I met Mr. von Hansemann, who had stayed in a different hotel, and he pointed out which carriage he would be travelling in. I would be four carriages ahead, and again he told me to come to him if I needed anything. At the entrance to my carriage I was met by two girls in uniform who, to my relief, actually spoke a little English. The Intourist man handed me over to them and left.

10

THE TRANS-SIBERIAN EXPRESS

I was led to a compartment, which was wide and roomy, with a big comfortable bed complete with brass knobs, crisp white sheets, and soft blankets. The floor was covered with a thick carpet, there was a sofa, a chair, plenty of space to store luggage, and an adjoining private shower, hand-wash, and lavatory. This was to be my home for the next twelve days.

I unpacked and set out to explore. My carriage was behind the engine, so I couldn't go forward. Instead I turned back along the corridor to see what sort of fellow passengers there were. The carriage immediately behind mine was taken by high-ranking (well, they had an awful lot of gold braid) Russian officers. Then came three compartments with some European families as well as a few Japanese. Farther along I found a dining car and finally the guard's compartment, beyond which I was not allowed.

When we drew out of Moscow, all blinds were pulled down so that we could not see out of the windows. Military police marched up and down the corridors to make sure we did not peep out at any possible military installation or armament factory. In fact, during the whole journey, it was one of the main tasks of the two stewardesses in each carriage to pull blinds down at mysterious moments. Suddenly, without warning, they would charge in, stumble over us, and drag down the blinds to hide we knew not what. These girls slept in small compartments at the end of each carriage. Here they had samovars and made endless cups of tea both for themselves and for us if we asked them.

One hour out of Moscow we were allowed to pull up the blinds. We were passing through a wooded area, dotted with sad-looking hamlets. In each carriage a map was stuck up, and every day at noon a small red flag would be advanced to show our new position.

As my grandfather had traced my journey for me on his globe before I left it, was somehow comforting to find the names of these lakes and towns again, as if they were old friends. What surprised me most was the slowness of the train—it hardly ever exceeded sixty kph. The guard told me the engine ran on a mixture of wood, coal and peat.

During the first day most people had their doors closed, but this was to change, and later we all relaxed and started to talk to one another. Some began to play chess or cards, and we would visit each other's compartments to help pass the time.

That first evening, between Moscow and Nizhniy-Novgorod, a steward in a white jacket went along the corridor beating a dinner gong. I followed him to the dining car and was placed at a table for two. The dining car was very grand, with red velvet upholstery and carpets, fancy curtains at the windows, and crisp white cloths set with silver and three glasses at each place. I knew one was for water and one for wine, but I couldn't make out what the little glass was for. The blinds were not down, and at each table a lamp was on, throwing pink shadows onto the passing landscape outside.

A few minutes after I sat down, a young Russian officer approached my table, bowed, and sat down opposite me. At first he spoke to me in Russian until I explained in English, German, and shaky French that I could not speak his language. At this he introduced himself to me in a heavily accented English—which later, in secret, I loved to imitate.

"Good evening," he said, "my name is Sergei."

He told me he was a major, thirty-five years old. I told him I was nine. We were to become good friends during the days we spent together, until he left the train at Irkutsk.

At that moment the waiter came in with a huge bowl full of a grey, slimy mess. It looked to me like frog spawn. A piece of toast was put on my plate and my little glass was filled with water from a frosted bottle. As I was thirsty I asked if my big glass could be filled up too, but Sergei stopped the waiter and they both grinned at me. A soup spoon with an enormous helping of the grey mess was ladled beside my toast. I sat looking at it helplessly. It looked utterly disgusting, and I asked Sergei what on earth it was.

"Just try it—you'll like it," he said as he piled some onto a piece of toast and took a huge bite. Of course I imitated him—and to my great surprise I found it delicious, salty, and cool. From that first meal I had caviar at every lunch and dinner, as it was served twice a day, every day. Sometimes red or black, sometimes grey. Sergei and I liked the grey best.

When I saw Sergei toss back the water in his little glass, I was about to follow suit when he said, "Better start with just a sip."

This I did, but even so I coughed and spluttered and felt my face go red. Sergei laughed and poured water from a carafe into a glass and I swallowed it down at a gulp. I left the vodka for him after that, but the waiter always put water into my small glass too so that I could pretend and return Sergei's toasts. The meals were vast—borscht, stroganoff, chicken Kiev, delicious sweet pastries, and brightly coloured, sugary ice cream were among my favourites.

The train continued eastward at an even slower pace after dark, and I slept wonderfully in my very comfortable bed. I can't remember how often I actually washed or changed my clothes during the journey, but I did brush my teeth every day, as I had promised my grandmother.

The next morning I woke to see deep woods and a broad, slow river outside my window. At breakfast Sergei told me it was the Volga—"The grandest river in the world," he said.

It narrowed and broadened out as it curved around the countryside, but even at its narrowest it was the widest river I had ever seen.

The stewardess had asked me the night before if I wanted my breakfast in bed, but I associated this with bronchitis and measles so I had opted for the dining room. I munched my way through ham and sausages with thick slices of grey bread and cheese as the train slowed down and pulled into Kazan.

The sky was a clear light blue. It was very cold, but there was no wind and it was quiet. I hadn't noticed the noise of the train until it stopped. We stayed in Kazan for three hours whilst we took on water and fuel. Passengers got off and on, mostly civilians, but there was always military about.

We set off again at noon and rolled through never-ending steppes, until at dusk the train slowed to a crawl and we began to climb. We were at the foothills of the

Urals. At about midnight we stopped again to bunker, this time at Krasnoufimsk. But before dawn we were off again, always climbing. Then at first light we were high in the mountains, chugging along at about thirty kph through snowy, wild peaks, where fir trees appeared about to slide down the slopes, some having already tumbled into the dramatic ravines, some clinging on for dear life under the weight of the snow bowing down their branches.

As the day began, I heard a commotion in the next compartment. Putting on my dressing gown, I went out into the corridor to see what was going on. There I found a Swiss gentleman who exclaimed, "Look out of your window, young man. There are wolves!"

I peered past him into his compartment and saw his entire family throwing bread out to the wolves as if they were feeding ducks. I dashed back to my window and spotted three wolves loping along close to the train, snatching at the bread before it fell into the snow. I had always imagined wolves to be huge, overpowering animals, so I was sad to see how emaciated, bedraggled, and dirty they were. Still, I was very glad to be up in the warmth of the train, as down there in the snow I knew I would not have lasted long, seeing how ravenous they were.

Every morning I checked the map to see exactly where we were. Our next stop would be the big, industrial capital of the Urals, Sverdlovsk. As we drew nearer to this town, we were asked to go back to our compartments where we found all the blinds had been lowered. Throughout our stay, which lasted several hours, we were not permitted to look out. This always annoyed me. Finally we were allowed to walk up and down the platform to stretch our legs. I peered about, curious to see what they had wanted to hide from us, but there didn't appear to be anything unusual. Even muffled up it was bitterly cold, so I did not stay long outside.

We took off again in the early afternoon, and it only dawned on me when checking the map that we had left Europe behind and were now in Asia, coming down the western Siberian plains. I went to find Sergei and ask him why the blinds had stayed down so long. He scratched his beard. "Sverdlovsk has many factories," he said, "big factories. Also many spies from Japan, Europe, America take these trains."

This was terrifically exciting and I began to inspect my co-travellers with renewed interest.

At that time, Russia was not at war. She had signed a non-aggression treaty. I knew that Poland, France, Denmark, Norway, the Benelux nations and the Balkans had already fallen to Hitler, and I wondered what had happened since I left Switzerland.

In my grandfather's study, after listening to the BBC and the Swiss news from Berne, he daily marked the movements of war, so I always knew where the armies were.

Now, instead of my grandfather, I asked Sergei for news, although stuck as we were in the middle of nowhere he couldn't have much fresh to tell. Anyway I asked him who was going to win the war. He looked very serious for once. "As it looks now, probably Germany," he said. "The European continent is on its knees and Russia is not involved."

I asked him whether he thought Russia would join in one day and whether he was afraid of dying in battle. He gave me a smile and shrugged. "A Russian is never afraid to die for his country."

The train stopped twice a day to rebunker and take on water, usually in remote villages or small towns. We rolled through endless beech forests, past vast steppes, and now the occasional lake. It had become monotonous, but it certainly brought home to me how enormous Russia was. It took us ten hours to reach Kourgan, another 500 kilometres along the way.

One day Sergei asked me to play chess with him. He must have been as bored as I was. He ordered coffee for us both and began to teach me how each piece moved. I had never had coffee before and, at the onset, I paid the thick black liquid, sticky with sugar more attention than I did the game but eventually I learnt the basic moves. At first I found it all utterly confusing but once I started to concentrate I began to enjoy it. How much fun it can have been for Sergei I am not certain...

Our next major stop was Petropavlovsk, and just before drawing into the station we came to a standstill and waited for several hours. We had no idea what was wrong. Eventually a stewardess admitted that we had engine trouble. The staff was very proud of the trains and hated us to think that anything could ever be amiss. But this time they had to explain that the wait was for spare parts, and nobody knew how long they might take to get to us.

Probably to keep us quiet, we were allowed off the train to walk up and down the tracks. It was mild, there were blue and yellow flowers in the fields, and it felt like spring. From the back of the train some of the Russian soldiers produced a football and, within minutes, there was an animated game. I was allowed to join in, even though I had little familiarity with the rules. This was one of the rare occasions when I saw Mr. von Hansemann, and I ran to ask him if he would like to play too. He said he would rather not, and warned me that a broken leg would be a disaster. Early in the afternoon the spare part arrived from Omsk—our next stop, about 300 kilometres away.

We arrived in Omsk late at night and were told that the engine had to be overhauled, so we would not leave for about twelve hours. The next morning we were allowed into town, and Sergei and I set off to buy a roast chicken. We had smelled it from the train and just followed our noses until we found the stall on a street corner. We ate it with our fingers standing in the road, and it was the best chicken I had ever tasted. I insisted upon paying my share and, after great protests, Sergei accepted. When he saw my money bag crammed with roubles, dollars, and francs, he was aghast that I was wandering around with all that money on me. I explained that my grandfather had told me to put it in the train safe, but there wasn't one. I had never had to pay for anything before, as everything was included in the train ticket, and Sergei had thought I just carried loose change in my pouch.

"Well hide the damned thing under your jumper or somewhere and don't let anyone else see it," he advised.

We ran into some of Sergei's fellow officers and we all went into a tavern. The men ordered beer and vodka, and I was allowed to have a sip of beer—which I found, to my disappointment, pretty horrible. This they all found very funny. They bought me a lemonade, which was great—sweet and bright yellow. On the way back to the train they started to sing, and I remember feeling very grown-up as I struggled to keep up with their long strides and sing along with them—even though I knew neither the words nor the melodies.

As evening approached, the train was ready at last and off we rode toward Tatarsk, in the steppes of Barabinsk, where we took on water and more wood and set off for Novosibirsk.

By this time we had all settled into a daily routine. Every morning I played chess with Sergei and his friends, who never complained about my amateurish efforts. In fact, trying not to beat me in three or four moves must have been quite an effort. But they good-naturedly always let me set out the pieces, and I must admit I watched them playing more than I played myself.

After lunch everyone napped, and I would be alone in my compartment, reading a little but mostly just staring out of the window. There was no rain, but it was always windy, and I would watch the clouds chase each other across the grey skies. For some reason, no matter how hard I tried to pretend that I was looking out of my window in Clarens, somehow the clouds just didn't look right.

Around Barabinsk there were lakes swarming with swans, storks, and many other white birds, swirling about and skid-landing on the water. As we only moved at about forty kph, I had plenty of time to admire them. Rabbits, hares, and foxes red and grey chased about and around the water, brightening up my afternoons with their antics.

Somewhere after Barabinsk, the train again broke down during the night and I woke up feeling extremely cold as the heating was off. Shivering under blankets in my big brass bed, I was not to be cold for long as a stewardess bustled in with a large eiderdown.

In the morning we set off again for Novosibirsk—where we arrived late, of course. We stayed for about six hours but were not allowed to leave the train as there were factories and military installations close by. Despite this edict, Sergei and some other officers got permission to visit a nearby garrison, and they took me with them. Sergei wanted to see some friends, and I wanted to see the tanks and cannons. I was allowed to crawl inside a tank, and they showed me how a cannon worked.

Afterwards we went to a little café. It was noisy and crowded. We had huge bowls of borscht, which was even better than on the train. This was followed by enormous platters of goulash. The officers drank endless vodkas, and one of them took a balalaika from a hook on the wall and they all started singing, thumping the table with their fists, pounding the beat out with their high boots, and roaring with great good humour. We were having such a good time that we nearly missed the train, and I would not have minded at all.

But off we set for Taiga, another seven hours away. Still the steppes stretched as far as the eye could see, and I thought they would never end. Taiga was very small and we didn't get off the train. We left after midnight and inched our way upwards, finally climbing out of the steppes.

We arrived in Krasnoiarsk early the following afternoon, where we were to stay for eight hours. The sun shone and the sky was blue, so I left the train without a coat and walked alone into town. I bought half a chicken for a few kopeks at a street stall and wandered along, eating it from its paper wrapper. Somehow it was not as good without Sergei.

When I opened my eyes the next morning I saw that we had finally left the steppes behind, and out the window I saw an arid, mountainous region. There was still some snow on the peaks, and noisy little swollen streams rushed down the hillsides. Once in a while I spotted a solitary wolf sniffing along the river banks, searching for food, whilst overhead eagles cruised in the clear blue sky. We stopped at Kansk for several hours, and then veered south towards the mountains and Lake Baikal.

I must have caught a cold in Krasnoiarsk because I felt a bit odd and stayed in bed most of that day. I lay staring unseeingly out of the window and tried to think of happy things. I was very lonely and a little anxious. What if my parents forgot to meet me?

Fortunately before I scared myself too much, the stewardess came to see if I felt better. I told her I did and she advised me to get up. We were on our way to Toulon, Zima, Sibirskoye, and finally Irkutsk. This leg of the journey would take about three days, passing through mountains and many tunnels. We passed several beautiful mountain lakes where the water was an incredible emerald green. They were bigger than any I had seen so far, much bigger than the Swiss ones I was familiar with. I knew that Lake Geneva was about ninety kilometres long, but these must have been closer to 1,000.

As day followed day, even in these wildernesses we often had to close our blinds for military reasons. Then about a day out of Irkutsk, Sergei told me he would be leaving the train there. He gave me a photograph of himself in uniform and I dug out a passport photo, which was all I had. We exchanged addresses and promised to write. His family came from Smolensk, about 400 kilometres west of Moscow. At that time, nobody thought Hitler would invade Russia.

Sergei advised me to buy presents for the stewardesses before I left the train at the Manchurian border. They had been so kind to me, and tipping was not allowed in the Soviet Union. At the next stop, Sibirskoye, half a day before Irkutsk in the middle of the Lake District, Sergei and I went into a little shop and I bought two very fancy pen and pencil sets. These were nicely wrapped, and then Sergei gave me a pencil that changed colours when you flicked a little lever. I had never seen such a pencil and was most impressed as well as grateful. He was a grand fellow, and I dreaded his leaving the train.

When we reached Irkutsk, we stood on the platform and said goodbye. I asked him if we would ever meet again and he said "Absolutely!" He gave me a great Russian bear hug and then a crisp military salute. About two months later, in Shanghai, I received a postcard from him just before the German-Russian war broke out. I never heard from him again, but I have never forgotten him.

What struck me most about Irkutsk was the sudden Asian atmosphere. The sides of the road were sandy, few of the roads were paved and most were dried mud where caravans of camels flopped their big feet as they loitered along, heads tilted back, looking curiously at everything down their long noses. The people had Mongolian features with brown, leathery skins, and most of the men wore coned hats and baggy blue trousers.

When the train took off again we circled around the south-western shores of Lake Baikal for about ten hours. The stewardess told me that this was the biggest lake in Eurasia and that it was famous for its sturgeon. "That caviar you like so much, he come from here!" she said.

The area was very beautiful, with dramatic mountains covered in snow, but I became fascinated by the tunnels. On one stretch I counted over seventy!

Onwards we chugged, ever eastwards, now parallel to the Mongolian border. Every morning I checked our position by the flag on the map, and I also drew lines across a small map of the world in the back of my notebook. Had I not known exactly where I was and thus been able to reassure myself that I really was getting closer to Shanghai and my parents, I should have felt even more abandoned and insecure.

Fortunately, after Sergei's departure, I had made good friends with all the staff in my carriage and the dining car. I thought it was an awful fate to have to travel back and forth between Moscow and Vladivostok forever and ever, but they assured me that they were very privileged and proud to have such excellent jobs.

My favourite waiter was Yuri. He was fat and jolly and always gave me a double portion, about three heaped soup spoons of my favourite caviar. After Sergei left, I was happy to have the waiters and cooks to chat with. One day it was the birthday of one of the cooks, and I was invited to his party. We had a huge cake and they all drank lots of vodka, then sang and danced to a balalaika and an accordion. It was, however, a poor show compared to the wild delight of Sergei and his fellow officers.

Once we had passed through all the tunnels, we continued eastwards for several days until we reached Tchita, where we were allowed to walk around the town. I was fascinated by the flamboyant bazaars, where you could find cutlasses and spices, fireworks, and all manner of intriguing objects. The streets were dusty and dirty, splattered with dung as horses, camels, and sheep wandered amongst the crowds. In the middle of all this, food stalls were set up with big pots sizzling over open fires and low tables where men would eat, oblivious of the people and animals pushing past them. I walked for hours, trying not to stare at the rather forbidding and unsmiling faces of the men with their fur hats and jackets and their slanted Mongol eyes.

I ran into two of the stewardesses, and they took me to a tea-room where a disgusting tea, oily with yak butter, was served in little cups without handles or saucers. I slurped manfully, then tried to get rid of the taste by eating the sweet sesame biscuits they plonked in front of us, but these too were greasy, sticky, and pretty awful.

On the way back to the train I suddenly realised that I had no gift for Yuri. I would have to find something now, as we would soon be in the town of Manzhouli, where I would leave the train because I was not going on to Vladivostok. I nipped into a shop in the bazaar that appeared to sell a little of everything. After a bit of hunting around I was shown a fancy Bakelite pencil in a box, which the salesman and I agreed would be just right for Yuri. With no common language, the shop keeper and I got along famously.

From Tchita we headed south-east to Karintskoie, where the train would split. Half of it would proceed to Vladivostok while the other half—my half—would continue to the Manchurian border, about one-and-a-half days' journey away.

Now that Sergei was no longer there to fill the days with fun, they seemed endless, and I felt as if the journey would go on forever. Eventually, though, we pulled into Manzhouli, Manchuria, the end of the line for me. Here I said goodbye to all the members of the staff who had become my friends and who had been so kind. I gave the fountain pens to the two hostesses and the propelling pencil to Yuri. I was very upset that I had not bought presents for everyone. In true Russian fashion they all had tears in their eyes, and I was hugged and embraced until I began to feel as bereft at leaving them as if they had been family.

Yuri helped me to the customs barrier with my two large bags, where a Russian Military Police platoon ordered all foreigners into a barrack for identification. I met Mr. von Hansemann, who told me they were looking for an international spy whom they suspected of having taken photographs throughout Siberia. How I wished I knew who it was! We were all interrogated and frisked, and our luggage was searched. But I don't think they found the man they were looking for. Finally they let us go and a customs officer gave me half a bar of Russian chocolate, which was very kind of him—even though I knew it would be inedible. We were told to cross the border on foot. Fortunately there were coolies to help—I would never have managed to carry my bags alone.

We walked towards an array of flags, including the Japanese war flag, as Manchuria was a Japanese Protectorate at that time. At the border control the Japanese officials gave Mr. von Hansemann and the other German nationals a great welcome. "Axis partners! Special treatment!" But upon seeing my Danish passport all I got were grunts as they thumbed me through.

Novosibirsk

Chita border between Soviet Union and Manchuria

Baikal Lake

11

THE TRAIN TO DAIREN

We boarded a Japanese train, which a fellow passenger from the Trans-Siberian Express told me included identical copies of an American Pullman sleeper car. The front of our train was armour plated and instead of compartments, the carriages had central aisles with two very comfortable leather seats on either side. The bunk beds were over our heads, to be let down at night.

I sat at the window next to a Japanese colonel, who gave me a friendly nod. We both said "Kon-ni-chi-wa," which was all I knew how to say. Across the aisle from us sat an elegant Chinese lady in European dress, who also smiled at me.

Before we pulled out of the station a platoon of Japanese Military Police boarded and again checked all our passports. It was the first time since leaving Germany that I had been checked so often and so thoroughly. Because the colonel was chatting to me in English and seemed to be taking a fatherly interest in me, the military police were extremely courteous, and the officer actually gave me a bow as he returned my passport. I was unaccustomed to being bowed to and much impressed. However, a few minutes later three Japanese men in civilian clothes, accompanied by two military policemen, charged into our carriage and came to a halt in front of the Chinese lady. One had a drawn pistol. They shouted at her, handcuffed her, and dragged her to her feet. Despite her pleas and cries she was not allowed to take her luggage with her, only her handbag. As they marched her roughly off the train our eyes met—and even at my age I could recognise her terror and despair.

It had all happened so quickly, and the train began to pull out of the station before I had time to realise what had just taken place. I was in a state of shock and begged the colonel to tell me why this had happened. He looked very stern and said, "This not my business. Army my business. Maybe she spy."

I had never seen her on the Trans-Siberian train, which I would have done when passengers had to get off and stand around on platforms. This meant that she could not have been the one they had been looking for before. Either the whole area was riddled with spies or a mistake had been made. She was so beautiful and so sad that I was sure the authorities would realise their mistake before long and let her go. Comforted by this thought, I began to feel better.

Because the Manchurian rails were back to normal European size the train was narrower and we travelled much faster. There was no dining car, but the food supply was ample and original. Every half hour three young girls in white uniforms and caps entered the carriage, bowed deeply, and offered us green tea in small cups. Like the Chinese, the Japanese slurp up their tea with noisy gusto, so I felt quite at home. Then followed a continuous supply of Japanese beer, ice creams, and dainty little lunch boxes containing complete meals. In the boxes were small pouches of cooked rice and compartments holding sushi, omelette, sword fish, and so forth, all in bite-sized pieces. We could also choose miso soup.

Chop sticks and soy sauce were free. It was all very cheap, and sometimes I ordered three boxes in one morning as I only liked bits of each—and anyway it was a lot of fun.

As the journey progressed, the Japanese travellers cast off more and more clothing until most of the men sat in their underwear and socks. The colonel only took off his leather belt with its holster and Mauser pistol, then the leather sheath containing his officer's sword. Last of all he removed a sword of about seven inches, which dangled in its own small sheath. I asked if I could look at his pistol and he took great pleasure in removing the bullets and letting me hold the Mauser. Then he drew his large sword and I was amazed at how sparkling and beautiful it was. He did not allow me to touch it because it was as sharp as a razor blade. I then asked him what the little sword was for. I thought it might be for fruit or to sharpen his pencils, but he smiled wryly and said, "Little sword for honour." When I gave him a blank stare he explained, "If Japanese officer make big mistake or become prisoner of enemy, he lose honour. This knife for Hara Kiri. Cut open stomach and die."

Quickly I returned his knife and said, "Well sir, I certainly hope you never have to use it!"

To change the subject, I asked him why the front of our train had steel armour plates. He laughed. "Communist guerrillas. Bad people. Shoot at train from gauleang."

I had no idea what gauleang was, so he told me it was a very tall plant which grew in plantations right up to the railway lines and was the perfect place to hide machine guns. He said most of the plantations along the rails had been cut down but not all areas were cleared.

"And who are the communist guerrillas?" I asked.

He grunted. "Bad Chinese people fight for big man Mao Tse-tung. No like Japan, like Russia."

I was becoming anxious now. "So will they know so many Japanese soldiers are on this train? Will they attack us?"

He gave me a happy grin. "Probably!" With this comforting news, we all prepared for bed.

Our bunks were over our heads and were now lowered for us. Each had a small ladder to climb, and a curtain that pulled across afforded the only privacy. My bed had crisp white sheets, a reading lamp, and a bell to call the steward. As everyone settled down, it was a bit noisy with lots of coughing and muffled laughter, but I thought it was all great fun. I rang my bell just to see what would happen, and within seconds the steward popped his head through my curtains and offered me more green tea saying, "Good for sleep, make good dreams." I lay awake a little longer, feeling very cosy and safe behind my curtain, but the tea must have worked because I soon fell asleep.

Around two in the morning, I awoke to a tremendous racket. We must have been somewhere between Tsitsihar and Harbin, and I could hear rapid rifle- and machine-gun fire, with the non-stop hooting of the engine adding to the confusion. The train had accelerated and we were racing along.

The shooting and general mayhem—officers jumping down from their bunks, grabbing their pistols, drawing their swords, bullets hitting the side of the train, women screaming, babies crying—made my head whirl. The Japanese officers opened the windows and shot blindly into the dark, aiming anywhere into the shadowy gaulean bushes where flashes of light betrayed our attackers. As suddenly as it had begun, all went quiet.

Nobody in our carriage was hit, even though there were bullets embedded around every window. My colonel, together with three junior officers, went to see what had happened to the rest of the train. There was an announcement over the tannoy in several languages asking for doctors to make themselves known to the staff. About twenty minutes later the colonel and his officers returned and ordered us all back to bed, but even under military command it was impossible to go to sleep as the train was still hurtling along. I, for one, was very keyed up and excited.

The next morning we arrived at Harbin, the biggest city in Manchuria, where we were scheduled to have a two-hour stop. As we drew into the station, we saw that the platform was bustling with Japanese military police, army medics with stretchers, and several ambulances. The colonel leapt down even before the train came to a halt. He ran up to a group of officers and everyone began saluting and bowing. I leant as far out of the window as I could and watched as stretchers were passed up and then handed down from the front of the train. Some were completely covered with blankets, and on others I could see wounded and bloodstained bodies. A Swiss man at my side told me that the covered bodies were dead. This was a tremendous shock as, naturally, I had never seen dead people before.

We were forbidden to leave the train at first, but about two hours later we were allowed off to stretch our legs. I ran into Mr. von Hansemann on the platform, and he seemed most upset. We chatted and exchanged experiences, but I could see he was more nervous about the events than I was. I know now that this was not due to any bravery on my part but more to do with my ignorance of our danger. At my age, danger meant excitement. I couldn't imagine anything really bad ever happening to me. He told me there were three dead and seven wounded.

We went together to the station buffet and were delighted to be able to order a European meal as the novelty of the Japanese lunch boxes had definitely palled. What amazed me was the number of Russians everywhere, and the fact that one heard more Russian than Chinese or Japanese. Mr. von Hansemann told me that Harbin had for years been a centre for White Russians who had escaped during and after the revolution. He told me that Shanghai also had a huge Russian colony, and I was glad to hear this as I was particularly fond of Russians.

Later that afternoon, the train continued its journey south via Sinking and Moukden to Dairen. This famous northern port, also known as Port Arthur, was where the Russian fleet had been caught by surprise when the Japanese launched an attack on Feb. 8, 1904. By January, 1905, after thousands of casualties, the Japanese Imperial Navy finally captured Port Arthur. Tsar Nicholas II had wanted to expand his empire, but so did the Japanese want to expand theirs—and China, unprepared for modern warfare, was caught in the middle. This defeat in Port Arthur was considered by the Russians to be one of the Tsar's most terrible blunders.

"And we all know what happened after that," concluded Mr. von Hanseman grimly.

We arrived in Sinking around midnight, and a second armoured locomotive was added to the train to give us more speed. A Japanese platoon with two machine guns also boarded to protect us should Mao Tse-tung's guerrillas attack us again.

My colonel left the train there. He gave me an untouched dinner box, slapped me on the shoulder, and shook my hand as if we were old friends. The train continued to Mukden, where we arrived early the next morning, and this town also was crowded with Russians.

"Amazing when you think about it, nearly 90,000 Russians died defending this town," remarked my new mentor. Mr. von Hansemann and I had met on the platform and had time for breakfast together in the station before re-boarding for the last stretch of the train journey to Dairen.

We were supposed to reach Dairen in the late afternoon, but we stopped shortly after Mukden, in Liaoyang, as one of the two locomotives had broken down. Everyone was tense during this long, forced delay—especially when darkness fell, as we were sitting ducks for any Maoist troops, despite our reinforced capabilities of repelling them. Fortunately, none could have been in the area as there was no attack, and we set off again, arriving in Dairen the following morning.

12

DAIREN

Dairen was the end of our train journey. Relieved to be on firm land again, Mr. von Hansemann and I each took a rickshaw and hired a third for our luggage. Then we set off to find a shipping agent. My grandfather's precise arrangements for me came to an end here, and somehow I had to work out the voyage to Shanghai, as this had been impossible to arrange from Europe. Mr. von Hansemann said we would just grab the first ship available. Apparently there was a Rickmers' ship in port, as well as one of my father's company ships, so we planned to try our luck with these first.

At the first shipping agency we found on the docks we were told that the Gustav Diederichsen was to stay in port discharging cargo for three days, and we certainly didn't want to wait that long. With our luggage piled up around us we hailed three more rickshaws in order to continue our search. There were plenty of shipping agencies to choose from, but the hustle and bustle of the heaving crowds, dashing between the cars, trucks, rickshaws, bicycles, and coolies laden with cargo on their shoulders, was chaotic.

We set off in the midst of this pandemonium, but almost immediately our three rickshaws became separated and I lost sight of Mr. von Hansemann and the luggage rickshaw. I couldn't communicate with my own rickshaw coolie, but I shook his shoulder and gestured wildly for him to stop the minute I saw another shipping agency. Paying the man—unfortunately half in American dollars, as I had hardly any local currency—I ran inside and asked the first clerk I saw for the next ship to Shanghai.

To my relief the man spoke English. I told him I had heard that one of my grandfather Rickmers' ships was in port. He checked and told me that the *Ursula Rickmers* was indeed sailing in four hours, which would have been perfect, except that she was sailing to Kobe in Japan. So that was another blank to add to the fact that I had lost Mr. von Hansemann *and* all my belongings. The clerk gave me the name of a Japanese shipping agent whom he thought would be able to help. Other employees had gathered around, and they all tried to be helpful, amazed at having to deal with a nine-year-old.

Before I set off again, I managed to change some of my American dollars as I most certainly had been cheated by the rickshaw coolie. As I stowed the wads of banknotes back into my pouch, the clerk hailed a rickshaw and told the coolie to take me to the Nippon Yusen Kaisha Line on such-and-such street. It took about thirty minutes of dashing around to find the place, and I had no idea if we were going in deliberate circles or whether we were actually lost. Eventually we arrived and I told the rickshaw coolie to wait for me.

As I marched up to the front door of the line's offices, I was suddenly jumped on by two Manchurian youths, who must have seen my money bag. I yelled and screamed, kicked and wriggled like an eel in their grasp, clutching my pouch to my stomach with all my strength. I knew that without it I would be lost. To my intense relief, the agency doors opened and a huge man with a blond beard came out, saw my distress and, with a roar of indignation, beat my assailants about the ears and chased them off. Terrified by this raging giant, the two fled.

My rescuer took me into the agency and asked me if anything had been stolen. I opened my pouch to check and when he saw my Danish passport he immediately switched into Danish. He told me to sit down as I was visibly shaken. He ordered a Coca Cola from a clerk for me. This was the first time in my life that I had tasted Coke, and I thought it was fantastic. Soon my teeth stopped chattering against the glass and I could really enjoy it.

My new friend turned out to be a captain for the Danish Great Northern Telegraph, the first company to bring telegraph and telephone to China. His ship was part of the Great Northern fleet, laying cables from Denmark to China, Manchuria, and Japan. He even knew my father! Immediately he sent clerks scurrying around and soon had booked me a passage on the Tientsin Maru from Dairen via Tsingtao to Shanghai. She sailed that evening and would arrive in Shanghai three-and-a-half days later.

I paid for my ticket from my wad of money which, I began to realise, was attracting too much attention. This, of course, was long before the days of plastic.

The captain promised to send my father a telegram, telling him of my travel plans and assuring him that I was well. This would be the first sign of life that my parents would have of me since I left Zurich a lifetime ago. Once again I was asked why I was alone and I explained about losing Mr. von Hansemann and my luggage.

"*Det er fan'me for dårligt!*" the captain exclaimed in amazement at the extent of my misfortunes. I asked if I should go to the police, which made everybody laugh. "Forget about them. We'll have to find him ourselves."

At that moment the door swung open and in burst Mr. von Hansemann, panting, sweating, and extremely upset. Never before had he been so happy to see me. Once he had caught his breath he explained how he had raced from one shipping agent to another, asking if they had seen a European boy. Finally he had been told to come here, and it had taken him all this time to find me. He also had our luggage outside, so all was turning out well.

He too booked a ticket on the *Tientsin Maru* and thanked the captain for having taken such kind care of me. I also thanked the captain profusely and he gave me a painfully firm handshake. "*Farvel min dreng.* Take care not to get lost again!"

Later I learnt that my father was so grateful to this kind man that he wrote to him with his sincere thanks and even invited him to stay in our house the next time he was in Shanghai. However, I never saw him again.

When Mr. von Hansemann and I had quite recovered, we went to the pier where the *Tientsin Maru* was berthed, but we were not allowed to embark for another three hours. We were both very hungry and tired from our emotions, so we found a decent-looking restaurant, piled our luggage around our table, and ordered a feast. We had bowls of noodles and dumplings, rice, chicken, and beef and vegetables, and soon we could hardly move. Mr. von Hansemann downed several cold beers whilst I continued with my new-found passion, Coca Cola.

13

The Tientsin Maru

Full up and content, we boarded the *Tientsin Maru* and followed a steward to our respective cabins. After the last cramped train quarters, I was delighted to find that I had a large cabin to myself with my own bathroom. The cabin was about three metres above the waterline and there was a large sign over the porthole saying, "Do not open when in port." The steward explained that this was to deter thieves who would row right under the portholes with children small enough to wriggle through when shoved up. The children would grab everything they could carry and slither back the way they came like little eels.

As I unpacked my bags, I saw they were beginning to look somewhat messy as nothing had been washed since the Russian stewardesses had taken care of my laundry. I wasn't too upset about this myself, but I did wonder what my mother would think of my grubby appearance.

Racing out to inspect the ship, I bumped into one of the junior officers and asked him how big the ship was. He told me she was 10,000 tons dead weight and that she carried cargo and about thirty-five passengers. All the crew were Japanese, of course, but most of the officers spoke passable English. They were extremely friendly, and even said I could go up to the bridge whenever I felt like it. This would be a treat indeed.

Next I found a large saloon already filled with Japanese businessmen and military officers. Some of the civilians had started the undressing ritual familiar to me from the train. I overheard a few Westerners complaining about the overnight stop in Tsingtao, which made the ship take longer than the train, but one red-faced

Englishman cut them off with the remark, "Better than having pot shots taken at one by Mao's chaps, I'd say."

I hadn't thought of this, but now I was very relieved to be at sea.

The *Tientsin Maru* gave a blast of her horn and began to slide slowly though the port and out to the Gulf of Korea. Hundreds of ships surrounded by lighters were anchored in the bay, feverishly taking on and discharging cargo.

Mr. von Hansemann joined me on deck and pointed to a freighter with a black hull and white superstructure. "There's the *Gustav Diederichsen*—the one we didn't want to hang around for."

I was glad we hadn't as she was one of the dirtiest ships in harbour. Mr. von Hansemann laughed when he saw my look of dismay and assured me that she was one of the smallest and oldest of the company fleet.

Once in the open gulf the dinner gong sounded and we went to find the dining room. This turned out to be more like a school dining hall, with a long central, communal table at which all the passengers sat together. Dinner was a hotchpotch of Western and Japanese dishes, all very tasty if unexpected. I remember there was a lot of rice, both raw and fried eggs, salmon, miso soup and wiener schnitzels. I drank Coke whilst most of the adults drank Japanese beer.

Mr. von Hansemann sat at the far end of the table with a group of Swiss businessmen whilst I found myself flanked by two Japanese officers who kept impressing on me how dirty China and the Chinese were compared to clean and beautiful Japan. I told them I had been to Karuizawa as a child and that I hoped to go again from Shanghai to Japan for our family summer holidays. They wholeheartedly approved of this plan, bowing and repeating, "Ah-so! Sodiska-ney," with great enthusiasm. After dinner many people began to play cards, but I wandered about the ship a bit and then went to bed early, as I was pretty tired.

I got up before dawn, dressed, and went up on deck where I found, to our joint surprise, about ten officers in kimonos. They stood at the railing, bowing and praying to the rising sun. I was fascinated and watched them closely until, caught up in the spectacle, I started to join in and began bowing when they did. This, however, caused one of the officers to give me such a glowering stare that I left immediately, feeling rather deflated, to have my breakfast.

When I came back on deck, all the officers had disappeared and we were just rounding the big peninsula at Tsinghaiwei. We were heading for the port of Tsingtao, where we were due to arrive around noon and stay until the next day, discharging and loading cargo. Mr. von Hansemann told me that Tsingtao had been leased to Germany in 1898, but in 1914 a large Japanese land and naval force had besieged and captured it.

I was getting very confused. "But I thought Japan was Germany's ally," I said.

"Not in the First World War," said Mr. von Hansemann. "The Japanese held on to Tsingtao until 1922, but there are still signs of its German past. I'll show you."

In order to explore the town, we took one of the horse-drawn carriages lined up on the quay. We were disconcerted to see how filthy the carriage was, but most of all I was upset at the state of our horse. I would have asked Mr. von Hansemann if we could take another but, as I looked around, I saw that they were all skeletal and in the same distressing state. The town was extremely dirty, full of beggars and starving stray dogs, and it was frightfully smelly.

Mr. von Hansemann pointed out the many white houses with red tiles, remnants of the German colonial days. They were now tottering and dilapidated, but it was easy to imagine how neat and smart they must have once been. The town was surrounded on three sides by the Yellow Sea, and I was made to admire the Bavarian-style railway station, the twin-spired Catholic Church, and the former German governor's residence.

We decided to have lunch in a restaurant overlooking the harbour. I can't remember what we ate, but I had several Coca Colas, and Mr. von Hansemann had a few of the local Tsingtao beers. "Best beer in China!" he declared. "Brewed by a German brewery." In fact its reputation is intact to this day, and it is still sold and enjoyed all over the world.

That evening after dinner, a Japanese officer tried to teach me poker. We made huge wagers—fortunately using matches, as I lost every time and ran up a debt of several million dollars. We all had a good laugh at this and even Mr. von Hansemann joined in.

The next morning I went up to the bridge and was allowed to steer the *Tientsin Maru* for about twenty minutes. I have to confess that an anxious helmsman was at my elbow the entire time, but even so I was extremely proud to think that I was in charge of a 10,000-ton ship plus her crew, cargo, and passengers. Perhaps it was just as well that the latter were not aware of this. (The *Tientsin Maru* hit a U.S. mine and sank in late summer, 1944.)

We sailed all that day, and the following morning I was astonished to see that the entire sea had turned a muddy yellow colour. I told the sea it could turn scarlet for all I cared. Soon I would finally be reunited with my parents—I was nearly home!

14
SHANGHAI

Heading for the delta of the Yangtze Kiang, we passed Wusong, the entrance to the Whampoa River, which would lead us to Shanghai. The ship slowed down and a pilot came on board. I wandered around, hardly able to contain my excitement for the remaining two hours before we docked. I had packed my things for the last time, cleaned myself up as best I could and was back on deck, eager to get the first possible glimpse of my parents. "Just let them be there! Please just let them be there!" I was surprised to find myself muttering under my breath.

Mr. von Hansemann appeared at my side and seemed as keyed-up as I was. We were fascinated by the maze of junks, sampans, riverboats and cargo ships, passenger liners, ferries and lighters, plus Japanese, British, and Italian warships which the pilot had to slowly and skilfully weave past. Without the fresh breezes from the open sea it was terribly hot and humid. One of the passengers saw me wiping my face with my handkerchief and laughed. "Ah, wait until you get ashore, you'll be amazed at the size of the mosquitoes!" But nothing could dampen my spirits.

The silhouette of the tall buildings along the Bund, Shanghai's waterfront, came into view and impressed me greatly. With the help of clever little tugboats, we were edged into our docking position—and then, as I nervously scanned the waiting crowd, I suddenly spotted Mother and Father on the quay, and my heart leapt. Father was waving his Panama wildly in great circles around his blond head, whilst Mother jumped up and down, flapping her handkerchief furiously to attract my attention. I also saw my old friend, Man Fat from Hong Kong, standing behind them, beaming from ear to ear and waving his cap at me. It was all too much and I found myself, for the first time since I had said goodbye to my grandfather, in tears.

After the excitement of reunion I tried to tell my parents everything that had happened during my long journey in the first five minutes. Father laughed and said, "Slow down, old man. You can take weeks to tell us about all your adventures."

I stared at him in delight. So I could!

We climbed into the car and Man Fat drove us to the Cathay Mansions, as our house was not yet ready. Our apartment consisted of a large living room, two bedrooms, two bathrooms, and a kitchenette—which seemed to serve mainly as a place to fix cocktails. I immediately pleaded for a constant supply of Coca Cola.

Breakfast was sent up by room service, and we took dinner up at the top of the building in the Sky Room restaurant, unless my parents had engagements—in which case I had a room service supper too. Adding to my happiness, I shared my father's bedroom whilst Mother slept in the other.

Every day after breakfast, Man Fat would drive my father to his offices in 110 Hankow Road, close to the Bund in the heart of the business district. He stayed there all day and usually returned around six in the evening. During his absence I drove around town with Mother, mostly buying things for the new house. We would lunch together in little restaurants where I would gobble Chinese food with my chop sticks. The Chinese around us would burp loudly and, seeing my surprise, Mother explained that this was considered to be a polite way of showing your appreciation. I had been too young to go out to restaurants when we lived in Hong Kong, so this bit of etiquette was new to me. When she was in an especially good mood, Mother would allow me to follow the local custom.

As soon as Father had a free afternoon, he took me to see our new house at number 11A, Route Francis Garnier. This road, together with Avenue Petain, was one of the nicest in the French Concession, itself a leafy residential district.

My first impression was of how big the garden was, and what fun I would be able to have in it. It was surrounded by a five-metre-high fence lined with tall trees. In the middle of the front lawn was a huge willow, and on the right a lot of Japanese apple trees. Father said he was going to have the willow moved to another part of the garden, closer to the house, so that my friends and I would have room to play soccer.

The house itself was full of carpenters, masons, and plumbers, but we clambered over their tools and under their ladders to have a look at everything. Last of all we wandered around the garden, then back to the waiting car. At the main gate was the watchman's house. There were to be two men, one for day and one for night. We were all three very anxious to move in and have a proper home again, but I could see that we would have to be patient.

As it was beginning to get very hot, and the house was far from ready, it was decided that Mother and I should take a ship to Japan to escape the Shanghai heat. Father would stay behind as he had a lot of work, and at the same time he would keep an eye on the completion of the house, which he hoped would be finished by the time we returned. I was a bit upset about this as I had only just arrived, but I could see how my mother had set her heart on it, so that was that.

Before we left, Father took me to see his office. Number 110 Hankow Road was a colonial-style building with a pillared entrance, very grand to a young boy. Unfortunately, this impression was marred by a beggar lying on the steps, his festering, swollen leg thrust out across our path. The flies, pus, and maggots caused me to avert my head and retch. My father spoke to the man sharply in the Shanghai dialect and rushed me into the building.

In the cool of the lobby we sat on a leather sofa and Father talked to me quietly, calming me down. "Beggars in Shanghai have their own laws and rules, Son. That man is one of the top chaps, and every evening he is picked up by car, so don't feel too sorry for him."

I couldn't understand why he didn't have his leg attended to if he were not poor.

"But that leg is his capital," Father said. "He catches all the newcomers with it. He's made a fortune out of that leg."

Still feeling rather queasy, I followed Father upstairs to meet his employees. We went into high-ceilinged rooms, where two or three Europeans per room sat under plunking ceiling fans, surrounded by their Chinese clerks. Big brass spittoons were placed about strategically, at which the clerks would hawk and aim, not always with the greatest accuracy. This did not help my nausea.

To my relief, Mr. von Hansemann came to say hello, and then I was introduced to Father's young cousin, Michael Jebsen, known in the family as Buele. He gave me a large box of sweets, which he had bought for my arrival. Thus our relationship started off on a happy note.

My father's Shanghai offi ce on Hankow Road 110

15

Unzen-Japan

A few days later, Mother and I took the *Nagasaki Maru* and sailed to Nagasaki, the main port of Kyushu. It took us forty-eight hours. Although the crossing was short, it was lots of fun as the ship was full of European families with children my age, all escaping the Shanghai summer heat for the cool mountains of Japan. There were at least thirty girls and boys, and we had terrific games of hide and seek throughout the ship, from the bridge down to the engine room, often to the distress of the Japanese officers.

When we arrived in Nagasaki, we asked our taxi driver to show us a little of the town before taking us on to Unzen. We saw the port located at the head of a narrow, deep-cut bay, with crooked streets and tiered houses clinging to the hillsides that enclosed the inner bay. Then we drove on to Unzen, about three hours inland, toward the mountains of Kyushu. Unzen lies high in the hills in the centre of a small peninsula surrounded by the Tachibanawan and Ariake-Kai bays.

We stayed at the Kyushu Hotel in the Unzen National Park, which was a westernised hotel. Most of the guests were European, and I found many of the children I had played with on the *Nagasaki Maru*. My mother found it quite amazing that the German, English, Italian, and French guests had perfectly amiable relations, playing bridge and golf together, even though their countries were at war. Japan, of course, was still neutral. Parties of hotel guests of all nationalities would often drive down from the hills to the wonderful beaches and the Amakus National Park, which was surrounded by forests and sulphur springs.

Once a week there was an English-speaking film show in Unzen, where we children always flocked. Before the main feature, usually a western, we had to sit through Japanese newsreels showing battleships, formations of Zero fighters, and military tank manoeuvres. Naturally we children had no idea that this glorification of the Japanese military might was a psychological preparation of the Japanese public for war. We also sat through short films showing the military conquest of China, where Chinese children offered flowers to Japanese soldiers to great applause from the Unzen audience.

The fact that we children believed anything we were shown infuriated one of the Englishmen who, back at the hotel, made us all sit on the hotel lawn whilst he gave us a lecture.

"Nanking was an old walled city with no defences and few Chinese troops. On Dec. 13, 1937, when the Japanese captured it, they began a reign of terror that lasted for six weeks. Up to 80,000 women from the age of seven to the elderly were raped and killed. Thousands of young men, not soldiers, were taken to the Yangtze River, where they were machine-gunned. Their bodies were swept away by the river. Others were used for bayonet practice. Thousands were decapitated, burned, nailed to trees, or hung by their tongues. Babies were thrown into the air and caught on bayonets. Pregnant women were bayoneted in the belly. The death toll is said to range between 200,000 and 300,000."

By this time, some of the parents were coming over to see what sort of game we were playing. The Englishman stopped speaking and marched off, still white with fury. One by one we stood up and slunk away—embarrassed as well as frightened by what we had just had to listen to. I don't think anybody explained to the grown-ups what had been going on. Not then anyway. Later, perhaps because of the nightmares some of the children had, a few parents complained to the Englishman, and we never saw him again. I didn't tell my mother. I could hardly believe that all those terrible things had actually happened—and if true, she would only be frightened. The hardest thing was not to hate all Japanese on sight. I thought of my charming Japanese train companion and could not reconcile his kindness with the atrocities I had just heard about.

Nanking massacres

The evening before we sailed home, Mother and I were driven down to the coast, where we spent the night in the Hotel New Nagasaki and had a last sukiyaki dinner sitting on the floor on straw mats. Then the holiday was over and we were on the *Kobe Maru* sailing back to Shanghai. Miles before we saw land, the sea changed colour as the mud carried by the mighty Yangtze Kiang stained it a muddy yellow. This time I knew the cause.

16

SHANGHAI DAYS

Above: Shanghai Bund
Right: Cathay Hotel (now Peace Hotel) where my parents met

As we drew into the port of Shanghai, we saw my father and Man Fat holding Alf on a leash. Father was eager to take us to our new house, which was now completely finished. Man Fat drove us through the gates right up to the front steps, past the watchmen standing in their khaki uniforms saluting us.

Mother and I admired the immaculate white walls, the red-tiled roof, and the bright green shutters. All the servants were lined up in crisp new uniforms in front of the main door. There was Number One Boy, Number Two Boy, Cook, Number One Amah, Number Two Amah, Coolie Boy, Coolie, and the gardeners. All these people I would soon get to know, but for the moment, as in Hong Kong, I only recognised them by their uniforms.

Father showed us the rooms he had so carefully furnished, but I was more interested in the security arrangements. On each corner of the house under the eaves were large searchlights capable of lighting up the entire garden and entrance. These lights could be operated from Father's night table. When he flicked them on for us after dinner, it became as bright as day. If needed, an alarm could be set off in the watchman's house, and if the watchman heard something suspicious, he could set an alarm off in my parents' bedroom. Both the watchmen and Father had buttons that triggered alarms in the French police station, which was two kilometres away. The watchmen and my father all had pistols, and both watchman were ex-policemen from the International Police Force. We also had two excellent watch dogs in Alf and Didi. Alf stayed in the garden at night whilst Didi slept inside.

All these security arrangements were necessary because of the great poverty in China, especially since the outbreak of violent and frequent skirmishes between the Chinese and the Japanese. During that summer of 1941, Colonel Samuel Howard, commanding officer of the U.S. Fourth Marines, which had guarded the International Settlement in Shanghai for over fourteen years, was given orders to withdraw the regiment on Nov. 28. When the marines paraded through the settlement for the last time, thousands of cheering people waving Chinese and American flags lined the streets. The liners *President Harrison* and *President Madison* had been chartered to pick the men up. The Fourth Marines were bound for the Philippines and Corregidor.

Into this vacuum, the havoc of war in the countryside caused thousands of homeless peasants to enter the city, and crime—especially burglary—was rampant. Because of this, despite all his careful arrangements for our safety, Mother still looked distinctly uneasy as Father tried again to reassure her. "My dear, even if burglars did manage to get into the garden, they would have a pretty tough time getting *away* with all these precautions."

But Mother was still nervous, so we went to look at the high fence around the garden, which had been topped with broken glass. Even the trees that hid the fence from the house now had electric sensors to detect any movement.

"Apart from an inside job, I don't think we have anything to worry about," my father declared stoutly.

"What do you mean, an inside job?" I wanted to know. This, apparently, meant that the watchmen or servants could be the thieves themselves, a disloyalty I could not imagine.

"Well, inside jobs do happen, I can assure you!" my father laughed. "Tell him about your bracelet, my dear."

So Mother told me about the magnificent bracelet her father had given her for a wedding present. He had bought it from a Russian Prince in Paris, one of many who had to sell their family jewels after the revolution. "It had square cut emeralds alternating with fat baguette diamonds, all set in white gold," she remembered dreamily. One evening in Hong Kong she had taken off this bracelet after a ball and left it on her dressing table. The next morning it was gone, and Number One Boy was gone too. Policemen swarmed everywhere, taking fingerprints, but neither the bracelet nor the servant ever turned up.

"I never dared tell your grandfather," Mother confessed, "and don't you dare tell him either!"

My father grinned at me. "Now that was an inside job."

Whatever doubts Mother had, I found all the arrangements perfect. I also knew that Alf was trained not to accept food from strangers as, even in Hong Kong, it had been quite common for thieves to poison guard dogs. Didi, on the other hand, was greedy and would accept anything from anyone so it was just as well she slept indoors at night.

Once we had moved in and more or less settled down, the question of my schooling came up. The American school was only 800 metres away, which would have been ideal. I was very keen to go there as, before they left, I used to watch the marines play American football against teams from the U.S. Army or Navy on the sports field. Unfortunately it turned out to cater only for children of the American Garrison, and the school closed soon after the marines sailed away.

The Chinese schools were out of the question, as it would have taken me years to learn how to read and write in this difficult language. The same was true of the Russian School, which catered to the large White Russian community. The International School was said to have a rather doubtful reputation regarding discipline, but the deciding factor for my father was that its scholastic record was not the best.

After long talks with his friends, Father decided that I should attend the German School. About fifty percent of the pupils were non-German—Scandinavians, Swiss, White Russians, Italians, and even a few Chinese from families who could afford to give their children a European education.

Father went to talk to the headmaster, Herr Direktor Gugel. Political aspects were discussed as well as educational. These were way over my head at that time, but I overheard my parents talking about Nazi propaganda.

"I specifically asked Gugel about Hitler Youth-type things but, fortunately, you have to be sixteen, and let's pray that this dreadful war will be over before we have to cross that bridge," I heard Father say. As I would be only thirteen when Germany lost the war, I was indeed spared that experience.

My parents were very anxious about this decision, so they spoke to as many people as they could who had children in the German School. They questioned a Mr. Hug, who was Swiss, plus a Captain Nielsen and a Mr. Ledertoug, both Danes. They quizzed Italian and Chinese friends whose children attended the school, and the father of my classmate-to-be, Zin-Ho. All assured my father that the school had an excellent scholastic standard and to just ignore any Nazi stuff.

On the basis of this, it was decided that I should go to the Kaiser Wilhelm School in the International Settlement, opposite the big Italian Club. As I had not been to school since Denmark over three years ago, having been taught only by private tutors in Switzerland, I was terribly nervous on my first day. I'd had very little contact with other children, and I was more scared of them than of the actual lessons. In addition, half the pupils were girls.

The day started badly as Man Fat drove me to school and, at the school gates, opened the car door for me. He was in uniform, of course. I was greeted with taunts of, "Look at the rich kid!" before I had even opened my mouth.

The next shock was that, as I followed the other children through the arched entrance, I saw each raise his right arm and shout, "Heil Hitler!" I passed through without saying anything and was instantly stopped by a teacher and told to re-enter the school properly. This I did, not really caring what I was saying, but I had overheard enough of my parents' conversations to know that they were not going to like this.

I was shown to my classroom and told to sit at a desk that I would share with a White Russian boy called Yuri Boiko. The headmaster came in and all the pupils stood up and said, "Heil Hitler." This time I realised that I would have to follow suit in order not to attract attention. It went on all day—at the beginning and end of every lesson and as we filed out at day's end.

Man Fat was waiting for me after school, which I already knew would cause me trouble. By the time Father returned that evening, I was in a state of high nervous excitement, pleading to be allowed to walk to school. Being chauffeur driven overrode any ethical qualms about Hitler.

Father explained that it would take me forty-five minutes, so I begged for a bicycle like everyone else. Mother exclaimed that the traffic would make it far too dangerous, but Father understood how vital this was for me and he promised to buy me one. To appease Mother, he said he would get himself one too and teach me not only the way to school, but how to cope with the crazy Shanghai traffic.

At dinner I told them about the "Heil Hitler" business, which upset them as much as being driven to school by Man Fat had upset me. Father was determined to have it out with Dr. Gugel the next day and accuse him of misrepresenting the facts.

He called up his friends to ask them why they had not told him about this. Captain Nielsen said he had instructed his sons to substitute the name of King Christian. "My boys spend their day celebrating our King and nobody ever notices. The Italian boys say 'Heil Duce,' and the Spaniards probably say 'Heil Franco,' so let your boy mumble whatever he likes!"

Nothing could be done about buying bicycles until the weekend, but I extracted a promise from Father that Man Fat would leave me to walk the last hundred yards to school so that nobody saw him. Although Mother thought this scheme could go on indefinitely, Father realised that I was growing up.

"If he can cross Russia, he can bicycle to school," he declared, so Mother gave up.

The school itself was in a large and spacious building with airy classrooms. There was an excellent gym, libraries and laboratories and a huge sports ground. A church adjoined the school where a pastor gave us religious instruction twice a week. Pastor Maass was violently anti-Nazi and took every opportunity to hit Hitler's regime under the belt so the classes took on a decidedly political tone at times.

Saturday morning arrived and Father and I set out to buy our bicycles. I chose blue, and my father black. Then off we rode through the French Concession and down Avenue Petain to the Picardie apartments—a good landmark—then up Avenue Joffre to the Wei Ha Wei Creek and back via Avenue Foch to the Clemens apartments, where my new Danish teacher lived. We finally headed back to our house, riding just past Chiang Kai-shek's villa, which was at present occupied by a Colonel Stinnes, his German ex-military advisor from the 1930s.

Practically the first lesson to catch my attention at my new school had been about Chiang Kai-shek. In 1920 he had joined Sun Yat-sen in Canton, where he became a top official in the Kuomintang, the ruling Nationalist Party of China. When Sun Yat-sen died, he became the leader of the right wing, and his followers joined him in distancing themselves from Mao Tse-tung's communists. However, after the Japanese invasion, he made a pact with Mao and now led the unified resistance from his base in Chungking. It all seemed more actual and exciting than the endless dates I'd had to memorise in my European history lessons, particularly since I felt some sort of connection to Mao, having been shot at by his guerrillas.

A few hundred metres farther on and opposite us was the house of the Sun Yat-sen family. Sun Yat-sen was called the founder of modern China, and amongst other reforms he had forbidden the cruel practice of binding baby girls' feet, and men were no longer allowed to wear the traditional pigtail. His sister-in-law, Soong Mei-ling, was Chiang Kai-shek's second wife. Because we were surrounded by the houses of all these Chinese personalities, our street was particularly well-guarded and quiet.

Not this morning, however. Before Father and I could enter our gates, we heard the crack of rifles and pistols. Father and I jumped off our bicycles and stood out of the way, pressed up against our fence. A Shanghai Silver Taxi charged past with two Chinese leaning out either side of the back windows, firing at a French police car giving chase with pistol shots and squealing tyres.

At breakfast the following morning, Father read out from his newspaper that three Chinese criminals from a famous Triad gang had escaped from prison. Although our neighbourhood had been praised to me as the cleanest and quietest, I thought things were looking up!

Father explained over porridge that the Shanghai Triads were mainly engaged in the drug trade, gambling, or prostitution. They were highly dangerous organisations with their headquarters in China Town, which at that time was a "forbidden city" to foreigners. It was in the centre of Shanghai, a rabbit warren slum of poverty and crime. The International Settlement Police, and even the Sikh Police, were not allowed to enter it unaccompanied. There was a saying that if a non-Chinese entered China Town, he would never come out alive.

I was to revisit Shanghai some fifty years later and explore China Town for the first time—still with some trepidation, I must admit—but by then it had become a relatively sanitised, safe tourist attraction.

The following day Father bicycled downtown with me in order to teach me how to cope with the traffic there—which was chaotic, to say the least. You had to wriggle between rickshaws, pedicabs, trams, buses, cars, and hundreds of other cyclists, and at the same time avoiding coolies racing along with no regard for anything as they balanced merchandise over their shoulders on bamboo poles. It was quite miraculous that, during the five years I zipped around Shanghai on my bike, I never had an accident.

Amongst my new school mates I was happy to find Gerhard and Henning Melchers, who were second cousins of mine via my Clarens Omi. Gerhard was a year older than I was and Henning a year younger. Uncle Carl Gerhard ran Melchers, which was one of the oldest and biggest trading companies in China, with its own fleet of ships.

Uncle Carl Gerhard and my father were the best of friends. They formed a trio together with Magge von Hassel, and I well remember them poring over maps with great anxiety, discussing the progress of the war. All three were vehemently anti-Hitler and, even as a boy, I was aware of how distressed they were about the rapid German advancement throughout Europe. Uncle Carl Gerhard swore he would not return to Germany until the Nazi regime had been defeated.

The Melchers lived in a three-storey house in Hung Jao. It was surrounded by a large landscaped park that had a small lake at its centre. At that time Hung Jao was outside the city limits, which also meant that it was outside the protection of the French Concession and the International Settlement, and the area was now controlled by the Japanese. There were soldiers everywhere, and to get to my cousins' house one had to pass through checkpoints. We would show our passports every time we arrived and again when we left, after which the Japanese Military Police would roll back the barbed wire to let us through. They were always surly, but never actually denied us entrance.

Hung Jao back then was a beautiful, unspoilt area where Europeans played golf, shot duck, or took long walks along the creeks. Numbers of Europeans had summer houses there, with swimming pools and tennis courts. I spent many happy weekends with my cousins whilst my parents played golf or tennis. In season, my father would shoot duck.

It was at this time, one evening after dinner at home in Shanghai, when we were still chatting at table, that my father told me about the egg of Columbus. I couldn't understand why Columbus had to smash his egg, as I was convinced that I could make one stand. Father leant back in his chair and grinned at me. "If you can balance a raw egg on this polished table, without a cloth, I will give you 1,000 Shanghai dollars."

This was a fortune for a boy my age. He pushed the linen cloth aside and called for the Boy to bring a raw egg. To his amazement I balanced the egg, and my mother burst out laughing.

"Well done!" said father. "I'll open an account for you and you can buy whatever you want until the money is spent."

The very next day I went on a shopping spree, with my best friends Gego and Yuri adding their ideas to mine. Gego's father had been captain of the *SS Clara Jebsen* and had married a Chinese woman, so Gego was half Chinese and knew great places to shop where Yuri and I had never been.

First of all I bought everything we needed to build a radio receiver. For weeks we had been poring over a magazine that explained exactly how to do this, and we were very keen to have a go. Unfortunately, despite our best efforts, the thing never worked, but we had hours of fun trying. I also bought a BB gun with a silver barrel and a reservoir of one hundred pellets. It worked like a Winchester rifle—or the salesman and I thought it did anyway. Finally Gego, Yuri, and I scoured Shanghai for something really special, and we hit on a Chinese crossbow with a reservoir for twenty hard clay pellets. To celebrate we went to Jessfield Park and raced about like mad things to get rid of some of our boundless energy.

After school I invited fifteen of my friends to the American Coffee Shop under the Picardie apartments, and we all gorged ourselves on club sandwiches and ice cream sodas. In this way the 1,000 Shanghai dollars, which had appeared to be such a fortune, soon evaporated.

Our House in Shanghai (note Danish flag)

Nine days later Japan attacks Pearl Harbour !

U.S. Marines leave Shanghai Nov 28th 1941

17

The War Comes Closer

During the winter of 1941, my father and his friends appeared increasingly grave. Added to their concerns about the war in Europe was the growing trade-war tension between the United States and Japan. I would sit at the top of the stairs, clutching the banister and listen at cocktail parties and dinners to the endless speculations about diplomatic stand-offs.

On the night of Dec. 7, I heard my parents come home early from a party. Father raced up to my room, thinking to wake me. He was a little tipsy and very excited. "The Japanese have attacked the Americans in Pearl Harbor and Roosevelt has declared war!"

No one could sleep that night. We scoured the radio waves for the latest news about the annihilation of the American fleet, and the human tragedies that unfolded were heart-breaking. During the following days we learnt that Japanese planes had also sunk a British battleship, the *Prince of Wales*, as well as the battle cruiser *Repulse*, off Singapore.

The Japanese were rapidly advancing throughout Southeast Asia, and all this appeared to me to be disastrous news, but Father was more cheerful than I had seen him for some time. "Now that America is in the war, both Germany and Japan will be defeated. This terrible world-wide conflagration will soon be over."

But for now the news was dire. On Dec. 8, the *HMS Petrel* was attacked at her mooring in Shanghai by the Japanese battle cruiser *Idzumo*. Despite brave resistance, the *Petrel* was sunk. The *USS Wake*, also at her Shanghai mooring, was boarded and forced to surrender.

The Japanese, already in Chinese Shanghai since 1937, now poured across into the International Settlement, and for the first time there were Japanese soldiers everywhere. Only the French Concession managed its own affairs more or less as before because Vichy France was considered an ally.

The next morning, Japanese Military Police barged into our class rooms, looking for "enemy" students. As Denmark was occupied by Germany and thus not at war with Japan, the Danes were left alone. This was also true for the other Scandinavians. The Swiss and other neutral nations were deemed "friends." We were the lucky ones.

At the end of this horrible day, when classmates were forcibly dragged away we knew not where, I cycled home past Japanese troops inside the International Settlement. Barbed wire roadblocks had been thrown up at the borders of the French

Japanese attack Shanghai (google)

Japanese armoured cars invade international settlement (google)

Concession. Nothing could have made it clearer to the thousands of foreigners living in Shanghai that our nations were now at war with Japan and that we were living in enemy-occupied territory.

Seven days later, on Dec. 14, 1941, Father came home sad, bearing a telegram announcing the death in Denmark of his partner, Jacob Jebsen, at the age of 70. He grieved openly as they had been close friends for many years. He had been a mentor to my father after my grandfather Jessen died, and Father must have felt very much alone at this moment. He had greatly admired his uncle's business acumen, and his death meant that Father was now the sole owner, responsible for both Jebsen & Co. and Jebsen and Jessen.

Japanese Navy on Nanking Road

Japanese Marines storming Shanghai

And...more massacres (google)

Entering French Consession (google)

There was little time to grieve though. Many of my parents' friends were British, and over the next few days we were to learn that one after another had been arrested and interned in the Lungwha camp. Those who had forewarning of what was to happen came and hid their moveable belongings with us. They left bicycles, hockey sticks, tennis rackets, cricket bats, golf clubs and shotguns, all shoved into our garages until the doors would barely close. Some left jewellery and paintings for us to keep safe for them until the end of the war. How we wished we could have hidden our friends too.

A few weeks later, officers from the Japanese secret police force—the Kempeitei—marched up to our gates very early one morning, and our Chinese watchman came to the breakfast table in great distress, teeth chattering with fear, stammering out that officers were demanding the keys to all storerooms. To Father's particular dismay they took all his good brandies and whiskies—and then, amazingly, gave him a receipt.

They asked if we had any weapons and wished to search the whole house, pointing out politely that undeclared weapons carried the death penalty. They searched the attic last and took four guns plus my father's favourite three-barrelled shotgun. They left him one shotgun when Father said he liked to shoot duck for our table. He was also allowed to keep his pistol and one magazine for home protection. The night watchman was allowed to keep his revolver and six bullets. As we were to learn, there was little logic in many of their decisions, and the officers themselves were quite unpredictable.

When they saw the unusual amount of bicycles in the garages, they took most of them away, leaving one for each family member and one for the servants, "For shopping or other domestic duties." They eyed the gleaming Buick and smiled. "Perhaps we come back one day for this. Good car for General. Ha, ha!"

They gave my father more receipts for the confiscated goods and then left. Everyone had shown exquisite manners during the whole exchange. Their parting shot had been, on requesting our passports one final time, "Denmark small country. No problem for Japan."

The next weekend father took me to Hung Jao for a long walk along the creeks. As he fetched his shotgun and I my BB gun, he told me that his gun would probably be taken soon so, "Let's have some fun while we can."

We walked for five hours and father shot three ducks. One fell into a creek and an old Chinese farmer fished it out for us with a long pole. I spotted a sparrow on a branch and shot it. I had never managed actually to hit a bird before and, devastated at what I had done, was close to tears. I hoped my father had not noticed, but perhaps he had for on the way home he told me long stories about his past shooting adventures and how the rule was, "If you are not going to eat it, don't shoot it."

His favourite expeditions had been for wild geese in Swatow on the South China coast. He would take his yacht, *Maski II*, and sail with friends for a week at a time. Maski is phonetic Chinese for "never mind."

We stopped under a tree to rest and he drew diagrams for me in the dust. "Geese sleep in large flocks on the ground—like this, with guards strategically placed to warn of any danger. If they do not get wind of you, never shoot a sitting bird, as this is poor sportsmanship."

So he and his friends would creep into hidden positions, and then sailors from the yacht would deliberately disturb the geese guards. Within seconds all the flock would rise up in a flurry. "Sometimes we got as many as twenty or thirty birds," Father remembered with pride. The sailors would gather them up, put them in the hold (which was full of ice), and sail back to Hong Kong as fast as they could. These shoots were often planned just before Christmas so that a goose could be sent to a friend as a Christmas gift. The geese were fat and tasty and much appreciated—especially by the Danes, who traditionally eat goose on Christmas Eve.

When we finally arrived home I was exhausted, but Father, who was very fit, was as cool as when we had set out. We gave the ducks to the cook, who promised to make one of our favourite dishes, Peking Duck.

We had a very powerful RCA radio and we listened to the Voice of America and the BBC every night, despite the fact that this was illegal and the penalties if caught were imprisonment or even death. Roosevelt and Churchill enthralled us. With the Japanese in the Philippines, Malaya, Singapore, and the Dutch East Indies, we certainly needed some stirring speeches. Every day the situation deteriorated on all fronts. The Germans were almost at the Suez Canal and advancing rapidly on the Eastern Front.

It was terrible to be without news of loved ones. We sporadically received telegrams from the family in Aabenraa or from my grandfather in Clarens, but they had to confine themselves to family matters. All we really knew was that they were still alive. Telephoning was impossible because it was reserved for the military, and it was useless to mail letters.

Father was always served a cup of strong black tea when he arrived home from work, and he would sit close to the radio so that he could have it on low, with the door locked. Mother and I would gather around too, and we would all listen with dread to the catastrophes of war.

Soon after Hong Kong fell to the Japanese, Father came home ashen-faced and wild with impotent rage. One of his best friends, Sir Vandeleur Grayburn, known to his intimates as "Tubby," was the Chief General Manager of the Hong Kong and Shanghai Banking Corporation. He had refused to co-operate with the Japanese—he would neither sign their new bank notes nor give them any information about the bank's clients. As punishment he had been stripped naked and forced into one of their diabolical bamboo cages, where his head was imprisoned at the neck and his limp body hung down inside the strips of bamboo, his feet dangling above the ground.

The cage was put in front of the Star Ferry landing stage, under the broiling sun so that Grayburn would die of thirst. Friends tried to splash him with water, but they were whipped away by Japanese guards. All too slowly this good man died. For days Father was grey with grief, not only at the loss of his friend but at the senseless cruelty of his death.

One evening a few months later our doorbell rang, and the night watchman was ordered to open the gates to the Japanese. We had not yet finished dinner when a Kempeitei officer and three soldiers charged into the dining room and demanded the keys of our car. The officer sat down without asking Mother's permission and proceeded to write out a receipt:

Imperial Japanese Army take 1 Buick, 1941 model.

The soldiers took the car out of the garage and the officer sat in the back with his sergeant. To Father's sorrow and Man Fat's outrage, they proudly drove away.

Exactly nineteen years later, to my utter astonishment, when I was working in Denmark I received a telephone call from the Japanese Embassy in Copenhagen. "We take one motor car from Mr. J. H. Jessen in Shanghai in 1942. You are Mr. J. H. Jessen? We have money for you."

They asked how they could get the money to me and I gave them my bank account number. They, however, preferred to send an embassy employee from Copenhagen all the way to southern Denmark to deliver the repayment in cash. I received about U.S. $3,800, which was roughly the value of the car when it had been confiscated. One has to give credit where credit is due, and this was an honourable end to the affair from the Japanese point of view.

As ever, Chinese ingenuity and entrepreneurial flair found solutions to the new difficulties of life in Shanghai under Japanese rule. When it became known that all

U.S. Marines Defend the Philippine Islands at Bataan and Corregidor against Japanese Imperial Army Attack Immediately Following the Bombing of Pearl Harbor in December, 1941

non-military cars had been confiscated, a flourishing horse-carriage trade suddenly developed. All sorts of vehicles in all price ranges became available, and Father bought a smart, black-lacquered, four-wheeled carriage.

Now we had to find a horse. Father knew a Captain Danilov, a Russian ex-cavalry man who ran the Cossack Riding School. He advised us to go to the horse fair held regularly outside some rather tatty stables by the Wei Ha Wei creek. On the day of the next sale, Father, Man Fat and I rode out on our bicycles to see what we could find. From the outset this expedition found no favour with Man Fat who, immaculate in his white chauffeur's uniform, tried to keep his distance from the farmers who touted, hopefully and raucously, donkeys, mules, and a variety of horses. The air was thick with dust, flies buzzed everywhere, and the stench of steaming, animal droppings was overwhelming.

It was difficult to circulate because we were pestered at every turn to admire some ill-favoured beast, but finally, tied to a tree, we saw the only possible candidate—a four-year-old stallion of good height. Its alert eye and eagerly pricked ears pleased Father, whilst I was lost in admiration of his glossy grey coat dappled with white.

The moment we stopped our tour, every farmer abandoned his post and gathered around to enjoy the bargaining. Man Fat came alive as he translated Father's offer and then refused to even repeat the outrageous asking price. I supposed, correctly, that the haggling would take some time, because as always in China a matter of face was involved. I took the opportunity to make friends with the grey and quickly decided that his name should be Winston.

Eventually a price was agreed upon, and then a stable had to be inspected and more monthly fees for food and general care sorted out. Our new carriage also had to be kept in some sort of a shack. Man Fat's face grew long as he realised he would have to cycle here every morning, groom Winston, harness him to the carriage, and be back to pick up my father in time to take him to the office. Man Fat detested horses and hardly knew the front from the back, so he would have to be taught the basics of horse management and how to keep the carriage spick-and-span instead of the Buick.

Now the trip to the office would take over an hour in the crazy traffic, which would be made worse by similar badly driven carriages with novice Shanghai grooms. My father enjoyed this new mode of transport only because it gave him time to read up on his business correspondence, but for Man Fat the entire new regime was a daily humiliation.

For several weekends Man Fat and I went by carriage to Hung Jao, where I also learnt how to handle Winston. I enjoyed this so much that it was decided I should have riding lessons and was enrolled at Captain Danilov's stables outside Shanghai. Kitted out in jodhpurs and boots, I would bicycle to the stables every weekend and daily during the holidays. We were taught to ride on Mongolian ponies with double bits because they were so frisky. Captain Danilov also insisted that his pupils learn how to ride bareback, which was a lot of fun. A group of us would ride out along the creeks, and Alf would run with me as we cantered along the paths.

Unfortunately, these excursions with Alf were not to last long. Very often Japanese Military patrols would jump out of the bushes and stop us in the middle of a canter, demanding to see our papers—which one always had to carry. One day I was riding on my own with Alf loping along at my side when I suddenly remembered that I had left my passport in my jacket at the stables. At that moment a soldier challenged me. As I could produce no identification, the man ordered me to dismount and began to frisk me. Watching this, Alf gave a deep growl and was about to attack. The soldier immediately let go of me and cocked his Mauser at Alf. I begged the soldier to spare Alf's life and tried, at the same time, to calm Alf down. The soldier finally relented, but as of that day I never took Alf with me again.

Man Fat was becoming increasingly sulky, and when the monthly bill came from the stables and it transpired that he had refused to groom Winston or clean out his stable, Father decided to employ a professional mafu, or groom, and a new job had to be found for Man Fat.

Because of rationing, we could no longer use the central heating and had to buy small stoves for each room. These stoves used wood and coke, and it became Man Fat's duty to keep them going all day long. He insisted on wearing his smart uniform for his new tasks—which was impractical, to say the least. As it lost its starched purity, so did Man Fat lose his prestige in front of the other servants, and he began to wither away like a plant deprived of water.

After a few months, Man Fat could take it no longer and asked if he could leave. He had been offered a job as chauffeur to a wealthy Chinese family connected to Wang-Ching-Wai, the puppet Prime Minister for occupied China appointed by Japan. Although Wang-Ching-Wai lived in the French Concession, the puppet government had its headquarters in Nanking, and Man Fat was to move there with his new employers. I, of course, had never forgotten the horrific stories of the massacre there and could only pray that all was calm now. We were all very fond of Man Fat and were sad to see him go as he had been with our family for twelve years, but we could quite understand how he wanted to get back into his real profession.

I was to meet Man Fat thirteen years later when I was working in Hong Kong. He was waiting for his current employer at the Star Ferry landing stage, where I was also waiting for the ferry to arrive. He jumped out of a car, ran across the road, and enveloped me in a surprising hug. I was somewhat startled as I had no idea who could be so pleased to see me.

"Young Master, you no remember me? Me Man Fat!"

Then of course I knew who it was, despite his grey hair. What was remarkable was that he should have recognised in me the twelve-year-old boy he had last seen in Shanghai. Before he let me go, he made me promise to make a lot of money, to buy a really big car, and to employ him as my driver.

Because Shanghai was the major port and trading town in China, the huge "go-downs," or warehouses, were never empty all through the war, and there was no shortage of food for those who could pay. Eventually the poor could not even afford rice but, for the fortunate, Australian canned butter, Heinz baked beans, Campbell's soups, English jams, et cetera, were available.

Surrounded by extremely fertile country, we could always buy chicken, pork, and vegetables. The latter were fertilised with human "night soil," which was to Europeans an astonishing and disgusting practice. At home our gardeners were strictly forbidden to use this ancient method, but anything bought at the open market had to be soaked in the large kitchen sinks in a solution of violet-red disinfectant granules to avoid the risk of typhoid or cholera. All water had to be boiled, of course—even the water for ice cubes—and during the heat of the summer, we would brush our teeth in water that had been boiled too.

Eggs were plentiful, but ever more expensive. Bought directly from the farmers, they cost about half the price charged in town, so whenever I could I would cycle out to the farms with several baskets attached to my bicycle. I would buy hundreds of eggs and cycle gingerly home with my precious cargo, selling it to my mother and other neighbours.

I was allowed to breed rabbits. Starting out with four, I had about thirty after six months, with cages and runs in a far corner of the garden. I tried not to get attached to them and, after my first traumatic attempt to kill one, I always took them live to the kitchen. I have never enjoyed rabbit, but it was served in many guises on many tables during the war.

Soon I diversified into duck breeding, but had to confine all my activities to the very edge of the vegetable garden. Between all the work involved both in feeding and cleaning my live stock; cycling about with eggs, plus school work during the term, I was kept pretty busy. But Mother paid me well, and I accumulated quite a lot of silver dollars—which were very pretty, with images of junks, Sun Yat-sen, and Buddhas stamped on them. If paid in paper money, I would change it at the market, and when I left Shanghai three years later I had managed to save over 300 silver dollars.

Life became more difficult by the day. Even if private cars had more or less disappeared, the street chaos did not improve. Buses and trucks could no longer find petrol so they, together with the famous "silver taxis," converted their engines to run on charcoal. Everything just crawled along, spewing out clouds of filthy smoke, making an incredible racket. The trams and buses were very overcrowded, and people hung out of them like grapes. Rickshaws and pedicabs—bicycle-drawn rickshaws—did a roaring trade, and many people who had lost their cars had to suffer the indignities of this means of transport.

The Chinese who could afford to had private rickshaws as the public ones were lice-ridden and often the cause of "rose spot" typhoid, which could be deadly.

My Uncle Buele Jebsen had managed to hang on to his big diesel Mercedes through his friendship with the German Consul General—who, in turn, as Germany was a Japanese ally, had special relations with the Japanese Military Authorities. He was, however, despite this connection, unable to procure diesel fuel. Then he remembered that the company go-downs were bursting with prime Italian salad oil. Uncle Buele and his chauffeur experimented with mixtures of salad oil and alcohol until they hit upon a ratio which actually allowed the car to run. It spat, sputtered, spewed out grey smoke. and had a top speed of about forty kph, but it certainly was faster than any other civilian means of transport. Thus my father was fetched every morning, and he and my uncle rode to the office in style.

Unfortunately, the arrangement was short-lived as the car was soon confiscated. The new Japanese owners were not to be overjoyed for long, though. They called upon my uncle a few days later complaining that the engine was completely ruined, and what on earth had he done to it? Was this sabotage? they wanted to know. The whole office rejoiced at this, but Father's enjoyment was mitigated by the fact that it was back to the carriage, and now it was his turn to fetch my uncle every day.

Soon this arrangement also came to an end. One evening, returning home late, Father was stopped, ordered out of the carriage on Nanking Road, and told to walk home. The mafu then had to drive the Japanese officers back to their HQ.

It was midnight before the *mafu* turned up on foot, heartbroken, begging Father to keep him on in any capacity as he dreaded working for the Japanese. He became Coolie Assistant Gardener and, unlike Man Fat, was quite content and relieved to have any job.

A few nights later our Number One Boy ran amok, screaming and yelling, brandishing a large kitchen knife and destroying vases. Father buzzed for the night watchman, and together they managed to disarm the servant, who was foaming at the mouth and quite out of control. He was a tough kick-boxing expert, so it was quite a struggle. Finally the French-Annamese police in their blue uniforms and blue helmets arrived in a van, handcuffed Number One Boy, and took him away. A week later he returned, quite his mild normal self again, and asked for his old job back. Mother, naturally, had lost confidence in him, so Father gave him a generous severance pay and we saw no more of him.

Well-trained Number One Boys—the sort of servant who could receive a phone call at six in the evening and arrange a dinner party for twenty by nine—were becoming a rarity. Course after perfect course would appear, and it was quite common for guests to recognise their own silver, china or crystal, as the boys would help each other out by lending equipment, whilst cooks from neighbouring houses would come and lend a hand in an emergency.

Due to the highly efficient "bamboo telegraph," four days after our Number One Boy had been dismissed, Kofa arrived asking for a job. He had been long employed by friends of ours, a Mr. and Mrs. von Schubert, who were Balts but British citizens, and now interned. Mr. von Schubert had been a prominent business man in Shanghai, and his wife, Quirly, was a highly esteemed painter. Several of her paintings had been entrusted to us and now, much admired, hung on our walls.

Kofa was somewhat cross-eyed and had a harelip, but he was a fabulous butler and Mother was delighted to inherit him. I also enjoyed his fund of fascinating stories. Once he told me that a cousin of his had fought with the Kuomintang in central China, where they greatly outnumbered the Japanese, but he and his comrades only had swords, lances and hand-grenades to fight with. There were some rifles, and a few lucky ones had pistols. Once the Chinese soldiers had thrown their grenades, all they could do was force themselves forward at the run in a human wave against the Japanese machine guns. Of course a massacre ensued, leaving few survivors. Kofa's cousin, despite a jagged thigh wound, was dragged away by friends and lived.

Sadly, these thrilling tales were soon to cease as a few months later Kofa announced, much embarrassed, that he was to marry. "So solly, me go mally Ningpo girl. She velly pleety, only nineteen, and father plenty gold bar." We were very sorry too, but happy for his good fortune.

After the war, when the von Schuberts were released, Kofa returned to work for them again. Perhaps the father-in-law had not had as many gold bars as expected, or maybe the pretty young bride felt she deserved a more handsome groom.

The war created ever more poverty and a level of misery unusual even for China. This in turn led to great cruelty. Live babies were left on street-corners as their parents could not afford another mouth to feed. On several occasions, when bicycling early in the morning, I came across clusters of dogs eating these new-borns. Nobody seemed to care. The police just shrugged their shoulders and looked the other way. All my parents said was that most of these dogs had rabies and I should avoid them at all costs. "Don't even look!" was Mother's advice.

One of Father's Austrian friends was indeed attacked a few days later. He must have been bitten by one of these rabid animals when cycling home, but he did not call his doctor or take any precautions. A few days later he began to foam at the mouth and attacked his house boys, who bravely cornered him and tied him to a chair before calling the police. By the time they arrived, the poor crazed man had thrown himself, still tied to the chair, out of his high apartment building, and there was nothing to be done for the crushed body in the street.

Not a day went by that one did not hear the gunfire of shoot-outs between rival Chinese gangs, not to mention the gunfire from the Japanese as they defended themselves against sniping Mao guerrillas. We certainly did not feel safe. Prior to internment, citizens of those countries openly at war with Japan, had to wear arm bands—"B" for British, "A" for Americans, and "N" for the Netherlands (because of the Dutch East Indies). All bank accounts were frozen, and foreigners could only withdraw 2,000 Chinese dollars a month from banks that were only open two hours each day.

School boys, however, carried on much as usual. One Saturday morning we played a school hockey match in Hongjao, close to a creek. As we searched for our lost ball, we saw several dead Chinese and a Japanese soldier drifting down on the current. After the game, as we cycled home, we passed Chinese peasants fishing out these corpses and stripping them naked. It was a grisly sight, but the considered opinion of our team was that the living needed the clothes more than the dead.

I continued to ride at Captain Danilov's, but one morning that too was over. I arrived to find him standing desolate outside his stables. The Japanese had taken all his horses.

By now, in April 1943, I often could not get home from school for lunch due to the hastily flung up road blocks, and on these days one of our Boys would cycle as close to school as he could, wait for me on one side of the barbed wire, and toss me an envelope with money inside. With these funds I would go to the Italian Club across from the school buildings and have lunch. On those occasions when getting home at night was also impossible, I had to sleep there as well.

It was not only on land that trouble erupted. In 1940 Italy had declared war on the Allies and joined forces with Hitler, and she automatically became an ally of Japan. Italy had therefore been allowed a military presence in Shanghai, where she kept several minor war ships, one of them the *Eritrea*. They were to be joined later by the *Conte Verde*, the very same ship on which my little brother Nicolai Peter had died. She became home to a unit of Italian marines, who must have enjoyed being billeted on board such a luxurious liner.

Now in September, 1943, when Italy surrendered to the Allies, General Badoglio dissolved the Fascist Party and, on Oct. 13, declared war on Germany. This *volte-face* immediately jeopardised the Italian presence in Japanese-occupied Shanghai. Italy became an enemy of Japan overnight.

As soon as they heard the news, the Italian marines scuttled the giant passenger liner in the middle of the Whampoa River, thus effectively blocking a great part of the harbour, to the hysterical frustration of the Japanese.

The Italian marines were interned immediately, together with all other pro-Badoglio Italians. Some Italians remained at liberty by declaring themselves still loyal fans of Mussolini, so the Japanese left them alone. They had other fish to fry. The Pacific Theatre of War and the gaining strength of the Chinese army in Central China overrode any thoughts of far-away Italy and her troublesome citizens.

Generalissimo Chiang Kai-shek and his Kuomintang forces were allowing Mao's communists to receive arms and advice from Russia as they moved closer to territory controlled by the Soviets. The faint hope of the Chinese and ever-present fear of the Japanese was that Russia would turn her attention towards China and force Japan to fight on yet another front.

Jewish settlements in Shanghai during war

18

Peking

Into these troubled times came the unwelcome news that my father was unwell. The headaches that had been troubling him for some time were becoming ever more frequent; he lost his appetite and had pains in his chest and groin. His doctor advised a complete medical check-up in Peking, after which we were to join him and go to Pei-ta-ho, a famous beach resort south-east of Peking. This was the best one could do, as obviously one was not allowed to leave China.

Father took a fast train from Shanghai to Nanking, stayed overnight in the bedbug-infested Yangtze Hotel, and then was rowed across the Yangtze to the Nanking-to-Peking train.

A week later Mother and I followed in his footsteps. On the train to Nanking, we were surrounded by Japanese top brass, and our papers were checked frequently by military police. One of the policemen was very rude to my mother, perhaps hoping to impress his superiors, and he threw her passport back into her face. At this a Japanese colonel leapt to his feet and severely reprimanded the man. The policeman bowed obsequiously to Mother and scuttled out backwards. The colonel then went over to Mother, bowed, and offered her his apologies on behalf of the Imperial Japanese Army. You really never knew where you were with them.

We arrived in Nanking in the evening. Standing on the platform with our bags, we were looking for a porter when three Chinese leapt out of the train, followed by a posse of Japanese soldiers who opened fire as they ran. One of the Chinese dropped, apparently dead, another was wounded, and the third got away. We dared not move a muscle. The wounded man was about five yards away from us, obviously

Temple of Heaven

in terrible pain. We watched horrified as the Japanese roughly tore off his clothes and shoved the man about despite his agonised screams. Hidden under his shirt was a pistol strapped to his waist, and as his gaiters were yanked off, gold coins fell out. One of the soldiers shoved a few of the coins into the man's mouth to shut him up. They grabbed him by the wrists and dragged him off, leaving a trail of blood in front of Mother and me as they went. About an hour later we were allowed to leave the station.

We took pedicabs to the same flea-bitten hotel where father had stayed, as this was the only "decent" hotel available for foreigners. When we awoke the next morning, we compared our swollen legs and arms in dismay. Then we too were rowed across the Yangtze and boarded the same train to Tientsin, where father was to meet us.

The train had comfortable sleeping cabins and a decent dining car so, after our night in the hotel of horrors, we felt as if we were in the lap of luxury. The train was heavily armoured against the frequent attacks from Mao Tse-tung's guerrillas, and indeed that night brought the feared attack. Fortunately, it was a feeble affair, and despite some exchange of fire, we slept well. Actually I did not. I spent most of the night on the lavatory, and Mother feared that I had contracted dysentery or typhoid in Nanking, always a danger in China.

The following afternoon we found Father waiting for us at Tientsin, and we were delighted that he had managed to commandeer a car for us from the Danish legation in Peking. We were driven to a hotel where we stayed for two days whilst Father attended to business.

Father told me that Tientsin was a major seaport that had been practically demolished during the Boxer uprising. Now it had no old charm left, and Mother and I found it pretty dull. "There isn't a thing worth buying," she complained.

The next day we were driven to Peking along a stunning highway, partially along the coast, which I could not enjoy due to my state of health. Things became so bad that it was decided I should accompany Father to the Peking hospital, where he was to be given the results of his tests. It was obvious that I needed a little help too, if anybody was going to enjoy this holiday.

Father only had to spend one night in hospital, after which he had a long talk with a specialist who led him to believe that his pains were due to TB of the bone marrow, which was curable. After the war he should go to Davos, where the bracing mountain air would do the trick. In the meantime he should eat plenty of good food and try to fatten himself up a bit as he had lost a lot of weight. "Work less and eat more!" seemed to be the gist of it. Our plans to go to Pei-ta-ho were excellent, and Father should proceed there at once.

"Your son, on the other hand, needs to stay a little longer while we run some tests," the doctor told Father and Mother. "Leave him with us and don't worry—it's nothing serious."

So Father went ahead to Pei-ta-ho and Mother moved in with friends, the Haas family, now to wait for the results of *my* tests. She arrived at my bedside one morning to tell me that a serious bug had been found in my intestines, which would require a two-week stay in hospital.

I had no time to feel sorry for myself for she went right on to tell me that father was much more seriously ill than he believed. Only much later was I to learn that he did not have TB, but an acute form of cancer known as Hodgkin's disease. She also hid from me the fact that the doctors did not give him more than six to eight months to live. It must have been dreadful for her to keep this tragic news to herself.

Up until almost the end she always managed to appear bright and gay, and I am sure this made things a little easier for us all.

During the many tests I had to undergo, it was discovered that I had the beginnings of trachoma, a serious but then-common eye disease in China and Mongolia—which, if left untreated, could lead to blindness. I was operated on by a famous eye surgeon, Dr. Bock. The surgery was successful, if painful, and I had to have both eyes bandaged for about ten days, which was beastly.

Mother stayed with me until after the operation, but she left before my bandages were off. At the time neither my father nor I could understand why she had abandoned me, but later I realised that she had so little time left to be with my father. Once she knew I was in no danger, his need was far greater than mine.

The Haas family visited me daily. Dr Haas had been the German ambassador to Peking, but under Hitler he had been relieved of his duties. The family had opted to stay in China, and Dr. Haas was now a successful businessman. They lived in a charming old Hong, a square one-storey house around an inner courtyard—a typical Chinese family home where one wing is occupied by the parents, one by the children, one by the grandparents, and one by the servants.

They had a son my age, Wilhelm, who visited me often and who promised to take me to the Mongolian bazaars as soon as my bandages were off. When this momentous day finally arrived, both Dr. Bock and I were delighted that I could see perfectly again. I had to continue to sleep in the hospital every night as I was still under observation, but during the day I could explore with Wilhelm.

We bicycled to the Chinese-Mongolian bazaars and bought no end of wonders. We were particularly proud of our Mongolian whistling arrows. The Mongolians used these in war to signal to their troops with sounds meaning, "attack," "advance," "retreat," and so forth, but as we never could remember which whistle meant what, it was just as well no Mongolian horsemen were in the vicinity as we would have caused havoc.

We bought crossbows with steel-tipped arrows, and I found a steel tube with an inner spring. In this you could hide an arrow up your sleeve as a secret weapon. All these deadly artefacts of war were freely available—even to youngsters such as ourselves.

While everyone else was napping after lunch, we would climb up to the roof and scamper from one Hong to another, firing our arrows at nothing in particular. We cycled through parts of Peking that we knew were out of bounds. Here foreigners never set foot, and we imagined we were proving our manhood. All this was highly exciting, but every night I had to return to the hospital as, despite all these activities, my eyes and intestines still needed attention.

Early one morning about two weeks later, my bedroom door was flung open and there was Father. We were overjoyed to see one another, and he said he had come to take me back with him to Pei-ta-ho. "Come on," he said, "let's pack your stuff—there's a train this afternoon."

He was horrified to see that my total belongings amounted to one spare set of underwear, one sweater, one pair of shorts, plus the clothes I had arrived in—all incredibly grubby, as I had been wearing them for weeks. Instead of clothes I had a whole armoury of weapons in my cupboard. He asked a nurse for a large carton, and dumped the lot inside. He called the Haas family telling them Wilhelm could pick up these "toys" if he wanted them, as I was not going to be allowed to take them with me.

Father, who was known by everyone for his gentle nature, was becoming increasingly quick-tempered because of his illness, so I dared not protest. He was furious with my mother as she had arrived from Shanghai with trunks of cocktail dresses and hats whereas I had left with what would fit in my satchel. Off he dragged me to the nearest Chinese bazaar, where he bought me sweaters, trousers, shorts, shirts, underwear, swimming trunks—the whole lot—plus a Gladstone bag to hold everything.

19

PEI-TA-HO

The train journey to Pei-ta-ho, to a village we all called "The Junction" took about three hours. Here we hired rickshaws, and for one-and-a-half hours we were driven for a spectacular ride over rugged cliffs, with bays, inlets, and the crashing sea far below us. We arrived at sunset, and I was thrilled to see how close our hotel was to the long beaches.

All the hotels were family hotels in those days, mostly operated by Europeans. Ours was a white, one-storey bungalow with wide terraces all around. Here we found Mother. The hotel was owned by a White Russian lady called "Ceezee," who catered to about twelve guests. We were just in time for dinner, which was taken at one large table with Ceezee at one end and Father, at her insistence, at the other. The food looked delicious—all the dishes I had grown to love on the Trans-Siberian Express—but, unfortunately, at first none of it was for me. Ceezee had been a nurse. Forewarned of my problem by Mother, and despite my insistence that I was cured, Ceezee promptly put me on a diet of barley soup. Fortunately not for long, though. It was so evident that I was in good health that soon all the delights of her table were for me too.

After Shanghai we revelled in the cool, fresh sea air, with the roar of crashing surf sometimes so loud that you could hardly hear yourself speak. There were lots of children staying in all the hotels, so there were bicycles to rent and horses for hire. We were all three sure this holiday was going to make us forget all our worries.

At breakfast I watched in amazement as father downed three or four fried eggs with bacon, four or five slices of buttered toast, and several glasses of very cold, thick cream. All this was on doctor's orders, but I failed to see any results as he did not appear to be putting on weight.

Soon even I became aware that his pains were getting worse. He had a code with my mother to let her know how things were, on a scale up to ten. In the morning he would tell us, "Two to three," but the pain always increased during the day so that a "good" evening would be an eight. More and more often, however, it reached ten, no matter how many painkillers he took.

The only time father could lead any sort of a normal life was in the early mornings, when he and I would go to the beach together. We would swim or hire sampans and row out to sea with our fishing rods. I only caught something once, and even that was only about twenty centimetres long. Ceezee had my fish grilled and it was passed around the table so that everyone could have a symbolic forkful.

In the afternoons, Father rested and, on good days, Mother would have guests for cocktails in their suite. A lot of their Shanghai friends were scattered around in various hotels. At these gatherings, Father would make an immense effort to live up to his nickname of "sunny boy," earned because of his happy nature and charm, but this left him utterly exhausted. Gradually Mother invited fewer and fewer guests, until only one or two really good friends came.

In the evenings, games of Shanghai Millionaire (Monopoly) or Mah-jongg were organised by Ceezee. I enjoyed them, but my parents never took part. The combination of excellent air, exercise, and sun soon had their effect—on me at least—and I began to feel normal again after so many weeks in hospital. Had Father been well, it would have been a dream holiday, but his sufferings cast a cloud over every day.

A Shanghai doctor known to my mother was also vacationing in Pei-ta-ho, and she asked him to come and see my father to give him some more powerful pain killers. Before leaving, when he was alone with Mother, this doctor told her that he suspected a brain tumour was causing these terrible headaches. Mother told me that this also must be kept to ourselves.

Sometimes one or other of the guests would invite a friend to join us for a meal. So it was that, one evening at dinner, I was aghast to see Herr Foerster, my math teacher, sit down next to one of the hotel regulars. As he entered the room he raised his arm and, instead of a simple good evening, cried out, "Heil Hitler!"

Father, whose temper was becoming ever more volatile, turned white. He informed Herr Foerster that in this gathering of Scandinavians, Swiss, and White

Russians, nobody desired to be subjected to Nazi rituals.

Herr Foerster started shouting that Germany was definitely going to win the war and be the "Master of Europe," at which time all the "silly little nations" would fall under the Nazi yoke and we "had better all start getting used to the idea."

This was too much for my father. Incandescent with rage, he stood up, grabbed Herr Foerster, and propelled him towards the door. By this time Father was beside himself. "They will never win! Hitler is a maniac and a disaster for Germany. I will not tolerate anyone saying 'Heil Hitler' in my presence!"

Despite his illness, Father was still surprisingly strong, and his arm muscles, from years of rowing, were still stronger than most. As he was shoved out of the front door, Herr Foerster yelled back with braggadocio, "You will regret this, Mr. Jessen! You will regret this!"

In actual fact it was I who regretted this scene, because when school recommenced in Shanghai at the end of the summer, Herr Foerster found a hundred small ways to make my life miserable, now that he was my form master too.

20

My Father

The day for our return to Shanghai arrived. We hired five rickshaws, and at 2 a.m., under a full moon, the journey along the dramatic coast left me with an indelible memory. A dark blue sea capped with white, a silvery sky full of scudding night clouds, the crash of the waves far below, a pale moon lighting our way along the cliffs, all made for a magical night which, because of our slow means of transport, seemed to last for ever.

When we arrived in Nanking, we were surprised to see such milling crowds of Japanese military at the station. Wounded soldiers lay on stretchers on every platform, waiting to be taken to any available hospital.

Violent battles in the interior of China between the Japanese and Chiang Kai-shek's armies had been stepped up, my father had explained to me during our long walks on the beach, due to the arrival of vast quantities of desperately needed military equipment for the Chinese from the Americans. A foreign ambassador also holidaying in Pei-ta-ho had told him that Chinese frontline troops had been re-equipped and trained by their own officers, who in turn had been trained by the Americans. No seaport was available on the China coast, and there was a limit to how much could be flown in, but anti-aircraft batteries, machine guns, anti-tank guns, mortars, Tommy Guns, radio and signal equipment, as well as trucks and gasoline, had arrived. Chinese and American officers were working together, creating a new force that was invigorated by the arrival of modern arms.

Now we were witnessing the success of this new army, surrounded as we were by stretchers and the severely wounded Japanese. Most of the soldiers could not

My father J.H.Jessen

disguise their terrible pain—which caused us great distress, no matter whose side they were on or where they came from. We tried not to stare, but in the chaos we had no idea which platform to go to. Soon we were noticed and hurried away to our waiting train.

When we arrived back in Shanghai, everyone remarked on how brown and well we all looked. Few could see past this to Father's actual state of health. The fact that he himself thought he was improving, despite his ever-present pain, no doubt helped.

To our relief we found that the heat had abated, but the food shortages had worsened. The black market continued to flourish, though, and we never went hungry—even if our diet was somewhat monotonous. Rice, chicken, and eggs were still available, I contributed rabbits and the odd duck, and our own gardeners supplied us with potatoes and other vegetables. Still, one couldn't help wanting to satisfy Father's longing for Swiss chocolate or ice-cold grapes.

Soon Father's condition worsened again, and he had to have radio therapy in the Country Hospital, which was close to my school. This treatment had awful side effects, and he became ever more irritable. Nevertheless, he continued to help me with my homework every evening. He had a gift for making everything appear easy, and he explained algebra to me in a way that no school teacher had been able.

In front of the fireplace in our drawing room stood a large, circular table from Jehol, which Father had bought when he first went to Mongolia in the late 1920s. Here we would spread my books and study together for about two hours every day. Now, however, I was often close to tears as I saw how he would fight his pain in his determination to help me, trying so hard not to lose his temper. Today this table, having been several times around the world, stands in my own living room as a vivid reminder of those evenings.

As Father's health deteriorated, several operations had to be performed to remove cancerous growths, but despite these and the ever-present pain, he continued to go to the office whenever he could, at least from 8 a.m. until 3 p.m. In this way he continued to run the company whose entire responsibility rested on his shoulders.

In the late afternoon, after our homework sessions, he would have to retire to bed. Soon he was moved into my bedroom, which was a little apart from the main part of the house and quieter. He slept in my bed, and a sofa and desk were brought in so that he could work whenever he was able. Often a secretary from the office came to take dictation.

I was moved into my parents' suite, and Mother now slept in her boudoir, which was large and comfortable, with a fireplace and long day beds upholstered in red silk. Despite the sadness of all this upheaval, I found myself in a huge room with its own bathroom and an adjoining closed-in terrace. Here I set out my entire train circuit, my Meccano construction set, and my school desk.

As Father's pain soared out of control, Mother engaged a Russian nurse from the Country Hospital to be with him at night. It was arranged that I should spend every weekend with my cousins Gerhard and Henning in Hongjao. The Melchers were wonderful to me during these difficult times.

Every Friday after school I would go home to pick up a small bag and then cycle out to their house, where I would stay until Monday morning. These rides were rather scary because I had to pass great Japanese barbed wire blockades at the end of Avenue Joffre, at the Wei-ha-wei creek, and another about a mile farther inland. My overnight bag was always searched, my passport examined, and then I would be allowed to cycle on, accompanied by sullen grunts.

These weekends were filled with games of hide-and-seek and tree climbing. When it rained we played board games, our favourite being Shanghai Millionaire. We improved this by adding two game boards together to form an "eight," and a game could last from one weekend to the next before one of us would finally emerge victorious.

My uncle would retire to his study after dinner to listen to the Voice of America and the BBC. He had large maps hidden in this room, and they now began to reflect the war's slow but gradual turnaround. We boys were allowed to come in after the broadcasts were finished and he would point out to us on his maps the Allied advances. He was convinced that Hitler's regime would collapse during the summer of 1944 but, unfortunately, he was over-optimistic.

One day whilst playing hide-and-seek, I hid in the crawl space under my uncle's house. It was about fifty centimetres high and ran under the entire building. Suddenly my hand touched something metallic and, switching on my torch, I saw a Mauser pistol. I shone my torch around and discovered a steel helmet, machine gun ammunition belts, and another pistol. All thoughts of our game fled as I crawled out on my belly and yelled to my cousins to come and have a look at my find. We were all very excited and decided to keep this as our secret.

Emboldened by this find, we decided to join the war. Close to the Melchers' house, parallel to the main road leading from Shanghai through Hongjao to the golf course, the Lung-Wha Pagoda, and the Shanghai hills, there was a railway line on which, once or twice every night, Japanese military trains would roll past at slow speed. We decided to try and sabotage it.

We took wrenches from the gardeners' tool shed and, at dusk, sneaked out to see what damage we could do. It was surprisingly easy to loosen the bolts, which we eventually managed to do over a stretch of 200 metres. As there could be Japanese patrols, we took the steel helmet and the two pistols with us. The helmet was a German one of the type used by the Kuo-min-tang troops in the '30s, when Chiang Kai-shek was armed and aided by the Germans. We took turns to wear it, as we did carrying the pistols. Thus armed, we imagined we could defend ourselves against any Japanese patrol.

All this resistance activity made us very secretive. We adopted a sign language when in the presence of adults, and our whispered, cryptic conversations at table made my uncle suspicious that something was going on. He called us into his study and demanded to know what we were up to.

Eventually we broke down and told him the whole story, at which point his face turned ashen and he became very angry. He called us "stupid little boys," telling us that, had we been discovered with our military gear, with loaded pistols, unbolting railway lines, we would have been shot on the spot, followed by the entire Melchers and Jessen families in China.

He ordered us to put what we'd found into a large box, and then he telephoned the police and told them that his nephew and two sons had discovered some old military equipment under his house. When the Chinese police arrived twenty minutes later, they peered into the box, questioned us, and then called the dreaded Japanese Kempeitei. Their irrational brutality was well known, and my uncle was as white as we became when they stormed in. No mention was made of our attempts to derail their trains, and we all stuck to the story that as soon as we had found these relics we had called them. The contents of the box were confiscated after we had shown where we had found them, and then all members of both police forces left. We had been incredibly lucky. My uncle made us promise never to go close to the railway tracks again and never to mention to anyone what we had done—and he, in turn, would not upset my parents with reports of our "activities."

Although our efforts never achieved a total derailment, about a week later we learnt that a Japanese train did stop for about seven hours during the night, exactly at the spot where we had tampered with the rails. To our immense satisfaction, its engine had been partially derailed. So much for the war effort of three boys!

Christmas, 1943, was approaching. Everyone looked forward to winter in

Shanghai, when the days were fresh and the skies high and blue. Even grey days were pleasant after too many months of sticky heat. Despite the war and the Japanese occupation, department stores like Wing-On were bursting with goods. Shops were decorated with Christmas trees, and men were hired to parade around in Santa Claus outfits. Confused Asian eyes peered out over large, false beards as cultures failed to meet. Apart from the small Christian minority, Christmas for the Chinese was just a splendid business opportunity.

Every year my parents invited all the European bachelors from the office to our house for a black-tie dinner on Dec. 24. The main course was always roast goose with red cabbage and roast potatoes, so it was just as well the heat was over. Usually the birds were shot by Father, but not this year. Flaming baked Alaska, my favourite dessert, always followed.

Whilst the Boys and Cooks were preparing this feast, my parents and I went to Pastor Maass's candle-lit Christmas Eve service. Pastor Maass was a great favourite of my father's. "Good man," he would always say whenever the pastor's name was mentioned. "Had he remained in Germany he would certainly have ended up in a concentration camp."

This was high praise. When we arrived at the church we sat at the back, but I soon caught sight of most of my friends sitting up at the front. I asked if I could join them.

"Of course you must," Father replied immediately, making way for me, but Mother held my arm in an iron grip and hissed, "Stay with us!"

I pulled away and pushed rather rudely past her. As I did I heard her angry whisper: "You stupid boy. You will regret this."

She was right, of course. The following Christmas, Father was no longer with us.

Before leaving for church, Father and I had gone to the kitchen to sample the goose lard, which each year the cooks made up into a Danish recipe using onions and chopped apples to concoct a delicious spread for bread. As we were in a hurry and our rickshaws were already at the door, we bypassed the bread and just dug in soup spoons, half ashamed, half laughing at our shared gluttony. The cooks shook their heads and sighed, "Velly heavy. Velly lich. You be sollee." But we did not listen.

The revenge soon came. Almost immediately after the service began I had violent cramps and had to dash to the lavatories, followed seconds later by Father. During the entire service we went back and forth to our pews, mine in the front,

Father's at the back, disturbing and irritating the entire congregation. Even Pastor Maass noticed our comings and goings and must have wondered if Father had taken a turn for the worse. Our stifled laughter surely made him realise that something else entirely was afoot.

On the way home, our rickshaws raced through the cold, dark night, and we froze. I snuggled closer to Mother's scented furs, and to warm ourselves we began to sing carols. To our amazement, the rickshaw coolies joined in. They knew the tunes but, if one listened carefully, the words they sang were mostly gibberish, a mixture of Shanghainese, Pidgin English, and made-up nonsense.

Before our guests arrived, Father and Mother changed into evening clothes and I struggled into a suit. Our cramps disappeared as quickly as they had come on, and Father and I were able to enjoy dinner with our usual gusto. I think Father was keyed up, living on his nerves—otherwise how could he have managed?

Presents were laid out under the Christmas tree in the drawing room, and after dinner we all went in to drink champagne and open them. I received a much longed-for and impressive array of lead soldiers to add to my collection.

To Mother's and my amazement, and certainly helped by pain killers, Father managed to be the life and soul of the party, cracking jokes and full of fun. Toast after toast was proposed, most for peace in the coming year of 1944. At midnight I was sent off to bed, but I lay awake for ages, listening to the music and laughter. This was to be the last night of laughter for a very long time.

In January, 1944, father became increasingly ill and weak. I continued to spend every weekend with the Melchers whilst father was in and out of hospital for weeks at a time.

In March he had a major operation. Dr. Bender from Vienna, a famous eye and neurosurgeon, operated for hours, using only local anaesthetics. He had to remove one of my father's eyes in order to get at a tumour, and then return the eye to its socket. My mother sat outside the operating theatre, and she told me that she heard my father cry, "Cut it out! Cut out all that damned shit. Come on!"

Afterwards, his handsome face was never the same, criss-crossed as it was with scars but, amazingly, he could still see. He stayed in the Country Hospital for nearly two weeks, and then the doctors sent him home.

He spent most of his days wrapped in cashmere blankets on a chaise longue out on a terrace, soaking up the Shanghai spring sunshine. Every afternoon he still asked me to come to him so he could help me with my homework. Because he was under sedation, his explanations were hard to follow, but he was desperate to help me and I hated myself for failing to understand. When he realised that we were both having a hard time, he decided to employ a math tutor.

A young Austrian student came to be interviewed. We three sat around the Jehol table in the drawing room, Father in his burgundy silk dressing gown, huge scars across his face, his eye back but never as before, and a bandage swathed around his head. He asked the young man to please excuse the fact that he was not dressed. "I have just had a minor surgical intervention." The student looked embarrassed and somewhat scared, but he made no comment.

By now, both day and night nurses were in constant attendance, and doctors came and went all the time. They told my mother that she had to find some morphine as they could not.

Mother had acquaintance with a Japanese diplomat who, educated in Europe, spoke several European languages. She took the desperate step of contacting this gentleman, Dr. Takashima, and asking for his help. He managed to get sufficient supplies from the Japanese Army, at exorbitant prices, to relieve Father of the worst pain until the end.

As I now took my after-school lessons with my new tutor, I missed the afternoons with Father. I asked Mother if I could just sit with him and what I could do to distract or amuse him. She told me to talk to him about our times together. "Whatever you remember doing with him," she said, "no matter how small you were, remind him of it. Bring his memories back to life for him." I shall always be grateful to my mother for this advice.

The following afternoon, after my tutor had left, I slipped into Father's room to see how he was. I sat by his bed and he gave me a little smile, despite his obvious pain. At times he spoke rationally, at others it was hard to follow his thoughts, clouded as they were by morphine. I never knew how I would find him, but today he spoke quite clearly and asked me how school was. We chatted about this for a few minutes, and then there was a long silence.

This was my moment, but how to begin? I dithered and dawdled, and then blurted out, "Do you remember the Coronation?" He looked at me rather blankly. "In Hong Kong," I persisted, "King George the Sixth."

Father's face cleared. "Fancy you remembering that. You can only have been quite small. It was in '37, wasn't it?"

I was so happy he knew what I was talking about. "You held me up in your arms. On the front terrace."

Now he beamed. "Ah, yes. Down in the harbour every ship was lit up with red, white and blue strings of bulbs draped up and down the decks and looped between the masts." His eyes were bright. "Then all the ships blasted their horns in unison and you practically jumped out of you skin!" He was silent for a minute. "We decorated Kik-Ud too. Coloured lights all around the roof—and the *fireworks!*"

He loved fireworks. From the Peak down to the harbour, from the anchored ships over to the New Territories, rockets raining stars and blooming chrysanthemums soared into the tropical night sky and lit up the surrounding hills. Draped from the stone balustrade at the foot of our garden was a huge Union flag, and I think it was the first time in my life I was given a sip of champagne—which I promptly spat out. My parents and I stood on the lawn overlooking Hong Kong and enjoyed the show for about an hour.

For a minute or two we were both lost in our memories, and then father tapped my wrist. "Do you remember our Chinese New Year's party?" I did, but I let him remind me. "We invited the entire Hong Kong office staff, and all the way up the walls of the house, ladders were erected with fire crackers attached to every step. When they were lit they gave out a racket like cannon fire!"

I could see it clearly. Father in a dinner jacket, Mother resplendent in red chiffon, and I in my dressing gown. At first it was true that I had been a bit scared, but being with Father always made everything safe and fun.

"And the women!" he grinned. "They all ran, screaming, holding their ears, into the house." We laughed, men together. "Do you know why we made such a noise? The Chinese believe it chases away the evil spirits until the next year."

We were not the only ones to produce such an incredible noise. The other houses on the Peak had fireworks too, and down in Hong Kong itself pandemonium reigned.

Even at this stage of his illness, on better days, Father continued to listen to the BBC and the Voice of America. There was also a German Shanghai radio station—XGRS—but it was full of Nazi propaganda, and unreliable as a source of news. In the mornings he still was able to read the English language Shanghai newspaper, but it was strictly censored by the Japanese and was, therefore, full of their latest victories, often imaginary. German successes on the Russian Front were reported too, despite the fact that the German Army was in general retreat now, in March, 1944.

Sometimes, when I came into Father's room, he would be smoking, although his doctors had forbidden him tobacco. Mother said we should close our eyes to the odd cigarette or glass of whisky, as he should be allowed whatever pleasures he could still enjoy. "It's not as if it's going to make any difference," she would add sadly.

Father himself remained, at least outwardly, full of hope. "Once this war is finally over and I can get to Switzerland, I'll kick this thing," he would repeat endlessly. This optimism, both on his side and mine, soon came to an end. Even I had to accept that he was sinking by the week.

Uncle Carl Gerhard often took me aside and talked to me during the weekends when I was at his house. Gently he tried to prepare me for the worst. "You know that your father is very gravely ill and that he might not make it?" he would say whenever we were alone. Mother never spoke like this, and I clung to the hope that, until she did, all could still be well.

One day, when I returned from school, I found Mother in tears, which was in itself most unusual. She told me that Father had spent the entire afternoon searching for his pistol. "'I can't take this pain anymore. There's no point in it. I'm not going to make it anyway,'" she told me he kept shouting. This was the first time he had ever spoken of dying. He had searched through the house in a frenzy for two hours, and then collapsed on his bed, exhausted. Mother said she had hidden the pistol, but she was terrified he would find it the next time. She had telephoned the police and was waiting for them to come and take the pistol away.

The S.S. Gustav Diederichsen on trial run in Aabenraa Fjord

The following afternoon I went to see Father, as I had not dared intrude upon him after the trauma of the day before. I found him drowsy, half adrift on a sea of morphine, but very affectionate. He patted his bed for me to sit next to him.

I had decided to ask him about the great typhoon of 1937 in Hong Kong. When I mentioned it his eyes widened. "What a storm that was! Many of the Wanchai houses were half blown away. Not only were the poor districts affected, but some of the houses on the Peak were damaged too."

I told him I remembered seeing roof tiles and shutters scattered all over town in the aftermath of the storm.

"Hundreds of Chinese lost their lives. Hundreds of sampans capsized or were dashed onto the rocks. It was a terrible sight." Father's eyes were closed but he continued. "Do you remember I took you out on my boat and we sailed around Hong Kong island after the typhoon?"

How could a son forget. "Wasn't a Japanese liner thrown up by the storm and left stranded on a hill?"

Father gave his new crooked grin. "Oh yes, and the 10,000-ton *Gertrude Maersk* was tossed up onto Green Island in Hong Kong harbour by the tidal wave. It took ages to refloat her and then months to repair her."

He was silent for a while. Then he said, "That was quite the worst typhoon I ever saw. Eyes still closed, Father continued. "Have I ever told you the story of the *Gustav Diederichsen* and the pirates?"

This was a favourite story of his, which I had heard often. "Tell me again," I said.

He settled back on his pillows. He must have known the story by heart. I knew I did. "In February, 1933, the *Gustav Diederichsen* left Hong Kong harbour on her way to Swatow and Bangkok. Amongst the passengers were forty Chinese who embarked in Hong Kong. The Danish Captain had no idea that these men were pirates."

He opened his eyes to check that I was paying attention. "Once the ship was on the open sea, the pirates split up into two teams. One group, armed with rifles and pistols, took over the bridge. The second team stormed the officers' dining room and immobilised the officers. Captain Jacobsen heard shots and tried to send off an SOS but was overpowered, and one of the officers was wounded."

He was silent for quite a while and, fearing he had exhausted himself, I was about to creep away when he carried on with his tale. "The pirates thought that the ship was carrying gold. When they found she was not, they took all jewellery and valuables from the passengers and forced Captain Jacobsen to open the safe. All the ship's money was taken too."

There was a tap at the door and a Boy came in with a carafe of fresh lemonade. Father took a gulp and went on. "Afterwards Captain Jacobsen told me that once they had some loot, the leaders of the gang became quite chummy. They ordered tea and biscuits to be served to the passengers, they handed out ship's cigarettes and, lounging about on the floor, lit up their opium pipes, counted the money, and admired the jewellery. This was not the gold they had expected, but they seemed quite content."

By now I was worried that father was over-tired, but he would not stop. "The swag was bundled up inside a carpet, and the ship's officers were forced to sail through fog into a bay. The sailors rowed the pirates to shore, together with three of the richest Chinese passengers who were taken as hostages. Once on land, the leader of the gang threw handfuls of silver dollars back into the boat as a tip for the sailors! When the ship finally sailed into harbour, they were the sensation of the week in Hong Kong."

By now Father was out of breath and pale. I held his hand and waited for him to fall asleep.

As I sat there, I remembered Gego's father, Captain George Hamman, telling us that when he was captain of the *Clara Jebsen* he had more than once come under attack from pirates. One of their favourite tricks was to have a manila rope, thicker than a man's thigh, connecting two junks. Full of armed men, these junks would approach a ship, one to starboard and one to port, the rope out of sight under water. Once the ship steamed into the rope she automatically drew the two junks together until she had one on either side, ready to board her. Knowing this was about to happen to him, Captain Hamman had ordered full steam ahead and, luckily, although the junks were drawing ever closer, the sharp bow of the *Clara Jebsen* had sliced through the rope, leaving the pirates screaming, yelling, and shooting their rifles in impotent rage as their prey raced out of danger. He also told us tales of pirates in the South China Seas throwing officers and passengers overboard to the sharks.

Father opened his eyes. "I had to go to their trial, you know. Months later, two of the pirates were identified and arrested. The hostages had been released against a hefty ransom, and one of them later recognised a couple of his captors. I had to be present at that trial and listen as the judge proclaimed the sentence of death by hanging. As owner, I had to witness this. It was horrible to have to watch those men die. I hope you never have such an experience."

As I waited, not knowing how to change the subject, Father fell back to sleep. I think I realised then that this would probably be one of the last of our chats together. How I wished it could have ended on a happier note.

Five or six days later I came home from school to find my mother feverish and tearful. She was lying on her bed and asked me to cuddle up beside her. I felt awkward as I had long grown out of such childishness, but I lay stiffly at her side in order not to upset her. She had tears stains on her cheeks and I found her strange. When I asked her how Father was, she said he was very ill and could not be disturbed. When she fell asleep I crept away.

A couple of hours later my uncle Carl Gerhard arrived. He took me into Father's study and put his hand on my shoulder. "You know how ill your father is and that the end is near?" I nodded dumbly. "Well, my boy, this morning, when you were in school, your father gently passed away."

My world collapsed. How could my mother have kept this from me? Why had I not been called back from school? I rushed to Father's sickroom, only to find the Boys stripping the empty bed and cleaning the room as if to erase every trace of him. I locked myself in my room, inconsolable.

Later I was told that my mother, meaning well, had thought it would be too difficult for me to watch my father dying. But now I would never be able to say goodbye to him or tell him one last time how much I loved him.

The funeral took place some days later, in the church next to my school. There were not enough places for all the people who wanted to come and bid farewell to my father. Flowers poured in as if the whole of Shanghai had sent wreaths, and they were massed almost to the ceiling.

Before the service, I stood at the entrance to the church with Mother, and many of my school friends came up to me. They told me that they had accompanied their parents yesterday to pay their last respects to my father, who had lain in the church in an open coffin. I was devastated. No one had told me. I had not even been allowed to do what my friends had done. Now the coffin was closed and I had lost my last chance to see him. I was his only son. I loved him so. Would he believe this now that I had failed him? If this denial had also been to "spare" me, how was it possible for Mother to have been so wrong?

The service was overwhelming, and I had to struggle to keep my self-control. Pastor Maass read the eulogy, which I was to treasure and know almost by heart:

"When looking at Johan Heinrich Jessen's life, one thinks of Goethe's words: 'The Gods give everything to their best beloved in abundance—both infinite joy and infinite sorrow.' And from the Bible: 'The Lord punishes most those whom he loves the best.'

"Johan came from the most shining and brilliant circumstances of an Aabenraa family that has been enmeshed for many years in trading and seafaring to China. Paternal love was the guiding star of his life—and then he had to suffer the premature death of his young mother and the fatal accident of his father.

"With his marriage to Etha Rickmers, he remained faithful to the seafaring tradition. The greatest happiness and the deepest sorrow had to be borne by both. During their honeymoon, the news arrived of his father's death. Later their happiness was severely dented by the death of two children.

"Blessed with a brilliant mind and an admirable, sunny character, J. H. Jessen was very popular and the centre of the business scene and social life in Canton, Hong Kong, and Shanghai. Then he was attacked by that treacherous, awful disease, which he fought with such bravery—a disease that tore him away from a successful life and separated him with such cruelty from his loved ones at the age of just forty.

"In 1922, as a young man of only nineteen, he stepped into his father's business—which, until the very last months of his life, he enlarged, preserved, and maintained as one of the biggest trading companies of East Asia. And yet the outbreak of the Second World War, the end of which he was not to see, must have filled him with great worries.

"We know that the deceased will not only remain in the thoughts and hearts of his wife and son, but others also will remember him for his generous and balanced nature, his high intelligence—which knew no ulterior motives, nor deceit, nor moods, nor capriciousness. A nature that in every sense of the word could only be called 'sunny.'"

21
Sad Days

Life was never the same again. I placed my father's picture on my bedside table so his face greeted me first thing in the morning and last thing at night. I was dazed with grief.

In a brave attempt to distract me, Mother decided that she and I should travel to Peking and then to Pei-ta-ho at the end of term, to escape the summer heat and the sadness that lay like a miasma over our house.

I continued to go to school, but no longer spent every weekend with the Melchers. I stayed with my mother as we both needed each other. Social life in Shanghai had pretty much ground to a halt, and suddenly, after the anxious months of caring for my father, her days were empty and she didn't know what to do with herself. Had it not been for the war, we would have returned either to Clarens or Aabenraa. As it was, we were lost without my father, our anchor in Asia—and yet we could not leave.

Our financial situation too was becoming difficult. No funds could be remitted to us from occupied Denmark or the United States, where my father had accounts, nor could my grandfather help us from Switzerland. Due to the political situation, business was pretty much at a standstill, but once a week Mr. von Hansemann and a colleague, Mr. Juergens, came to our house with a suitcase full of money. Due to the rampant inflation, the bundles of Shanghai dollars became ever larger and bought ever less. This delivery of funds was also somewhat risky, as an attack and subsequent robbery was always possible. Fortunately our lifestyle had become simpler. We were never hungry, as so many millions around us were.

My schoolwork suffered and my grades fell. Direktor Gugel had told the whole school at assembly about the death of my father, so both pupils and staff were understanding and kind. Even Mr. Foerster became almost human.

22

FRIENDS TO THE RESCUE

It was at this time that Gego Hamman, Yuri Boiko, and I decided that we should organise a football team, with the lawn in our garden as our club grounds. My mother allowed us to erect goal posts, which we painted white so they looked pretty good. We named our club "Mars," and designed a uniform of green-and-white-striped knee socks, green shorts, and a white shirt with a green "Mars" logo on the back. My shirt had a red armband. I was to be captain, as it was my idea and my garden.

We selected a team from amongst our friends, winding up with four Danes, three Koreans, three White Russians, plus three Chinese, and we practised twice a week. We arranged matches against other Shanghai junior teams on most Sundays, and soon, out of eight teams, we were usually ranked second or third.

Our football cleats created havoc in the garden, and Mother had to ask the gardeners to patch up the lawn with fresh sods of grass. The "Weedy-Weedy" women, who had previously come just twice a year, now had to come more often.

This meant about several dozen Hakka coolie women would arrive and line up in a row, each with her small knee stool, scissors, and tools. Like an advancing army formation, they slowly inched across the lawn, snipping away at the grass, removing every weed in their path. They came at dawn and left at dusk, and they always took three days. For the whole of the time they worked in the garden, they chattered like magpies—non-stop—and one could hardly hear oneself speak or even think. Our servants distrusted them and would stand guard at every door and window, convinced that a mass attempt at robbery was imminent.

After the Weedy-Weedies left, the garden was immaculate again. In the place of every removed weed, they planted fresh grass. Sadly, though, our football mania soon reduced this splendour to bare patches around the goals once more. Fortunately, Mother was so happy to see me occupied and enjoying myself that she rarely complained.

One night Mother came to my bedroom and woke me. It must have been about eleven, and she had just heard on the Voice of America that the Allies had landed in Normandy. It was June 6, 1944—D-Day! Just two months after my father's death, the breakthrough in Europe, which would have so elated him, had begun. My mother rang down to wake the Boy and she told him to bring champagne and two glasses. We sat on my bed, I still groggy in my striped pyjamas, and we toasted to victory. Mother, between tears and laughter, repeated every few minutes, "If only your father had lived to hear this!"

We were both convinced that the Nazi regime would collapse now, not only due to the Allied advances, but also from within. Many people thought that German officers themselves would now rise up against Hitler. Tragically, the few heroic attempts failed.

In school things became tense. The pro-Nazi teachers tried to brainwash us that the Führer's final victory was merely postponed and that he had secret weapons up his sleeve, which would reverse the entire situation. Some chose to believe this, others amongst us did not.

In an attempt to persuade us that Germany's place in China was assured, no matter the outcome of the war, great emphasis was placed on the friendship that had existed between Chiang Kai-shek and the German military in the 1920s. "Remember Colonel Bauer, children," these teachers would say. "The Chinese Army was trained by German officers to German standards of excellence under this man. German-Chinese aviation companies such as the Eurasia Fluggesellschaft flourished. Chiang Kai-shek will not forget how we helped him at the beginning of his career. He cannot forget the uniforms, guns, munitions, railroad technologies, even submarines that the beloved Fatherland bestowed on China."

Without Father, there was no one with whom I could discuss all this. But with the confidence of youth, I refused to believe that what had happened so long ago would have any bearing on what the future held for us all now. Like my father, I was firmly on the Allied side, and nothing Germany had done in pre-Hitler days counted in this war.

Mother bought a fresh map of the world from the French Bookshop around the corner, together with red flags and thick coloured pens to track the Allied advances every evening after we had listened to the Voice of America.

"Hang on, Darling," she would say every night as I went upstairs to bed. "Soon we'll be able to go home!" But for me, Shanghai was home.

Just two days before we left for Peking, our Number One Boy came in, breathless with fear, to tell us that two Kempeitei officers were demanding entrance. "Velly bad. Velly angly."

We were in the middle of dinner when the officers burst in. "Where is your radio? Show us all your radios at once!" they shouted.

Mother took them into the drawing room where the large RCA radio stood. One of the officers switched it on and, of course, it was tuned to the Voice of America. "Ah so!" he crowed. "Do you listen to this legulaly?" We swore we did not.

"It is just a coincidence that you have picked up this station," Mother protested. Her face was ashen and I saw her clasp her hands behind her back to hide their trembling.

"We are Danish," I announced as firmly as I could. "The war does not interest us."

I was terrified that they would search the house and discover the map in Father's study. It not only showed the Allied advances in Europe, but also the Japanese defeats in the Pacific. We were asked if we had any other powerful radios, and my mother said she only had a small one in her bedroom, which was incapable of receiving anything but local Shanghai stations. The officers bounded up the stairs, insisting on seeing for themselves, but fortunately they were satisfied when they saw the little thing and did not search any further. Upstairs in the attic there was still my father's shotgun, together with two guns belonging to Mr. von Schubert, our British-Baltic friend, but by now the men seemed bored with us and checked no further.

Finally the officers went outside and yelled into the night. A large black van bristling with antennae pulled up in front of our entrance and two Japanese soldiers jumped out. They ran to the officer, who brought them into the house and told them to remove our RCA radio. The officer barked at Mother, "Japanese Army confiscate radio. No receipt!" And as quickly as they had come, they left.

Frightening as this had been, we were very lucky. Chinese friends of ours told us that listening to the Voice of America usually meant severe beatings, jail, and sometimes even death.

23

PEKING AND PEI-TA-HO AGAIN

How relieved we were that our change of scene was imminent. Two days later we took the train to Nanking, spent yet another night in the "hotel of horrors," crossed the Yangtze River, and boarded the train to Peking. Both Mother and I were overwhelmed by a completely spurious sense of freedom from the moment we left Shanghai.

In Peking we stayed in the huge Hong of Baron von Maltzan, a family friend. The profusion of fine carpets, silk hangings, precious vases, dark carved wood, candles, and incense created an aura of exotic luxury. The baron was interested in furs—and, I thought, in Mother too. Every day several Chinese traders came to spread out their finest sables, minks, and tiger skins over the silk carpets. Surrounded by such opulence, it was difficult to remember we were in an occupied country. Mother adored sables and bought enough for a coat to be made up for her in Shanghai. We stayed for four or five days, during which the Haas family invited us several times for lunch or dinner. Everyone had been very fond of my father and all were especially kind to us because of our loss.

When we arrived in Pei-ta-ho, we stayed again at Ceezee's. Every nook and cranny was full of memories of my father and our last visit, but neither my mother nor I mentioned this, in order to protect the other. We each dreaded breaking down.

Early before breakfast every morning, I hired a horse and galloped along the damp sands whilst they were still empty. The resort was becoming crowded with visitors of all nationalities, and we came across a friend of my mother's amongst them.

Dr. Huber was a Swiss gynaecologist from Shanghai, and he invited me to join him on a shark fishing trip. One morning at 5 a.m. we climbed aboard a junk manned by four Chinese fishermen and sailed far out into the Gulf of Bo Hai. Here the waters were pretty rough, but we set out seven lines and bloody bait was thrown overboard. Soon a large shark circled our junk over and over again but he, too smart for us and bored, glided away. We trawled up and down for six hours in the choppy sea, but caught nothing.

Dr. Huber had been on a similar outing the year before, when four sharks had been caught. He described how they had thrashed around violently on deck until the crew had literally hammered them senseless. Hearing this, I was less unhappy. I was not sure that I would have liked to witness such slaughter. Finally, cold and empty-handed, we sailed back to Pei-ta-ho.

On the beach a small, forlorn Chinese boy stood with two baskets at his feet. Dr. Huber and I passed him on our way back to my hotel and peered inside. In one basket were six baby hares, and in the other, two puppies. As a consolation for not having brought back a shark, Dr. Huber bought the six hares and one of the puppies for me.

Mother was not amused. "What on earth are we supposed to do with hares and dogs in a hotel?" she demanded.

Ceezee, however, could cope with anything. She gave me a large cardboard box, lined it with straw, and we put the baby hares inside. She gave me an eyedropper and showed me how to dribble warm milk into their eager, pink mouths. Feeding them took up most of my day, but I was determined to take them back to Shanghai and cross-breed them with my rabbits. Unfortunately, and to my despair, they died one after the other despite my best efforts.

I was luckier with the puppy. About three months old, it was able to manage without its mother and thrived under my care. Soon he could race up and down the beach after me, he slept on my bed, and ate whatever I gave him. For both of us these were halcyon days.

I had no doubt that we would take the puppy back home with us, but here I hit a brick wall. Mother pointed out that we already had two dogs in Shanghai and, in such uncertain times, we could not adopt any more. Sadly I approached many people on the beach, asking if they would like to have Terry. In the end a retired Swedish captain who lived in Peking agreed to adopt him. He left with the puppy a few days later and kindly said I could visit Terry whenever I passed through Peking.

When our holidays were over a few weeks later, we returned home via Peking so Mother and I visited the captain, who lived on a farm far out of town. Here Terry seemed fat and happy, and I knew I had done the best I could for him.

24

1944-The Danish Consulate

Back in Shanghai, in this autumn of 1944 when I was twelve, we learnt that Japan was being forced out of many Pacific strongholds. As we no longer had a radio at home capable of receiving the BBC or Voice of America, it was at school, during our breaks that my friends and I would cluster together, each eager to impart the latest news gleaned from their fathers. All I could do was listen.

The U.S. counter-offensive against Japan, which had begun with the invasion of Guadalcanal in August 1942, continued year after year as bitter fighting brought the Americans slow advances from island to island. The losses on both sides were enormous. By now, in July, 1944, Saipan, Tinian, and Guam were in American hands, while in October a fierce battle in the Leyte Gulf caused heavy Japanese naval losses. With bases in the Philippines now, the Americans could bomb mainland China—for us a mixed blessing.

In the interior of China there was severe fighting between the Japanese "China Army" and the Kuo-Min-Tang forces led by Chiang Kai-shek as well as fierce attacks on the Japanese in the north by Mao Tse-tung's communists. At the controls and check points in and around Shanghai, the Japanese soldiers, probably aware of the way the wind was blowing, were nervous, aggressive, and even brutal, if not to us.

The Japanese "China Air Force" was obviously short of fuel as more and more American planes were able to reach, with no counter-attacks, the outskirts of Shanghai, bombing factories with little chase from Japanese planes.

One evening a bomb fell about a half mile away from our house. We could see flames light up the sky. Gego and I raced out on our bicycles as close to the site as we could, fascinated by the struggle of the fire-fighters as they fought to extinguish the fire. The house had been occupied by a large Chinese family known to my mother, and this stray bomb practically wiped out the entire clan. This was the first time we had seen a civilian house bombed flat to smoking ruins.

After this, Mother and I each packed a small suitcase with our most precious belongings and kept it beside our bed. Mother had her jewellery, money, our passports, and some clothes. I had my father's picture in its silver frame and over a hundred silver dollars wedged in between my sweaters. Should a stray bomb hit our house and not kill us, we would be able to make a quick getaway.

Because the water table in Shanghai was so high, underground air-raid shelters, basements, or cellars were not feasible. An architect friend took a look at our house and advised us to use my father's study in case of an attack as the strong beams there would give us the best protection in anything other than a direct hit.

Air raids became more and more frequent, but eventually we all became quite blasé about the wailing alarm sirens or the single note of the "all clear." We were acutely aware of how incongruous it was that we were in grave danger of attack by "our" side.

Crime was all that flourished in those days. There was a White Russian Mafia to rival the traditional Chinese Triads, and the puppet Chinese Wang-Ching-Wei troops were corrupt and capable of anything. Street battles between these groups raged day and night. Banks were robbed constantly, and houses were burgled on a nightly basis. The Japanese occupation forces played an increasingly passive role in policing the city as their own hopes plummeted, with the Imperial Japanese Armies in retreat from the advancing Americans on all fronts.

Life was pretty difficult on the home front, too, and our financial worries became quite severe. At a cocktail party—they were still held occasionally as alcohol was readily available and people needed cheering up—my mother chatted to the Danish Consul General, Poul Scheel, an old friend. He mentioned that he was looking for new offices for the Consulate in a more tranquil part of Shanghai instead of the present downtown premises.

Mother told me she took a deep breath and suggested the ground floor of our house. A royal rent was quickly offered and accepted, thus solving most of our financial difficulties.

We felt much more secure under the Danish flag. A large red-and-gold shield shone from the front door, stating boldly that this was the "Royal Danish Consulate General." An armed and uniformed Chinese guard watched over us during the day (we had long since been unable to employ our own) whilst a White Russian called Ivan guarded the Consular premises from inside the house at night, armed with a Smith and Wesson.

The new arrangement meant that Mother and I lived in the upper part of our house only. My bedroom was converted into a sitting room, and the guest apartment at the back of the house became our dining room. The Boys loved this, as it was much closer to the kitchen and easier for them to serve our meals.

For Mother and me, this new set-up was ideal as now we felt physically safe as well as more financially secure. The grounds were still entirely ours, so Mars Football Club could continue. This was the most vital clause in the contract, as far as I was concerned.

We no longer used the front door nor the main staircase during office hours, but Didi and Alf considered the lower floor still to be part of their domain and continued to circulate freely among the diplomats.

Soon it was December and this first Christmas without my father was a subdued affair. We went downstairs to the Consular Christmas lunch, and upstairs we dressed a small tree in Mother's boudoir, which was always cosy in winter with a big fire roaring in the grate. We had a few people over for drinks on Christmas Eve, but our traditional party was out of the question. There was no getting away from the fact that it was a very emotional time for us, and we didn't even go to church. Christmas day we spent with the Melchers, who were always so kind to both of us.

25

America to the Rescue

At the beginning of 1945, the American Fourteenth Air Force stepped up their air raids on Shanghai. They concentrated mostly on Japanese warships in the harbour and Japanese factories on the outskirts of town. By mistake a bomb would fall from time to time on the residential sectors, which was pretty unsettling, so we prayed for the pilots to get their targets right. These raids were usually at night, so Mother and I would take temporary shelter in my father's old study downstairs, with Ivan helping to keep our spirits up until the all-clear sounded and we could go back up to bed.

One afternoon when a school friend and I were shooting our air rifles in the garden, the air-raid warning sirens went off. Mother was out, so Walter and I climbed through Number One Boy's bedroom window onto the sloping tiled roof.

Despite the grip of our gym shoes, it was quite scary to creep upwards, and had there been a loose tile we would have hurtled down to an almost certain death—but at thirteen, one doesn't dwell on such possibilities.

From the top of the house, we had an excellent view of the action. As we straddled the peak of the roof, three planes, with a mighty roar, raced over our heads at an altitude of about 600 feet. We saw the white tiger teeth gleaming on the red noses of the planes and each pilot in his cockpit as they zoomed over our heads. We waved frantically and one plane made a wide circle, flew back over the house and, to our astonished joy, dipped his wings to us in greeting. Walter and I grinned at each other. We felt at one with our heroes, sharing in their glamour, convinced they would liberate us within a matter of days.

Our euphoria was shattered by a screech from my mother. She was standing in the drive, head tilted back in horror, imploring us to come down, to hurry, to be careful, and other conflicting demands. The air raid was now in full swing, bombs were falling, and Japanese anti-aircraft guns chattered away in the distance.

Mother hustled Walter and me into our new dining room, which was lower than the rest of our top floor and therefore supposedly safer. She seemed quite hysterical. "I lost your two brothers, I lost your father, and now I could lose you!"

She was trembling in a mixture of rage and fear. Walter looked distinctly uncomfortable, and I was not surprised when he suddenly remembered a pressing appointment. He could not leave until the all-clear sounded, but once we were alone I promised Mother never to go on the roof again, and she became calmer.

The whole situation was certainly getting the adults down. They talked of nothing but war, and everyone wondered what would happen next. All of Shanghai knew that the Japanese had painted their war flag—a red sun with red rays—on the roof of the barracks where they held as prisoners the Italian marines and some Chinese military. The Americans obviously were not aware of this. They attacked the buildings, fortunately hitting only one out of six or seven.

Outside Shanghai, in Hongkew, was the infamous Bridge House, an eight-storey apartment building now converted into a prison, where the most dreadful tortures took place. I learnt about this from Gego, whose Chinese mother heard things we never did. The prisoners—men, women, foreigners, and Chinese—were all crowded together. There was no water for washing and one bucket per room where everyone had to relieve himself. Rats and lice were everywhere, dysentery and typhus raged. There was one meal a day—of rice, bread, and tea.

When prisoners were interrogated, they had to strip naked and kneel. First they were beaten with bamboo sticks until they bled. Metal spikes or bamboo slivers were forced under their nails. For water torture, they were strapped down and dirty water was poured down their nose and mouth through bamboo pipes until they passed out. The prisoner would regain consciousness to find himself tied by the ankles so that the water drained out of his body. Both sexes had their genitals burnt with cigarettes or electric wires. Many died, some committed suicide, and a few were set free in order to tell the tale and act as a deterrent. It was from one of these sad cases that Gego's mother had heard his terrible story. Surely all those poor prisoners would have been grateful for the quick release of a direct hit from an American plane.

British, American, Australian, New Zealand, and Dutch civilians were held in camps such as Lungwha. These were known to the American pilots, thanks to Chinese Intelligence. For the most part, with skill and a certain amount of luck, they managed to avoid them.

26
DINO

In the middle of all this, my mother met an Italian businessman. Dr. Dino Tirinnanzi was then in his fifties whilst my mother was thirty-seven. Elegant, sophisticated, monocled, and polyglot, he had been in the import-export business in India and Singapore before moving to Shanghai. A confirmed bachelor, he now seemed determined to court my mother, and soon they saw each other daily.

Perhaps feeling that things were moving along rather fast, Mother wrote to her sister Ursula, now that mail could be sent to Europe via Siberia. When Ursula's reply finally arrived, my mother was overjoyed to learn that Ursula had actually *met* Dino on the *Conte Verde* between Italy and China in 1937. They had developed quite a friendship, enjoying long discussions on Asian culture and philosophy. Matters were clinched when Ursula wrote, "Obviously a ladies' man, Dino was kind enough to spend hours with a cripple like me."

When Mother read this aloud to me in triumph, my bitterness spilled over and I was cheeky enough to ask her how she was going to discuss philosophy with her new friend. My punishment was the worried frown that marred her beautiful face.

Mother's elderly beau now decided to try to win me over. I learnt that he had fought with the Bersaglieri, the famous Italian Alpine troops, against the Austrians in W.W.I. During a battle on the Stelvio Pass, he had been wounded by four machine gun bullets, three hitting him below the knee and one over his left eye. He had refused to allow his leg to be amputated, and had lain for two agonising years in a Florence hospital. His leg, shrunken and scarred, was functional, but he would always have a limp. His damaged eye was almost useless—hence the monocle.

One day he told me how he had lost most of his money. When Italy stopped being a German ally in 1943, the Japanese promptly confiscated all Italian-held property in their occupied territories. Dino owned many Yangtze river cargo boats, and these were confiscated. Then soldiers came and searched his house on Magnini Road, forcing him to open the safe where they found and removed all his gold bars.

In their usual manner, they gave him receipts but it was over fifty years later, after his death in Florence, that Mother was finally reimbursed by the Japanese government. She received a small part of the riverboats' value and repayment of the gold based on its 1943 price.

I was invited to Dino's impressive house on many occasions, but I never got used to the fact that, apart from his Number One Boy, all his staff of butler, cook, gardener, and dog handler were Italians from the Conte Verde. He had managed to get these prisoners of war released by convincing the Japanese that they were Tyrolian of Austrian descent, therefore more German than Italian. Naturally these men were devoted to Dino. They spoke a weird mishmash of Italian, German, and English, and the butler, Hermann Goetsch, was to remain in Dino's employ long after we had all left China.

It would be an understatement to say that I resented the intrusion of Dino in our lives. I was jealous of him and fiercely loyal to my father. Mother spent more and more of her time at his house and very little with me. Of course some of this was my fault. Again and again my friends and I let the air out of Dino's tyres when he came to visit. He had to ride a lady's bicycle because of his leg, so we branded him a sissy and sniggered whilst we sabotaged it. Of course Dino knew what I was up to, and whilst a Boy pumped up his tyres he would look at me with distaste, calling me a "bad, mischievous child."

Although Dino was probably very amusing in society, he knew nothing about young people. I am sure he felt as uneasy with me as I did with him, but I did not know how to hide my resentment. Perhaps he thought to appeal to me with his dogs. He had six Afghans, and sometimes at the weekend he and his dog handler would walk over to our house with them. They were beautiful, elegant creatures, with surprisingly large teeth. Apparently they had been bred originally for tiger hunts in Afghanistan.

On one occasion our Cook arrived home from the market with two live chickens. As he re-locked the gate, he put the basket down and the birds escaped, fluttering into the garden. As quick as a flash the Afghans flew at them and tore them to pieces in seconds.

I was forbidden to touch these dogs, as they were so unpredictable. One afternoon when my rabbits were in an open run nibbling away at a corner of the lawn, Sultan and Rajah, Dino's favourites, leapt over the wire netting and killed about seven rabbits in the blink of an eye. So much for making friends through our "shared love of animals."

The only advantage this new phase in my life brought was that I was allowed to invite friends to sleep over whenever I was alone at night. This soon came to mean every weekend, and many times during the week too. The house continued to run on oiled wheels, regular meals always appeared upstairs, the Consulate functioned decorously downstairs, and I certainly was surrounded by a lot of people. I was provided with pocket money, which I could use to invite friends to the movies or to anything else that took our fancy. I think it would be fair to say that I began to run a little wild. Well, wild for 1945 . . .

27

The Boxing Mania

It all began when Dickie Kask Alfierieff, an Estonian-Russian member of our Mars Football Club who lived opposite us, suggested that we should start taking boxing lessons. The Kasks were very Americanised, and I admired Dickie as he knew every single American car ever built. (I came across Dick decades later and he is still a friend and a great guy.) I thought it would be neat to be a boxer, and soon Gego, Axel, and Palle Nielsen said they were game.

Axel found an Italian boxing instructor who was the middleweight champion of the Italian Naval Forces in Shanghai, and it was agreed that we should have lessons from him twice a week on the broad terrace of the Nielsen house. We quickly became besotted with boxing and could talk of nothing else. Even football took a back seat.

Our instructor, Alessandro, gave us free tickets for a boxing event in the Shanghai Auditorium close to the big jai alai courts. The evening began with flyweight, lightweight, and bantam matches leading up to the main events of middleweight and heavyweight. The bouts lasted from twelve to fifteen rounds. Alessandro fought at middleweight but, to our chagrin, he lost on points to a Russian.

The whole atmosphere was thrilling, and the general pandemonium was intense. The noisy betting that went on throughout the evening fascinated us almost as much as the matches themselves. Alessandro had warned us about the corruption where some boxers were bribed by the heavy gamblers to lose. He, however, was as clean as a whistle.

Despite Alessandro's defeat, we still hero-worshipped him and our lessons continued. However, he wasn't satisfied with our progress for, despite our football and school sports, he thought we were all a bit soft—"a bunch of wimps," to be precise. He decided to take us along to a gym run by Maestro Marelli, a friend of his.

Maestro Marelli had once been the weightlifting champion of Northern Italy. We joined up for lessons here too, twice a week. In between our football training and matches, our boxing lessons and now body building, we hoped to get seriously fit. Fortunately, school was only from 8 a.m. to 12:30, so there was plenty of time for all these activities. Homework, of course, took a back seat.

Then one day Gego came up with a scheme. He had learnt that an old, second-hand ring with canvas, ropes, and bell was for sale for a song. I was to finance the purchase of this equipment by selling some of my cache of silver dollars—which, Gego assured me, I would get back. Alessandro would be paid to help us install everything in our garden, and then we would organise junior boxing matches. Gego was confident that we would be able to sell enough tickets not only for me to get my money back, but for all of us to make a nice profit and have some fun.

The contestants were to be Axel and Palle Nielsen, Gego, Boiko, Dickie, and me, with Froessel, who was older than the rest of us, as our champion. To this core we added some Chinese and Korean friends from our football club. Between bouts we were all to take turns as seconds, and Alessandro was to be our referee. Matches were to take place on Saturday and Sunday afternoons when the Consulate was closed.

We placed small ads in the local Russian, Chinese, and German newspapers, and leaflets were printed with a programme that gave the venue, date and time of the event, plus a list of the contestants. We chose great names. Gego's fighting name was Bronze Bull, Boiko was Siberian Bear, and I was Daring Jessy. White tickets for adults cost about U.S. $2 and pink tickets for those under fifteen cost U.S. $1.

Once the ring was erected, we "borrowed" a desk from our house, which we placed at our main gate. Boiko provided a large metal box with a padlock for the take. Gego, Boiko, and I took turns as cashier and assistant cashier, armed with a blackjack that we hid under the desk in case someone tried to run off with the cash. We also designated one of the taller boys as security guard. He wore an Italian marine steel helmet with a silver anchor emblem. This was an early gift from Dino, but I doubt if he expected it to be used at boxing matches. The security guard also had to carry an air rifle and keep the peace in case of disorder. We were confident we had thought of everything.

Our very first match was scheduled to begin at 4 p.m. one Saturday, but to our surprise people began to arrive at 2.30. It must be remembered that in Shanghai at that time there was not much in the way of entertainment. By four o'clock, about a hundred people had turned up. Many were family and friends who had brought their own folding chairs, as we had suggested. The rest had to make do with the straw mats we had placed on the grass around the ring.

The afternoon was a resounding success. As we were about fourteen boxers, we were able to stage seven matches. In the intervals we played records on my gramophone and made announcements with a microphone lent by one of the fathers.

At the end of that first, momentous event, after paying Alessandro U.S. $25, enough money was left over to cover all expenses and I was reimbursed in full. From now on we figured that the take would be "pure gravy."

Our success was such that we started to add refinements. We asked some girls from school to go around with trays selling sweets and soft drinks at, I must admit, rather inflated prices. All in all we soon began to net over U.S. $100 per afternoon, which was fairly distributed amongst the boxers whether they won or lost. The girls made a commission on their sales.

Alessandro saw to it that all matches were fair and clean and, as we were all the same light weight, there were no fouls or knockouts.

We were jubilant, but the fun was not to last. We had a good run of about eight weekends, and then it all fell apart. In the beginning, Mother, rarely at home at the weekends, had no idea what was going on at the bottom of her garden. Unfortunately, on that last Saturday, she had come home to change for a dinner, and was disturbed by the amount of people milling about. From the window of her boudoir she inspected our activities through her opera glasses.

The following Sunday she decided to stay at home, and I invited her to come and join in the fun. This was not a good idea. In a flowery chiffon tea frock she sat perched on a high stool and gazed around in amazement through her dark glasses. All still might have gone well had it not been for a nasty, little Swiss man who she had been snubbing for years.

As soon as he caught sight of her he sidled up with a leer. "Ah, my dear Mrs. Jessen. You must be making quite a tidy profit from these children. Is this how you keep up your standard of living?"

I saw Mother go white with rage, slip off her stool and, with a ferocious frown in my direction, stalk back to the house.

At that moment the heavens opened and a tropical downpour drenched us all.

There was no shelter available, so our disgruntled audience was quickly soaked to the skin, and the Chinese in particular began to demand their money back. We were completely at a loss as to know what to do. Our "Security guard" had already left with the take, as per his instructions, but Alessandro came to our rescue by grabbing the microphone and offering free tickets for the following Saturday. With rain streaming off our embarrassed faces, we sheepishly handed out soggy tickets and the grumbling crowd faded away.

But there was to be no match the following weekend—or indeed any other. Mother's fury at my "incredible lack of sense" was kindled anew when she received a telephone call from Poul Scheel wondering gently whether the rumours he had been hearing were true. Was it possible that boxing matches were being held in the Danish Consulate gardens?

My argument that our garden was not part of his deal was brushed aside. When I protested that we *couldn't* stop because of the free tickets we had handed out, Mother coldly told me to give the people their money back in cash and let that be the end of it. She didn't want to hear another word.

I called the team together for one last general council held in Dickie Kask's house as nobody wanted to run into my mother. I told them that the game was up, and they all understood. At the end of the day, we agreed that it had been great fun while it lasted. Gego even managed to sell our equipment for half of what it had cost, so on the whole it had been a pretty good show.

A few weeks later Mother received a letter from the Municipal Council enquiring whether we had a licence for public sports performances. If not, all such performances would have to cease. "Well," I said crossly, "they have, haven't they?" Mother just looked at me over her teacup in silence.

For the next few weeks it was almost like old times at home as Mother decided to go to Dino's less often and have dinner again with me, much to my delight. When she wanted to, she could be the most wonderful companion. It was agreed that I should be allowed to continue to have boxing lessons and work out at the gym twice a week—but this, of course, meant that I was out more than she.

So Dino began to have dinner at our house nearly every night. Not that we all sat down together. Gego and I would be served at about seven and my mother and Dino at eight. Afterwards they would invariably go out to play bridge. My mother's friends were Dino's now, and she moved almost entirely in the Italian business and consular community. Soon after they left, Gego would have to go home and I would have only the servants or Ivan to talk to. But things were about to look up.

28

The Concubines

On the right side of our garden, two large houses had been built and were now surrounded by a beautiful landscaped park with small fish ponds, little bridges, water falls, and bamboo thickets. Despite the war, for the past two years earth-moving and construction had been going on, but in those days no cranes or pneumatic drills were used and the lines of coolies carrying buckets had barely disturbed us.

The owner of this compound was one of Shanghai's richest Chinese who, according to the servants, never left his property as he was terrified of being kidnapped. Apparently he owned most, if not all, of the Western and Chinese pharmacies and herbal health stores. I never caught a glimpse of him, but Number One Boy said he was a fine fat man of about sixty.

He lived in the main house on the corner of Avenue Dufour together with his first, second, third, and fourth wives plus his Number One Son and *his* first and second wives. The house closer to ours was for the remaining wives and between fifteen and twenty concubines.

In those days in China, it was perfectly normal, even expected, that a man should have as many wives as he could afford. It was a status symbol. Even our Head Gardener was the proud "owner" of two wives.

Scouts would scour the countryside for the prettiest girls, who would then be sold to Shanghai tycoons. Ningpo Province in particular was famous for the beauty of its women. The girls led rather boring lives once they became concubines, for they rarely saw their master and there was absolutely nothing for them to do except make themselves pretty and wait to be summoned.

From the paths on the other side of our garden fence, soft giggles and whispers could now be heard. One afternoon, when six or seven of us were kicking a football around, someone missed his shot and the ball soared up in the air and over the fence into the park next door. It was greeted by excited laughter and small shrieks, so we ran over to the fence and peered through. Half a dozen young girls dressed in colourful silks were throwing our ball to one another then collapsing in graceful heaps, overcome with giggles.

I yelled through the fence, "Please, will you throw our ball back?"

But the girls were having such fun they had no intention of giving up their game. Then Gego shouted out in Shanghainese, "Hey! Send that ball back," but with no greater success than me. We had no idea how to talk to Chinese girls, let alone exotic concubines.

Boiko found the reserve ball and we half-heartedly started to kick it about when suddenly our original ball landed at our feet. Gego and I raced to the fence, shouting our thanks in Shanghainese. One young girl came close to the fence and whispered that they would love to come and play with us but did not dare. At that moment a gong sounded, and all the girls fluttered about, then drifted away toward their house like a cloud of brilliantly coloured butterflies.

The following Saturday, Gego and I bought a big coloured beach ball and we asked our friend Zinho to write a note for us saying, "We hope you have fun with this."

Although Gego's mother was Cantonese, his written Chinese was more than shaky, and even his Shanghainese was not entirely fluent. People from one province to another in China spoke completely different languages, and it was only much later, under Chairman Mao, that Mandarin became the official language.

We stuck the note to the ball and threw it over into the garden next door. It was greeted with excited laughs, and three girls came up to the fence and thanked us with dimples and smiles. Most of the girls started to play catch with the ball, but two stayed at the fence to talk with us. They told us they remembered seeing the boys in their village kicking balls about, but they had never seen a proper football (soccer) field with goal posts and organised games. Just before they left, one asked us what the funny, green markings on our white shirts meant. Gego tried to explain that they read Mars, the name of a planet, and he pointed to the sky, but the girls burst into another fit of giggles having only heard the word "ma," which meant "horse" in Chinese. They seemed to imagine we were playing at being horses!

This bantering and flirting through the fence went on for several weeks as we learnt their names and teased each other. Then Gego had one of his ideas. He thought the girls were lonely and bored and that it was up to us to cheer them up. He decided that we should visit them. His plan was that we should dig a tunnel as in the best prisoner-of-war films, so after dusk when no gardeners were about we took spades and started to dig. It was extremely muddy and we began to worry about the state we would be in when finally we managed to crawl through to the girls. If they were anything like our mothers, they would have a horror of mud. Our second fear was that the gardeners next door would notice the hole and report it to their master, who was bound to think of kidnappers and make an unholy fuss. The third fear was that there might be guard dogs or watchmen to take pot-shots at us as obviously we would be trespassing. In other words, we were in a funk.

But we didn't want all that effort to go to waste, so we cycled to Bubbling Well Road to the Kiesling and Bader chocolate shop, where we bought the biggest and fanciest box of chocolates I could afford. We attached a note saying how much we would like to meet, wrapped the lot in a jute sack, shoved it under the fence, and called to the girls with low whistles.

Several girls ran up, unwrapped our gift and, like children, danced with excitement, stuffing their painted mouths with sweets. Now all came to the fence and chattered away in their high little voices. Unfortunately my Shanghainese was not up to the job and I kept having to ask Gego, "What did they say? What does she mean?" This caused him intense irritation, as he was getting along famously.

The girls told us they would love us to visit them and suggested that late afternoon would be the safest time.

Now we were in a dilemma. The muddy hole would obviously not do, but once again Gego came to the rescue. He fetched a carpenter who agreed to cut a small door in the bamboo fence behind our greenhouse at the very bottom of our garden. It was about two feet square, just enough to wriggle through, then close with a latch. Fortunately, at this chosen spot the girls' side was thick with flowering bushes, so the door was quite hidden from view.

The following evening, Gego and I, hair slicked, finger nails scrubbed, and wearing our best flannels, slipped through into the girls' garden laden with bags of sweets and lollipops. We sneaked along the fence making "psst" sounds to attract the girls. One, the least pretty but by far the bravest, came at once and couldn't believe that we were on her side. She called softly to two of her friends and we gave them the sweets. Everyone was whispering and laughing, but underneath we were really nervous.

Still, Gego asked if we could take tea with them. We had worked out that asking for tea was a pretty adult thing to do. They agreed that it would be lovely, but not today. The day after tomorrow, at the same evening hour, we should meet again, when most of the others would be having supper. Then they asked us to leave as they were scared that their Amahs would discover us. As we left we got gentle little kisses on our cheeks, soft nose rubbings, and hand squeezes. Gego and I hardly needed our door because we could have floated over the fence.

The day of our tryst arrived and, with bumping hearts, we slipped through our little door and crept along the fence behind the bushes. The girl Gego fancied was waiting for us, but not with the welcome we were expecting.

The girls had decided that we could not go up to their house as it was far too risky. If they were discovered, they would be punished, probably beaten, stripped of all their beautiful clothes, and delivered back to their villages in disgrace. They were terribly sad and apologetic, but there just was no solution, and they felt guilty about having raised our hopes. We could go on chatting through the fence if we felt like it, but the tea party was definitely off.

We trudged back the way we had come in the depths of gloom and sat on a bench in the vegetable garden. Then, for once, I had an idea. If it was too dangerous for us to sit on their terrace, where we realised that we would be conspicuous and compromise the girls in front of their servants, then why not invite them here? "They could easily slip through our door, and we could entertain them in the greenhouse!" I said.

Gego looked at me with scorn. "I know how keen you are on this greenhouse of yours and, for a greenhouse, it is pretty smart all painted green inside and out, but even so, we can hardly expect girls to want to sit on a damp floor between tubs of plants."

I gave him a grin and dragged him to his feet. "Come and look at this," I said. I pulled him through the greenhouse and down to the very end, where a door led into a small room. Here a bedroom had been fixed up for the Head Gardener, but it had never been used as he slept in a house of his own with two wives to look after him.

There were two iron beds with straw-stuffed mattresses and pillows, a green table, and a bare electric light bulb hanging from the ceiling. Leading off this room was a smaller one with a lavatory and a make-shift water pipe shower. Gego seemed to think it was a paradise. He turned to me and declared, "This, my friend, is it. We can give a party!"

The following day we cycled to Wing On, and at the money changer I gave up some of my cherished silver dollars so that we could shop. We bought the cheapest white sheets and pillow slips we could find and raced back to make up the beds—not very neatly, it must be admitted, as we had never done this before. Next we raided our kitchen and came away with a kettle, but then realised that we had no stove. Back to Wing On we went for a sort of camping stove, plus four white-and-blue tea cups and a matching bowl for biscuits. On our way home, we stopped at our corner shop for tea, cookies, and sweets. Our final purchase was an ashtray and a packet of cigarettes. We didn't smoke, but Gego said all Chinese did, and we pictured ourselves, like Cary Grant, casually lighting the girls' cigarettes.

Considering that the girls had not even agreed to visit us yet, I was beginning to think that this was quite a financial gamble, but Gego was sure they would be unable to resist.

As a final sophistication, we lugged my gramophone down from my bedroom together with several suitably romantic records, such as "The Blue Danube" and "Stardust" pinched from my mother's collection. The gramophone usually ran on electricity, but it could also be hand-wound. We lugged in a pot from the greenhouse, one full of little pink flowers, and stood it on the floor in a corner. On the green table we put the gramophone, the cookie bowl, the ashtray, and the cigarettes. Then we stood back and reviewed our efforts with satisfaction.

The next evening we were back at the fence waiting for our two favourites. My girl was called Yim Mung, but I can't for the life of me remember what Gego's girl was called. Finally they arrived, flustered and fluttery, because now even chatting to us was beginning to seem dangerous to them. They told us that we would never be able to go into their garden again as they had been getting funny looks from their Amahs.

But Gego was superb. Older and much more mature than I was, he began to soothe and entice them. He said we had a really secure place where they could come and take tea with us in complete safety. Nobody in their house or ours would ever know they had been. The girls began to perk up.

"And we have cigarettes," I added encouragingly. Now they were laughing and giggling again, but they would not allow us to set a date. They would have to think about it.

Then, just before they ran off, they relented. "It is not entirely impossible," they whispered coyly. "Perhaps three days from now? At dusk?" And with this they blew us kisses and ran away.

We had to get through the next few days. We were not only excited, but very nervous too as we were both entering unknown territory here. Then Gego remembered the bibos (loquats—a Chinese fruit). Some time ago, on the advice of the under-gardener, we had put some of these fruits into a biscuit tin together with a little water and lots of sugar. On the afternoon of the big day we dug out this tin and prised it open. The smell of fermentation was pretty ghastly. Nevertheless, we tasted the fruit, if rather cautiously, and found them quite excellent. Primed with this Dutch courage, we waited at our "gate" for our dates.

Finally the girls arrived, beautifully dressed and even more carefully made-up than usual. They were almost as nervous as we were, if for different reasons. Etiquette required us to help them through the opening, but unfortunately, in his eagerness, Gego pulled his girl too fast and her elaborate coiffure got caught up in the bamboo and one of her combs came out. She was furious and all for going back, but Gego pulled himself together and managed to pacify her with soothing words in Shanghainese.

We led the girls through the green house which they admired greatly but when they saw the gardener's bedroom, despite our heroic efforts, they doubled up with laughter. Once she had caught her breath and noticed our shamed faces, Yim Mung mused, "If only it were not so dangerous, I really think our house would be better after all!"

To this Gego assured them that naturally we could quite understand that this accommodation was not up to their usual standards, for which we apologised, but it was the safest place we could think of.

Despite his fine words, Gego and I were both very disconcerted. To stop the girls from making a hasty retreat, Gego began tea preparations whilst I offered bibos. I wound up the gramophone and put on "The Blue Danube," then plied the girls with cigarettes and biscuits. Poor Gego was having a hard time with the stove and just couldn't get it going. I lit the girls' cigarettes with panache, and then unwisely took one myself.

So there we were, Gego crouched desperately over the stove, Yim Mung nibbling at a bibo, Gego's girl refusing everything, whilst I spluttered over my cigarette. Fortunately the girls began again to see the funny side of all this. Yim Mung took pity on Gego and took over the tea-making. The worst seemed to be over.

Then I sat on one bed with Yim Mung, Gego sat with his girl on the other, and we all delicately slurped our tea in silence. Gego then suggested that we dance. There was not much room between the beds, the cement floor was rather uneven, and Gego and I were no Fred Astaires, but the girls were good sports. For us, holding their delicate waists and tiny hands made us forget everything else.

Soon they asked for Chinese music, but we had none so we continued with "Stardust." The girls taught us how to dance cheek-to-cheek, and Yim Mung gave me my first kiss on the mouth. I became so excited that I knocked over the little table and broke the cookie jar. Gego and I were down on our knees trying to clean up whilst Gego's girl whispered to Yim Mung in the other corner of the room.

Yim Mung pulled me up from my efforts and made it quite clear that we were to leave the other two alone. She took two cups of tea and we went out to sit on the bench at the back of the vegetable garden. The combination of the bibos and the tobacco had made me feel a bit sick, so I was grateful both for the tea and the fresh air.

We couldn't communicate without Gego, so we just smiled at each other. The only words we had in common were, "Jessy, you okay," from Yim Mung, to which I would reply fervently, "Yim Mung, you okay too!"

We repeated this to our mutual satisfaction many times. When we had finished our tea, she took my hand and we walked around the neat beds, where she pointed to various vegetables and fruit bushes, teaching me their names in Chinese.

This went on for about twenty minutes, and then Gego and his girl came out to join us. I thought Gego looked pretty silly, grinning like a Cheshire Cat, but for once his girl seemed to be in a good mood too. Then Yim Mung took my hand and led me back to the gardener's room. My heart was pounding as I didn't really know what was expected of me.

Despite her childish ways, Yim Mung of course knew what to do, but my inexperience and confusion seemed to bring out her maternal instincts, which was not what I had been led to believe would happen. Then I remembered that Gego had told me that I, as the man, had to take the initiative. We sat on the bed and cuddled, which was very nice, but I couldn't get her to take off a single piece of clothing. Gego had stressed the importance of this, but I was getting nowhere.

At this point the other two came back and, with Gego's translation, Yim Mung managed to explain that she thought I was too young for more "elegant pleasures." I was furious with myself and couldn't hide my disappointment. I'm afraid I sulked and did not even have the courtesy to help Yim Mung back into her own garden. Thus ended my first lesson.

29
The Last Days of the Japanese Occupation

Time to turn to more serious matters. Even now, in March, 1945, with the German armies collapsing on all fronts, German films still highlighting the glory of the Luftwaffe continued to be shown at all local cinemas. One might have imagined that Germany's imminent defeat would have caused some embarrassment to their Japanese allies, but apparently not. We, the public, however, had had enough of lies and propaganda. The only available films we were prepared to believe in were Russian.

We and the rest of the Shanghai public sat happily through endless love stories where Russian fighter pilots and female tank commanders would praise in unison the glorious Soviet Union and the Communist cause. Major battles such as heroic Stalingrad were favourite subjects. These Soviet films had only Chinese subtitles, so I always went with Dickie or Boiko, Russian friends who could tell me what was going on.

Once Mother was bored enough to want to join us. Boiko sat on her right, I sat next to her, and Dickie was on my left so that they could translate. Their running commentaries and disagreements over finer points of dialogue got quite heated as these two exiled sons of Tsarist Russia became momentarily proud of their Soviet compatriots. The rest of the audience, who either understood Russian or could read the Chinese sub-titles, became increasingly annoyed with us, and as their hissing and shushing had no effect, the manager was called. He bustled importantly up to us, shining his torch in our faces, all ready to kick us out—until he caught sight of my mother, whereupon he merely pleaded for somewhat quieter translations and slunk back into the dark. Mother could always upstage everyone without even lifting an eyebrow.

Life at school was changing. Discipline became lax and the morale of the teaching staff was low. Most had lost relations either to the bombing in Germany or on the various fronts of war. Some began befriending the non-German students, hoping that we would vouch for them—or at least store their valuables should the war be lost completely.

"What, more stuff?" Mother exclaimed, but actually, as we had no car, there was plenty of room.

The German teaching staff had good reason to be fearful. They could be interned locally, or shipped back to a bombed-out Germany in chaos, both terrifying possibilities. Nobody knew exactly how bad things were in Europe. In fact, all foreigners in Shanghai had nightmares of their own.

The Americans were coming ever closer, and although we definitely wanted them to *win*, we all knew that the Japanese "China Army" was still pretty well intact, and we were terrified that it would put up a major last-ditch stand and turn Shanghai, until now more or less unscathed by war, into a bloody battleground.

My friends and I feared losing touch with one another should the school really close, and we made plans to try to stick together. Apart from Gego, Dickie, and Boiko, I was quite close to Hans Meiser and Dieter Flamme—as well as Zin Ho, of course.

One of the last big receptions given at this time was the funeral luncheon held in a famous restaurant for Zin Ho's grandmother. Our entire class was invited, and we all sat down in one enormous room to a fifty-course banquet with rather special musical arrangements. In one corner of the huge dining room, Chinese Boy Scouts blasted out military marches. In the opposite corner an ensemble played Chinese classical music. In the third corner a band played modern Chinese dance music, whilst in the last were the "Cry-Cry" women, hired to sob and wail at the top of their voices all through the day.

For the most part the four groups entertained us in turn, but after about five hours, during which quite an amount of alcohol was consumed, all performed enthusiastically together. This built up to a cacophonous crescendo when fireworks were set off and the guests all rose, cheering and toasting the old lady who lay in a coffin in the centre of the room. Zin Ho gained a tremendous amount of face with this party.

Now in May, news came of the fall of Berlin at last, with Hitler's presumed suicide and the end of the Third Reich. For the Chinese, these events were too far away to really matter—and even for us, despite our jubilation, we were still living in an occupied country, still in the middle of a bitter war. There were no victory parades in Shanghai.

In July, the worst air raid yet targeted the Japanese radio station in Hongkew district. Tragically it hit the Jewish ghetto there as well. Thirty-one refugees were killed, 500 wounded, and 700 were left homeless. I remembered Father talking to Uncle Gerhard back in 1943, when the Japanese had forced all "stateless refugees," their euphemism for the Jews, to live in a designated area of Hongkew. They were given three months to move their households and businesses there. About 16,000 refugees were crammed into an area of one square mile, where 100,000 Chinese were already established. Now most of both the Chinese and Jewish homes were in ruins.

Starved for real news, we lived on gossip. A well-loved old German gentleman, Herr L., had, at the age of eighty, married his twenty-six-year-old niece, and the couple lived in a grand house in the French Concession. They had a large garden in which there was a well. In the undisciplined chaos of those days, a group of drunken Wang Ching Wei soldiers burst into the house, pulled Herr L. and his wife out into the garden, and tied him to a tree. These Chinese soldiers, fanatically loyal to the Japanese, began to scream insults, accusing the old man of being a German coward, like the Germans who had surrendered to the Russians in Berlin instead of fighting to the death, "Which the great Japanese would have done."

Then they gang raped Herr L.'s young wife in front of him. Once they had finished, they poured gasoline over her and set her alight. They left when she was dead, leaving also behind a broken, half-insane old man.

The end of this story came a few months after the liberation of Shanghai, when a group of Kuo Min Tang soldiers arrived at the German gentleman's house with six or seven beaten up Wang Ching Wei prisoners in handcuffs. They asked if these were the rapists and murderers of his wife. Herr L. said he recognised them, whereupon the Kuo Min Tang soldiers slowly drowned the Wang Chin Wei men in the well, dropping each man in and hauling him out once he was dead. Before leaving, the Kuo Min Tang soldiers stood to attention in front of the old man and cried, "This is Chinese Justice."

Apart from discussing these lurid tales, my friends and I lived for sport. One day Alessandro did not turn up for our boxing class, and we learnt in the gym that he had left Shanghai in a desperate attempt to return to Italy. Maestro Morelli said he was a fool. "We all wait so long. Why he no wait a leetle longer?" Alessandro's departure left us with only football and the gym to keep us out of mischief.

Girls were always on our minds. My favourites at school were Sonja Sachert and Babsy Dietrich. I thought they were both stunning, and Sonja was our class pin-up. She was dark and Babsy was blond.

Sonja lived in the Plum Villas on the eastern outskirts of town, and she would cycle in most weekends. Whenever we managed to meet, we would either play records in my room, go to the movies, or listen to an open air concert in Jessfield Park. There was never any question of showing her the gardener's room.

We would bicycle along Bubbling Well Road to the Majestic, into Nanking Road and Avenue Edward Seventh for the Nanking Theatre, or along the race course for the Grand. We understood very little if the movie was Russian, but this did not matter much as the main reason for going was so that I could hold her hand in the dark or, on special occasions, put my arm around her shoulders.

But our meetings were soon to come to an end with the closure of the Kaiser Wilhelm school following Germany's surrender. Parents desperately tried to improvise a series of lessons, with teachers giving classes in private homes in the most essential subjects. I attended in the beginning, but it was poorly organised, and after a few weeks Mother decided that I should stick to my own tutors, who were more reliable.

Fru Kristensen had been giving me Danish lessons since 1943. She was a beautiful young woman with a small child, the widow of a Danish captain. Now she added literature, and her explanations of Holberg and Oehlenschlaeger's works were the only lessons I really enjoyed in Shanghai. She made everything so real. She still lived in the Clemens apartments on Rue Lafayette, and two afternoons a week she served me home-baked cookies and coffee after our lessons. As she spoke excellent English, she took over my English studies and geography.

For some time, Max Schubert had replaced the young Austrian tutor my father had engaged. Max taught me Latin, algebra, geometry, and math, but in actual fact we spent most of the time just talking. He was a very wise man, and the wonderful discussions we had about life in general were certainly more useful to me than Latin or math could ever have been.

Max was Jewish. Shanghai had two enormous foreign communities; the White Russians who fled to Shanghai in the 1920s, and the Jews, who later had escaped from the Nazis. From our house doctor, to our vet, to our dentist, to the eye doctor who operated on my father, to the doctor who operated on me in Peking, many professionals had found sanctuary in China. After the outbreak of war, late arrivals all had to wear yellow arm bands and live in Hongkew. The fact that Max had one of the prized passes, which allowed him to circulate outside the ghetto, meant that he could find work in Shanghai.

Max was about fifty, and he had to walk for at least two-and-a-half hours from Hongkew to our house three times a week. He always arrived with a big grin, and never complained about those long walks. We had no car to fetch him, of course. I asked him once what he thought about during these hikes, and he told me that he usually worried about his family members who had not managed to escape from Germany, and whose fates were unknown to him.

He kept up his spirits when he felt too depressed by singing, of all things, German army songs. Apparently he had been a sergeant in the German Army in the Great War, and his commanding officer had been Jewish too. When he saw my astonishment, he told me there had been many Jewish officers in the German Army during W.W.I.

"But if Jews fought for them *then*, how can they treat you so badly *now*?" I just couldn't understand this, but Max lifted his hands, palms towards heaven, and gave me one of his famous shrugs.

After the desperate years of waiting, now that Germany had finally surrendered, good news seemed to come in every day. When Denmark was liberated, a big cocktail party was given in celebration downstairs in the Consulate, and feelings of relief and pride kept bubbling up to the surface all through the International and French Concessions, carefully hidden of course in front of all members of *our* local Master Race.

The Japanese became very anti-Nazi, and the papers were full of how much they despised Germany for having "thrown in the towel so prematurely." Their boast was that Japan would never surrender. In the unlikely event that the Americans should ever invade their islands every man, woman and child would "fight to the last drop of Japanese blood."

It was hot, it was summer, but nobody even thought of holidays. Everyone waited to see if the Soviet Union, now that it no longer had to worry about the Germans, would turn its might against the Japanese "China Army" and invade Manchuria. This would certainly speed up the end of the war, but nothing happened during the early summer of 1945. The suspense was nerve-racking.

30

JAPAN SURRENDERS

At the beginning of August rumours ran around Shanghai like wild fire that Japan had received a terrible blow from America. A few days later, we boys met at the gym and Maestro Morelli received us with full Italian exuberance. "The war is over! Finished!"

We were well accustomed to his exaggerations. "Says who?" we rudely replied.

Somehow he had managed to hang onto his powerful radio, and he had heard on the Voice of America that on the morning of Aug. 6, the B 29 Superfortress *Enola Gay* had left Tinian in the early morning hours to drop an atomic bomb on Hiroshima. Today, Aug. 9, a second device had been dropped on Nagasaki. Both bombs had been delivered to Tinian days earlier by the United States cruiser *Indianapolis.*

"This is the *second* one!" Morelli crowed. I had heard nothing about the *first!* Few people had a decent radio, and the only news we heard was from the local stations, which were under Japanese censorship. No mention had reached us of Hiroshima. Now, three days later, I learnt about both bombs at the same time. Then the sad news came crackling over the airwaves that, after delivering its cargo, the *Indianapolis* had been sunk by a Japanese submarine. It was all too much to grasp.

At that moment Gego burst into the gym, late and breathless, full of news. His father was now Harbour Captain for China Merchants, and he had heard from Chinese associates in Woosung at the mouth of the Yangtze that strange flashes of light had been seen on the eastern horizon. Gego was convinced that they had seen the explosion on Nagasaki but whether this was actually possible or not I never knew.

Gym was forgotten as we gathered around Morelli's radio daily. Soon news came in that Soviet troops had begun massive offensives against the 750,000-strong Japanese Manchurian Army. Over the next days we cheered as we learnt that the Japanese defences in Manchuria, North Korea, and Mongolia all fell to the Russians. I went to Morelli's every day and brought home the exciting news. For once I had Mother's and Dino's entire attention.

Now it was the turn of our enormous White Russian population to be alarmed. Would the Japanese take reprisals against them? If the Russians ever made it to Shanghai, would they?

Everything was topsy-turvy. The Chinese movie theatres blithely continued to feature Soviet propaganda war films, even though Russia and her heroes were now arch enemies of our Japanese masters.

Shanghai waited with bated breath for the next move. Were we about to witness the long-feared last stand of the Japanese "China Army" that would bring a blood bath to the city? We felt like rabbits caught in a car's headlights—terrified, but unable to run.

Hostilities officially ended that August, but we had to wait for the news that finally came over all radio stations, local as well as international—Japan had surrendered unconditionally on Sept. 2, 1945.

After our initial exhilaration, there were many of us unable to hide horror at the photos in the newspapers, which became front page news now that there was no Japanese censorship. We were appalled at the utter devastation of Hiroshima and Nagasaki. The ghastly pictures of the burnt and maimed survivors wandering like ghosts in the ruins of their cities filled our days and gave us nightmares. Could this violence on civilians really have been necessary?

It was Pastor Maass who called his remaining pupils together to answer some of our questions. He did not try to defend the moral position of the Americans, but in his usual pragmatic way he pointed out to us that, without the atom bomb, Japan would never have surrendered, and that her claim she would fight until "the last drop of blood of the last Japanese" was no empty threat. More lives than the two bombs had shattered would have been lost on both sides if the war in the Pacific continued.

Unashamed in *her* joy, Shanghai exploded. Firecrackers went off day and night. Weeks ago the Chinese entrepreneurial instinct must have seen a gap in the market, and within hours, American, British, and Kuo Min Tang flags were for sale on every street corner.

Gego, Boiko, and I stuck American and British flags on our handle bars and cycled off to the nearest Japanese garrison, where sentries with rifles and fixed bayonets still stood guard. They had been commanded by the Allies to keep law and order until the first American troops or the Kuo Min Tang forces of Chiang Kai-shek could get to Shanghai. This was in the Japanese soldiers' own interests, as four million Chinese, crazed with victory, anger, and revenge—not only against the Japanese, but also against the hated Wan Ching Wei troops—would have caused bloody riots if left unchecked.

We foolish boys cycled back and forth in front of the garrison, waving our flags in derision. It must have been tempting for the guards to take pot-shots at us, and it was only their innate Asian stoicism that saved our lives. There they stood in their crumpled khakis, their puttees, and those caps with neck cloths, symbols of all we had hated for so long. Fortunately for us, they merely ignored our antics.

A few days after we learned of the official Japanese surrender, a wave of transport planes thundered over Lung Wha, most carrying American soldiers, but some with Chinese Nationalist troops. Crates of food were dropped over the internment camps outside town, the first unfortunately killing a few prisoners who had just stood and stared up at the sky in bewilderment.

Then American jeeps full of lounging, grinning GIs drove through our streets, and ecstatic crowds appeared as if by magic, cheering wildly. Excitement grew to a fever pitch on Sept. 13 when the *HIJMS Ataka*, flying American colours above her Japanese flag, entered Shanghai Harbour, escorted by the *USS YMS 49*. A great sight, it would be followed over the next few days by many more American Navy ships, spilling thousands of white-uniformed sailors onto the streets of Shanghai. Amongst them were Marines marching in crisp, close formation to their old garrison where, as a nine-year-old in 1941, I had watched their buddies play football before being shipped to Corregidor. Now they were back as liberating heroes.

The Chinese Nationalist troops, smartly turned-out, were also cheered as they marched into town, but it was the Americans who had won our hearts. Whether Navy, Army, or Air Force, they were feted wherever they went, and customers rose to applaud them in all the bars and restaurants.

Chinese troops entering Shanghai

The internment camps were opened up, and out poured thousands of elated British, American, Dutch, New Zealand, and Australian civilians. Now, at last, we were to learn about Pootung, Chapei, Lungwha, Ash Camp, Yu Yuen Road, Lincoln Avenue, Haiphong Road, and Great Western Road. Nearly 14,000 men, women, and children, mostly of British or American nationality, had been incarcerated in these camps. We learnt that there had been no torture of the horrific type carried out in Bridge House, but there were constant rape attacks, solitary confinements, and punishments of days standing under the blazing sun. Foul food of probably about 300 calories a day; filth, bedbugs, a lack of latrines and running water had been suffered by all. The greatest stress, they all agreed, had been the constant threats of reprisals, the roll calls in the middle of the night, and the uncertainty of their future. The inmates of Haiphong Road Camp had been herded into cattle trains bound for Manchuria, and their fate was still unknown at that time.

It was remarkable how quickly the ex-pats slipped back into their old way of life. On the whole their houses had been untouched, and the von Schuberts, for example, returned to find their home just as they had left it. British companies reopened for business, and life slowly returned to almost pre-war conditions, despite the crippling inflation.

Many of the families released from the camps asked to be repatriated to Europe

U.S.Navy arrives!

with all speed. They couldn't wait to get the dust of Asia off their feet, but for those who stayed, the quicker they could forget the nightmare of the past four years, the better. Parties went on non-stop as people celebrated both victory and freedom.

Now it was the turn of the remaining Japanese troops to be interned in the recently vacated camps outside Shanghai, where they had treated the Chinese so atrociously. The Chinese revenge was terrible as their fury was unleashed on the hapless Japanese, but slowly they too were repatriated on troop carriers to Japan, to their own and everyone else's relief.

But I had never forgotten what the Japanese colonel who had befriended me on the train to Dairen had said—no Japanese was ever supposed to allow himself to be taken prisoner. He had told me it was considered the final disgrace. Hara-kiri was the only honourable answer. I could not help wondering how these men were going to deal with their shame, and how they would be treated once they arrived home.

Now Shanghai was trying to turn itself into an American city. Everything American was admired by the Chinese. American bars sprang up, and the shops were flooded with American cigarettes, chewing gum, and other goodies previously unknown to us. A tidal wave of American movies arrived, and the cinemas were open all day.

Liberty at last!

You could go to the Majestic at 11 a.m., see a film, then have a dim sum lunch in the cinema cafeteria, after which it was back to the big screen for another film, then tea and sandwiches before the final film of the late afternoon. These day programmes were very popular as the Chinese were always fanatic film fans. But never before had there been such choice.

Gego, McGregor, Boiko, and I went to everything on offer. We saw *The Battle of Bataan* several times, and never tired of watching Robert Taylor cut down waves of Japanese with his machine gun before falling into the grave he had thoughtfully prepared for himself beforehand. *Anchors Away, Over There,* epics of the battles of Saipan and Iwo Jima thrilled us without fail as we chewed our gum, cheered our heroes, and caught up with the events of the past war years, about which we had known so little.

Soon any amount of Army and Navy surplus was for sale. Tommy guns, 9 mm Mausers from the Chinese troops, and .45s were there for the asking—and even tanks, jeeps, and personnel carriers could be bought if you had the money. The Triads went on major shopping sprees. We boys contented ourselves with pilots' leather flight jackets with fur collars, the stars and stripes across our backs.

Thus attired, we hired a sampan at the Bund in order to get a closer look at the American warships in the harbour. As we rowed around the cruisers and destroyers,

More U.S.Navy ships arriving in Shanghai

the sailors on deck waved to us—and some, to our astonishment, flipped nickels and dimes down into our boat.

We also rowed around a British cruiser, the famous *Belfast*, which is now anchored in the Thames in London. Here the sailors put their fingers in their mouths and emitted shrill, joyous whistles as they waved to us from high up on the deck. A basket with several bottles of English ale was lowered down, which we opened with a pocket knife and swigged to the health of our new friends. We rowed back somewhat haphazardly, singing "Here Comes the Navy!" at the top of our voices, to the cheers of the American sailors.

Sometimes, at the beginning, it seemed as if things were really getting out of hand. We witnessed unbelievable scenes: teams of American sailors having rickshaw races, with the coolies sitting as passengers; army jeeps full of drunken GIs being driven around by bar girls. The Chinese were unaccustomed to seeing Westerners behave badly in public. The young laughed, but the older generation was shocked and looked away. These displays of high spirits were harmless enough, and order was to be restored before long by the MPs. The men had seen such fierce fighting for so long, now that they were victorious even the military police often turned a blind eye.

For some, there were no good times left. Now many of my school friends and most members of the German community were deported by the Chinese Repatriation Committee. Some managed to bribe the right person and were allowed to stay, but most were put on troop ships and repatriated to Germany.

31

"Celestial Pleasures"

In the middle of this chaos, Gego decided that it was time for me to erase the memory of my failure to seduce Yim Mung. He was to take me to one of Shanghai's better brothels on Bubbling Well Road, number 199. So one day in Oct., 1945, a month before my fourteenth birthday, we cycled there with a bag holding our pooled silver dollars. Nervously, we rang the bell, and the door was opened immediately by an enormous Mongolian who asked us politely what we desired. Gego explained that we would like to meet some young ladies. We were looked up and down with surprise and then, with a big grin, the man let us in.

He motioned to a shiny, stuffed sofa, where we sat down, feeling utterly ridiculous in our shorts and white cotton socks. The lobby was full of elegantly dressed Chinese businessmen, who came and went between the waiters circulating with trays of drinks and canapés.

After a few endless minutes, during which I hissed to Gego at least a dozen times that I was getting out of there, an elderly Chinese lady, resplendent in silks and jewels, came and sat down beside us. She smiled tenderly and asked, "Is it true that you wish to experience celestial pleasures?" She spoke excellent English and we both nodded enthusiastically. "Do you know how much this will cost?"

Of course we had no idea, and when the price was mentioned, we must have gone rather pale. "How much can you afford?"

Full of hope, we showed her our silver dollars, but she tinkled with a little silvery laugh. "My boys, you are going to have to bring me three times as much for even the briefest of encounters."

When she saw that we were about to abandon the whole enterprise, she rang a small bell and two exquisite girls not much older than Gego appeared, even more beautifully turned out than my neighbour's concubines. The girls took one look at us in our shorts and smothered their giggles behind their red lacquered fingers. The kind lady frowned at them. "Come back tomorrow and these beauties will be waiting for you. Bring anything you like, silver dollars, American dollars, Shanghai dollars or Customs Units—I accept them all."

We had no Customs Units, but we knew that they were a special currency created during the great inflation. We had no American dollars either, but between us we would be able to scrape up enough silver and Shanghai dollars.

As we stood up to leave she whispered to us from behind her fan, "Better wear long trousers, heya?

As we cycled home, we discussed finances. I had enough, but Gego would have to ask his father for an advance, using some phoney excuse. I can't remember what it was, but it worked, and that was the main thing.

The next day, sartorially correct, we returned to Bubbling Well Road. This time the Mongolian did not laugh, but ushered us in immediately. We were served tea as we perched on the sofa, puffing nervously on cigarettes. The kind lady appeared, nodded approvingly at our attire, and asked if we had the correct funds this time. We handed over a vast sum, which she assured us would be just enough—"For a little while. Now, choose your partners!"

This time four girls arrived in long Chinese dresses slit high on the thigh. They sat around us and two of them spoke a little English. "Take one minute, make up mind," one said sweetly, but I had already decided on a girl in white silk with a white flower in her long black hair who reminded me of Yim Mung. As we left to go upstairs, Gego still hadn't made up his mind between the remaining three candidates.

My girl led me to a small room with an extremely large bed. Soft music wafted over our heads from a speaker, her perfume was heady, and very soon, to my relief, I was gently and expertly led to "heavenly bliss."

When she took me back to the Mama-San, I was told to sit down and have another cup of tea. Gego had taken such a long time to make up his mind which girl to choose that his celestial pleasures were not yet over.

Afterward we had enough coins left to buy a couple of celebratory beers before going to our respective homes—well satisfied with ourselves that we were men at last.

32

Mother Takes Over

Mother began to pay me a lot of attention almost immediately. Could she have learnt of my escapade? Did it show? For whatever reason, she seemed to want to remind me of how life used to be. She assured me that Father had left her properties and shares, which soon she would be able to access.

Our house itself in Shanghai represented an immediate asset, and Father had left seventy-five percent of it to me and twenty-five percent to my mother. Real Estate values after the liberation of Shanghai had jumped sky-high, and Dino thought we should sell. In addition to this, an education trust had been set up years ago so that I would be able to go to good schools. In other words, I was not to worry.

My education became a priority once again, and there were endless discussions about where I should go. For my father's sake, Mother wanted me to be educated in Denmark, and she had decided that I should leave just as soon as possible. She herself was toying with the idea of moving to Italy with Dino, so a buyer was needed to take the house off our hands.

For the time being, though, I couldn't even get to Europe as there were no civilian airlines or ships available in the aftermath of the war. Europe was in turmoil, and I would just have to be patient. This didn't disturb me at all as I was quite happy to remain a "Shanghai kid."

Cars now became available again, with shipments arriving from the States. One day Mother came home triumphantly at the wheel of a new Ford. She had always been an excellent driver, and we were both heady with freedom as she drove us into the surrounding countryside.

I was confident that I too could manage a car, so one day, when the Ford was parked in the driveway and Mother was out, I turned the key in the ignition and stepped on the gas. Somewhat to my surprise, the car leapt forward onto the lawn. Still, I thought, this would be a good place to practise, and I drove around and around the willow tree, having a grand time. More by good luck than good management, I got the car back onto the drive in front of the house and turned off the engine, persuaded that Mother would never know. Unfortunately the lawn was scarred with wheel ruts, and once again the Weedy-Weedies had to be summoned. I, of course, was back in disgrace.

The entire house became ours again when the Danish Consulate moved into bigger premises downtown. My mother was thrilled to redecorate as, quite apart from the pleasure it gave her, she said it would help fetch a better price when buyers came. To my disgust, many of Dino's extra pieces of Florentine furniture found their way into our rooms—but not into mine!

Life began to return more or less to a pre-war routine. A chauffeur was engaged, and Mother started to entertain again, giving many dinners and cocktail parties for Dino and his Italian crowd. Now I was glad to be leaving Shanghai soon, as I no longer felt this was my home.

Efforts were ongoing to find a way of getting me back to Europe, and my uncle Buele Jebsen finally found a solution. The P&O passenger liner *SS Strathmore* had been converted into a troop ship in order to ferry thousands of British Navy, Army, and Air Force personnel back home. About 800 Annamese French Colonial troops, who had been guarding the French Concession, were to be taken to France too, but this still left space for a couple of hundred civilians. Women and children under twelve were to be assigned cabins, and everybody else would have to sleep in hammocks.

As Uncle Buele explained all this over the dinner table, my eyes must have gleamed. What an adventure! A basic fee of £90 had to be paid for the voyage, but men and boys over twelve had to be prepared to work their passage as well. The voyage would take about five weeks, with many stops.

Whilst my passage was being arranged, Mother talked to me about what I should do once the ship docked. It was all a bit hazy, but the general idea was that I should make my way from Southampton to Aabenraa, where I should stay with my step-grandmother, who would make arrangements for me to attend either Herlufsholm or Stenhus. Mother's idea of planning a trip was not as precise as my grandfather's had been, but then, as she kept reminding me, I was now fourteen and no longer a child.

Because we were allowed only one piece of luggage, I sold all my treasures. I was to take my father's overseas trunk, which was a monster, but I still had to get rid of my electric trains, my Meccano sets, my rifle, my birds, and my bicycle. I was not unmoved by this, but I reassured myself that these possessions were part of my past and I had outgrown them.

On my last evening, Mother gave a small dinner, inviting Uncle Buele and several other friends of my father's. Then it was the big day. We drove to the port where a coolie lugged my huge trunk on board and I had to say goodbye to my mother. This was not as heart-wrenching as it might have been, as I was quite convinced she would follow me soon to Europe. When she had settled down in Italy with Dino, I was to join them for every school holiday. The last thing she said to me was, "Don't forget to tip your cabin steward and the dining room steward, so that they take good care of you, my Darling." Little did she know what this trip had in store for me.

33

TROOP SHIP *Strathmore*

I followed in the wake of the coolie as he shouldered my trunk down to Troop Deck E3, where hundreds of men milled about. Most were Annamese soldiers from the French Concession. Hammocks hung in layers of three in surely a hundred rows. I was assigned a hammock that, unfortunately, was not only a middle one but also in the centre of the deck.

My trunk was shoved under the lowest hammock, to the great delight of its occupant, who said it would make a great step-up for him. On top of me was a charming, elderly Danish gentleman, Mr. Ledertoug, a manager of the Danish Great Northern Telegraph Company. He was the father of Joergen, a school friend of mine. Joergen and his mother had stayed in Shanghai and were to take a later, more comfortable, ship. "Like my mother," I said confidently.

It became obvious that Mr. Ledertoug had great problems getting in and out of his top hammock, so I offered to swap with him. He preferred my sandwich bed, as it was easier to climb into. My head was now only about twenty centimetres from the ceiling, so for the first couple of nights I cracked my head whenever I got up to pee. I had to scramble up and down the ropes, always waking the Annamese soldier and Mr. Ledertoug no matter how hard I tried not to, but nobody complained as it was the same for us all.

I counted about twelve portholes, all just at the waterline, so that in port you could see out but when under way the glass was sometimes completely under water. It was very disconcerting and rather nauseating to veer between nothing but sky, then crashing waves, then nothing but green water.

T.S.S. Strathmore

The 23,500-ton *Strathmore* was escorted out of Shanghai harbour and all the way to Hong Kong by a British frigate and a light cruiser. They were there to warn us of mines and to rescue us should we be hit, which was not entirely the most comforting of thoughts. The South China Sea was awash with mines that had been laid by all sides, so we had to zigzag about according to endless signals from our escorts.

Our entire crew was Indian, from stokers to donkey men to the bosuns and the kitchen personnel. All the officers were British or Australian.

A Mrs. Ratje, a Dutch acquaintance of Mother's, came to find me. She was travelling with her young son in a normal cabin on the boat deck, and they took their meals in the passenger dining room whilst we men ate in the troop mess under the waterline. We had to queue for half an hour before each meal, and the air was heavy with kitchen smells so we always knew what was in store for us—usually beans. There was no choice. We held out our plates, food was slapped on, and we sat at long tables to eat. The food was pretty disgusting but plentiful.

One day out of Shanghai, we were summoned in front of officers and had duties assigned to us—which, although certainly not hard labour, were pretty unpleasant. I had the bad luck to be part of a team cleaning the showers and lavatories. The ship was so overcrowded that queues always formed in front of the lavatories, which made cleaning them tricky. It was a disgusting chore. One day a week I had dining-hall duty, which was better. Even scraping plates into garbage cans, wiping down tables, and swabbing floors was a pleasure after the latrines. Our ship was not built for such numbers—over 5,000 were crammed on board. It was hot, about to get hotter, and the decks below the waterline were poorly ventilated and smelly.

I wrote to my mother when I could. This was the first letter I wrote from the ship.

TSS Strathmore,
Troop Deck E3,
5 April 1946,

Dear Mami,

Please forgive this awful paper but it is all that is available on board. The airmail paper you gave me I have used up as in the lavatories here they use cut up news papers! Yesterday afternoon we left Hong Kong where we had been for 4 days but we were only allowed ashore on the 3rd day. Mr. Wiele was not allowed on board so I went with Mrs. Ratje and her son to Jebsen and Company which consisted of one small room. Mr. Wiele was terribly nice and after Mrs. Ratje had talked with him she took me shopping. She bought me a topi and some sweets. She spent HK $18. The topi was 10 and the sweets 8. Then we took the tram up to the Peak where we walked around for about an hour and stopped at a restaurant for ice creams.

Downtown Hong Kong seems to be undamaged but on the Peak most houses lie in ruins. Kik-Ud still stands but the servants' quarters are gone. Then we took the tram down again and had Chinese Chow with 15 courses! Mr. Wiele invited us then he gave me 12 bars of chocolate which I ate over the following two days. The food on the ship was OK for the first 3 days but since then it has become terrible. For the last few days we have had black bean soup for lunch and for dinner a thin slice of corned beef with beans and vinegar! Today for lunch we got a piece of fish and this morning porridge without milk or sugar. Every third evening they give us an orange. The women and children get wonderful food on Deck F2 and they can order whatever they like. Please don't come on one of these ships with Dino. He would not survive.

At night I go to bed as late as I can as the air is terrible and it's very hot. We have to get up at 5:30 in the morning and then stand in a queue to go to the lavatory. In Hong Kong 2,500 British soldiers boarded the ship so now we carry 7,123 people including crew.

I am so happy that I didn't take Micky on board. It would be terrible here for a cat. In my dormitory we are now 254 people in hammocks side by side and over each other. All the men snore and it is very stinky.

We have to sleep in our life-vests which is hot and uncomfortable. We eat the same food as the Indian crew but theirs is curried and ours is not unfortunately. I still have a sore throat and the medicine is coming to an end. In 4 days we will reach Singapore where I will mail this letter. Please telegraph me how you are. You only have to put Troop

Steam Ship Strathmore and it will arrive. My Swedish friend received a telegram from his father in Peking so it works.

The weather is wonderful but there is too much noise and walla-walla with all these people. It is terribly boring and one never knows what to do when the work is done. Most people are in a very bad mood. From time to time we see sharks. Have you sold the house? How are Micky and Didi? Yesterday evening a Mrs. Elster gave me a banana. I hope you are well. Have you married Dino? Please follow soon. Many greetings and kisses,

Your loving son.

P.S. Please follow soon! I am well, don't worry! I am very tanned.

Letter No.1

As the *Strathmore* drew into Singapore, I stood on deck and watched as she dropped anchor. It was a fine, fresh morning, and all around us were British and American Navy ships, ferries, and little inter-coastal steamers. The water was iridescent with oil and utterly calm.

Almost immediately immigration officials came on board, and soon an announcement over the Tannoy dismayed us: "Military personnel only have shore leave. All civilian refugees are to be restricted to the ship."

We muttered and fumed. "We were not 'refugees'—how dare they!"

Fortunately we had no idea then that we would not be allowed ashore in Colombo or Port Said, and we refused to believe the pessimists amongst us who grumbled that we would not be able to get off the ship until she reached Southampton. "They treat us like *lepers*," was a common complaint, which made everyone's mood plummet.

Over 500 or so British troops came aboard in Singapore, so that now we were close to 8,000 people crammed on the ship. We stayed in port for three days, bunkering coal, water, and food, our frustration fed by the tantalising closeness of the town. It became ever hotter and the humidity rose steadily.

At last we sailed out into the open sea, which immediately revived our spirits. A group of army entertainers had embarked with the latest batch of British troops, so soon pianos, drums, and loud speakers were set up on the main deck, and every evening from then on there was a concert of music and comedy sketches, primarily for the soldiers—but anyone could join in.

We sat cross-legged on deck, thousands of us squashed together like sardines, roaring with laughter at the jokes and singing along with gusto. The soldiers' spirits were sky high, of course. The war was over, they had won, and they were on their way home, whilst most of the civilians had no idea what they were returning to.

The show always ended with requests, and they were always the same. "Don't Fence Me In," "It's a Long Way to Tipperary," and, "There, I've said it again!" were the great favourites. All the soldiers joined in, yelling lustily at the top of their voices, and soon I knew every word too. We probably scared all the marine life for miles around, but on those hot, breathless evenings in the middle of the Indian Ocean, our massed voices soaring up under a brilliant canopy of stars were unforgettable.

Sometimes I preferred to stand at a railing, watching the ship's wake lit by the moon, listening to the music from a distance. Unfortunately, being alone gave me time to remember Shanghai, my friends, and my old life with such nostalgia that I would force myself to think of the future—but this was pretty scary because there were so many unknowns.

Once when I was standing there, Fox came up to admire the night sky with me. Fox had been a gunner on the *Prince of Wales* when she was sunk by Japanese torpedo planes off Kuantan, Malaya. I had heard him tell this to other sailors, but I felt it was not proper to ask questions, so I knew no details.

"So lad, what sort of a war did you have?" he asked me. "Where were you anyway?"

After I have given him a potted history, I felt I could ask him a few things because he had asked first. "What was it like on the *Prince of Wales?*"

I thought he was not going to answer at first, but then he said, "We left Singapore on Dec. 8, put out to sea and headed north up the Malay coast to where the Japs were landing. Dec. 10 and all hell broke loose. They say eighty-eight torpedo bombers attacked the *Repulse* and us. Old Admiral Phillips of Naval Force Z had ordered no air support. We didn't stand a chance. He called the Japs 'Those little yellow chaps,' and he thought we were in no danger. Stupid really, it being only three days after Pearl Harbor! Anyway, we get a direct hit and start to sink. I jump into the drink and find meself surrounded by dead bodies and screaming wounded. Nothing to be done. Sharks arrive and then panic really sets in I can tell you."

I was all agog. "Then what happened?"

Fox lit another cigarette with an unsteady hand. "Picked up by a destroyer and returned to Singapore. Bit of bad luck that. Had to start fighting them Japs on land. Got caught and ended up in a prison camp." Suddenly he stopped.

"What was that like?"

Fox turned away. "You don't want to know, Lad, you just don't want to know." And off he strolled back to his mates.

Six days after Singapore, we arrived in Colombo, where we picked up another couple of hundred troops and fifty-odd civilians. I was delighted to see projectors and reels of film come aboard, and soon yet another effort to ease our boredom was organised.

Each day at noon a lottery was held to see who could guess the speed of the ship. A guess cost five shillings, and I participated every time. The very first day after Colombo, I bet that the speed was seventeen knots and I was one of the winners. I had to split with five or six others, but I still won £12. Later, the day we entered the Red Sea, I won again, this time £14.

Ever since Singapore, the temperature in our quarters had become quite unbearable, so many of us took to sleeping on deck. I would take my life jacket as a pillow and curl up in a corner on the warm planks, relishing in the clean air and occasional breeze.

One day it was announced that there would be a dance on the main deck the following Saturday. All the women passengers, the nurses, and the female crew were asked to do their best to dance with as many partners as possible. This was quite a tall order as there were only about five dozen woman and thousands of men. I was certainly not a candidate and only went along to watch.

There was such a crush that one was pushed here and there, and suddenly I bumped into Michèle, a pretty seventeen-year-old Belgian girl with whom I had chatted a bit in French. The minute she saw me, she asked me to dance with her, as she was tired of being clutched by sweaty soldiers. I told her I couldn't dance, but she led me to the floor and took great pains to teach me the foxtrot. I stepped on her feet and bumped into everyone around us, but I was reassured when Michèle told me how handsome I looked. I was in long, white trousers, a short-sleeved white shirt and tie, and even I thought I looked pretty mature.

After our dance we strolled around the deck, and Michèle asked me where my cabin was. I told her about our hammocks under the water-line and that I slept mostly up on deck. Cheekily I asked her, "Is there room for me in your cabin?" Unfortunately, she was sharing with an aunt. "Oh well, *qui ne risque rien ne gagne rien*," I quipped in my best French.

She asked me where I usually slept, so I showed her my favourite spot. "I'll come and visit you one evening," she teased.

Now it was my turn to laugh. "Once the music is over, there will be hundreds of men sleeping up here, so perhaps you had better not." She took my face in her hands and gave me a quick kiss on the mouth and left.

That night I stared up at the stars thinking only of Michèle, but next morning my hopes were dashed when I caught sight of her walking hand-in-hand with a smart young English officer. Nevertheless, we remained good friends, and the three of us would often while away the afternoons playing cards.

By now the men knew how fascinated I was by their war, as distinct from mine in China. They probably remembered asking their own fathers and grandfathers about the Great War, so with great good nature they would draw diagrams for me and tell me about the fall of Singapore on Feb. 15, 1942.

"She was supposed to be impregnable," one man said, "and she would have been had the Japs attacked from the sea. We never thought they'd come through the jungle and mangrove swamps of the Malay Peninsula, but that's just what they did—and us lot sitting with defences locked in position pointing out to sea—I ask you!"

There was a mutter of disgust, then another spoke up." They told us them Japs couldn't fight, but most of 'em had seen a load of action while lots of our boys had never seen combat."

Another took up the sorry tale. "Don't forget our valiant officers—'ad those gentlemen spent a bit less time in the Long Bar of the Raffles Hotel they might 'ave seen what was going to 'appen."

An emaciated youngster, who already looked like an old man, downed his beer and carried on. "What about old Lieutenant General Arthur Percival? He had 90,000 men to Yamashita's 65,000, but he spread us out too thin and them devils broke through."

Then off they would drift to get more beer or smoke another cigarette—sick again of this eternal rehashing of their humiliation.

Before Aden, I received a severe blow. I went down to my trunk for fresh clothes only to find that the lock had been picked and the trunk was open. I searched feverishly under my shirts and my worst fears were confirmed. Not only had my cache of silver dollars been stolen, but the beautiful mother-of-pearl cuff-links, circled in diamonds with central sapphires, was gone. They had been my father's favourite dress cuff-links, and Mother had given them to me as a farewell gift, together with a collapsible silver goblet that my father always took with him on shoots. Also gone.

I dashed to find the purser, but when I reported the theft he said, "We'll try our best, Sonny, but there's not a lot we can do with so many people on board."

I was desperate. "Can't you search people?"

He was a fatherly man and tried to be kind after I had explained about the cuff links and the silver goblet. I told him it wasn't the money so much as the last souvenirs of my father. "Well, Lad, on your deck, with all those chaps, it's not really feasible."

Still, he came down to look at the trunk, and the next day he brought me a new padlock and chain, which he had had made for me at the locksmiths. He was very nice, but of course it was too late. I never saw my things again.

Apart from this piece of bad luck, I have to say that during the six weeks of the trip, despite our cramped quarters and the thousands of men on board, I never saw a single scuffle nor any really disorderly behaviour from any British sailor, soldier, or airman. Sometimes they would have a beer too many, but they were always good-natured, and some of them were very funny.

As we approached Aden in sweltering heat, it was announced that there were to be boxing matches. Just the thing to cheer me up. Contests in all weights were to be fought between the various services. I watched them all and judged them to be of a pretty high standard. Of course I considered myself to be something of an expert after my Shanghai experiences.

We stopped to bunker in Aden, but nobody was allowed ashore, and then it was, "Next stop the Red Sea." Although I had been this way three times before, I had been too young to be interested in my surroundings. Now I marvelled at the bull sharks, tiger sharks, and hammerheads that followed us. Manta rays abounded, and flying fish skimmed tirelessly across our bow. At first I couldn't see the flying fish everyone exclaimed about because I was looking too high. Eventually I caught sight of them, just above the water, more fish than bird, of course. I recognised some storks and other birds unknown to me as they cruised in the clear, blue sky. Most stunning of all were the wild, painted Egyptian geese.

Day after day the heat was unbearable, and even the nights on deck brought no relief. Whenever we grumbled, however, there was always someone to tell us that soon we would be in the Mediterranean, where it would be cooler—and anyway, once in England, we could forget about the sun. "Rains every day, it does," one soldier from Manchester announced with satisfaction.

A few days later we sailed into the Gulf of Suez, between the Sinai Desert and the Eastern Desert of Egypt. Even when we could see neither shore, the desert winds blew hotly and the decks of the *Strathmore* were powdered with fine sand that crunched beneath your feet.

Morale was not high amongst the civilians as people were bored and hot, with little to do once work was finished. My chores in the wash-halls and lavatories became particularly unpleasant in the heat with no ventilation. When I cursed my bad luck, someone laughed and said, "Lucky for you we're not all sea-sick." One had to be grateful for small mercies.

A military police sergeant offered me a cigarette one day. His name was Walter—only first names were ever used. "Anybody ever tell you about the Alexandra?" he began.

"You mean the military hospital in Singapore?" I asked.

"That's the one, Sonny. I was in there, wounded, when the Japs came. They raped all the nurses, then bayoneted them. The Nip officers took their swords and decapitated the wounded. Any nurse left alive went down on her knees begging for mercy. Made no difference. There was no mercy. Some of us wounded who could walk were rounded up by Japs reeking of saki with blood all over their uniforms. They threw us into trucks. I must have passed out because when I came to we were crammed into a go-down.

"Days later we were marched off to a camp. Seventy percent of our men died on that march and of those left more than half died in the camp." He shook his shoulders, as if to get rid of a burden. "My sister's a nurse, you know. Not the sort of story I'll be telling at home."

I wondered if he had been in Changi. So many of the men had been, but none would talk about it. If a man screamed out in his nightmare when we all lay uncomfortably on deck during those hot nights, someone would always get up and pull the man's blanket up around him, whispering to the others just one word in explanation, "Changi." The men would nod grimly and curl up again, trying to recapture sleep.

Soon there was an announcement that the ship would anchor in the Bay of Suez, which cheered us all up—especially when we were told that, "Civilians will be taken ashore between Port Taufiq and El Shatt for 'Desert Entertainments' and 'Clothing Stalls.'"

Once we had anchored, navy launches pulled alongside, and about 300 of us boarded in great spirits. Military trucks awaited us on shore and drove us through the desert to an army camp. This was the Fanara-Bitter Lake Camp 307, which seemed to consist of a smart brick entrance gate and wall, behind which there was nothing much but rows and rows of tents lined up in the sand. Here we jumped out and were told to form columns and march off to an enormous canvas "hall." We joked to one another that we were being enlisted!

On the truck I had been surprised to see men in khaki trousers with a black stripe down the outside leg and short sleeved shirts with a black lozenge sewn on the back. Nobody said anything, but it was quite obvious that these were not British troops. I wished Mr. Ledertoug had been along to ask, but he had preferred to stay on board.

Under the big canvas were many more of these curiously uniformed men, standing at trestle tables laden with piles of clothing—trousers, jackets, sweaters, shirts, underwear, and shoes. We had expected to haggle at an oriental bazaar!

Deep, metal trays were handed out to us as we were told to queue up, and we inched our way along the tables in front of the uniformed men. They asked us our size in halting, heavily accented English. I picked out a pair of grey flannel trousers and several warm shirts, despite the fact that I had a trunk full of my own clothes, as did quite a few of us. We did not want to attract attention to ourselves by refusing, especially as many amongst us really were in dire need of warm clothing for the cold that surely awaited us. The clothes were not new, but of good quality and in excellent condition, and to turn them down would have been churlish.

Once everyone was satisfied, we were led into an adjoining large tent with tables and benches, where we were told to sit down and put our bundles of clothes at our feet. About a dozen uniformed men entered carrying enormous platters of sandwiches and cakes, whilst bottles of soft drinks and urns of tea stood on every table. I sat at the end of a table, and a grey haired man came and poured me a cup of tea.

As I thanked him, I asked him where he came from, and he said, "I am German." So I switched languages and asked him what he was doing there. *"Wir sind deutsche Kriegsgefangene."*

It turned out that he had been a major in the German army, and that now he, like all the men, was a prisoner of war. A few of them were from the Africa Corps, but most had been taken in Italy or Greece and shipped here to Egypt. I asked him what it was like, here in the desert, and he gave a tight smile. "We are reasonably fed, not ill treated, but the climate is hard, with sandstorms and incredible heat followed by extreme cold at night. It hardly ever rains, but when it does it is so heavy our tents collapse and we have to start all over again. Even so, we are probably better off here than in poor, devastated Germany."

After the meal, we were led outside for "rides." To my surprise, I found myself perched on a dromedary, quite unlike the camels I had seen in Mongolia and China. After this, a couple of dozen Arabs held mock war games, charging each other astride their camels, brandishing scimitars and giving bloodcurdling yells. To one side, a small band played weird music on strange instruments, whilst a fat, middle-aged woman wriggled her belly about.

That was it! We returned to the tent, picked up our belongings, and then the German major came up to me and held out a bar of Cadbury's chocolate. "Here, take this. I know you refugees don't get much of this stuff."

I blushed to be taken for a refugee again, but thanked him for his kindness, pocketed his gift, and wished him luck.

Back on board, refreshed by the day's events, I had to try to cram all this new stuff into my already over-full trunk. It was a good thing I had the new chain to keep it from bursting open but then I didn't really have anything left worth stealing anymore.

I was woken on deck at dawn by strange sounds, camel grunts, and loud Arab voices. We had reached the Suez Canal! I jumped to my feet and saw, about thirty metres away and far below me, men in long robes riding their camels alongside us, chattering away, apparently oblivious of the ship towering above them. In the distance, a slim minaret stood out against the lightening sky, and suddenly came the wailing call to early prayer. As the sounds reached the Arabs, they slid off their camels, unrolled small carpets, and knelt down with their heads touching their knees. It was an amazing scene, with palm trees and rolling sands on either side as far as the eye could see.

All that day I remained on deck, fascinated by the fleeting snap-shots of Arab life that slipped by—the vivid colours, the tall dusty trees, the strange sounds, and smells, and always the yellow desert beyond.

Once through the canal, we anchored in Port Said, again to take on supplies. To our frustration, nobody was allowed ashore. Mr. Ledertoug had promised to show me the pyramids, and I was bitterly disappointed. Despite the heat, all portholes were ordered closed to avoid the sort of pilfering I had been warned about on the *Tientsin Maru* in Tsingtao.

Word must have spread like wildfire in the port that 8,000 potential customers were aboard the Strathmore, unable to go ashore, a captive clientele for the Egyptian merchants. They swarmed out in boats, barges, and dhows, waving their wares at us and yelling their heads off. The noise was deafening. Hundreds of merchants offered us everything from dates, figs, and Turkish Delight to fruit and coconuts. An abundance of cheap handbags, wallets, belts, and Arab robes were touted as the finest for sale anywhere in the world.

Prices were haggled over in shouting matches, and intense bargaining went on even for a box of figs. Once a price was agreed upon, money was lowered in a basket and the vendor counted it carefully. Then he put the purchases in the basket to be hauled up on deck. With a cunning learnt in China, I managed to get most of the items I bought at less than half the price originally quoted, although whether I would consider them bargains today is in some doubt. However, at the time I was thrilled with the three handbags I bought for my Laimun Omi and aunts Elke and Evchen. I also bought three wallets, a belt, boxes of dates, and a bag of Turkish Delight. My prize acquisition was a scarlet fez with a black tassel, which I wore all the way to Southampton until Mr. Ledertoug advised me to take it off. My last purchase was a large canvas bag, as my trunk could hold no more.

Bit by bit, the soldiers became more and more infuriated as the Arab vendors cheated them, giving incorrect change or sending up the wrong bag. There were endless disagreements. Finally tempers snapped and a couple of soldiers grabbed one of the ship's fire hoses and aimed at the boats, practically submerging them in a powerful blast of water. Egyptian knives were waved in drenched fury as the dhows beat a smart retreat just out of range, but half an hour later they were back in business on the other side of the ship. It was quite a show, lasting the whole day with neither side giving up. The merchants continued to cheat the soldiers until the soldiers lost patience and gave them a dousing.

After a while I lost interest and retired to a quiet spot, put on my fez, and munched my delicious dates. Michèle strolled by, and I gave her some Turkish Delight and a wallet. She rewarded me with one of her quick kisses and a racing heartbeat.

The following day we were in the Mediterranean, and there was an outbreak of dysentery amongst the Annamese soldiers. Leaflets were promptly distributed, warning us against drinking tap water. Only the boiled water in the dining halls or bottled sodas from the canteen should be consumed. Of course my lavatory-cleaning duties became even less jolly, but by now I was used to them and, with my fez firmly on my head, I scrubbed away singing, "Don't Fence Me In" at the top of my voice. If my mother could have seen me now . . .

Actually I had received no word from Mother since leaving Shanghai, even though I sent her long screeds from every port. It continued to be warm and I still slept on deck. Close to Sicily schools of dolphins followed us, laughing and leaping in and out of the water, their wet grey bodies sleek in the sunlight. It was a great spectacle and I watched for hours.

Rumours now abounded that the French Colonial troops were to disembark in Marseilles. This would mean that not only would our sleeping quarters be considerably less crowded, but that we might be allowed ashore. There was also talk of Gibraltar, where some British Navy units were to get off, and where we would be allowed to visit The Rock. Unfortunately, none of this came about. Orders were received to proceed directly to Southampton, where we were all to disembark together. So there were no more hopes of any landings.

As we inched our way up into the western Mediterranean, the weather cooled to about twenty-four degrees C., and now there was heavy sea traffic. Just before Gibraltar we passed an enormous American Battle Group consisting of an aircraft carrier, heavy cruisers, and destroyers, all heading in the opposite direction, toward Naples.

A great deal of signalling went on between the Americans and the *Strathmore*, and one destroyer came quite close to us. We lowered the red ensign as a courtesy, and the destroyer replied by lowering the Stars and Stripes whilst its loud speakers blared out "Anchors Away," to my intense delight.

Once through the Straits of Gibraltar and into the open Atlantic, the weather turned cool and foggy, but I still preferred to sleep on deck. It was only off Vigo that the cold sent me reluctantly back down to my hammock.

A few days before our final destination, Bob, an Irish airman, approached me and asked whether I would lend him my gold Omega watch. He explained that he was to meet his girlfriend in Belfast, and he really would like to show off to her with my watch on his wrist. He solemnly swore to mail it to me in Denmark in a couple of weeks. Despite the fact that I considered myself a street smart "Shanghai kid," I agreed. As one might expect, I never saw my watch again.

Excitement on board soared to a fever pitch as we sailed up the Channel. Many of the servicemen had not seen home for many years, and for all of us the long trip was almost over. I knew that the men who had been prisoners of war were not as excited as their fighting comrades. The men who had fought in Europe would all be heroes, they thought, but the POWs were not sure what sort of a reception they would get. From the terrible stories they had told me, I was pretty sure they would not be repeating many of them to their wives and children. They had suffered so much and been so kind to me that I worried almost as much about them as I did about myself and my uncertain future.

The first thing that struck me about England was that all the dock-workers were white. I blurted out to the English officer standing next to me at the rail, "The coolies are white here!"

He roared with laughter and slapped me on the back. "You're not in Asia now, Sonny."

How true. As I gazed in despair at the drab skies of post-war England, it seemed as if all the adventures of my youth were well and truly over. For the rest of my life I would forget neither the sorrows nor the excitements of those Shanghai years. My father's death was the worst part, but all my happy memories of him are part of China too—all stored away in my sometimes uncomfortably accurate memory, forever indelible.

34

ENGLAND

There must be a better time to first set foot on English soil than the aftermath of six years of war, and more welcoming places than a dilapidated house full of elderly folk in Chalk Farm.

After docking in Southampton, I found myself herded into a bus with the rest of the *Strathmore's* small Scandinavian contingent. At that time, all foreigners arriving in England were treated as refugees, so we were kindly but firmly told what to do and where to go. Our temporary abode was to be The Chalk Farm Retirement Home, where we were to stay until we could continue our separate journeys.

When first I heard the name, I imagined a farmhouse surrounded by the white cliffs of Dover, but Chalk Farm turned out to be a dingy suburb of London and the large old house where we were billeted was dismal and in disrepair. A group of elderly, whey-faced men and women were gathered on the front porch, eyeing us with cold curiosity. Nobody spoke.

A matron in starched white marched us up to an attic that smelled of damp, where about thirty army cots were lined up in rows. My elderly mentor, Mr. Ledertoug, cried out with delight at the sight of them. "A bed! What luxury after those dreadful hammocks."

We were shown a rather rusty bathroom, and after "cleaning ourselves up," we were told to assemble downstairs in the hall where our duties would be assigned—"To pay for your keep," sniffed the matron.

I was seconded to the kitchen and told to set about making sandwiches. The cook soon became enraged, accusing me of "wanton extravagance." I had to learn to scrape the merest hint of "marge" on one slice of bread, lay a wafer-thin slice of spam on it, then top it with an "un-marged" slice of bread. One sandwich per person was lunch.

There was no time to feel hungry. Two Danish boys and I were given sponges, buckets, and cloths with which to clean all the downstairs windows. We were not very good at this, and the results of our efforts were considered far from adequate.

Dinner that evening consisted of cabbage and potato soup in which a few chunks of grey boiled meat floated. We soon realised that not only would the meals be meagre, but the ingredients would be of poor quality and seriously overcooked. We each had been given one week's supply of temporary ration cards, which had been immediately snapped up by the cook upon our arrival. We were convinced she would have let us starve without these.

Fortunately, our uncomfortable stay at Chalk Farm only lasted a week before arrangements were made by the Danish Consulate for Mr. Ledertoug and me to sail from Harwich to Esbjerg on the *DFDS A. P. Bernstorff.* She seemed very small after the *Strathmore*, but with her red carpets and piped soft music, we found her most luxurious after our weeks on a stripped-down troop carrier.

As an officer took my ticket I asked when I should report for duty. He looked at me in amazement. "What duty are you talking about?"

I was embarrassed by his stare. "Well, Sir, shall I work in the kitchens or what?"

He burst out laughing and slapped me on the back, thinking I was pulling his leg, and told a steward to show me to my cabin. As I left he called out, "I think we'll manage to run the ship without you this time, Lad!"

What a relief. All I had to do then was send a telegram to my step-grandmother, alerting her of my imminent arrival.

35

DENMARK

I woke early to find the ship had docked in Esbjerg. I threw on some decidedly grubby clothes and raced up on deck to watch the bustle of the busy port.

When unloading appeared to be over and the quays had emptied, I saw, far below me on the quay, a young woman looking rather lost. I called down, "May I help you?"

She stared up at me. "I'm waiting to meet my nephew from China."

It was Evchen, as I had hoped. Each was as surprised as the other, but of course we had not seen one another for eight years or so. I couldn't remember exactly what my aunt looked like, and with my newly brilliantined hair and dark tan, I certainly could not have looked familiar. I wished I had thought to give my step-grandmother a clue regarding my appearance, as in my favourite detective novels. I could have worn my fez!

On the train to Aabenraa, Evchen told me that we would not be going to "Laimun." The big family house had been requisitioned by the Danish government as a home for pregnant refugees. Hundreds of East German women had fled from the Russians and been taken by boat to the nearest Danish islands, from where they were assigned shelter. Bad luck if you had a large house in southern Denmark with more bedrooms than you needed—you just had to move out and make other arrangements for your own family.

In the small town of Aabenraa, my step-grandmother owned two apartments, which she had turned into one large flat. She was living here with her two daughters, four grandchildren, and their nursemaid. Together with me we were to be nine.

As surprising as this news was, I was so delighted to be with family again and my welcome was so warm that I didn't think twice about the crowding. Once I had recounted all my adventures and heard all of theirs, step-grandmother said it was time for bed. I was far too excited to sleep, but it immediately became apparent that my unruly ways would have to change drastically. Did anyone even realise that I was now a young man? There seemed to be some doubt about this.

At breakfast, I found a timetable in step-grandmother's hand by my plate, from which I learned that I had been enrolled in Aabenraa High School. Term would begin in seven weeks. Until then I was to have daily lessons in Danish from nine to noon, while every afternoon from two to five I would be tutored in math. From five to seven there would be homework, followed by dinner and then bed. On Saturdays I need only study in the morning, as after lunch there would be weeding and fruit gathering in the Laimun gardens. I was to receive five kroners pocket money a week, enough for one cinema ticket at 3 kr. 50. I could spend the remaining 1 kr. 50 on ice cream, et cetera. I did not think there would be much et cetera.

In such confined quarters, it was difficult not to be under people's feet all the time. I recalled the big house with its forests to roam in, the orchards where apples could be pinched, the pebbly beach where I would launch my small person into icy waters. Now a clumsy teenager, I was expected to take up as little room as possible, rapidly perfect my Danish and German, and read aloud from the classics to assembled family members after dinner.

Since the death of my father, I had been practically without adult supervision as Mother became more and more involved with her Italian gentleman. My school in Shanghai had closed towards the end of the war, so the strict regime I was to follow under my step-grandmother's roof came as a short, sharp shock.

Even though Mother had written that I was to be sent to boarding school near Copenhagen, being enrolled in the local Danish school did not really upset me, as I had no friends in either establishment. But I did worry that father's wishes, which he had made known to me before he became ill, were being totally disregarded.

In Denmark as in England, everything was still rationed, so the first thing I had to do was visit the Town Hall to obtain a ration card and clothing coupons. My step-grandmother had taken one look at my clothes and did not seem to approve of even the clean ones. She came with me to choose a suit of green knickerbockers with a matching jacket, which I instantly and passionately loathed. My step-grandmother, however, nodded happily when I tried on these garments. "Just the thing for school," she beamed.

At last a letter arrived from Mother, in which she described in detail her life in Shanghai—but already it all seemed so far away. She and Dino planned to come to Europe next year, but there was no mention of the sale of our house or their move to Italy. I perked up when I read that she had met a Captain Andresen, who would pass through Aabenraa on his way home to Norway. He would bring me three metres of camel hair for a coat; three metres of grey flannel for a suit, and three metres of Harris tweed for two jackets.

I could see an end to the hated green knickerbockers, but when the materials arrived my step-grandmother was not well pleased. "You may go to the tailor and have these items made up, but you will not wear them in Aabenraa. It would not be appropriate. They are to be put away until you go to boarding school. The tailor must take this into account when measuring you."

As I stormed out of the room I overheard her say to my aunt, "A camel coat for a school boy—can you imagine!" It was obvious that she and Mother would rarely see eye to eye about anything.

School began, and I was relieved to get away from women and babies. Of course I was quite a novelty for the small-town school, and the English master asked me to give a talk on China to the top three classes. Funnily enough, I was treated less of an oddity after this, and was accepted almost as one of them. Well, to be *really* accepted, I would have had to be born in Aabenraa, and my father before me. Unfortunately, though, we had both had the curious notion of getting ourselves born in Hong Kong.

On Sundays after church, I would visit my Great-uncle Johan who, now blind, lived in what had been the family home when my ancestors had been ships' captains. Uncle Johan had also spent many years in China, and told me exciting tales of warlords, bandits, and the Boxer Rebellion. He claimed my Sunday visits were quite the highlight of his week. I suppose everybody else had heard all his stories already. Before I left, he always offered me a glass of port and a cigarette. Although I didn't really smoke, I would cross my legs and puff away with him, swapping tales and feeling quite the old China hand.

Lensnack, the big Jebsen house adjacent to Laimun, had also been taken over to accommodate refugees, and my Great-aunt Kaethe had moved into the old Jebsen family home in Aabenraa. Now news came that the Lensnack refugees were to be repatriated, which meant that Tante Kaethe could return home with her son, daughter, and three grandchildren. Lensnack was huge, much bigger than Laimun, and as we were so many in step-grandmother's apartment, it was decided that I should go and live there also.

Tante Kaethe loved to play cards, and every evening after dinner she and I would have battles of gin rummy or double patience. She cheated outrageously, peering at me out of the corner of her beady eyes to see if I had noticed, but I always pretended I didn't. It was like playing with a naughty little girl hiding inside an extremely large body. She had to walk with two sticks and was something of an invalid, but her mind was sharp and she could be great fun. Between battles she would always say, "Why don't you fetch a little glass of something for us both?" and then, sipping delicate glasses of sweet sherry or Madeira, we would pick up our cards again. Between my various relations, I was in danger of becoming over-fond of sweet wines.

But all was not fun and games. Here too I had to collect fruit from the orchards in summer, and in winter chop firewood and shovel peat into the central heating furnaces, as coal was still rationed. It was a good thing I had learnt on the *Strathmore* to put aside my spoilt Asian habits, where there had always been a Boy to do the dirty work.

A few months later, just when I was beginning to feel at home in Lensnack, Aunt Elke left Aabenraa with her children in order to join her Doctor husband, who had just been released from the Navy. Now there was more space in my step-grandmother's apartment, so back I went. Luckily I had made some friends at school and my initial loneliness was over, so it didn't seem to matter much where I actually slept. This was fortunate as I was about to move again.

Arwed, my step-grandmother's younger son, now returned to Aabenraa. The plan was that he should go out to Hong Kong, but in the meantime he was to work in the Jebsen Shipping Office. Naturally he expected to live with his mother, so a room was found for me with an elderly widow.

Her house was reasonably large, but I was confined to one small room. Here I slept, did my homework, and ate my breakfast. Apart from the lavatory and bathroom, I was not to enter any other room. I had a cupboard where I kept Cornflakes, sugar, and milk, as well as black bread and cold cuts with which to make my school sandwiches. Dinner I took at my step-grandmother's.

This was not a happy time. The widow and I did not hit it off. Reprimands about muddy feet and noise escalated to a full-blown row when one night, returning from a bridge party, she found she had forgotten her keys to the front door. I was woken by a fearful banging on the side door, the one for which I had a key. Like most healthy youngsters, I slept like a log, and it was some time before I heard anything. I stumbled downstairs, still half asleep, to find the widow beside herself with rage. She had been knocking for "over an hour," and I had "deliberately ignored" her, leaving her out in the snow. "This is the last straw, and you have one week to find other accommodation."

For the rest of that night I tossed and turned, making wild plans to bicycle up north to the port of Fredericia, where I would look for work on a ship—any ship, going anywhere.

At school the next morning, I talked this over with a friend whose father was First Mate with the East Asiatic Shipping Line. He told me that you had to be at least sixteen and have written parental consent. As I was not yet fifteen and Mother would never agree to my plan, it was obviously out.

As it happened, before the week was over I was sent back to Lensnack, so my dreams of escape became less urgent. I moved into my old room and played cards again with Aunt Kaethe. Just as I had resettled, my uncles Arwed and Jocko left together for Hong Kong on the East Asiatic Company ship Kina, so I returned to my step-grandmother's apartment. How I wished that this game of musical chairs would end.

Now talk finally turned to boarding schools. Letters were written to Stenhus and Herlufsholm. I was accepted by both, and lists of items I should bring with me kept arriving. Then suddenly all talk of these Danish schools stopped, and I was told that I was to go to school in Switzerland.

Apparently my mother's brother Claus had suggested that I be sent to the Lyceum Alpinum, a boys' school in Zuoz, in the Engadine. I would have preferred to follow my father's wishes and stay in Denmark, but nobody was interested in my opinion. When I asked why there had been this sudden change of plan, I was told that as my mother had mentioned the possibility of settling in Italy with Dino, it only made sense for me to be closer to them. I had been waiting for this move to happen for so long that I no longer believed she would actually ever come.

Then I had to go to hospital to have my tonsils removed—for the second time, which seemed singularly unfair. The day after the operation, a telegram arrived for me at St. Ansgars. Mother's sister Ursula had died in Clarens of pneumonia. She had been very dear to me, and I was miserable to think I would never see her again—especially now that I was so soon to be in Switzerland myself.

Before I left St. Ansgars, I received yet another telegram. This time I read of my grandfather's death from peritonitis in the Clinique La Prairie in Clarens. I didn't even know what this was. My grandfather and Aunt Ursi were both gone. I could not even begin to think how terrible this must be for my poor Clarens Omi. I had just written, telling her how happy I was to stay with them in the Empereur on my way to Zuoz, and how I looked forward to being reunited with my Rickmers family after so many years. The letter I had to write now was the most difficult I had ever composed.

Arrangements went ahead for my journey to Switzerland. I took the fast train to Copenhagen, and was fascinated to watch as it rolled onto a ferry between the islands of Fyn and Zealand. I was met in Copenhagen by a Mr. Hans Hennig, a family friend who put me up for the night. I had been given instructions to invite him to dinner, and he chose the Scandia restaurant. Afterwards he took me to Tivoli Gardens, which were in full swing with international bands playing under the stars and all the fun of the fair. We rode a roller coaster, and from the top we could see the lights of the whole of Copenhagen spread out beneath us.

The next day I flew to Zurich on the Danish airline, Det Danske Luftfartselskab (DDL). It was my first flight ever, and I was in a state of high excitement. In Zurich I was met by my uncle Claus, who wore a black tie and a black arm band. How I wished I had thought of this.

After lunch, Claus had to meet his lawyers, and I was to wait for him in the station. To pass the time, I went into a newsreel cinema, where I watched the funeral of King Christian X of Denmark, a suitably sombre subject before arriving in Clarens at a house in full mourning.

36
Switzerland

When Claus returned, we took the trains to Lausanne and then Vevey. He was obviously exhausted by his meetings and lounged across from me in the carriage, eyes closed, long legs stretched out interminably. I reckoned he must be over six-two, a giant compared to my grandfather, but he had inherited the Rickmers beaked nose and black hair. As I studied him surreptitiously, I envied him his careless elegance.

The eyes that now opened and caught me staring were very blue. I blurted out how shattered I was at the loss of his sister and father. Fortunately I was old enough to realise that my grief for a beloved grandfather and aunt could not compare to his, but I tried to explain just how much they and my years in the Empereur had meant to me. Only a few weeks ago I had written to ask my grandfather if we could do all our old walks together in the hills above Clarens.

Claus sighed. "He could have pulled through you know. He just gave up. The entire shipping fleet gone, the shipyard bombed to smithereens, the incalculable financial disasters, all left him a broken man."

I gazed at Claus miserably. What on earth was there to say? Then he added, thinking to cheer me up, "Oh, he was looking forward so much to seeing you again, young Jessy! When we knew you were coming, he really perked up, I want you to remember that. But then Ursi died, and he got sick, and nothing seemed to matter anymore."

During the four hours of our train journey, Claus filled me in with what had been happening. "This way you won't ask awkward questions and upset your grandmother."

Once grandfather had stopped going to Germany on shipping business, he lived in a cocoon in Switzerland all through the second half of the war. Of course he followed the progress of military action, but he just refused to believe any disturbing rumours of the ghastly excesses committed by the SS that filtered through to him. Even when defeat seemed unavoidable, and friends in the Swiss government approached him with an offer of Swiss citizenship and the possibility of registering his remaining ships under the Swiss flag, he refused. He may have been proud of being half French and enamoured of Switzerland, but he loved Germany, his father's country, the country he had grown up in, the Germany of Goethe, Schiller, and Beethoven. How could he turn his back on her in her hour of need?

Claus lit a cigarette with a slightly shaky hand, the only sign of distress I was to see. "After the war, Father followed the Nuremberg Trials in dazed disbelief. When films of the camps were shown, when no secrets remained hidden and he had to look at the horrors done in Germany's name, he lost his will to live."

I thought he had finished but there was more. "The only real asset left was his art collection, most of it in bank vaults. Soon a Corot here, a Holbein there, had to be sold to cover expenses. As the market flooded, prices dropped, but enough came in to allow Mother and Father to continue much as before."

But eventually, he explained, it became impossible for them to keep up the Empereur, with all its necessary staff. Alone now, my grandparents moved into Le Petit Cret, the five-bedroom guest house at the edge of the park. All cars were sold except for one small Fiat, which had been up on blocks for some time. I must have looked so utterly dumbfounded at this litany of catastrophes that Claus was forced to laugh. He punched my shoulder affectionately. "Don't look so miserable young Jessy! You will see. Le Petit Cret is very cosy, and your grandmother is busy turning the garden into a small paradise."

Somehow, despite the war, it had never occurred to me that things would ever change in neutral Switzerland; that my grandparents would ever move from the house which I loved so much. "But I addressed all my letters there!" was all I could think to say.

"Yes, well, it's rented out now, but we got all your letters, don't worry about that."

I couldn't quite take it all in. "But who lives there now?" I had longed for years to return to this house—half my dreams took place there. Was it possible that it was

Claus Rickmers

to remain forever out of my reach?

"It's rented to a Dr. Wilhelm Furtwängler—a friend of ours. Do you know who he is?"

I had never heard of this gentleman, but apparently he was a famous musician, a world-class conductor. Claus grinned. "He's very temperamental, of course, so watch your step! He can be utterly charming one minute, but woe betide you if you make a noise when he's working."

I could quite appreciate how renting out the big house would solve money problems, just as the Danish Consulate's lease had helped Mother and me in Shanghai. And of course a rental contract did not mean the house was lost to the family forever!

From the time our train arrived in Vevey, as we walked past the taxi rank and together lugged my stuff to take a tram to Clarens, then trudged up from the lake past the St. George's School and along the avenue Bosquets de Julie into the garden of le Petit Cret, I slowly began to realise quite how much life for everyone had changed.

However, past glories were forgotten when I saw Omi, now completely white-haired, standing at her new front door. She took me in her arms and, without a word, made me know I was home. Behind her stood Claus's twin sister Moni, who hugged and kissed me and teased me about my smart clothes. Every few minutes one or other would exclaim, "Oh, if only your grandfather could see you now," until Claus put a stop to this female fussing by dragging me off to the cellar to choose a couple of bottles of champagne.

It was cool and dark down there, and as we walked along the wine racks I saw they were still stacked with family Delamain cognacs and the vintage wines, my grandfather's pride and joy. By the time we went upstairs to celebrate my arrival, I had pulled myself together and the champagne chased away all tears.

I had imagined we would have long talks about Grandfather and Ursula, but these never took place. Omi was greatly influenced by the theosophical theories of Rudolf Steiner and a firm believer in reincarnation, so for her it was just a question of time before she would see her beloved husband and daughter again. How glad I should have been to have had her at my side with this comforting philosophy when my father died.

The weather remained superb during the weeks I spent in Clarens before school commenced. We could still use the Empereur's grounds, which meant Omi, Claus, and I played croquet on the big lawn every fine afternoon. Claus was our champion and won without fail. Moni could rarely join us as she was working as Dr. Furtwängler's secretary, a job she loved.

Then out of the blue a telegram arrived from Shanghai—Mother and Dino were to take an Air France flight to Geneva. The trip would take four days in a propeller plane with many stops en-route. I was overjoyed at this news, but Omi confessed to being somewhat nervous about meeting this unknown Italian who apparently had become her son-in-law. Moni, who spoke fluent Italian, reminded her mother that Ursula had met Dino on board some ship and had pronounced him a charming man. Strangely enough, nobody asked me what I thought of Dino, so I kept my opinions to myself.

The four of us went by taxi to meet the newlyweds at Montreux station. Mother stepped daintily down from the train, fresh as a daisy after her long journey, as elegant as ever. Dino immediately set out to charm us all.

We had to take three taxis home because of Mother's luggage. I rode with Dino and Claus. The moment the doors closed Dino asked why we had no car. We explained that the one remaining Fiat was blocked up in the garage due to lack of funds.

Mother took over my room at the top of le Petit Cret, whilst I moved to the Hotel Ketterer with Dino. I quite enjoyed this, as Mother had given me my first radio and I could roam the airwaves undisturbed far into the night.

As tea drew to a close the following afternoon, Dino pulled wads of banknotes out of his pocket and peeled off a pile, which he thrust at Claus. "This should be enough to get your car back on the road. Etha doesn't like being without one."

Grandmother flushed, and Mother looked daggers at Dino. There was a sudden confusion of clattering cups and plates as we gathered up the tea things, so I think I was the only one who heard Mother hiss at Dino that perhaps he could be a little more discreet in future.

Before I left for school, Dino invited us all to an extravagant ten-course luncheon in the Hotel Belmont over Montreux. The main topic of conversation became our house in Shanghai. Dino had found Chinese buyers who were willing to give us 200,000 American dollars for it, payable in San Francisco. I started to grin at Mother as three quarters of this, then a considerable sum, would be mine.

"Unfortunately," said Dino "that uncle of yours—and you have so many, let's call him your Number One Uncle in Asian fashion—does not appear to trust me. As executor of your father's will, he has blocked the sale."

There was a hubbub of outrage until Dino, polishing his monocle, announced that as he had now washed his hands of the entire affair we should change the subject of conversation. I was dying for details, but was silenced by a look from Mother.

The news she wanted to talk about was the Buddhist marriage a monk had arranged for them in Shanghai. We admired the red Chinese scroll with black characters and heavy scarlet seals, which she unrolled for us. This was their wedding certificate, and Dino was now officially my step-father. Amid the relieved congratulations, I kissed my mother and shook hands with Dino, determined to give him the benefit of every doubt from now on, as I had not seen Mother so radiantly happy in years.

As we were leaving the restaurant, the owner came over and asked if everything had been satisfactory. It had, until he held out his hand to shake my grandmother's. She drew back as if he were about to bite her, and her look of hauteur as she swept silently out of the place was so funny that we laughed all the way home. Naturally she could not see the joke.

The next day, Claus and I fetched the Fiat from the garage where we had taken it to be overhauled, and then Mother drove us for a spin over the vineyards towards Mont Pelerin and Les Pléiades, which were looking especially beautiful. As we drove higher, the alpine meadows were yellow with wild daffodils under the spring sunshine, just as I remembered them when Grandfather and I would gather great arms-full of flowers to take home to Omi. Sadly one was not allowed to do this any more.

Too soon it was time to leave. My trunk and bicycle were sent ahead by rail whilst Mother and Omi accompanied me by car. We drove through Bern, Zurich, and Chur into the Engadine Valley, spending the night at the Hotel Concordia in Zuoz before Mother drove me to meet the school director the following day.

37

Lyceum Alpinum

One's first term at boarding school always comes as a bit of a shock. Not only do you have to get used to living in close proximity to hundreds of boys, you can never get away from them. When I arrived, the school had a large and growing complement of the sons of post-war Italian millionaires. I shared a room with one of these boys. Wads of banknotes were constantly flashed under my nose, and my meagre pocket money of the regulation four francs a week was the cause of much scornful hilarity.

Sport was to be my consolation. There were courts for tennis and open-air fives, a cricket ground complete with traditional club house, ski lifts, a rink for ice hockey and skating, plus a large indoor swimming pool. Every afternoon was devoted to one sport or another, depending upon the time of year. That summer our sports master, a Scot with a passion for cricket, had us play an awful lot of his favourite game. It must have looked odd to visitors to the Engadine—wickets and cricket whites on the mountain lowlands of Switzerland, with the Union flag flying over the cricket pavilion.

Unlike most schools, our long break was in March and April during the snow melt, and in summer we had just three weeks of freedom. That August, before Mother and Dino returned to China, I took a yellow mountain bus to the top of the Passo Stelvio, one of the highest passes in Europe, where Switzerland, Italy, and Austria meet. Here Mother and Dino were waiting for me, together with Signore Lungo, a chauffeur who whizzed us down the hairpin bends in a convertible Lancia to the valleys of the Italian Tyrol.

From Canazei we made excursions to la Marmolata in the Dolomites, to Lago Carezza and Cortina d'Ampezzo. These were happy days, probably due to the fact that at nearly sixteen I had better manners and had made my peace with Dino. We spent the last week in Bellagio on the Lago di Como at the Hotel Villa Serbelloni. Every evening we dined on the terrace overlooking the lake and talked of China, and their plans to settle in Florence. I couldn't understand why they were taking so long to move, but in that summer of 1947 the Communist threat in the north seemed just a distant rumble to the old China hands of Shanghai who had survived the Japanese occupation. Mother was in no hurry to leave. They would take their time and get the best prices for our house, Dino's warehouses, and his remaining Yangtze riverboats. This was to prove a disastrous attitude. Once the Communists began to pour down towards the south, prices plummeted—and in the end, everything had to be left behind. They escaped only with hidden gold bars and smuggled cash.

But all this was yet to come. For now they happily left back to China in blissful ignorance of the future—and I, rather less cheerfully, returned to school. Then Moni arrived one weekend to drive me to St. Moritz where the Furtwängler family had a house on the lake. On the Saturday of that weekend, Moni and I swam in the icy water and then rushed back to the house to warm up and change for lunch. When I was tidy, I ran downstairs and into the first room I came across where, unbeknownst to me, Dr. Furtwängler was composing at a piano. As I opened the door there was a terrific draught, and all his music sheets flew up into the air before gently drifting down like giant snowflakes into disordered heaps. I was paralysed as Dr. Furtwängler leapt up in a violent rage, yelling at me to clear out. I offered to help pick everything up, but he was beside himself with fury. "Out, out, you stupid boy!" So out I fled.

At luncheon his serene wife Elisabeth calmed us both down and thanks to the antics of their small son Thomas, a curly headed white-blond four year old, even Dr. Furtwängler recovered his good temper, brushed aside my apologies and told me to call him "Fu." This nickname was used only by the Rickmers family, I believe.

Christmas came, and le Petit Cret burst at the seams as Bertram and Peter joined their mother, Claus, Moni, and me for the festivities. My uncle Bertram must have been about thirty then. He had lost his fiancée Doerthe, in Hamburg, towards the end of the war. Just before Bertram arrived for the official announcement of their engagement at the end of 1944, there was an air raid. Doerthe and her father waited for the "all clear" before going to the garden door to see what damage had been done. As they stood peering out into the dark, a dud bomb, which had fallen onto their frozen lawn, suddenly exploded, and a splinter flew off, directly at Doerthe. She fell back against her father exclaiming, "I think I have been hit!" The splinter had gone straight to her heart and she died almost instantly.

Since then, Uncle Bertram had buried himself in feverish work in Bremerhaven, trying to rebuild the badly bombed family shipyard. His post-war plan was to start on a small scale, building modern fishing trawlers.

Uncle Peter had divorced his first wife and just become engaged to Ilse, who had also been married before, and she would come into the family with her young son, Wolfgang. Peter was planning to manage the new Rickmers Line from the badly damaged Hamburg offices.

There was much talk of lost ships, especially those that had been seized in foreign ports by Britain and put under the British flag, only to be sunk by German U-boats. Others had been scuttled by their own captains on orders of the German government to keep them out of Allied hands. Such are the vagaries of war.

Peter and Bertram kept urging Claus to join them in their efforts to rebuild the family fortune, but he was adamant that his role was to arrange for the sale of his father's art collection. "Where else are you going to find the money to get things going again?" was always his trump card.

When not planning for the future, there was fun in the kitchen. Lunch was prepared by Madame Bouvard, who came in daily, but in the evening each made his own supper. Peter would challenge us to the most improbable contests, one of which was a spaghetti marathon. We all consumed mountains, but Peter, who was not only taller but already possessed of quite a paunch, won of course. Then there was the egg-eating competition. Peter claimed he could easily eat thirty eggs, so we challenged him to prove it. His trick was to hard-boil the eggs, then chop them up and fry them in butter. This method resulted in a greatly reduced volume, which he was able to eat, but the concoction was so heavy that he had to confess to feeling "somewhat out of sorts" afterwards.

I settled down quickly once back at school. To keep us entertained, the Day Girls who took some lessons with the senior boys were allowed to return for school dances and act in Drama Society productions. However, bursting with teenage energy, these highlights were too rare to keep us occupied, and some of us would accept dares and make night commando raids on St. Moritz.

On the first of these dares, a couple of friends and I hid our bicycles in the bushes under my bedroom window, and after "lights out" slid down a rope and rode off into the dark. It took us about forty minutes to battle our way along the mountain road, hampered by a sudden rainstorm. By the time we arrived in the village, we were soaked to the skin. We slipped into the Kulm Palace by a side entrance and dried ourselves off as best we could in the men's' room before heading straight for the dance floor.

As we were in suits and school ties, we passed the headwaiter's scrutiny and were shown to a table, where we ordered Campari sodas with great aplomb. These we had to drink slowly as they had to last, and between sips we peered over our glasses to see if any available girls were sitting with their parents. One of us finally plucked up courage and approached a table where a suitable girl sat. He asked her father if she would be allowed to dance with him and, upon his nod, off they twirled. Seeing his success, we all followed suit—and soon, much to our own surprise, we were on the floor too, clutching young maidens to our rather soggy chests.

At breakfast the following morning news of our exploit circulated and it became necessary for other boys to out-do us. In the end, the winner was Hans Joerg Badrutt, whose father owned the famous Palace Hotel in St. Moritz. As luck would have it, Rita Hayworth was staying there and, to cap us all, Hans Joerg invited her to visit the school. Incredibly, she accepted. As Hans Joerg and I led her around in her tight white sweater and little white shorts that showed off her long tanned legs, even the masters were wide-eyed. Cricket ground to a halt, and swimmers missed their strokes as we gave Rita a full tour.

Not content with this, Hans Joerg invited her for a picnic that weekend. The Palace Hotel prepared us a sumptuous basket, and off we dragged Rita, up into the hills. We spread a plaid blanket under a tree and sipped wine as she enthralled us with tales of Hollywood. Finally we had to pack up and take her back to the hotel. She thanked us both and rewarded us with quick kisses. Needless to say, I carefully avoided her lipstick smudge when washing and managed to keep it for a long time.

So I was enjoying the Lyceum Alpinum, and all would have been well had I not described to Claus, during a holiday break, the lifestyle of the Italian pupils. He listened with dismay to tales of polo ponies stabled in St. Moritz, of personal chauffeurs with fast sports cars at the ready for these scions of the Mafiosi, of the heavy gold rings and chains and the endless flashing of wealth. The last straw was when I told him that some had even found it a good joke to shit in the school pool. Inexorably these careless confidences led to a radical shift, and I soon found that I was not to return to Zuoz.

I should point out that the influx of sons of racketeers was a product of post-war Italy and in no way a reflection on the Lyceum Alpinum today, which is still one of the finest schools in Switzerland.

38

Institut auf dem Rosenberg

Elisabeth Furtwängler's nephew, Peter Gaefgen, was staying at the Empereur on holiday from the Institut auf dem Rosenberg in St. Gall. He was a year older than me, and he told me a bit about his school, so when Claus advised me that I was to go there too I was quite keen. Thus began some very happy years.

The school stood above the small town of St. Gall on the Rosenberg hill, with 465 steps leading down to the town—so the way back up was quite a trek. There was no tuck shop at school—quite a sore point, as practically all the staff and seniors smoked in those unenlightened days. Of course I had to start a cigarette business. The largest tobacconist in St. Gall agreed to sell me packs at a twenty-percent discount, as long as I bought a minimum of twenty cartons. Always short of funds, I needed a partner.

My good friend Edu Weidtmann, whose father was a banker in Istanbul, had inherited entrepreneurial genes as I had, and agreed to join me. We stashed shoe-boxes full of different brands in our rooms, and at weekends and during breaks we did a roaring trade, selling out our first quota in two days. When the headmaster asked for cigars to be added to our stock, profits rose so that my meagre weekly allowance grew nicely.

Back in Denmark, my step-grandmother finally could return to a newly emptied Laimun with Evchen and her two small children, so now I stayed with them during the summer holidays. Once I rode out on my bicycle to see all my grandfather Rickmer's old estates and farms, which were now Danish State Property. It made me very happy to meet gardeners and agents who remembered him.

I spent Christmas and Easter in Clarens. One Christmas the Furtwänglers asked us over to the Empereur for a small concert. My grandmother, Moni, Claus, and I joined Elisabeth and Fu in the main drawing room, where we sat entranced as Yehudi Menuhin, accompanied by Wilhelm Kempff, played violin sonatas for us. Kempff then played parts of Furtwängler's new symphony. It was an evening to remember.

The entire summer of 1949 I spent working in the Aabenraa Kreditbank, after which Great Aunt Kaethe and Evchen accompanied me as far as Zurich, where we stopped at the Glockenhof for three days. We had tickets for *Die Fledermaus*, and I began to realise how lucky I was to hear so much world-class music.

That December, Uncle Bertram married and came with his new wife, Christa, to stay in le Petit Cret before continuing on to Crans sur Sierre for their honeymoon. Bertram told us with great roars of laughter how he had seen Christa's photo on an aunt's desk in Hamburg, and had asked to be introduced. The next time he was in the vicinity of Christa's parents' house in Duisberg, it was arranged that he should come to dinner.

Here Christa interrupted, saying she had known perfectly well the whole thing was a set-up. When Bertram drove up that late afternoon, she was preserving " a mountain of beans" with her sister in the kitchen. She took one peek from the window and declared, "He's not my type at all!"

On Rosenberg with Gerhard Melchers

Nevertheless, she had to show him the local sights, and slowly her opinion of him changed. She visited the aunt in Hamburg the next Easter, and was colouring eggs when Bertram turned up out of the blue and joined in. The two fell in love and were married a few months later.

Every morning before breakfast, it was a Rickmers tradition that the family should join Omi in her bedroom for coffee and to plan the day. These were moments we all treasured, as Omi was much loved. Now Christa joined the three brothers and me at Omi's bedside, and it was at these early morning chats that I really got to know and feel affection for my new aunt.

The following Easter holiday in Clarens was so unusually sunny that Claus and I checked out the state of the croquet equipment. Soon Moni burst into the garden shed to ask us to put up the ring tennis net, as Fu and Yehudi Menuhin had decided to come down and challenge us. I played with Fu, and Claus teamed up with Yehudi. The game became very rowdy, with these two intellectuals shouting and calling out childish insults to one another. Fu must have been in his sixties at this time. He was tall and thin, with a long, rather sad face, so it was good to see him laugh and let his hair down—figuratively speaking, of course as Fu's head was almost bald, with just a friar's fuzz of white hair. Fu and I won the match. Yehudi was not a good loser.

Even though I realised that I was lucky to hear such superb music, it could sometimes be too much. One day Dr. Lusser, Rosenberg's headmaster, called me to his study with the news that my uncle Claus had just telephoned to ask if I could have a week off to go to Italy where Furtwängler was to conduct Wagner's

Renée, Omi, Elisabeth Furthwängler+ daughter, Moni, me

Nibelungen Ring at the Scala di Milano. Dr. Lusser said the decision was mine, but that I should not forget exams were near. I had to call Claus and tell him I really couldn't afford to miss a whole week of school just at that moment. I don't think he ever forgave me.

I redeemed myself a little when Moni turned up at school to drive me to Winterthur to the museum owned by Herr Buerle, CEO of Oerlikon, one of Switzerland's prominent industries and a great patron of the Arts. In a small music room, about twenty of us had the privilege of listening to Furtwängler play excerpts from his own symphony for the first time in public. My genuine enthusiasm at the end of the evening satisfied even Claus.

During my final year, my cousin Gerhard Melchers came to the Rosenberg and we shared a room for a couple of terms and in my last term his brother Henning arrived which was great as we had all been good pals in Shanghai.

It must have been about now that Claus married the beautiful Renée. Her father, James Gueydan, a Swiss lawyer, lived with his family in a country house set amid its own vineyards over the Tour-de-Peilz, between Clarens and Vevey. We were all most impressed with tall, elegant Renée, who was as musical and intellectual as a partner would have to be for Claus.

That summer I passed my Swiss Finals and celebrated in Lugano with friends before taking the train up to Hamburg. I had been apprenticed to Rabbow and Company, an old, established import-export firm where I was to receive a solid training before being sent out to Hong Kong to join the family business.

39

HAMBURG

Hamburg at the end of 1950 was in a mess. The building where Rabbow and Company had their offices was half in ruins, and over the lavatories were sheets of corrugated iron which didn't fit properly, so you could either admire the sky or get wet, depending upon the weather. There was bomb damage everywhere, and the people were sullen and hostile to all who had not been through what they had.

Alongside the gaping craters, cranes careened about, caught in a frantic reconstruction boom. Food rationing was over, but salaries were small and everything so expensive that times were still grim.

My grandfather Jessen's house on Bellevue had been razed during the air raids, and on the site an apartment house had been built, from which I received some rental income. Added to my fifteen dollars' monthly salary, it just about kept me fed and a roof over my head.

Mother sent me the addresses of many of her Hamburg society friends, but as I had no money for the mandatory flowers or chocolates needed in order to call, I contacted none of them. After office hours I would sit, lonely, at my window, and gaze out over the Alster. As my pension stood where the Intercontinental is now, at least I looked out over water instead of the ruined city.

Some 200 yards from my pension on the Alte Rabenstrasse lived Uncle Peter and Aunt Ilse with Wolfgang, now a mischievous seven-year-old, and their baby son Paul. This warm, merry household was to become my haven. On the morning I arrived in Hamburg, Peter had fetched me at the railway station and taken me home for breakfast. Our happy reunion had been interrupted by the abrupt arrival of my uncles Bertram and Claus, both in a feverish state of nerves.

What had them in this state was the seizure of the *Mai Rickmers* by the Taiwanese navy, which they first learned of in a cable from the ship's captain, and then from headlines in the local newspapers. As she had been in international waters, it was an obvious act of piracy. The *Mai Rickmers*, their new post-war pride and joy, was the first German vessel to head for China since the end of the war, and she had been taken hostage as she entered the Taiwan Straits.

I saw the three brothers in action for the first time over congealing eggs and endless cups of coffee as they thrashed out a press release. It soon became clear that Bertram had the business brain. Time and again he brought the other two back to a rational approach to the crisis. Claus, the intellectual, was new to the game, and Peter was still a fun-loving sailor at heart. Bertram had obviously inherited his father's talents.

Over the next days it became evident that the Taiwanese did not want shipping and commerce to pick up again between the West and Communist China. The *Mai Rickmers* was held by the Taiwanese government for several weeks until diplomatic pressure finally secured her release, although she was not allowed to continue her route to China.

During my first months in Hamburg, loneliness brought me back again and again to Peter and Ilse's house, and Peter became my hero. Never still, his hobbies were land hockey, tennis, and ninepin bowling. I often went with him to the Club an der Alster to watch him play hockey, after which we would celebrate his side's victory or defeat in the club bar.

Sometimes Ilse, Peter, and I would go bowling, and these evenings were very jolly as the games were interspersed with beers and schnapps, often followed by supper in their favourite cellar café, the Alsterdiele, where vast quantities of the traditional waterfront fare known as *Labskaus*, a stew of potatoes and corned beef served with beetroot, were devoured with gusto.

In winter we would go to international Catch-as Catch-Can matches, where "Ivan the Terrible" would pin "Henry the Lion Tamer" to the canvas. Long hair would be grabbed and yanked, noses twisted, and ears ripped, as the contestants generally pretended to kill one another. These matches could last up to three hours, during which Peter and I joined in the betting and yelled our hearts out in rage or approval amid a crescendo of noise, reminiscent—to me, at least—of Shanghai boxing matches.

We would pour beer down our throats to soothe the hoarseness from all that shouting, and generally have a whale of a time. Once, when Claus was visiting, Peter cheerfully described one of these evenings. That got *me* an icy stare from Claus, which clearly showed that he would have preferred me to attend evenings of chamber music.

Finally Mother and Dino announced their return to Europe, and I asked for leave from Rabbow in order to meet them in Genoa. They were to arrive on the Danish East Asiatic ship *India* from Shanghai, and I was convinced that the three of us would continue on to Tuscany to look for a new home.

Before they disembarked, I joined them on board for lunch, during which Dino calmly announced that they were just "passing through" Europe on their way to the West Indies. Ignoring my protests of dismay, Dino tried to impress on me the sense of their new plan. French friends in Shanghai had convinced them that their future lay in Haiti. Try as I might, I could not picture my elegant, cosseted Mother, nor the elderly, semi-invalid Dino, in the mountains of Haiti. I mean, none of us really knew where it was!

I was sick with disappointment that Mother had no intention of making a home for us in Italy, now that her Asian adventure was over, and that all she could think of was to dash off on some half-baked scheme to the other side of the world. When

Ilse, Wolfgang, Peter & Pollo Rickmers

I complained that we were turning out to be no better than gypsies, Dino told me to stop upsetting my mother—and anyway, "Only trees need roots."

My pleas and arguments continued on the train all the way up to Hamburg and only ceased when we arrived at Claus and Renée's, where we were all to stay for a short visit.

Mother's days were spent saying hello and goodbye to family and friends before sailing off again, this time for the Caribbean.

Lutteroths and Muenchmeyers entertained us—ever charming, if somewhat bemused by the turn of events. The Muenchmeyers lived on a beautiful private estate near Rissen, side by side with the Lutteroths. The two families had created a sort of compound, with houses added in the park for children when they married—very Chinese, in a way. Ascan Lutteroth had been one of father's best friends and sailing companion. He was noticeably cool to Dino.

My step-grandmother Jessen had not seen Mother since before the war, and of course had never met Dino. She came down from Denmark and stayed with Evchen in Blankenese. Evchen was in a state of euphoria. Her husband Max had just returned from Russia, where he had been in a prison camp for six years. He was emaciated and had a bad heart, but he was alive. I will never forget him telling me how he had kept himself going for a long stretch on bread and Red Cross toothpaste sandwiches!

My Rickmers grandmother arrived from Switzerland and stayed with her son Peter. Many family reunions were organised, and I met my grandfather's brother,

Shanghai Cocktail party: Arwed, Danish Consul, mother & Dino (background)

Rickmer Rickmers, for the first time. This great uncle of mine looked a bit the worse for wear, and his suit was distinctly shabby, but he was so like my grandfather that I loved him from the moment we met. Then Dino, our great diplomat, came across, was introduced, and immediately asked my great uncle how he was doing. Charming and soft-spoken, Rickmer Rickmers confessed that life in post-war Germany was not easy. I cringed as I saw Dino's hand go to his pocket. Sure enough, out came his elastic-bound roll of bills. He peeled off six or seven hundred dollars and offered them to my great uncle. Rickmer Rickmers just lifted his hands in disbelief, then turned away without a word.

When everyone had left, Mother tried desperately to explain to her new husband that his behaviour was unacceptable to proud old family members. I don't think Dino saw any harm in handing out chunks of what I later learnt was Mother's money, and he certainly never understood why anyone would take umbrage. Things must be different in Italy, I decided.

Finally there was a moment alone with Mother, and I asked her what had happened to our Shanghai house. She went off into a long tirade against my uncle, who had continued to turn down all the prospective buyers Dino had found. "Handsome prices were offered, Darling, but your uncle refused to budge!"

I looked at her in dismay. "So did you just abandon it?"

I knew her so well, and she was looking definitely uncomfortable. "Well of course I didn't, *mein Liebling!* I sold my quarter of the house to your uncle—well, we had to have some money immediately as we were leaving. You do see that don't you, my love?"

I was speechless, and after a moment I walked away. She ran after me and wrapped me in her arms. "My dearest boy, your uncle has promised to try to sell your part, but in the meantime it is going to be used as a company house for partners, et cetera, and you will receive a monthly rent when it is occupied. Isn't that something?"

And so it was that my father's house became known as "Villa Jebsen." It was the Shanghai residence of many company managers, including various uncles and their families, all living there for extended periods. For a while, small rental sums were dutifully banked for me, but there were no offers to buy me out nor to find other buyers. I was underage, far away, and helpless. After many letters, I eventually received U.S. $5,000 as compensation for my seventy-five percent of the property.

Mother knew I thought she had let me down, so I had to listen again to all the drama of their departure. "We risked our very lives, Darling, just taking out the gold bars and cash. We really couldn't stay another minute, house or no house. You do see that, my love, don't you?"

There was no point in being hurt or angry. When Mother decided upon a course of action, she went ahead with it no matter what. If I had pointed out that she had managed to hang on to her Asian inheritance while I had lost mine, she would love me a little less, that was all.

In 1950 Peter, Ilse, and I took Mother and Dino to the Hamburg docks, where they boarded a French freighter bound for Port au Prince, the capital of Haiti. As we stood on the grim dock and waved goodbye, it was worse than when Mother had sent me away from her in Shanghai or left me behind in Europe so often, parked with one long-suffering grandmother or another. Then she had told me each time that we would be together again a few months later. Now, after years of waiting for her, she was off on some wild goose chase, and I knew in my heart of hearts that all she really wanted was to be with Dino. She supported him financially, and in return he treated her like a little girl. He called her "Missy," and promised to look after her. Perhaps he made her feel safe . . . I don't know.

At first there was practically no news from Haiti. I received pretty post cards of the Bou Lélé Hotel, the village of Kengskoff high over the capital, and carefully photographed, artistic scenes of Petionville. Then months of silence. Suddenly, out of the blue, a letter arrived from Ciudad Trujillo, as the capital of the Dominican Republic was then called. By now I had looked up Haiti, and knew it was part of the island of Hispaniola, with the Dominican Republic the greater part.

Haiti was African- and French-speaking, whilst the Dominicans prided themselves on being of European descent (if a little mixed down the centuries) and they spoke Spanish. Haiti was desperately poor, whilst the Dominican Republic, under the iron fist of its dictator, Trujillo, was safer, cleaner, and definitely more prosperous.

Mother wrote that Haiti was "impossible." Now new friends had convinced them that planting coffee and breeding cattle in the fertile mountains of Cibao, in Santo Domingo, would be an unbeatable, profitable venture. They had just bought a coffee plantation high over Moca, and photos were included showing the lush landscape. Seen from drab Hamburg, it all looked so glamorous and exciting that I couldn't wait to fly out at the end of my apprenticeship.

I had not counted with my feisty grandmother Rickmers who, despite her seventy years, was determined to accompany me. Of course I would rather have flown out alone, but I could hardly object after the years of care and kindness she had lavished on me.

Probably the main reason for her wanting to get away was that she was now alone. Her son Peter was happy with Ilse, Bertram was married to Christa, Claus to Renée, and Moni had married André Thaon de St. André, the son of a French count and an Italian marquesa. The count was dead, but *Maman* and her son lived next to the Empereur in a large house called Le Pré Choisi. There had never been much contact between these neighbours as far as I knew, but somehow or other Moni and André had fallen in love, married, and now lived together with the garlic-chewing marquesa.

With all her children settled, Grandmother obviously thought it was time to have a last fling, and I was to be her escort as she visited Etha, her eldest daughter.

Grandmother arrived in Hamburg, and together we arranged our trip. As she had never flown before, the mere idea of taking a plane terrified her, so we had to go by sea. We were advised to take the Spanish ship El Marques de Comillas (built in 1913!) from Bilbao to Ciudad Trujillo. My grandfather had taken his wife on his ships many times before the war, so the thought of an ocean voyage seemed to fill her with a childish delight.

40

Travels with my Grandmother

Omi and I took the Paris train from Lausanne, and twelve hours later arrived at the Gare du Nord, where we were met by Moni and André, who were in Paris for a reason I don't recall. They had taken a day room for us in a hotel near the Place de la Concorde, where Grandmother and I washed, changed, and set out for a potted tour of Paris. We whizzed up the Eiffel Tower, lunched in a fabulous Belle Époque restaurant on the Champs Elysées, then took a nap before boarding the night train to Irun on the French-Spanish border. I think I was more tired than my grandmother.

Although we were armed with visas that had taken weeks to obtain, Franco's Spain was still pretty much a closed country, and we were checked, frisked, and interrogated by the Guardia Civil—to the intense irritation of my grandmother. Despite her denigrating remarks about their headgear and general demeanour, which fortunately were not understood, we were finally let through as if into the promised land.

The train we took to Bilbao stopped at every little pueblo along the way so the journey seemed endless. "We have been trapped here for hours and hours!" complained my grandmother. I was not as bored as she, for I had taken Spanish lessons in Hamburg and was quite keen to practise my rather shaky language skills, but I found the peasants spoke an incomprehensible dialect, and the rather pompous businessmen simply refused to understand me.

In Bilbao we stayed at the Hotel Torrontegui. My room was directly under the penthouse suite, where a raucous party was taking place with music, singing, heel-clicking, the snapping of castanets and many enthusiastic "olés!" Every time I took the elevator, it was packed with pretty girls going up to the top floor, so I asked Pepe the bellhop what was going on up there. He told me, with a wink and a nod, that the suite had been taken by a group of high-ranking clergy from South America, who had been organising these fun and games for the past three days and nights. "We call it the Synod," he grinned.

Dinner in the shabby elegance of the hotel's old-fashioned dining room was not a success. Our first course had a fancy name and turned out to be eggs fried to a crisp in a pungent oil. Before ordering the main course we cautiously asked for a translation and when we found it to be octopus cooked in its ink we ordered steaks instead but this was not a wise choice as when they finally arrived, under ancient silver cloches, they were like shoe leather. Our need for sleep was greater than our appetites so we gave up on dinner and retired for an early night.

The following morning we took a 1928-vintage taxi to the docks of Portugalete, only to find ourselves abandoned on the quay, surrounded by our mountains of luggage, listening with dismay to the news that the ship had engine trouble and would have to remain in port three more days before she could sail. Our journey was not starting out well, and Grandmother was not pleased. She sniffed and remarked coldly, as if it were my fault, "These things never happened with your grandfather's vessels!"

Back at the Torrontegui we were greeted like old friends and led back to the same rooms which now began to feel like home. As a consolation we dined that evening in the town's finest restaurant which cheered us both up considerably.

By now, Pepe the bellhop had adopted me, and later that night he showed me the bright lights of Bilbao. With a dashing flamenco show in the background, we devoured dozens of oysters, myriad tapas, and several bottles of wine—all for the princely sum of five dollars. The local beauties were most welcoming and generous with their favours, which greatly enhanced my opinion of their town in particular and Spain in general.

A routine developed. During the day I accompanied my grandmother to every museum and cathedral she could drum up, after which we would rest then dine together. After a small glass of some dessert wine, she would go happily off to bed whilst I would slip out to join Pepe.

The day before we were due to sail, a group of Mexican bullfighters and their entourage descended upon the Torrontegui, also due to take the *Marques de Comillas.* For an hour they created havoc at reception. Finally they went up to their rooms and the accustomed hush was restored, only to be disturbed again by a huddle of Cubans with camel coats draped over their shoulders and cigars between their teeth. They too were keen to check in. All these flamboyant types fascinated me, and I could not help staring as I had never come across such high spirits in adults before.

That evening I slipped out of my room as usual, and found myself jammed in a lift that was full of these gentlemen. They were wondering where to go and what to do in "this dump," so I plucked up my courage and, in my best Spanish, told them. They were highly amused, either by my accent or my youth, and adopted me as their guide.

On the day of our departure, a bus was sent to the hotel to ferry all the passengers to the docks. Grandmother and I were the first to climb aboard, but when she found herself gradually squeezed between guitars, moustachioed Latinos, and gold-toothed, garlic-smelling bullfighters, she was all for getting off and taking a taxi. When I told her that we would be sailing with these people, who would find her departure very odd, she simply closed her eyes and pretended she wasn't there, a female trick I had already noticed in my mother.

The *Marques de Comillas* turned out to be very old but well-run and spick-and-span. We had outside cabins that, although neither big nor luxurious, were adequate. At tea and over dinner, a violinist, a pianist, and a cellist played their rather limited repertoire, mainly of Zarzuela, but Grandmother said they were doing their best and we should show our appreciation. This meant that they adored her and never failed to play at our table. During the entertainment all conversation was out of the question as we listened with cocked heads and fixed smiles. The food did nothing to brighten things up either, but we learnt to stick to chicken and rice and ask to have our eggs softly boiled.

We had not been told that our itinerary included six Spanish ports. We stopped at San Sebastian, Santander, Gijon, La Coruna, Vigo, and Cadiz. Grandmother was outraged. "What a waste of time. We could have taken the train straight to Cadiz and boarded there."

But I liked the slow discovery of ancient ports, where we unloaded goods whilst South Americans boarded, on their way home after having visited their families in the Tierra Madre for the first time since before the war. They were a fun-loving mix, and I enjoyed this happy, noisy Latin crowd. My Spanish improved by leaps and bounds, especially when I became infatuated with a dark-haired girl called Consuelo, who was on her way back home to Santiago de Cuba. As we set out from the Canary Islands bound for the open Atlantic at last, we two stood on deck and wished the journey could go on forever.

41

In the Wake of Columbus

S.S. Marques de Comillas, built 1913(!)

Now began long uninterrupted days at sea when we slipped into that enchanted, lazy rhythm of doing absolutely nothing. We lay about on long deck chairs, read and ate. Lunch was at three and dinner at ten but small collations kept us going in between. After dinner I walked grandmother around the deck and then took her to her cabin. After a dutiful good night kiss on her lavender-scented, petal-soft cheek I would race up to the top deck to join the happy Latins and rumba the night away with Consuelo under a canopy of brilliant stars until, at three every morning, a large tortilla was served and we all stumbled off to bed.

Our first port of call was San Juan de Puerto Rico. The entrance into the old harbour with its Spanish colonial fortifications and watch towers could have been the set of an old pirate film and one had to pinch oneself to remember that this was real.

As we had no US visas we were given Day Passes. My grandmother and I walked for miles through the old town of Santurce with its lacey balconies jutting out over the narrow streets, guitar music seeping through the closed wooden shutters, banana and mango trees heavy with fruit in the tiny front gardens. Soon the over-ripe tropical scents in the close, steamy heat began to make our heads swim.

When we came to a more modern section of the town we saw a restaurant discreetly advertising its air-conditioning on a shiny brass plaque so we decided to stop for lunch. We took the lift to the top of the building and, as we entered the fantastically icy foyer, a maitre d'hotel swept towards us asking to see our Membership Cards as this was a Private Bankers' Club. Grandmother drew herself up to her full height and deigned to reply.

We do not need to be members. I am Mrs. Rickmers of the Rickmers Shipping Line.

Pronounced with such authority, the staff, who had certainly never heard of Rickmers, quailed before this indomitable little old lady and to my amazement, allowed us in.

High windows dominated the whole of San Juan and as we sank into the cool of deep leather armchairs grandmother gave me a wink and said,

I think we deserve a drink don't you?

We found our first daiquiris so unexpectedly delicious that each ordered a second and I had the secret delight of seeing my grandmother become a little tipsy.

That night we sailed for Santo Domingo where our sea journey ended. The rest of the passengers were to continue to La Habana, La Guaira or Veracruz and such is my addiction to life at sea that I would gladly have stayed on board with them.

42

THE DOMINICAN REPUBLIC

We sailed into the port of Ciudad Trujillo on a glorious early morning to see Mother and Dino waiting for us on the quay. We collected our belongings, and Mother drove us in her new convertible Oldsmobile to the Hotel Jaragua, where we were to spend the night before the long, hot drive to the coffee plantation.

The hotel was on the sea front, and in our rooms Grandmother and I were fascinated to find television sets. Neither of us had ever seen television before, and for the first hour of our siestas we were glued to the black-and-white screens. However, as the programmes appeared to consist entirely of political speeches mostly by President Rafael Leonidas Trujillo, the great *Jefe* himself, we soon got bored and switched him off.

After dinner that night, I stood entranced on my balcony. The tall rustling palms, the moonlight on the silver sea, and the insistent beat of merengue music were the stuff of romantic dreams. All that was missing was Consuelo.

Next morning I had my first papaya sprinkled with lime juice, followed by eggs, rice, *carne mechada*, and *platano frito* (beef cooked to shreds and fried green bananas), a hearty start to the day, and then we were off. Once out of the capital, we drove past sugar plantations, over lush green hills, and along mile after mile of palm-lined roads empty of all but the odd peasant on a plodding donkey in those days before mass tourism. Sometimes a hamlet of wooden houses painted in rainbow colours with bright blue shutters and corrugated iron roofs clustered around the road and made one want to stop.

And stop we did, for the blackest coffee I had ever tasted, in Bonao, where the gaudily painted "*guagua*" buses would pull in, jammed to the roof with cheerful, noisy people. Shoeshine men and boy peddlers with trays hung around their necks, piled precariously with cigarettes and brilliantly dyed sweets, proffered their wares and services.

Past La Vega, we drove to Moca, where Hermann Goetsch, Dino's Tyrolean butler-chauffeur and now farm manager, whom I remembered from Shanghai, was waiting for us. In Moca we stopped for lunch at the local "Chino." This entailed pointing to cans on the shelves of a small shack, which the Chinese owner then heated up for us to eat standing at his counter. Fortunately, Mother had warned us not to expect dim sum and glass noodles.

Hermann had come down to Moca in the Land Rover for the weekly shop, and I drove back up to the *finca* (estate) with him. Stacked behind me were sacks of rice, beans, sugar, flour, and so forth—for us, the five women who worked in the house, and the roughly twenty families who worked in the fields. Mother had told me with pride that the finca was self-sufficient in eggs, milk, meat, chicken—and, of course, fruit and vegetables.

We drove up into the hills in convoy on narrow gravel or dirt roads, winding through avenues of palms at a speed of not more than ten kilometres an hour as we kept passing locals on mule or donkey, ambling along in the middle of the road. They would greet us with wide grins, shouting out "*Abul, abul*," which apparently was patois for "good day." Hermann explained that the people of Cibao could not pronounce the "r," so doctor became "dotoi," which was what everyone was calling out to Dino: "*Abul, abul, Dotoi!*" I wasn't sure how he had become a doctor, but I could guess how he would like this.

We drove on through the lush rolling hills until we reached a plateau at about 1,300 metres. To the north was the green Atlantic, and to the south the blue waters of the Caribbean. We drew to a halt in front of a Chinese-style arched gateway with "Hacienda Palo Blanco" burnt into the top bar. This looked very grand, but we had already learned that the Dominicans always ignored this and just called the estate "La Finca."

Mother, Grandmother, and Dino climbed into the Land Rover, as the Oldsmobile was never taken down to the house in case of mud slides, which always followed heavy rains. To our left was a large warehouse with enormous cattle scales, and to our right the guard house, now Hermann's home. As we began the descent along a vertiginous drive, a herd of cattle wandered across our path. Hermann told me they were a mix of Holstein and Cebu, a local breed, which accounted for their long horns and slight humps.

"Ideal not only for meat and milk but able to withstand many tropical diseases," Dino announced with authority.

"And their udders are tough so they don't get cut in our sharp grasses," added Mother, not to be outdone. Grandmother and I were suitably impressed, but I noticed Hermann's private little smile.

At last we pulled up in front of a large two-storey house, and I saw Grandmother immediately make a brave attempt to hide her dismay. I think we had both imagined a pillared Tara straight out of *Gone with the Wind*. The house was built of red mahogany and had bright green shutters. Covered terraces ran around both floors, and steps led down to a rather patchy lawn surrounded by scraggy beds of flowers. To one side stood a large water tower and a gas-powered generator for electricity.

Inside things improved. Chinese carpets, old paintings, lacquered chests, silk hangings, and silver all gleamed against the warmth of the red wood. There was a lingering scent of those green mosquito coils, which took me straight back to the East. In the middle of the drawing room stood my father's Jehol table, which he had found as a young man in Mongolia. This piece alone said "home" to me.

Upstairs there were three bedrooms, complete with mosquito netting as well as Dino's office and my mother's study, all beautifully furnished and carpeted. There was no air-conditioning, of course, but the wide-open windows let in fresh hill breezes, and overhead fans plunked away pleasantly.

Back downstairs, Juana came to greet us. She was young and pretty with fine Carib features, barefoot in a blue uniform and white apron. She carried a silver tray with glasses and champagne. As we celebrated, Isolina, the coal-black Haitian cook, came in to have a look at us. Later I was to learn that she had seventeen children by an unknown number of men. When not actually working, or rather when Mother did not notice, she clenched a foul-smelling pipe between her broken teeth. She cooked well enough, and anyway nobody else had been found who could do better.

The locals lived in a very basic world. None of the servants would use a lavatory, preferring the great outdoors. When Nature called, they would gravely announce to Mother, "Doña Etha, I'm off to the hills," to which she would reply, "Go then with God."

And that would be that. They were all very clean, however, and every evening would shower, wash their hair, and put on fresh uniforms before serving dinner. If any of the women had their menses, they would not wash their hair, iron, or even open the refrigerator—three activities thought to cause sudden death at this time. Shoes were always out of the question, of course, having run barefoot since childhood the soles of their feet were like leather and were comfortable in no shoe except perhaps felt slippers. Mother preferred bare feet to those.

As we sat sipping champagne that first evening, two German shepherds and two cocker spaniels lay at our feet, which made the scene very cosy if rather hot. This peace was interrupted when Hermann brought in our luggage. We watched as he took several large leather suitcases upstairs, but when nothing more appeared, Grandmother became alarmed. "Where is my big brown bag?"

After searching both cars, Hermann and I had to drive the one-and-a-half hours back to Moca, to the nearest telephone. I finally got through to the Hotel Jaragua, but after keeping me on the line for fifteen minutes, the concierge declared himself distraught with sorrow but the bag was not to be found. "Now there's a surprise," was Hermann's jaundiced reply.

We drove back through sudden torrents of rain and, to cheer me up, Hermann stopped at three or four little "*pulperias*," or grocery shop-bars, where we stood at the counter and downed several shots of the local Ron Bermudez at ten cents the go. Thus I was in a quite contented frame of mind when we reached the house, and Grandmother's anguish at her loss scarcely got through to me. I beamed benignly at her as she described in detail the contents of her bag; all her newly tailored tropical outfits *plus* the camera she had bought in Switzerland for Mother, *plus* my grandfather's Zeiss ship binoculars, which were to have been for Dino.

After an early breakfast, a tall West Indian with a huge belly, khaki-cotton tracker's hat, and a revolver slung at his hip came to fetch me. This was Maygaro, the foreman. He presented me with a leather pouch containing a revolver plus a belt with thirty-six bullets. Then he gave me a gleaming machete. As I stood there, bewildered, a weapon in each hand, Maygaro explained that a man needed a machete to cut his way through the undergrowth, and the revolver was for self-defence as vagrants or even farm workers, high on cheap rum, would attack for as little as five dollars. Furthermore—and he flashed his white teeth at me—a revolver gave a man "*mucho prestigio*." I was to learn that Maygaro was very hot on prestige.

We walked down to the stables past our prize bull, eight months old and freshly imported from Denmark. It was to cover the Cebu cows when it was old enough and improve the herd. Of all possible names for this animal, Mother had chosen my own nickname, Jessy. I didn't know whether to feel flattered or insulted, but in the end Jessy and I became great chums, and I was happy to share my name with him.

We strode disdainfully past the sties, where the 500 or so pigs were kept, and went on to the stables. Maygaro had put aside a horse and a mule for me. The horse, el Moro, was a black stallion, and the mule, Amapola, was a pretty palomino colour. "The horse, he for the road, the mule, she for the finca."

Apparently Amapola would be much more sure-footed up and down the steep hills of the plantation, but to visit other farms or villages, el Moro was "*Mucho mas prestigioso.*"

We saddled up and Maygaro led the way on his mule, Canela, whilst Amapola and I followed. I had my revolver on my right hip and my machete in its leather sheath bumped against my left thigh. This was the stuff of the dreams I had woven in my pension in rainy Hamburg.

Mother's finca had cattle and pigs, but the major crop was coffee, of course. Bananas, tobacco, coconuts, maize, and yucca were also grown commercially, but this first morning we were to concentrate on the cattle.

We stopped under trees at the edge of large fields where the cows grazed. Black women in colourful, flounced skirts squatted beside each animal in turn, lazily squirting milk into pails, chattering all the while, whether to the cow or their friends I never knew. I was pretty sure most of it was for the cow's benefit, however. When the buckets were full, the women trudged over to enormous churns that stood in the shade and poured in the milk. Maygaro told me that it was collected at the end of every day by donkey train, which carried the churns up to the main road. A truck fetched them at dawn and drove them down to the milk co-operative in Moca.

We rode on to have a look at the little castrated bulls that were being fattened up. Once a month, cattlemen from the Sosua region drove their herds to us to graze on our rich fields. Maygaro would occasionally bid for some of these animals to increase Mother's herd. It was so strange to hear her being talked about as if she were a cattlewoman born and bred!

After five hours in the saddle I was pretty sore, and famished too, so we stopped in a neighbouring hamlet that consisted of about six or seven rough shacks and a bar. We tethered our mules and sat at a trestle table in the dust under a flamboyant tree, our boots ankle-deep in scarlet blossoms. Maygaro ordered two large bottles of ice-cold Presidente beer plus tin plates piled high with rice, yucca, beans, and goat stew—all utterly delicious. When we had eaten our fill, shots of rum were offered, and Maygaro encouraged me to sample the charms of one of the local ladies. On the ride home, Maygaro confided that he thought he was the proud father of thirty or so children in this area. "Through your children you are immortal, young man. One day these hills will be full of little Jessies if you put your mind to it."

This was certainly a novel philosophy, and would account for the incredible amount of children all the women seemed to have at their skirts, with never a father to be seen.

Back home, showered, changed, and relaxed, I listened to Grandmother's excited account of her day. She had ridden out with Mother and Dino, all on mules, for nearly two hours—which, for a sedentary seventy-year-old was extraordinary.

"I intend to do better," she declared, but I shall need a machete like Etha's to slash away those pesky branches. Once I have my machete I will ride all day, but I would prefer not to have to carry a firearm."

On learning that this would not be necessary, she went happily off to bed.

We settled quickly into the normal hacienda routine. Every morning after a gargantuan breakfast, Dino would prepare his speciality, Isolina would solemnly trudge into the breakfast room with a jug of thick cream, into which Dino poured lethally strong coffee plus heaps of sugar, all of which he stirred vigorously and then tipped into freezer trays. The resulting ice cream was a daily treat at the end of a hot day.

Driving mother and Omi in our landrover to Moca (nearest town), D.R.

After breakfast, Maygaro would be waiting for me with Amapola and we would ride deep into the finca accompanied by seven or eight peons, the local cowboys. From the herds we sorted out the animals that needed to be branded, castrated, vaccinated, or weighed. This took entire mornings, after which we grabbed a makeshift lunch, had a bit of a snooze in the shade of the trees, and then back to work. First all the animals were herded into separate corrals. One by one they would be let through into a holding pen, where I had to stand with Maygaro. My first job was to learn how to use the long-handled branding iron. I was as nervous as the calves.

The iron was held over an open brazier until it was white hot. Then the calf was grabbed and held as I touched its rump and burned DET, for Dino Etha Tirinnanzi, into its hide. The poor animal screamed until a bucket of cold water was thrown over the steaming flesh and it was allowed to scamper off. I had to do this over and over again. At first I was hesitant, until Maygaro yelled at me to "Get on with it," as it would hurt less that way.

Cows coming in for milking. Finca ends on hill crests on horizon

The following day the little bulls were to be castrated. Apparently this would be my job too. They taught me how to use the newly imported castrating machine, which neatly clipped and did the job in the wink of an eye. Lurid tales were told of the "real" way to do this, with one's own knife and a quick flick of the wrist. I was grateful that the machine had arrived before I did. After a while, Maygaro complained that I was too slow and mercifully took over, instead giving me the job of jabbing the animals in the rump with antibiotics, for which I was profoundly grateful. Finally we patched up any wounded cattle, giving them injections and cleaning their cuts and scratches with hydrogen peroxide. I was happiest doing this, as it required a less strong stomach than the branding and castrating. I was always aware of the nudges and laughing eyes of Mother's cattle hands as I tried not to disgrace her.

Later that week we were visited by the local vet and two cattlemen from Sosua, who all rode up to have a look at their own animals. Sosua was a Jewish settlement about twenty miles away on the northern coast, perched over a fantastic little bay with a sugar-white beach. In the 1930s, many German and Austrian families had sought sanctuary from the Nazis in the Dominican Republic and, probably to their own surprise, Generalissimo Trujillo had given Sosua to these Jewish immigrants to develop as a colony.

Most of the families were involved in cattle in some way, but others had little shops or grocery stores and there was a sausage factory in the village. Only German or Yiddish was spoken, which seemed exotic under the tropical skies.

Once in a while, as a special treat, we would drive to Sosua for supplies and spend a couple of days in the small hotel, where we were glad to have a change of menu and enjoy the swimming. Every evening Mother and Dino were delighted to find bridge partners, whilst I was taught how to dance the merengue by the local belles. The secret of this was to drag one foot as if you were a shackled slave!

When Joshi Milz, Moishe Meyerstein, and Dr. Blut, the vet, arrived up at the finca with a herd of about 300 heifers, it took two days of bargaining for them to persuade us to buy some of these animals. Each beast was inspected by Maygaro, with the help of Mother, Dino, my grandmother, and me—experts all. I was glad to see the huge cattle scale I had shipped out from Rabbow in Hamburg put to such good use. Once business was completed, the men loaded up the wagons with the bulk of their fattened cattle and took them off to the slaughter house and meat packers in the valley. Those days of cattle buying and selling were utterly exhausting, and I admired Mother and Grandmother, both kitted out in boots and jeans, haggling away as if they had been doing this all their lives. They might not have known much about cattle, but they could spot a lame animal or a sick one as well as the next man.

However, coffee was the heart of the plantation, and I had to learn the various stages of its growth, from seedlings sprouting into saplings until the young trees were planted out on the hill slopes, each with a yucca plant or banana tree for shade.

Unhappy with her harvest, Mother invited a specialist to come to the finca and give advice. This man arrived from El Salvador and took days to walk over the several

Me on finca´s verandah - checking on cows 3 miles away

thousand acres where the coffee grew. We were an anxious retinue slowly following our expert from section to section. Mother, Dino, and I stretched our Spanish to the limits in order to understand what needed to be done, whilst Grandmother became a bit huffy as she could not follow a word.

The main problem seemed to be that many of the trees were old and a lot of pruning and replanting would have to be done. This promised to be a lengthy and expensive process as coffee can only be harvested after many years of tender care. The news was a blow as market prices had fallen, but they would have to afford the cost somehow. I realised that Mother was over-stretched financially, and asked her if I could invest in the finca myself. A flurry of telegrams had to be sent back and forth to banks, but eventually everything was sorted out and finally I could consider myself Mother's junior partner.

This turn of events made it even more difficult for me to accept that my time in this small piece of paradise was coming to an end. Soon I had to begin my obligatory eighteen months of Danish National Service. Before this, however, Mother had one more adventure lined up for Grandmother and me.

Mother on finca

43

Haiti

And so it was that a few days later we three drove to Ciudad Trujillo and took a Pan Am flight to Port au Prince. This was Mai Rickmers first flight and she bubbled with a mixture of excitement and trepidation. Upon arrival she declared that this was the only way to travel, if one no longer had a husband with his own ships, *bien entendu*. "I refuse to go back to Europe trapped with all those tedious people for weeks on end. I shall return to Switzerland by air."

Now as we emerged from the customs shed into the glare of the fierce morning sun, Port au Prince felt like Africa, and we seemed to be the only whites around. Suddenly police in khaki uniforms bustled up importantly, pushing a way through the good-natured crowd.

"Le Président arrive!" they shouted. *"Le Président lui-meme arrive!"*

We all stood back, obediently waiting for the arrival of this eminent person. A cavalcade of official cars screeched to a halt, and out of the longest limousine a large black man emerged and made his way towards the airport building as the crowd yelled "Magloire—vive Magloire!" at the top of their voices. The great man bestowed a gleaming smile to left and right until he reached our part of the assembled peasantry. When he caught sight of my grandmother, he came to an abrupt halt and bent graciously over her hand. *"Je vous souhaite le bienvenue à Haiti, chère Madame."*

He bowed to Mother, then gripped my hand and said with a wide grin and a twinkle in his eye, "Bonjour jeune homme!" Then off he was whisked by his minders. We three were stupefied, and could only imagine that our pale faces had caught his attention. The crowd was terrifically impressed with us.

Our taxi drove us high up over the city, where French-looking villas lined the road and we saw a few European faces making us feel less conspicuous. The Bou Lélé Hotel, perched at the top of a hill, appeared to be losing its struggle to emerge from a riot of bougainvillaea, and we were welcomed with ice-cold rum punches in the cool lobby, where ceiling fans stirred the air.

After lunch in the patio and siestas in our shuttered rooms we took a car up to the small village of Kengskoff which had so delighted Mother and Dino. Here we were immediately surrounded by a large chanting crowd wearing white masks, brandishing white sticks and pretending to attack us. We had arrived in the middle of some sort of party. We took refuge in the one small hotel as my grandmother was ill at ease.

The manager told us that this was only a rehearsal for Carnaval but that, should we be interested, there would be an authentic voodoo celebration that very night in a village a few kilometres away. "Of course, in some districts of Port au Prince, tourists are taken to voodoo shows. Not very authentic. What will happen tonight will be the real thing."

He went on, however, to warn *"les dames"* that although there was no danger, there would be a lot of drinking and things could get out of hand, so Grandmother and Mother decided to go back down to our hotel, leaving me to find out about "the real thing" for them.

After dark, the hotel handyman drove me in his rust-eaten jeep through mountainous jungle to his village. For the last kilometre, the road ran out so we continued on foot, slashing our way through the undergrowth with the machetes my new friend had thoughtfully provided.

We arrived at a small clearing, where fifty or sixty people were gathered. Some wore masks, some had white-painted faces, some were in jeans, some in African robes. It was full moon, the Caribbean glittered far below, and huge stars studded the tropical night sky. Had nothing else happened that night, just to see these people in such surroundings and to hear the gentle puttering of drums would have made the trek worth while. The atmosphere was subdued but expectant, the quiet of the crowd broken by just a smattering of smothered, nervous laughter.

Almost imperceptibly, the drum beats accelerated and the women began to croon African chants. A tall, thin, almost naked man leapt into the centre of the crowd, followed by two enormously fat, swaying women, amazingly light on their bare feet.

They wore long, white, flounced frocks with white kerchiefs tight over their frizzy hair. Men and women began to dance, gyrating faster and faster around the open fire, arms high, gleaming with sweat in the firelight, leathery bare feet pounding the packed earth. Tin cans and metal mugs circulated, filled with a rough, fiery rum quite unlike the smooth, delicious Barbancourt rum served in the Bou Lélé.

As the women's voices rose ever higher in wailing trills, three or four chicken were dragged out of a basket and, quick as a flash, beheaded. Blood spurted out and was caught in a large jug. A white painted cross was held on high, and the chants reached a feverish crescendo. The two fat acolytes poured liquids, herbs, and powders into the blood as the dancers rolled back their eyes until only the whites shone, and they seemed to enter a trance. All the while the pot was stirred, sometimes on the fire, sometimes sitting on the dirt floor.

To my discomfort, more and more faces were thrust into mine, with mock threatening gestures and wild laughter. Suddenly they all fell back as one of the fat women came towards me, bearing the pot. Men all around grinned maniacally through sweat and blurred paint as the woman mumbled to me in local Patois, but all I could catch was, "*Bois ti blanc, bois.* Drink, little white man, drink."

My companion, ever at my side, gave me a nervous nudge. "You first, Sir. You white man. Is honour."

There was nothing I could do. I had no idea how I would manage to swallow this mess, and could only hope that all the stuff they had added would disguise the taste of blood.

The crowd swayed ever closer around me. I gathered up my courage as the woman poured from the pot into my tin can until it overflowed. Then she filled my companion's, who again hissed, "Go first! Drink now!"

So I did. Holding my breath, I swallowed the lot in one go. It was sticky with molasses, rough with rum, and fiery with peppers, so my worst fears that I would emerge as Dracula were unfounded. Now everyone drank, and in my relief I joined in the dance, which became faster, insistent, impelling—impossible to resist.

Many hours later, my new friend and I bade drunken farewells to all still standing and stumbled back to the jeep, where we both collapsed into an exhausted sleep on the torn plastic benches as dawn lightened the sky.

Later that day I drove back to the Bou Lélé with a fearsome hangover, and before I had recovered it was time to accompany Mother and Grandmother on a rusty old DC-3 belonging to the Haitian army. We flew to Cap Haïtien in the north of the country, where we stopped at a charming old-fashioned colonial hotel.

Six the next morning saw us bouncing around in a jeep driven by a local driver with aspirations to win le Mans. We were on our way to visit the Chateau Sans Souci, a fortress built in the early 1800s by forced labour under the dictates of the ex-slave Henri Christophe, who was later to proclaim himself King.

The French revolution had stirred men as far away as Saint-Domingue, as the island was then known, and a group of black soldiers, deserters from the French Colonial Army, had organised an uprising in what is now known as Haiti. Headed by Jean-Jacques Dessalines, there was a rebellion against the French, whose army was already decimated by yellow fever.

Only ruins remained of what must have been an imposing chateau at Sans Souci, so we continued on horseback up the mountain to La Citadelle. This gigantic stronghold had been held by the French, who had resisted fierce attacks from the rebels until sickness and hunger finally forced them to withdraw, allowing Haiti to promptly proclaim her independence.

The ride up was long, hot, and dusty but my grandmother refused to even flinch. Our Haitian guides could not get over her stamina. They had tried to dissuade her from even attempting the ascent, but she would not be daunted.

The Citadelle proved worth it. Perched high, it was a four-cornered stone fortress straddling the crest of a hill, with massive walls and impregnable bastions. It had caused countless deaths during its construction, and immeasurable slaughter on both sides during the siege. It had, in the end, forced the departure of the French and witnessed the birth of Haiti.

After dreamy wanderings amongst the imposing ruins, we sat in the central courtyard in the shadow of its crumbling walls and were served a typical local meal of goat, fried beans, yucca, and rice, all washed down by three-star Barbancourt and Coca Cola (later to be known as Cuba Libre), followed by sliced mangoes. It could have been straight from Isolina's kitchen.

The steep screes back to the valley were tougher to ride down than up, both for the horses and for us, so it was with some relief that we flopped wearily onto the hard seats of the jeep and allowed ourselves to be hurtled wildly back to Cap Haïtien.

The next day we boarded the same DC-3, and this time the pilot treated us to a circular tour high above the Citadel for one last look before flying us back to Port au Prince. Our Haitian trip had been exhausting but unforgettable.

44
Time to Leave

Dino was certainly glad to have Mother back, but soon a couple of unfortunate incidents were to mar my last few days on the finca. First Jessy, our prize bull, was bitten by a tarantula, one of those huge, black spiders that Isolina swore could jump.

Maygaro burst breathlessly in to our lunch table to tell us that the bull had been "Attacked in his testicles!"

I threw down my napkin and dashed out with him to have a look. It certainly appeared as if the poor animal was at death's door, but Maygaro summoned three peons to hold Jessy down whilst he took out his knife and, with one swift slice, castrated the bull in the time-honoured way. Poor Jessy screamed blue murder, but Maygaro had saved its life. Sadly it would never be able to improve the bloodlines of our livestock, but Mother and I felt sorry for him, so Jessy was allowed to spend the rest of his days roaming our hills, getting fat, a farm favourite.

The night before I was to leave for Europe, I woke to a terrible racket from the kitchens. Isolina and Juana were shouting their heads off, and in the background I could hear the drunken rumblings of a man. I went to the top of the stairs and recognised the blurred voice of Tomas, usually the mildest of men, now roaringly drunk and threatening the two women with his machete. He kept yelling for more rum and "lots of money!"

I picked up my revolver and was about to go downstairs and throw him out when Tomas lurched into the hall and caught sight of me. He stumbled to the stairs and began to stagger up, brandishing his machete, berserk with drunken rage. To keep him away, I shot into the air, but, undeterred, he came at me even faster so I aimed for his thigh. Fortunately I just grazed him, but the shock and noise stopped him in his tracks and he sat down and began to wail like a child.

Suddenly there were people everywhere. Maygaro and Rafael rushed in, alerted by the uproar, whilst Mother and Dino peered over the banisters in sleepy confusion. The two German shepherds began to bark, and the two cocker spaniels joined in. They had been of absolutely no use, as they knew Tomas and hadn't made a peep until now, when it was entirely too late and only added to the general mayhem.

At last Hermann arrived and order was restored. Tomas's scratch was patched up, the dogs were told to shut up, and everybody was sent back to bed. Hermann took Tomas down to the little police station, where he was to sleep it off in one of the cells. Unable to sleep, I dressed and waited for Hermann's return, as he was to drive me to Ciudad Trujillo and the airport.

I sat on a rattan basket chair on the front veranda and watched the night sky turn rose and gold as dawn approached. I had said my goodbyes to Mother, my grandmother, and Dino last night. Grandmother was to stay on for a few more months and then fly back to Switzerland alone.

Finally the lights of the jeep crested the top of the hill and Hermann came to fetch me. Now I really had to leave. The grillis—crickets—and frogs would continue their early morning chorus, the tall palms would still sway, the Atlantic would shimmer in the light of the rising sun, all without me. Adulthood and the Royal Danish Navy loomed.

45

Boot Camp

On a cold April morning, twenty-four hours before I was due to report to the Danish Naval Station "Holmen," I arrived in Copenhagen. With eighteen months of probable discomfort ahead of me, a last fling was in order. I checked into the Palace Hotel on Rådhuspladsen. It lived up to its reputation, and my brief dive into its lap of luxury came all too quickly to an end in the Palmehaven restaurant, which was decked out as a tropical oasis overlooking floodlit palm trees and tropical gardens, incongruously frosty outside. Everything had a special flavour, from the cocktails to the gourmet dishes and fine wines I treated myself to. I knew it would be months before I tasted anything like it again.

I arranged for a wake-up call at 5 a.m. and asked a bell hop to bang on my door then too. Finally, I set my own alarm clock. If the navy said arrive at 6:30, I imagined it meant it.

Resplendent in a grey flannel suit under my camel coat, I was driven in a hotel limousine with my three suitcases to the Naval Station Recruiting Centre in the port of Copenhagen, opposite the Royal Palace.

We rolled up to the gates, where we were halted by military police—who, somewhat briskly, I thought, told me to get out and walk. I gathered up my belongings as well as I could and turned to find myself under the bemused gaze of about 1,500 recruits. Somehow or other I advanced, clutching my bags, which were covered with labels from exotic places. I noticed to my horror that there was not another suitcase to be seen—although fortunately, in those far-off days, all were dressed like me, in a suit and coat. Despite the obvious surprise my arrival caused, two recruits immediately offered to help me out, each of us then carried a case.

Over the tannoy, instructions boomed for us to line up in rows of four, in silence, and to walk in an orderly manner to the Naval Hospital for medicals. Twenty military police sergeants took command, and we set off. After a few steps, an irate sergeant stormed up to me and asked me where the hell I thought I was going with all my fancy gear. "That stuff should have been left at home!" he yelled, grabbing my arm and pulling me and my belongings over to a desk. I had to hand everything over to a corporal, who noted my Danish Laimun address, where my possessions would be sent at the navy's expense. By now this was quite a relief.

In lieu of my matching pigskin I received, along with everyone else, a large paper bag and a label. We were ordered to strip, place all garments into said bag, fill out the label with our home address. Our belongings would then be forwarded to our respective homes. Then 1,500 guys waited, naked, for the medics. To add to my distress, I had to ask for a second bag, as my heavy coat would not fit in the first. Later I was to learn that a navy van had driven up to the steps of Laimun and, to my step-grandmother's consternation, had dumped my three suitcases plus the two paper bags on the gravel and then immediately screeched away without a word. Lehmkul, the old gardener, had hauled my stuff up to my bedroom. and neither he nor my step-grandmother had been amused.

In a cavernous hall, white-coated doctors x-rayed us, poked us about, and tested our blood pressure which, still stark naked in front of young nurses, cannot have given very accurate readings. Then still as God made us, we were marched briskly across the parade ground to another building, where each received a seaman's bag with kit from underwear to navy blue jackets with gold buttons. The latter were certain girl-bait, as we were all happily aware.

In the buses that drove us off, destination unknown, I was subjected to a barrage of questions. Where on earth had I come from? Was I really Danish? But despite the fact that no one had ever seen such an odd creature before, my inquisitors' manner was friendly and I began to breathe more freely.

Close to Frederiksvaerk, we found our boot camp scattered around the shores of Lake Aresoe. After a quick meal, we queued up to receive steel helmets, gas masks, semiautomatic rifles (no ammunition) and Madsen or Husquarna submachine guns, bayonets, etc.

Each man was assigned a serial number, by which he was always to be known. Since our last names, in Scandinavian fashion, were all too likely to be the same, if "Hansen" or "Petersen" had been yelled out, half a platoon would have answered.

I was number 9244178, but in my company this was shortened cosily to "24"—although my new nickname, "Hong Kong," was used more and more by the men.

Drill began with our sergeant explaining the function of the weapons. A great fuss was made about bayonets. They were to be kept as clean as a surgical instrument—being, after all, "designed for meat."

The next ninety days were gruelling. From 6 a.m. to 7 p.m. we drilled endlessly on the parade ground, struggled through obstacle courses designed by the U.S. Marine Corps, crawled on our bellies through mud, or ran uphill in gas masks with thirty kilos of kit on our backs, sometimes even carrying a buddy in a fireman's lift plus *his* gear. Live ammunition was fired over our heads for battle realism as we snaked in churned-up dirt under barbed wire. Then up we sprang to race to the lifeboats and row them across the lake in all weathers. Sometimes we were sent to hand-grenade practice. In close-combat training, we were taught the kinds of dirty tricks that would help us beat our enemies—who, unfortunately, would have learnt these too.

Our platoon was nicknamed "The Running Stags," as our sergeant was a marathon runner who made us sprint everywhere. Many years later I sailed from St. Thomas to Denmark with my fiancée, who was mystified when one of the ship's officers came up to me and remarked, "Weren't you one of those crazy Running Stags?"

To feel at the peak of one's physical condition is cause enough for pride for any young man, but for me there was something else. I had never before been thrown into such a varied group of men from all walks of life. From tough North Sea fishermen to placid farmers to the sons of professionals—we all got on famously together. It was a great lesson for me—I was accepted as one of their own, and I really enjoyed their company. If our sergeants and officers were tough, they were always fair. I found the food both excellent and plentiful (although guys from the least privileged homes complained almost on principle). We all turned flab to muscle, and were ready to tear out trees.

After three months, we found ourselves back at Naval HQ in Copenhagen, where we were split up into different branches of the navy—some to be trained in artillery, some in torpedoes, submarines, et cetera. We all had stints on patrol boats, minesweepers, and submarines, which gave us a basic knowledge of naval warfare.

I was assigned to IFF (Identification Friend or Foe) Radar and ASDIC (said to be named after Anti-Submarine Detection Indicator), which is familiarly known as sonar. For this I had to spend an additional two months at radar school, after which there was a short spell of night military police/shore patrol duties These were very popular, as one left the confines of the garrison and patrolled Tivoli and and Copenhagen's red light districts—always in groups of three under a sergeant.

Once we had to intervene in a wild brawl in the port where, for some reason, Danish Army soldiers attacked British sailors from the Royal Navy. The soldiers had the upper hand until some passing Danish sailors immediately joined the British sailors—naval solidarity being stronger than nationality. When we tried to break up this mêlée, swinging our clubs and madly blowing our whistles, our sergeant saw how our task was impossible and called for backup. By the time it arrived, the bar was in shambles with shrieking whores and blood all over the place. Brits and Danes were all force-marched into trucks and taken to the garrison to be patched up and sober down. The next morning I awoke to find myself the proud possessor of an impressive black eye.

At last our radar station postings were announced. These stations were scattered from Greenland to the island of Bornholm. My destination was Moens Klint, perched high over the chalk cliffs of the Baltic.

On the station we were thirty men working long shifts with varied duties—memorising the complicated procedures needed to operate the radar; shinning up the high tower as lookout should the radar fail; plotting the location, speed, and movements of East German, Polish, or Russian naval units in the Baltic and reporting them every ten minutes to Central Command in Copenhagen.

Every night, each man had to do at least four hours of sentry duty—which, in winter meant coping with eighty kph winds and temperatures as low as minus twenty C., so that our trigger fingers, which could not be covered with a glove, were regularly frozen blue.

In summer, civilians often walked around the barbed wire perimeter of the station, especially German tourists. All pestered us with stupid questions when we were on sentry duty and forbidden to answer. They were always surprised to see us carry submachine guns with fierce Alsatian guard dogs at our heels in the middle of the peaceful Danish countryside. "Think you're at war, lads?" was the jibe considered the height of wit.

One night, when I was freezing my butt off on sentry duty, three drunks tried to climb over the fence into the Station. I blew my whistle and ordered them to climb down otherwise I would have to shoot. These were our instructions. Roaring with laughter, they kept on climbing, so I fired the regulatory three shots over their heads—which seemed to sober them up as off they whooped into the woods. I was relieved as next I would have had to fire at their legs.

Fishermen from the Baltic told us one day that they had spotted a mine floating close to the beach. This was more like it! We raced our jeep down to the little port of Klintholm, where a patrol boat was waiting for us. Two mine disposal experts were flown in by helicopter from the island of Falster, and off we bounced on choppy seas to search for our mine. It took us two hours to find it. Great excitement. It was a German W.W.II horn mine, and our two experts lost interest. This was a job for us. The horns were easily visible, so we were told to just shoot at them. We took turns at the machine gun and, despite the rough weather, soon had a hit, which caused the acid in the horns to be released into the detonator, causing an enormous explosion that shook the windows of a nearby light house. The only use the experts had been was to tell us what distance to fire from, and for that I suppose we had to be grateful.

Our duties were twenty-four hours on and twenty-four off. Some twenty-five kilometres away was the quaint old town of Stege, which became our favourite spot for R&R. We spent most of our free time there, when we were supposed to be resting. The navy, resigned to the ways of young sailors, had rented a room in Stege for those who missed the last bus back.

We spent most of our time off searching for girls. My pal Nulla and I found two lovelies working in the tea room in Stege. My girl, Henny, was blond and blue-eyed, with the most accommodating parents I had ever come across. On our first date, Henny invited me home to meet them, and after a slap-up dinner her mother asked if I would like to spend the night. I was shown to the guest room, and then found, to my amazed delight, that Henny was to join me there. The following morning, to cap everything, her mother tapped at the door and brought in our breakfast tray. She also politely asked how we had spent the night—a far cry from the protocol of the Dominican Republic, where a girl invited to the cinema expected to bring along her sisters, aunts, and younger brother as chaperones.

My education in Denmark, however, was not entirely amorous. On duty one clear early morning, I was walking back from the radar barrack where I had just shut down all our radar when I heard a plane approaching at about 500 metres altitude. It was not a NATO plane, and I identified its markings as Polish. It circled slowly over the station, and I ran to press the alarm button. Immediately havoc reigned. The three men in charge of our 40 mm anti-aircraft guns raced to their posts whilst I fired off the entire magazine of my submachine gun, but of course the plane was far out of range and maddeningly disappeared before the gunners could get it in their sights. Now across the sky three Danish Air Force jets streaked in hot pursuit, chasing the Pole out of Danish air space. To our disappointment, they must have been under orders not to fire because, without a sound, the skies soon became clear. This excitement was about as close as I got to action.

And so the eighteen months of service quickly passed. At the end of it, our crew left Moens Klint and raced up to Copenhagen to collect our final pay packets and treat ourselves to a last fling in the "Gold Digger" night club. In the early hours of the morning, we all drifted off, each with a girl on his arm, far too busy to exchange addresses. And so we slipped out of each other's lives, if not our memories.

One of the last things I did on the island of Moen (not to be confused with Moen's Klint or cliff) was to buy a 9 mm pistol and get myself a license so that I could take it with me to the finca. From the time of purchase until I left Denmark, I was obliged by law to carry it with me. After our night of carousing, I found myself, somewhat the worse for wear, on a park bench in the early hours of the morning. I was awoken by a friendly policeman who said he was very sorry but he would have to arrest me as I was sleeping on a public bench with a pistol sticking out of my jacket. It is amazing how such news can sober a chap up. I told him I had just finished my National Service, showed him my honourable discharge dated just the previous day, and the licence for the pistol. Danes are pretty good guys. He drove me in his patrol car to a taxi stand, told the driver to take me to my hotel, pick up my bags, and then race to the airport. With luck I would just make my flight to the Dominican Republic—a place neither the policeman nor the taxi driver had ever heard of.

The months I had dreaded had turned out to be hard to forget. I never saw the friends I made again but I remember my buddies to this day with affection.

Above left & center: me on naval radar station

My idol: A. P. Møller

Mœrsk Star -7 points =7 workdays week (at sea)

46

Copenhagen

Before beginning my shipping training with A. P. Møller, I had time to make a quick dash to the coffee plantation, a welcome chance to warm up after all that freezing Baltic weather. I would have six weeks in which to slip back into the routine of the finca, to see how happy Mother and Dino were, and to have some good times with Hermann and Maygaro.

Then early in the November of 1954, my apprenticeship at A. P. Møller-Maersk Line began. At this time, the company only had fifty-odd ships compared to its fleet of over 900 today, but what a company it was even then. The enthusiasm of the staff was infectious, and the long hours, sometimes from 8 a.m. to 10 p.m., flew past. I spent time in the line department, the tramp department, the insurance department, and the ship brokerage department. A. P. Møller himself, then in his seventies, remembered my parents well from his visits with us in Hong Kong, and he kept a fatherly eye on me. His son, Maersk McKinney, then in his late thirties, was already in charge of the day-to-day running of the company. In the summer, father and son sailed together from their house in Gentofte on the Baltic to the office. The old man still ruled with an iron fist, and usually ate only a frugal sandwich for lunch at his desk. On one occasion, when Mother had flown in from the West Indies to see me, she paid a courtesy visit to A. P., who promptly invited us both for lunch at the Hotel d'Angleterre, which was just opposite the office. Without consulting either of us, he told the waiter to bring us the dish of the day, which turned out to be a large bowl of pea soup with croutons. This, with a glass of water, was our entire luncheon. Mother, however, asked for a pre-lunch cocktail, to which A. P. smilingly agreed.

Another time, Maersk McKinney would invite me to dinner in the same hotel, which was certainly more satisfying. Afterwards, he had tickets to the Kongelig Teater, and together we saw a fine performance. I was actually closest to A. P.'s nephew, Georg Andersen, who was director and partner in charge of the line department. We would often lunch together, and once he joined me on a trip to Flensburg for the launching of the *Michael Jebsen*. Georg was six-four, ex-Royal Guards, and extremely proud of it. Whenever the Guards and their rousing band marched past our office windows, we all had to stand and applaud until they were out of view. I found a decent apartment overlooking one of the many lakes inside Copenhagen, and my entire training period was most enjoyable—perhaps because shipping has always fascinated me, but also because of the good friends I made, such as Poul Rasmussen, with whom I correspond to this day. When it was time to leave, old A. P. Møller wished me good luck and told me I would always be welcome back. Maersk McKinney gave me a copy of Hemingway's "*The Old Man and the Sea*," which was one of his father's favourites.

Poul Rasmussen, my very good friend from Mærsk Line; former board member of Rederi Foreningen and Knight of the Dannebrog

After Copenhagen, I spent the next six months working in Hamburg at the Jebsen and Jessen offices before taking the *Hulda Maersk* from Genoa to New York. This freighter only took a few passengers, and I was delighted to meet a friend from A. P. Møller on board and even more delighted to find that we were to cross the Atlantic with nine American army nurses on their way home, who obviously would need cheering up.

From New York I flew down to the mountains of Santo Domingo, where I spent two weeks on the finca, then took a flight to Panama in order to board the old *Laura Maersk* as she sailed to Los Angeles, and then on to Yokohama. In Japan we called at six ports, which allowed me to meet all the local Maersk Line agents, whose legendary hospitality I greatly enjoyed.

47

HONG KONG

Finally, after so many years away, I beamed with delight as we sailed through the myriad of islands in the South China Sea which lead into the stunning Hong Kong harbour, teeming as usual with foreign ships, sampans and walla-walla boat taxis. It was as if time had stood still.

I spotted a familiar face in a boat approaching the *Laura*. It was Arwed, my father's young half-brother, smart in crisp white shorts and shirt plus white knee socks with tassels. He waved cheerily up at me and came on board, had a chat with old Captain Slotoe Madsen, ordered my luggage to be lowered into his water taxi, and accompanied me to the Star Ferry terminal on Hong Kong side.

My thrill at finally arriving where I had longed to be for years was, however, soon to be punctured when Arwed informed me that I would commence work the next day in the chemical dyes department. I had been sure that all my training was to lead me to the shipping department, which acted as general agents for Maersk Line, Hapag Lloyd, Rickmers Line—and, of course, the Jebsen Line. What did I know about chemicals?

I had the sense not to let my disappointment show and followed Arwed to 16, Conduit Road, which was one of the many "chummeries" the company maintained in Hong Kong for its bachelor employees. Life in these chummeries was pleasant, and we were spoilt by our Boys and Amahs who cleaned our rooms, laundered our clothes, and prepared delicious meals.

My first task was to kit myself out with the mandatory white shorts, knee socks,

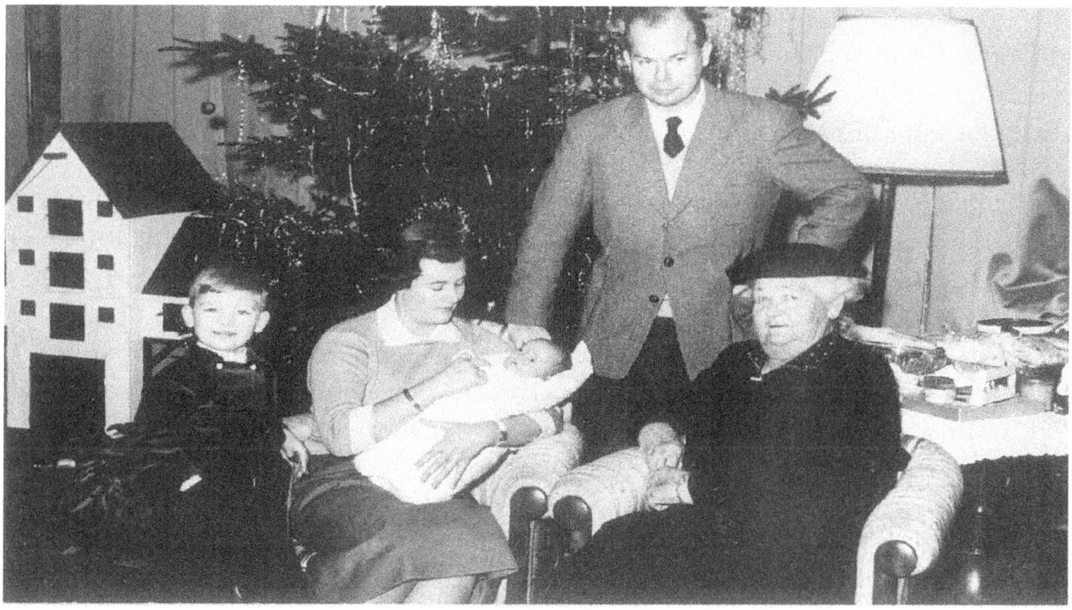

Hans Julius, Juliane with baby Hans Michael, Jocko and Tante Kaethe

shoes, and short-sleeved shirts. I was uncomfortable about the latter, as I would have preferred to hide the tattoos on my forearms that I had acquired in the navy, but the office dress code was strict.

Trying to shine, like all new employees, I befriended the manager of China Resources HK, an arm of the Peoples' Republic of China's Purchasing Agency, and through this contact sold tens of thousands of BASF tapes as well as shiploads of sulphate of ammonia and Nitrofoska fertiliser.

A shipment of chemicals arrived from Germany in partially damaged bags, which I had to arrange charter for on a small French tramp ship to Taku-Bar. Only bags in an acceptable condition were to be loaded, and I decided to supervise this myself. Throughout the night I sat in a steaming go-down, which was not only hot and humid but foul with the stench of sweat, urine, and human excrement. The coolies moved in almost utter silence. These men earned one Hong Kong dollar a day, and when not working most of them bought brief oblivion from their drudgery by spending half their pay on opium. The dim flickering light from Petromax kerosene storm-lamps glistened on their emaciated chests as they staggered up and down the creaky ladders with bags far heavier than their own body weight. It was a scene out of Dante's "Inferno."

Once the bags had passed my inspection, they were transferred by the thousand onto barges that took them alongside the rusty old freighter. I followed aboard and watched as each bag was stowed in the stinking holds, supervised by a drunken first officer who appeared not to care how well or badly this was done. The whole scenario couldn't have differed more from the spotless light blue Maersk Liners, with their efficient officers in crisp white uniforms.

At dawn the freighter was finally loaded, and I could take a walla-walla back to Hong Kong where I went straight to the office, dirty and unshaven. I had to send telexes to China Resources and Tientsin advising them that their order had sailed.

After this, knowing I would be late, I nevertheless raced back to the chummery to shower, shave, and change, arriving back at the office only twenty minutes late at ten to nine. As luck would have it, Number One Uncle was standing in the lobby, looking at his watch.

"Late I see!" was his only greeting. Had I been less in awe of him, I would have told him where I had been all night, but as usual he stalked off before I could open my mouth.

Undaunted, I continued to strive to win approval. It struck me that the enormous shipments of fertiliser and dyes from BASF to mainland China only generated a meagre commission for us. I approached Number One Uncle as well as the general manager, suggesting that we could buy these shipments ourselves, paying for them by 180-day sight drafts, then sell the shipments to China directly, thus earning perhaps three or four percent rather than our current two. As these shipments would only have to be paid 180 days after being loaded in Antwerp or Hamburg, and the Chinese always paid us ninety days after unloading in Shanghai or Taku-Bar, there would be absolutely no financial exposure on our side whilst doubling our profits. To this day I shall never forget the look of disdain I received from my uncle as he pronounced from a tight mouth, "We do not make unethical deals in this company, young man." And off he strode.

Above: H.E. Sir Alexander Grantham visiting my agri fair

I did not understand then or now how this method of doing business could be considered unethical, but once more I was made to feel unsatisfactory.

The New Territories represented only a very small agricultural area, but after doubling our sales of Nitrofoska to it in my first year, I was allowed to organise an agricultural fair with our New Territory agents. As I guided H.

E. Sir Alexander Grantham, the Governor of Hong Kong, around, he slapped me on the shoulder twice and said, "Well done, young Jessen." Welcome balm to my wounded pride.

My enthusiasm still was not dampened. I had met a Dutch-American financier, Andrew DeWitt, who had set up financing for the automobile market in the Dominican Republic. In Hong Kong our motor division had the exclusive agencies for Porsche, Volkswagen, and BMW. Sales were limited to a modest fifteen to twenty vehicles a month—cash only.

I talked to the head of the motor division and with his blessing asked for a meeting with Number One Uncle. I explained the simple mechanics of car-sale financing: the client pays thirty percent down and signs a promissory note for the remaining seventy percent plus interest.

We in turn could discount these notes with HSBC, for example, thus immediately obtaining the full price of the car whilst the client paid back his loan plus interest to the bank over a three-to-four-year period. In this manner we should be able to boost our sales to perhaps 400 vehicles a month.

When I had finished there was a long silence. With a sigh my uncle stood up. "I just do not know where you get these outlandish schemes from, but you try my patience, you really do."

And that, of course, was that. Obviously our competitors soon embarked on financed car sales, dramatically increasing their volume, whilst we dragged along for years with our cash-only system.

My very last attempt to come up with new ideas was in shipping. On the *Laura Maersk* I came across a fellow passenger, Mike Rosen, who worked in the Tokyo office of a U.S. ship owner. He had been hit by a taxi in LA, and doctors prescribed a relaxing voyage, which was where we met. We had twelve days to talk about shipping, and I learned a lot.

Mike told me that he could arrange a five-year charter contract from Esso-Standard Oil for Jebsens for a medium-sized tanker. With this charter contract, we would easily obtain a loan from any major bank

Above: Hosting China Resources, Hong Kong

to finance the building or purchase of such a tanker. Tanker business was booming, and Jebsen Line would have paid back the loan in seven years at most, whilst the tanker could be operated profitably for another ten years. With one operating tanker, we could order a second tanker, and eventually operate a small fleet of three or four ships.

Of course I got nowhere with Uncles One and Two. When I approached them on this subject the reply was as I had expected. "No more wild schemes please! We are not interested in the tanker business."

Fortunately, life outside the office made up for the disappointments within. I was enchanted by the beauty of Hong Kong, which I had been too young to appreciate as a boy. I took long hikes around the Peak and the New Territories, which were still almost unspoilt. Sundays were spent on Shek-O, Deep Water, or Repulse Bays, and Uwe Thomson and I joined the HK Royal Yacht Club, where we rowed in an eight. We practised once or twice a week, starting at Deep Water Bay, weather permitting. Rudi Kardel joined Uwe and me, and sometimes tiger sharks would circle our flimsy craft about twenty meters away, which was rather nerve-racking as they could have easily capsized us.

There was always fun in the chummery too. Once we were given a case of twelve bottles of Napoleon Biscuit Cognac by one of our suppliers for Chinese New Year. Although none of us drank brandy due to the heat, we noticed that, one after the other, the bottles were being emptied. We were convinced that our Boy Ahtung was the culprit, as the Chinese love brandy. When the last bottle was half full, someone suggested that we play a trick on him by peeing into what was left. Within a week the bottle was empty. Trying to stifle our laughter, we called Ahtung to the breakfast table and asked him how he liked our cognac.

"Oh no, young mastas," he replied, "Me no likee blandy. Me use plenty blandy when cooking for you." Hoisted by our own petard indeed.

But dark clouds began to appear. I was dismayed to learn from my colleagues the slander being spread about me by a few executives and Number One Uncle. At cocktail parties, they were overheard to claim that I had been kicked out of the Danish Navy because I was too fat! I could hardly go around distributing photos of myself, trim in uniform, nor put my honourable discharge certificate up on the notice board.

Apparently not to be outdone, Number Two Uncle unfailingly remarked, whenever my name came up at meetings discussing the possibility of a partnership, "The soup is getting too thin! No more partners!"

From as far back as I could remember both Father and Grandfather Rickmers had stressed that I had to do well in school and in life in order to prepare myself for a career in the family company, where a partnership would eventually be assured. Apparently the uncles were determined otherwise.

I could not help wondering if I was being punished for having a Chinese girlfriend, or whether this was just a pretext to rid themselves of me. The non-official company attitude towards the fraternisation of their unmarried employees with bar girls was tolerant—and even encouraged in a "boys will be boys" sort of way. A steady relationship was another thing altogether.

My girl friend was the twenty-five-year-old widow of a Kuomintang Air Force pilot, whose transport plane had been shot down by a MIG over Shanghai in 1949. Naturally we did not live together, except for the odd weekend, but we did see a great deal of each other. My friends were jealous, as she was both beautiful and educated, but for my uncles she could as well have been Jezebel herself. Criticisms and a general unpleasantness grew to the extent that I needed desperately to get away. I decided to take my leave on the finca.

I flew to Ciudad Trujillo via Tokyo, spent a few days in Honolulu, and continued to Los Angeles on a Pan Am Stratocruiser—which, in those days, had a lower deck where cocktails and canapés were served by candlelight and a live pianist played softly in the background. Not a good atmosphere for the heartsick. The Pan Am clipper was named "*Romance of the Sky*." Two days after my arrival in LA, the headlines in the papers read, "Pan Am "*Romance of the Sky*" crashed off Honolulu—no survivors." There but for the grace of God . . .

In LA I checked into my room at the Statler Hilton, then went straight out to the street to look for my brand of cigarettes. To our joint astonishment, I bumped into Ole, one of my A. P. Møller buddies from Copenhagen. He told me that A. P. was in town, giving a cocktail party that evening, and pressed me to go along with him.

We joined a crowd of about a hundred Maersk Line employees and agents, but when A. P. caught sight of me across the room, he gave me a wink and beckoned me over. "Let's find a quiet corner to talk."

After the treatment I had become used to in Hong Kong, this friendly and unexpected encounter cheered me up no end and I began to feel less like a leper. As we sat down he patted me on the knee. "Well, young man, are you happy in Hong Kong?"

I shook my head with a wry smile, but gave no explanation as I thought this would be disloyal to my family. He put his hand on my shoulder and continued in Danish, "Come back to us. There is a free desk for you in the line department. *De er velkommen tilbage.*

Shipping was a small world then. Could he have heard of my difficulties? I thanked him and said I would think it over. Such is destiny, when she opens a door one is not always ready to pass through. Had I known then of the letter that awaited me in the Dominican Republic, I would have accepted A. P. Møller's offer there and then.

48

The Finca

Mother was at the airport to meet my plane in Ciudad Trujillo, and we stayed for several days in the Hotel Jaragua. I could tell from the first moment that something was upsetting her. That first evening she showed me a letter she had just received in which my Number One Uncle wrote that my return was not encouraged. My relationship with a Chinese woman was reflecting negatively both on the family and the whole company's reputation.

Although I knew things were bad, I had not expected such devastating news. Pulling myself together, I told Mother the whole miserable sequence of events since my arrival in Hong Kong, most of which I had never mentioned to her before in my letters. She listened in silence, then gave a great sigh. "My poor boy, they seem determined to get rid of you. Some time ago I heard that there was a plot brewing to get you out, and that phrase, "'The soup is getting too thin,'" was passed all around the family. They are just using this woman as an excuse."

The next day we drove to the finca and Dino. His Italian blood had been outraged by my uncle's letter, and his anger knew no bounds when Mother told him the whole story. Looking back, I am aware that both Mother and Dino influenced me in my final decision to resign when probably I should have fought back. With my father long dead and nobody in my corner, I allowed myself to be persuaded that there was no future for me in my family's own company—even though I was the direct line, the first-born son of a first-born Jessen. I should have given it one more try, for my father's sake as well as my own. But night after night as Dino, Mother, and I sipped our whiskies and rehashed over and over again everything that had been written and said, Mother and Dino's indignation fuelled my own, and the die was cast.

Now I had to sort out what I wanted to do with my life. At first I seriously considered taking A. P. Moller up on his offer, but in the end decided that I would feel a traitor. Jebsens were Maersk's HK agents. The businesses were too close. Finally I agreed to meet some friends of Dino's in Ciudad Trujillo.

Hermann drove me, and on the way we passed new, enormous posters of Generalissimo Trujillo on either side of the road. Huge letters proclaimed him as the Great Benefactor of the New Fatherland, and sometimes as Our Beloved Chief or Our Saviour. This hagiography was getting worse. Now one could not read a newspaper nor listen to the radio without being swamped with praises to the glory of Trujillo. I had learnt quite a lot about the man over the long evenings without radio or television, whilst Mother, Dino, and I sat on the long terrace, the dark nights lit only by the stars and the glow from the green anti-mosquito coils.

Rafael Leonidas Trujillo Molina, "Benefactor de la Patria Nueva"

Born in 1891, son of a Spanish Army sergeant and a Haitian farmer's daughter, Trujillo was, from his youth, always touchy about his mixed blood. As a young man, he served in the Dominican National Guard, then had a lightning career, in the army being promoted from second. lieutenant to brigadier in less than ten years. He began to dabble in politics and, after a coup d'état in 1930, was elected president. Since then, his presidency had become brutal and fascist, good for some but disastrous for dissenters.

One of his first efforts to "improve the race" had been to order the Dominican Army to slaughter 10,000 Haitian labourers who habitually crossed the border to work on Dominican sugar plantations. This, together with the arrival of European

Jews, tipped the ratio slightly, but Trujillo's aim to have a "white" Dominican Republic in contrast to black Haiti was never going to happen.

But he had achieved some things. Under his dictatorship, roads, schools, and hospitals had improved immensely. There was no crime as the punishments were too severe. On the debit side, Trujillo's vast personal fortune came from terrorising the rich and appropriating their lands and factories.

This picture, of course, gave me pause, and I would have to be convinced that investing more money here would be a sound idea. Admittedly this once bankrupt, miserable, three-quarters of a small island state, riddled with disease and corruption, had been transformed under Trujillo's regime into a prosperous little country, but it could easily become as unstable as its neighbours.

Once in Ciudad Trujillo, I met Dino's Italian friends, the d'Alessandro family. The father had come from Calabria as a young engineer and married Dona Carmen, a local girl, daughter of the Gobernadora of Monte Cristi Province. Trujillo was family. After the wedding, an avalanche of major construction contracts appeared out of nowhere, and the young couple quickly amassed a fortune.

Soon the senior d'Alessandro was joined in partnership by another Calabrian émigré called Grisolia, and together they went from strength to strength. The Grisolia side of the business exported coffee, copra, and tobacco, whilst the d'Alessandros had exclusive rights to import Olivetti office machines, Danish air conditioners and vacuum cleaners, plus a wide range of Italian comestibles—and finally, Old Smuggler whisky, a local favourite. They were also general agents for Alitalia and the Italian Line.

Armando, son of the original Alessandro, was U.S. educated and now in his late twenties, headed the concern, whilst his younger brother, Guido, managed their wholly owned subsidiary "Automotiva", which was sole agent for Fiat, Pirelli, and Piago Vespa.

The brothers and I hit it off immediately, and they soon put my fears to rest. With their Trujillo family connections, there was nothing to worry about. They offered me a partnership. Old Señor Grisolia had long wished to retire and would sell me his shares. They suggested that I take over their import division, and as the offer was both interesting and promising, I decided to accept.

With my immediate future now settled, I wrote a letter of explanation to my Chinese girl friend—we had, after all, never been engaged—and one to my Number One Uncle, officially handing in my resignation and requesting the sale of my shares in the shipping company.

49
Ciudad Trujillo

When I started my new job in the capital, I spent two months in the Hotel Paz whilst looking for a suitable apartment. During this time, two major South American dictators sought refuge with Trujillo from the aftermath of regime changes at home, and lived in the same hotel. Not a day went by that I did not dine with Argentina's ex-President Peron sitting together at a large table with wife Isabelita to my left whilst to my right sat Venezuela's ex-President Pérez Jiménez, also with wife and cronies.

Peron

Isabelita Peron was always elegant, entirely dressed in white, fingers laden with impressive diamond baguettes and solitaires, heavy ropes of pearls draped across her breast. Her two white poodles sat on chairs at their table and well-armed body guards stood stiffly around. Outside the hotel, Trujillo's secret service agents waited for heaven knew what in strategically placed armoured vehicles. For ordinary guests, all this was a blasted nuisance.

I never spoke to Dona Isabelita, apart from small pleasantries should we happen to meet in the elevator, but I sometimes shared a night-cap with Peron at the Round Bar, and once or twice chatted there with Pérez Jiménez. Both men were keen for me to understand that, like their host Trujillo, they had taken over destitute, corrupt countries and transformed them into prosperous, law-abiding republics, only to be ousted by their ungrateful compatriots. Both were frustrated and needed an audience—as luck would have it, sometimes me.

Peron told me scary tales of the harsh military school he had attended in Argentina before becoming a full lieutenant in the army at twenty. Head of a nationalist clique of young officers, he had played an important role in the coup d'état that overthrew President Castillo in 1943. A year later, Peron became war minister and then vice-president under President Farrell, later succeeding him in 1946 and being re-elected in 1951. All this he told me with cold, military precision, until he mentioned his first wife, the famous Evita, whom he married in 1945, and then his voice roughened and we had to have another drink. The beautiful Evita had been a tremendous asset to him politically until she died in 1952, mourned not only by him but by the entire Republic. It was obvious he mourned her still.

Evita

I kept looking over my shoulder to see if Isabelita, the new wife, might appear, but of course she never joined him in these late-night reminiscences. Peron had not a single bad word to say about her, but it was obvious that his luck had changed. The Argentine people accused her of trying to take the place of their beloved Evita, and Isabelita was most unpopular. In 1955, Peron had been ex-communicated (he didn't elaborate), and when the army rose up against him, he fled Argentina to begin his long exile.

Perez Jiménez

I did not find Marcos Pérez Jiménez as charismatic as Peron. Balding and chubby-faced, he lacked Peron's military bearing—and, although younger, appeared older. He too had risen to power from a military career, and five years after his election to the Venezuelan presidency in 1952 was considered to be the finest leader in Latin America. He had modernised the country and its economy thrived, thanks mostly to its oil riches, but his authoritarian dictatorship was not what modern Venezuelans wanted, so in 1958 there was a military coup and he had to flee to his old friend Trujillo.

Castro

Both Peron and Pérez Jiménez fretted not only about their own futures but also about the situation in Cuba, where a student rebel named Fidel was making dangerous waves in the Sierra Maestra, uncomfortably close to Haiti and the Dominican Republic. They feared for their friend President Fulgencio Batista's personal safety as well as the rise of unrest in Cuba, which could easily incite the chronically poor of Haiti and perhaps even disturb the peasantry here, causing Trujillo's downfall. Then where would they go? When I thought of Maygaro and the happy field hands on the finca, I tried to reassure them, but they had lost confidence in the good sense of the people after what had happened to them both so recently.

Batista

I was to leave the hotel before either of these two illustrious guests did and, once installed in my new apartment overlooking the sea, my letters, full of descriptions of my new job, new friends, and general happiness, apparently caused Mother some discontent. Seen from seven years on the finca, life in Ciudad Trujillo must have appeared sophisticated and appealing. After all, when had she last spoken to a president, even an ex? when she had last been to the cinema or joined in the round of parties she loved so much. The finca had no telephone, no TV, and no radio to speak of. She began to complain of the hard work that running the finca entailed, and kept reminding me that Dino was sixty-three and she was over fifty. I felt she expected me to do something.

After much thought, I put a proposition to Armando and Guido, and together we decided to offer Dino a position as vice-president at Grisolia, with a decent-enough salary to enable him and Mother to move to Ciudad Trujillo. Hermann and Maygaro could be left in charge of the finca, with Mother and Dino visiting several times a month to pay wages and keep an eye on things.

This was not pure generosity on our part. Dino had been a seasoned business man in the Far East, he spoke four languages—and, most of all, he was a sophisticated Italian who would charm our major Italian principals out of the trees.

When the plan was put to Dino, Mother was over the moon, so there was never any doubt that he would accept our offer. A house was found, they descended with all their possessions on the capital, and soon were launched on the local society scene, with Mother the elegant envy of all her new friends and contemporaries. Those who had not seen her wield her machete from the back of her mule would never have believed it possible.

On the business front, I added several lucrative new European agencies to our stable, and profits steadily improved in both import and export. We sold thousands of Fiat cars, trucks, jeeps, Vespas, and buses to the Dominican military—all vehicles being sold with financing! Practically every second car in the Dominican Republic ran on our imported Pirelli tyres, Bosch spark plugs, and batteries.

Thanks to our contacts, we supplied most government offices with Olivetti machines, winning almost every tender. Our food and liquor business increased dramatically, except the import of Danish butter. All foreigners complained about the rancid Dominican butter, so I decided to get the agency for "Lurpak" butter. The first trial order of 5,000 kg of this prime butter arrived from Denmark, but was instantly rejected by the Dominican public. They claimed it tasted "*muy raro*"—very odd. Apparently years of consuming their own rancid butter made them prefer it! So we and our foreign friends ate the Lurpak with great gusto, until sadly it came to an end.

We exported thousands of tons of coffee, copra, and tobacco to the markets of Europe. The coffee was sorted, in triage fashion, on the open ground floor of our office building, where hundreds of raucous black women pawed over the beans, fought, and sang lustily under the stern leadership of Don Cecilio, our Dominican foreman, who tried to run a tight ship.

I made regular trips to Europe to visit our coffee and tobacco importers, usually ending up in Italy, where I set up long-term financing from Olivetti and Fiat. Whenever Dino knew I was to be in Italy, he insisted that I call on either a cousin of his who owned one of the larger Italian banks or some other well-heeled family. All appeared to have daughters of a marriageable age, but however charming and educated these heiresses were, none of them exactly bowled me over like the Italian beauties I caught sight of everywhere else. No introductions were necessary in order to get to know these girls, but they were probably not marriageable.

I was not safe either in the Dominican Republic from Dino's match-making. The daughter of the owner of one of the largest Caribbean rum empires was invited to dinner but however well-endowed she was financially, money could not make up for the rest of her.

On many occasions, I left our offices to travel deep into the interior in order to buy future crops of coffee and tobacco. For this I had to carry large amounts of cash, as the canny Dominican farmers would only bargain when hard currency was on the table, and I was glad to have my pistol—even if I never had cause to use it. Each time there would be hours of stubborn bargaining over many bottles of rum, always ending with back-slapping, emotional outbursts, and declarations of eternal friendship to seal the agreements.

But despite our rosy financial circumstances, the d'Alessandro family and many influential Dominicans in Ciudad Trujillo were becoming increasingly impatient with the unrestrained greed of the Trujillo clan, whose members all expected kickbacks. Rumours swirled around of several assassination attempts on the Supreme Leader and his cronies, but none succeeded. After each failed attempt, stories of unbelievable cruelty and perverse tortures came to light.

Fathers whose sons had been imprisoned and who would not act as informers on their boys' friends were also hauled off to jail. If the usual tortures did not succeed in breaking their silence, the men would be told they would be released the next day for lack of evidence. To show there were no hard feelings, a proper meal would be brought to them on the evening before their release. Once the half-starved men had devoured their dinner, they would be told that they had just eaten part of their son's leg, and if they still refused to talk, more pieces would be removed and cooked. No father could continue to resist.

Huge properties were expropriated. Friends of ours owned an enormous sugar mill and were offered one fifth of its value. When the owner refused to sell he was told, "Sell at this price, or do not be surprised if you or members of your family suffer car accidents in the near future."

Naturally our friend sold at a huge loss and the entire family left for Miami to join the growing number of discontented Dominicans already there.

To get away from this increasingly menacing atmosphere, Guido and Armando took their wives, Dolly and Josefina, for their first visit to Italy. They toured extensively, saw all the cultural sights, and returned full of enthusiasm for the beautiful countryside, the food—and, above all, the shops. Venice, Florence and Rome, however, failed to please.

"*Todo es tan viejo!*" the women wailed. "Everything is so old. They talk of architecture, but they should see Miami!"

At this time, Mother and Dino also took a prolonged trip to Europe, so I moved from my flat to their house to look after the dogs and enjoy being spoilt by their servants.

Across the avenue, an English girl was staying, and I tried hard to befriend her. Every evening I walked the dogs, and every evening I saw her sitting in the cool of the garden. No matter how I tried, I never got an answer to my pleasantries. Naturally she became a challenge. I sent her a note via Mother's cook to invite her to spend the evening with me. After that she simply disappeared from view.

Our neighbour, U.S. Ambassador McFarlaine, invited me to his annual New Year's Eve cocktail, and when I telephoned with my acceptance I asked him if an invitation could be sent to *la señorita Inglesa*—the young English woman—as she was known on our avenue. I did not even know her name.

Having no idea that I had anything to do with it, the invitation was accepted. After a frosty beginning over cocktails, she thawed enough to agree to have dinner with me and bring in the New Year at the Hotel Embajador, probably because every other guest at the party was at least the age of our parents, and all appeared to be ready to go home to bed at the twelfth stroke of midnight, if not before.

The girl next door...

Seated by the dance floor of the Embajador, I plied Jennifer with champagne and finally got her to tell me why I had received the cold-shoulder treatment. Apparently I had an abysmal reputation on Mother's avenue, due to the fact that, since my arrival, girls came to the house and left at all hours. I had to admit that some, very few—air hostesses from Varig and Carib Air—would pocket their per diem and stay with me instead. I had asked for their respective air line flags and I would fly them according to who was visiting me.

It took a little time before I could persuade Jennifer that the above was greatly exaggerated, and that my relationship with all these girls was purely platonic. Naturally.

On her side she confessed that she had come out to the Dominican Republic to marry, but things had gone wrong and she was about to break off her engagement. It came as a great relief to me that she was soon to be free, as I had already recognised her as the one I had been waiting for. A few months later I proposed to her—three times in fact. Twice she refused to take me seriously, claiming I had had too many Cuba Libres. On the third attempt I tried again, without my Dutch courage, and she said yes.

On learning of this, the ex-fiancé's blood boiled, and one evening I received a panicky phone call from Jennifer, telling me not to come and pick her up as her discarded beau was waiting for me in the garden with his shark harpoon. Not to be outdone, I wore my pistol openly and was quite prepared to duel at dawn. Unfortunately, I could not demonstrate my courage to my love as the harpoonist fled. How right Maygaro was—a pistol will always trump any blade.

This exciting romance took my eye off the political ball, but gradually I became aware that danger was brewing. The professional classes and businessmen had had enough, complaining that the Trujillo gang was simply "Pushing their luck too far."

As the Dominicans' discontent grew, rumours reached us from Cuba of that pesky young revolutionary who was gaining popularity. Tired of our own dictator, the initial reaction to the news from Habana was one of envy. Little was known about Fidel Castro at that time, other than that he was a student attempting to lead a large group of dissatisfied field hands in a coup to oust President Batista. Nobody imagined that Cuba would eventually become a full-fledged communist state under Castro's endless rule.

Unlike the ex-Presidents Peron and Pérez Jiménez, Cuba's current Gran Jefe, Fulgencio Batista, had humble beginnings. He had not attended expensive military academies nor formed part of a young army officers' clique. Born in 1901, he joined the Guardia Rural in his early twenties, rising to the grade of Sergeant in Cuba's State Army. During the 1930s, the Cuban government was overthrown several times—each time Batista rising in the ranks, until 1933, when he became a colonel and Chief of the Army. From 1933 to 1940, Batista violently opposed the rise of communism and socialism amongst the sugar field hands, and in 1940 he achieved his ambition and was elected President. After only four years he was overthrown, but eight years later, in 1952, he was re-elected to the presidency.

During Batista's time in office, Cuba saw great changes in the island's infrastructure. New auto routes, improved train services, and a spanking new airport, astonished the natives, but the persecution of all radical elements increased, fuelling the hatred of the impoverished sugar workers.

In early January of 1959, the long-expected but nevertheless astonishing news of Castro's successful coup in overthrowing Batista reached us in Ciudad Trujillo. We read the news with wonder. Within hours, Fulgencio Batista, his family, and a large entourage took refuge in the Hotel La Paz. By now the previous residents, Peron and Jiménez, had long moved on, so there was no commiseration in a club of ex-presidents in the bar for poor Fulgencio of course.

Now Castro held Cuba in a firm fist. Flushed with success, he was said to be eyeing the Dominican Republic as his next prize, our own dictator supposedly being ripe for the picking. The whole island, from peasant to millionaire, held its collective breath.

Excitement grew to a fever pitch when a group of Fidelistas from the Sierra Maestra in Cuba landed on our island and made camp in the mountainous regions of Constanza and Montaña. When it became apparent that the youngest of the d'Alessandro brothers had left for Montaña and intended to join the Fidelistas in their attempt to form a bridgehead into the heart of the Dominican Republic, Guido and Armando raced up to the mountains and began a desperate search for their teenage brother. The boy was far from ready to be "rescued," and practically had to be kidnapped in order to bring him back to his distraught mother.

The damage, unfortunately, was done. Once young d'Alessandro's "treasonous" escapade became known to the Trujillo clique as well as some of his older brothers' critical remarks about members of the family, not even Josefina, wife of Guido and closely related to the Trujillos, could intervene now.

With its usual severity, the government clamped down on both our companies, strangulating every phase of our business. Export licences were denied; import licences were blocked; agreed Government purchases cancelled. All our automotive and produce stocks in the go-downs were confiscated. Business simply ground to a halt.

I had endless talks with the d'Alessandro brothers over the next fruitless months, and we finally agreed that, if for them there was no alternative to keeping a low profile and hoping for better days, for me it was time to move on. Jennifer was anxious to return to Europe, where she wanted her family to meet me and for us to get married from her parents' house. Before that I would have to find a new job—and then, together, we would begin a new life.

Although I left behind a great deal of money tied up in the Dominican Republic from my share in mother's hacienda to my shares in Empresas Dominicanas, Automotiva S.A. and Grisolia, there was no way I could sell anything at this point. All I took with me were cherished memories of happy years spent on that beautiful island—and Jennifer, of course.

50

A New Beginning

Early in Nov. 1960, Jennifer and I flew to St. Thomas, from where I had booked passage to Europe on a freighter that would sail in ten days time, so we decided to take our honeymoon there and then, before our wedding, as a more romantic spot would have been hard to find. We were never to be very orthodox, I'm afraid.

From our bungalow on a sugar-white beach, a few steps away from the turquoise sea and sheltered by tall palms, we lazed the days away. I rented a pink jeep with candy-striped, tasselled awnings, and we explored the island from Sapphire Beach to Morning Star and Magens Bay, where we were warned about sharks that waited patiently. We drove up into the hills, where we found a straw-thatched bar that made banana daiquiris, so delicious, so unexpectedly lethal. On our way down, a sudden tropical storm drenched us, and only Bacchus kept us on the twisting dirt road back to safety.

The island had been Danish until 1917, and many streets still had Danish names despite the fact that it was now an American Protectorate. Our only misadventure was that I found myself stopped for speeding by a burly black policeman on a motor bike, who insisted that we follow him to the local police station. I tried to get him to allow me to leave Jennifer at our hotel, but he refused. He must have regretted this.

The little police station was crammed with U.S. Marines, all apparently from Georgia, hauled in for some unacceptable behaviour. They lounged against the grimy walls and grinned at us with faultless American teeth. After an interminable

Jennifer

wait, one of them found a chair for Jennifer. The moment she sat down, another huge black policeman stormed over to her, told her to stand up, and asked who the hell had given her permission to sit anyway? At this there was a rumble of discontent that rose to a roar as twenty marines pushed themselves away from the walls and surrounded the policeman in a threatening manner, their Southern sensibilities outraged by such treatment to a white girl. The black cop blanched, if this is possible, and made himself scarce. Within seconds I was summoned to pay $20. and then we were almost shoved outside—suddenly they couldn't get rid of us fast enough.

Our ship, the East Asiatic Company's MS *Magdala*, sailed the next day, and off we went on a three-week ocean crossing, ending with stops in Dublin, Liverpool, Le Havre, Antwerp, Rotterdam, and finally Copenhagen.

Mid-Atlantic, encouraged by our bored fellow passengers (we were only about fifteen in all), who seemed to find us a most romantic couple, we asked the rather grumpy Danish captain if he would marry us, and then we could all have a jolly party. He smiled grimly and asked if Jennifer were either pregnant or suffering from a terminal disease. As neither case applied, he claimed new rules forbade such ceremonies. A damned shame, we all agreed, and had the party anyway.

Our first port of call was Dublin on a cold, wet autumn day. As we wandered, shivering, around the town I was astonished to see so many filthy children, dressed in rags, begging in the street. I was dismayed and whispered in Jennifer's ear, "I never realised the standard of living was so low here!"

She collapsed in laughter at that. "It's Halloween, you silly!"

And so began our long education in one another's folklore, customs, and eccentricities when an understanding of language is not enough.

Our next stop was Liverpool. We had cabled Jennifer's parents that she would stay on board with me until Copenhagen and then fly home, but their impatience to see their daughter and, probably, vet me, led them to brave the complications of the maze of Liverpool's docks to come and have lunch on board. To everyone's relief, we got along like a house on fire—even if Beth, my future mother-in-law, took me aback somewhat when she announced that I had chosen her most intelligent daughter, but also the most difficult! To this day the three sisters have not forgotten her remark. It is pleasant to be considered intelligent, but one would rather not be labelled difficult—nor the reverse, of course.

My future father-in-law, Bill, was one of the cleverest men I have ever met, and the breadth of his knowledge astounded me. Although his love was poetry and literature, at well over eighty and only a few months before his death I found him reading up on quantum physics. When he saw my surprise, he shrugged and replied, "One has to keep up, you know."

After a few days in Copenhagen, Jennifer flew to England to make wedding arrangements whilst I began a frantic job hunt, as soon I would have to support a wife. Two weeks later I had an offer from Danfoss, a major electronics and refrigeration industrial concern. They seemed to think I would be perfect for their export division, and what actually clinched the deal for me was that the job came with a house.

With this offer in my pocket, I sailed to Harwich, where Jennifer and Bill picked me up and drove me to Huntingdon, where I met her beloved sisters, Elizabeth and Susan, and my new brother-in-law, another John, who was to become a great friend. On Dec. 17, 1960, in the company of various aunts, uncles, and cousins, Jennifer and I were married.

51

The Island of Als

The outskirts of a small town on a quiet island in southern Denmark is probably the ideal place in which to slow down and become accustomed to married life. The hours of my new job were so regular that Jennifer could set her watch by my arrival home for dinner, in true Danish fashion, at six o'clock. Her culinary efforts were described by her father as "either a burnt offering or a bloody sacrifice," but I didn't really care.

We had to wait a few weeks for our new house to be ready, so we stayed in a small hotel in Sønderborg. We were only a few miles away from Laimun, where my Jessen step-grandmother still lived. The first time I took Jennifer to meet her was a bit awkward. Our reading lights happened to be lethally placed above our pillows—and Jennifer, sitting up abruptly, had nearly poked an eye out, with the upsetting result that she had a magnificent black eye. Makeup could not conceal it, so despite the January gloom, my nervous young wife wore sunglasses to meet my step-grandmother, who was kind enough not to make a remark.

The two of them actually became fond of each other, and when our little house was finally ready, my step-grandmother and Emmi, her housekeeper, took the bus from Aabenraa to Nordborg, armed with baskets, one full of a picnic lunch and the other full of cleaning products. The three women set to remove all trace of the workmen with vigour, and ended up polishing all windows until they glittered. Naturally I drove the two home, but had not been able to fetch them as theirs was a surprise visit. As Step-grandmother was about eighty at this time, her kindness cannot be overestimated. During the entire time we stayed in Denmark, we visited her often, and she delighted in practising her excellent French with Jennifer.

In February we learnt to our joy that a baby was on its way, and soon our visits to Laimun took on an entirely new atmosphere as my step-grandmother insisted upon our arrival, after only forty minutes in the car, that Jennifer should rest in a small room where a rocking chair with warm plaids and a tray with milk and biscuits had been arranged—delicate, old-fashioned attentions for a still invisible pregnancy.

On weekends, Jennifer and I enjoyed Als, with its deep forests and wild beaches, but work at Danfoss was unexciting. Engineers and scientists thrived developing the new refrigeration and electronics technologies that were to make Danfoss the giant it is today, but the commercial side was less inspiring. I worked in the export department, marketing compressors to Germany. The highlight of the year turned out to be the Cologne Fair. Had it not been for the novelty of our cosy domestic life and the excitement of our coming baby, I would have quit sooner, but I knew that I had to hang on to give Jennifer a peaceful pregnancy and the baby a secure start. For these reasons, Als was ideal.

Even in this tranquillity news reached us of the world outside. Letters arrived from the Dominican Republic about the many failed attempts to oust Trujillo, but one day a coup was successful. Trujillo had driven incognito, in a beat-up old Chevy, to visit a favourite mistress in San Cristobal. It was dark, and tropical rain sluiced down, concealing the ambush. A group of businessmen and doctors (including my own dentist) strafed his car with rifle fire. His bullet-riddled body was stuffed into a jute sack, thrown into the trunk of my dentist's car, and swiftly driven back to his house and parked in his garage. The dentist then promptly disappeared.

Next morning a lonely policeman on his normal beat saw pools of dried blood, which must have seeped out of the car, under the garage door, and into the street. He raised the alarm and pandemonium reigned.

Trujillo's playboy son, Ramfis, Chief of Staff of the Armed Forces, conducted a witch hunt unparalleled even in that country, during which hundreds were questioned, tortured, and executed. I was pretty sure that the d'Alessandro brothers were part of this final coup, but they were never arrested, and later claimed to have had nothing to do with it. It does not do to boast about such things, but it is significant that Guido d'Alessandro went into hiding for several months, in the tender care of old Italian friends of his father.

Far more important to us than this distant skulduggery was the birth of our first son, John Henry Rickmer, on Sept. 24, 1961. Amongst all the blond, blue-eyed Danish babies in the Sønderborg hospital, his dark curls caused him to be nicknamed Fidel Castro! Both Jennifer's mother and mine soon arrived to inspect their new grandson, and joy reigned in our little house. Visits continued to Laimun, where my step-grandmother now had Jennifer's ritual glass of milk replaced by half a pint of malt beer—just the thing for breast-feeding mothers !

With the New Year, however, came a resurgence of my restlessness, and I began to scan newspapers for some more challenging position. It was Jennifer who pointed out to me the amusing advertisement in the *International Herald Tribune*, which spoke of travel and riches. The travel alone was lure enough for me!

That weekend I wrote off to Investors Overseas Services in Switzerland, little realising that our humdrum lives were about to be turned upside-down.

I was invited to visit the IOS headquarters at 119 rue de Lausanne in Geneva for interviews, and once these were over I agreed to participate in the next training session in February, 1962. I returned to Denmark to hand in my resignation to Danfoss. We bade a fond farewell to our first home and put all our furniture into storage, little realising that we were to see none of it again until we watched our crates being unpacked in Beirut in 1967.

52

THE I.O.S. YEARS

Much has been written about Bernie Cornfeld, but for those of us who knew him in those early days, he was like no one else we had ever met. Short, plump, and not particularly attractive physically, he radiated energy, magnetism, and optimism. He had a vision. We were to bring financial security to all and, in the process, spread wealth around the globe. We, his foot-soldiers, would live where we pleased, open markets wherever we saw an opportunity—and if, by spreading the word of "Peoples' Capitalism" we made our own fortunes, then so be it. He entranced us all with his ability to communicate his exciting vision of the future. With an eloquence worthy of a messiah, we were to leave our nets and follow him. Like the children after the piper, we did.

The group of men on my initial training course was a mix of cultures—Hong Kong Chinese, Brits from Sierra Leone, Argentines, South Africans, Canadians, and Europeans. The products we were introduced to were mutual funds, little known in the early sixties outside the U.S. and the U.K. These funds enabled the small investor to globally diversify his assets by pooling his money together with thousands of others and thus be able to benefit from expert management.

The past performance of our flagship, the Dreyfus Fund, was excellent, but we also had our own in-house funds to market, such as the International Investment Trust—IIT—as well as the Research Investors Fund, both outstanding performers. Now a small investor with an initial down-payment of as little as $1,000 could participate in a well-diversified portfolio of stocks and bonds. Of course we were also encouraged to find more affluent prospects who could afford substantial investments, or companies that could divert part of their pension plans into our funds.

Sales Techniques and Psychology classes helped us to perfect a "presentation" and taught us how to answer clients' questions or erase any doubts. We learnt how to recognise body language and thus understand our clients better. In the early 1960s, such an educated sales approach was quite new—not only to us, but to practically all non-U.S. investors.

With all these new ideas buzzing around my head, I met Jennifer and baby John for lunch every day in the little Hotel Eden around the corner from IOS head office. I was unaware that my enthusiastic reports of all I had learnt were being overheard by a man at a neighbouring table, whom I subsequently knew as Ted Price, then right hand to Bernie Cornfeld, to whom he related, with quiet amusement, this new trainee's enthusiasm. But Bernie liked a dedicated convert and did not forget my name.

At the end of the training period, each man had a personal meeting with Bernie. When he and I met, he seemed fascinated by my colourful background, then offered me a choice between two locations: Manila, to work with Allen Cantor, the manager of the Philippines, because of my strong ties to Asia; or Mexico City, under Robert Sutner, as I was a "born Latin" and spoke Spanish.

I opted for Mexico for family reasons because, as Bernie himself pointed out, "You have a five-month-old son—he'll be eaten alive by Manila's giant mosquitoes. I know I am!"

Finally a send-off dinner for our group was held in the Hotel du Rhone, at the end of which Bernie gave one of his uplifting speeches, always in his soft-spoken way so that his audience really had to listen. He sent us all off to the far corners of the world with his blessings and our enthusiasm redoubled.

53

Mexico City

Although at that time the Capital of Mexico had a population of only 4 million it was still a daunting sight after the tranquillity of a Caribbean island, a small Danish town and sleepy Geneva. Both Jennifer and I were overwhelmed by the sheer NOISE of it as Mexicans are an exuberant lot. However, after two weeks in a hotel on the hurly-burly Paseo Reforma, I found an apartment which came with a maid in a quiet residential district. After installing Jennifer and baby John I could at last get the bit between my teeth.

The first words Bob Sutner said to me in the IOS offices were, "Anyone who parachutes down with his small family into unknown territory, not knowing a soul, to start selling Mutual Funds shows an almost heroic enthusiasm. You'll do fine."

There were about twenty-five representatives working the Mexican market—Austrians, Germans, Americans, Swiss, Spaniards, Brits, and now me. The office had been open for about a year, and business was growing steadily. Although we were all "competitors" on a strictly commission basis, there reigned a comradely, team spirit, which I was to find everywhere throughout the IOS world over the next decade.

The centrepiece of the office was a giant blackboard, where the secretaries logged each associate's monthly sales according to volume. As soon as I saw it, I promised myself that by my second month my name would be at the top. I told this to an amused Bob—not as a boast, but to spur me on, as my honour was now involved.

The first step towards my goal was to get hold of a Mexican version of "*Who's Who*" as well as directories from various chambers of commerce. Step number two was coaching Jennifer so she could act as my secretary and get me appointments. She charmed her way past even the most impregnable of secretaries with her fluent Spanish, French, or clear English. Her opening remarks never varied: "Mr. Jessen is a financial advisor who has just flown in from Geneva and would like to meet Mr. X."

For the next couple of years, it appeared that I flew in from Geneva on a daily basis. Jennifer opened all doors for me, and I was never refused an initial interview.

Appointments were made with captains of industry, importers, exporters, shipping company executives, and top professional men of many nationalities. So successful was our campaign that soon I found myself racing all over Mexico City and we had to pin up a large street map so Jennifer could plan my appointments efficiently, enabling me to get from one to another without wasting half a morning.

I gave at least four new presentations daily, and soon second and third follow-up visits had to be made to interested clients as well, so my evenings were also hectic.

My first sale was to an American engineer. I only had to visit him twice before he made an investment of $30,000 in the Dreyfus Fund. My second was to a Swiss industrialist, who put $50,000 into our in-house IIT Fund—which pleased Bernie particularly, as this was his baby. Then I closed a German, who took out a $250-per-month Dreyfus Savings Plan over a ten-year period. A day later I added a Swede to my list of clients, who invested $75,000, and in the first couple of weeks I made the equivalent of more than twice the annual salary I had earned in Hong Kong. Best of all, I found this new job not only challenging but exciting.

The following month my sales increased enough to put me second on the famous board, and by the third month I achieved my goal and saw my name at the top.

Jennifer wrote long, weekly letters home to placate her parents, who had hoped that she would settle down somewhere nearer to them. When she told them of my first commissions, I received a cable from my father-in-law: "Now is the winter of your discontent made glorious summer!" (With apologies to W.S.)

Very apt—very Bill-like.

The men I worked with were a gregarious lot and we received a constant stream of invitations. In some ways, being an "IOSer" was like joining a club. Next to Bob and Charlotte Sutner, I particularly remember Ward Griffin, a charming Louisianian who dreamt only of huntin', shootin', and fishin', so it was a surprise to meet his gentle, artist wife who came from top Mexican society. Then there was José Arechebala, who was to remain a friend for decades. José was a Spaniard raised in Cuba and heir to the Arechebala sugar empire, who later married Perla, heiress to the Cuban Partagas Cigars fortune, sadly all confiscated and nationalised by Castro.

Years later, José invited Jennifer and me to a shoot on an estate outside Madrid, where I bagged seventy-five partridges in the morning before sitting down at an exquisitely laid table under a large marquee in the middle of nowhere, where we were served an outstanding luncheon with impeccable decorum. That evening we all celebrated in an exclusive Madrid club, where José's guest of honour was one of the princesses of Savoy. José was to remain a friend until he died tragically early from cancer.

One day Bernie arrived in Mexico on one of his world tours to visit all the IOS offices. He gave a great dinner party in the Alameda Hotel, firing us up all over again, reiterating that we should remember to be proud that we were or could become co-owners of IOS, thanks to the IOS Stock Option Plan. Acquiring Options at book value in the expectation of selling them at a later date with an enormous profit greatly fostered company spirit and sales. The minimum requirement for men in the field to qualify for the plan was a sales volume of a million dollars U.S., and as one rose in the company hierarchy, at each promotion one was allowed to buy more stock.

As usual, Bernie was accompanied by his current girl friend—this time a Japanese beauty. Charlotte asked Jennifer to help her entertain this young woman, so whilst we men were in meetings they picked her up from her hotel, armed with a list of cultural sights. Immediately it was made clear that their ideas of entertainment were out of order. Only jewellers were to be visited. In their naiveté, Charlotte and Jennifer told her of their own favourite artisans, who made beautiful modern pieces in gold or silver based on ancient designs. This would not do at all. Madam simply wanted to be taken to the best jeweller in town, so that evaluations could be made of the rings, brooches, and necklaces Bernie had bought for her over the past few weeks. Nothing more was required of them.

During this visit I asked Bernie for advice with a particularly difficult prospect, and he immediately offered to go with me. This man, a native Pole, was toying with the idea of investing $500,000 in the IIT Fund. However, there had been a constant stream of objections, which I had not been able to overcome during three visits.

The Pole received us pleasantly enough, and listened to Bernie as he slowly and softly explained once more the basics of IIT—but added that it was not very well diversified geographically.

"What? exclaimed the Pole. "I understood it to be in the Far East, Europe, and the Americas.

Bernie was silent for a minute. "Well, that's true, but have you considered the tax implications?"

Here the Pole jumped in again. "But Mr. Jessen told me there are no taxes to be paid by a non-Swiss resident."

Back to Bernie. "Ah yes, in your case that is so. But the performance of IIT is not our most stellar example, you know."

The Pole was getting annoyed. "That is not correct, Mr. Cornfeld. IIT has an excellent performance, which is the reason why I intend to invest half a million dollars in it."

And he did.

This was a prime example of Bernie's negative approach, which prompted my client to sell the product to himself. From then on I used this technique many times during the days of my personal selling career.

Despite the fact that business was going better than I could ever have dreamed, we were only to stay in Mexico for six months. When Ed Cowett arrived—IOS General Counsel and Executive Vice-President at that time—he strongly urged me to move to Argentina, where the market was ripe and where I would be made branch manager in due course. This was enticing, especially as Mexico City's altitude of 7,400 feet caused me constant and severe headaches. On my frequent trips to Toluca, where I found many clients amongst the Swiss engineers, I suffered even more as the altitude there rose to 8,500 feet. Buenos Aires was at sea level.

Our departure was a Mexican fiesta in itself. First José Arechebala arrived at our place, leading an entire mariachi band that paraded around our small apartment, blasting out "Adelita," "Las Mananitas," "El Rey," and many more old favourites at full volume. Down in the street the entire IOS crew were lined up in their cars, and as we set off for the airport they followed the mariachis who followed us in a long and noisy cortège. We were accompanied by this motley crew, serenading us across the tarmac and right up to the gangway—still possible in those days. José wore baby John's sun hat, and I was given one of the band's huge cartwheels—which unfortunately I had to give back, as it would not fit through the cabin door. The air hostesses found it all very funny, and a welcome change to their daily routine. But not all the passengers agreed, so we three behaved ourselves in an exemplary manner for the rest of the flight.

We had decided to break our journey in Rio de Janeiro, in order to give John Jr. a break, but as it turned out it would have been less tiring for us all had we flown straight down to Buenos Aires. It appeared that the Brazilian Consulate in Mexico City had mistakenly stamped our passports with permanent resident visas, which did not allow us to spend just one night in Brazil before continuing down to Argentina. I spent the next three days racing from one Government office to another, pleading and bribing my way through kilometres of red tape.

Finally, armed with the correct visas, we prepared to leave, but at the airport a new complication arose. To enter Argentina from Brazil, smallpox vaccinations were mandatory. Jennifer and I had these, but the Mexicans had not required them for a baby. Argentina, however, did, and so we were marched off to the airport health authorities where, to our consternation, a metal tray holding a pile of rather rusty-looking household nails was produced, and our baby son's arm was scratched with one of these before the vaccine was dabbed on. It was not little John's outraged howls that frightened us so much as the fear of tetanus, but the deed was done.

54

ARGENTINA

At last we landed in Buenos Aires. In the Ezeiza Airport, I raced off to find our luggage, which had been checked through on our original flight from Mexico, and thus had been standing around for several days. When we unpacked later we were not surprised to find that many items had disappeared.

I took a suite in the City Hotel as a base until we could find a suitable apartment. The separate living room fast became my office and a quiet place for Jennifer to make appointments for me when baby John was asleep. Should he wake, she became adept at quickly hanging up—then, once he had settled down, calling back, pretending the connection had been broken—a common occurrence anyway. After Mexico, we found BA very European, and even decorous. The hotel restaurant trolleys were always laden with delicious hors d'oeuvres, and the general high quality in all the restaurants turned us into instant foodies, after the monotony of tamales, guacamole, and refried beans—however much we had enjoyed the Mexican cuisine at first.

Here in BA, the IOS offices were very grand, in an old-fashioned, elegant building between Billinghurst and Avenida Libertador San Martin—a prestigious address in 1962. The General Manager for Argentina and Uruguay was a tall, charming, much-travelled American called Bill Hovan. He made me welcome and introduced me to about twenty-five associates, who were all gathered there for the weekly meeting. Most seemed to be Anglo-Argentine, more British than the British, in old school ties or tweeds. There was also a Polish count who wore his jacket draped across his shoulders like a cape, as well as several Germans and Swiss. They seemed a pleasant group.

Their top producer was a German-Argentine called Carlos Luetjohann who, at seventy-seven, out-performed everybody. I, of course, immediately made myself a silent vow to overtake him. Just as in Mexico, I had arrived in an area where I had absolutely no contacts, but this was never to deter me.

Very soon we found a charming apartment that came with Fanny, a live-in maid, who promptly fell in love with little John and neglected most other duties for him. From the small study we set up our campaign room, with street maps and lists of prospects culled from our usual sources. Jennifer was soon making me almost more appointments than I could handle.

Buenos Aires

An early client was the president of Mercedes Benz-Argentina, William Mosetti. This charming Triestino-Austrian not only invested with us, but also introduced me to many of his friends, who soon became my clients too.

At that time, Mercedes employed about 8,000 workers in Argentina, assembling mainly trucks and diesel taxis. During my frequent visits, William Mosetti and I became friends, and over drinks one day he told me that in the 1950s he had an assistant who would constantly bob in and out with papers to be signed, or other annoying interruptions. This man was extremely servile, always bowing and muttering apologies in German. No one ever suspected that this obsequious little man should turn out to be the infamous Adolf Eichmann! One morning he did not turn up for work and was never seen again, having been tracked down by the Israeli Secret Service. Mosetti remembered how often he had blasted out at the man for always hovering about, and we had a good laugh when we realised how easily Eichmann could have poisoned his coffee!

Early in 1963, just before we moved from our small apartment into a larger one overlooking the Botanical Gardens—for Jennifer was pregnant again and we would soon need more room—we witnessed the beginnings of a civil war, South American style. One morning before leaving for the office, I happened to take my coffee out to our front balcony, which overlooked the always busy Las Heras street. To my surprise, there was no traffic at all. Suddenly Fanny appeared at my elbow in a state of high excitement. She had been listening to her radio and told me that our very lives were in danger.

"Look!" she whispered dramatically as she pointed to both ends of our wide avenue.

Sure enough—a lot was going on in the distance. Tanks were stationed at either end, flags fluttering in the morning breeze—red to the north and blue to the south.

What appeared to be hundreds of troops milled around, jeeps and revving motor cycles adding to the uproar. With the French windows now open, the noise reached Jennifer, who came out with little John in her arms. Fanny was horrified.

"*Damelo señora!* It is far too *peligroso* for the *angelito* out here," and grabbing our son from his surprised mother's arms, she dashed inside with him.

"Oh, has it started?" Jennifer asked, curiously peering up and down our street. I was flabbergasted.

"How do you know about this? Why didn't you say anything?" But having witnessed the London blitz as a small child, she considered these affairs to be small potatoes.

Apparently over the past few days, the women in the markets and the cashiers in the local shops had all warned her to stock up on essentials, as trouble was on its way. To please them, she had built up a small supply of staples, but she had not thought anything serious was going to happen. As it turned out, this English sangfroid proved not to have been misplaced.

We stood waiting for things to begin for hours, but neither the red nor the blue general appeared to be quite ready. Apart from a constant exchange of insults yelled over loudspeakers from the troops and bursts of rapid rifle fire into the air, nothing happened. Just before noon, rain began to fall, and soon it turned into a veritable deluge. To our astonishment, both sides rapidly appeared to be in full retreat. We went inside to have a quick lunch, fully expecting both "armies" to return with the sun, but nobody ever did. We could only suppose that diplomacy had won the day. A comic opera indeed.

Business continued to flourish, and I was soon the region's top salesman. A few months later I received the million-dollar IOS award, a Patek Phillipe gold watch, and was appointed branch manager, which meant that I could recruit and train my own sales team. My clients were happy, I was making heaps of money and my family was growing. I felt I deserved a break.

To escape from the suffocating heat of BA, I took Jennifer and little John to Punta del Este in Uruguay. We relaxed for a few weeks, then, refreshed, returned to Argentina for the last months of Jennifer's pregnancy. On Aug. 2, 1963, Paul Nicholas was born in the Little Company of Mary hospital, which was run by catholic nuns. When John arrived to inspect his new brother, he was far more interested in the crucifix hanging over his mother's bed and now, at almost two, very curious, asked, "Why is that man wearing nappies?" Even the nuns were amused.

Our second son had to have an Argentine passport as soon as he entered the world. The Danes were prepared to wait, presuming correctly that the babe was not about to travel alone. Instead of a signature, the Argentine passport carried one-minute fingerprint and his new name—Pablo Nicolas. We were told to be proud that we had an Argentine son (Puro Porteño in fact, meaning born in Buenos Aires) who, in due course, would have the honour of serving in the Argentine armed forces. Jennifer and I exchanged glances at this news, which we both knew meant, "Over my dead body!"

He also had to be vaccinated against smallpox, but the cow pox that was administered to three-month-old Nicky was so virulent that his little body was covered with scabs. In order to avoid pox marks, we first put cotton mittens on his hands, then, as the itching intensified, we had to bind his arms to his body. Marie, our housekeeper, and Jennifer took turns at his bedside and managed to keep him from scratching so that, in the end, his skin was unmarked, apart from one small scar on his forehead.

At this point, Ed Cowett arrived from Geneva and appointed me Regional Manager of Peru. Jennifer's mother was visiting us in BA at the time and became quite flustered with this sudden change of plan, but for Jennifer and me it was exciting news. For the next few weeks I flew back and forth between Peru and Argentina, until Jennifer felt strong enough to move, and then the four of us left for Lima.

Just as in Mexico, we had not taken the time to visit all the places we longed to see in Argentina. In both countries we had imagined our stays would be much longer, so we never got around to seeing the Aztec pyramids or the Argentine gauchos on the pampas. I promised Jennifer we really would see something of Peru, quickly, before we were again sent off somewhere else at a moment's notice.

55

Peru

On the drive from the airport, Lima seemed very small after Buenos Aires. It also looked extremely poor as we drove through the outskirts. Of course Argentina had its slums too, but its capital was so big we never saw them. Here there were few impressive boulevards or tall buildings, only a few vestiges of Lima's proud past, such as the historic Colonial Square, La Plaza de Armas with the Cathedral Basilica, as well as a bronze Baroque fountain from 1650—all of which were proudly pointed out to us by chatty taxi drivers.

We stayed in the Hotel Crillon, comfortably cushioned from the real world, as large hotels always are. This cheered Jennifer up as she was becoming a little nervous about the whole Peruvian enterprise—especially with two small sons in tow.

On the plane she had asked me if there were ever earthquakes in Lima, as she had been quite scared by one in Mexico City, when we had had to run down the stairs in our night wear, clutching baby John as the hotel elevator tolled like a church bell.

"No," I assured her. "No earthquakes here."

Naturally that very first night we woke to find the chandelier in our hotel bedroom swinging like a pendulum as mirrors cracked and pictures crashed to the floor. Aghast, Jennifer leapt out of bed and grabbed Nick. I swept up John and we dashed along the corridor to the stairwell. In the lobby, hotel employees were soothing the jangled nerves of frightened guests, sending us back to bed like little children.

"All over now. *Todo ha terminado,*" they repeated endlessly. Everyone obeyed, but I don't think many of us slept that night, and it was quite some time before Jennifer forgave me—the earthquake obviously being my fault.

Fortunately help was easy to find, and soon a happy, fat woman with fine Inca features would sit at night with the sleeping children whilst I tried to whip up some enthusiasm from my wife for our new posting. The first time we had dinner in the Sky Room of the Crillon, Lima glittered at our feet like jewellery on a display cushion, and over a glass of wine she relaxed a little. Unfortunately the same view at luncheon showed only miserable hovels, dusty and dilapidated, their flat-topped roofs littered with piles of junk and discarded mattresses. The fairy landscape had disappeared at day break. I was going to have to come up with something good to cheer Jennifer up.

The early delights of Lima proved to be gastronomic, and in the renowned restaurant Trece Monedas we were introduced to the local cocktail, pisco sour. Pisco is an alcohol originally made for centuries by the Incas, but improved when the Spaniards arrived and introduced Muscat grape vines into the country. The famous drink is made with the addition of lime juice, whipped egg white, and sugar, the resulting frothy concoction finally sprinkled with Angostura Bitters. Ambrosia indeed.

Local custom has it that one begins dinner with ceviche, a raw fish dish. The firm white flesh of corvina is cut into bite-sized chunks and marinated in lime juice with chopped coriander leaves and little chilli peppers until the fish becomes opaque. The result is both devilishly hot and icily refreshing. For a hangover, one drinks the juices alone, and this is called "*leche del tigre,*" or tiger's milk, and one does indeed feel quite ferocious after it. Aji de gallina (chicken), or lomo (beef) saltado served with papas (potatoes) a la Huancaina were our favourite dishes, so fiery with chilies that our palates had to be soothed with suspiro Limeno—a rather boring pudding, but we loved the name, which meant "sighs of Lima," so we ordered it anyway.

However, we could not just eat and drink. Quite apart from Jennifer's doubts, I also wondered if I would be able to build up a prosperous operation in such unpromising surroundings. When I met the small, demoralised group gathered in the shabby IOS office, I knew I had a major job on my hands. My first move was to relocate the local branch manager back to Canada. Next I had to find new premises.

On the outskirts of town, we were delighted to find pretty residential districts with wide, tree-lined avenues and colonial-style houses. In one of these, San Isidro, we were shown a large house flanked by embassies and close to the country club. Although number 120, Avenida los Andes was too big for us as a family and too big for the office, it would be ideal for both purposes. The ground floor, with its imposing entrance hall, reception rooms, dining room, kitchen, and smaller salons, would make perfect offices and entertainment facilities. Upstairs there was loads of room for us, with bedrooms, bathrooms, a playroom, and den, plus a wide covered terrace that we thought would be ideal for rainy days—until we discovered that it never rained in Lima. In fact, our new Pontiac was delivered without windscreen wipers! The large walled garden would be a paradise for the children, and their mother immediately insisted that it should be their domain. However, I would be allowed to give parties there in the evenings. In front of the house was a patio where an ancient fig tree stood—which, we were assured by the agent, had been planted by Pizarro himself. Hmm.

Now everybody cheered up. The boys were delighted with their new home, and at last all their toys, records, and books could be unpacked. Jennifer was so busy finding a full domestic staff that she had no time to worry about anything else. She was greatly helped by Hilda Mørck, the wife of the Danish Consul General, who told her that a *mayordomo* was essential in Lima, quite apart from a nanny, cook, maids, washer woman, and gardener. Fortunately an agency supplied us with trained people, all of whom seemed to know exactly what to do, so the house soon ran on oiled wheels. This was a lifestyle I had not seen since my childhood in Asia, but how quickly one can become re-accustomed to it!

My own initial task was to install some enthusiasm as well as product knowledge and sales psychology into my small group of South American businessmen, Lebanese, Italians, Germans, Swedes, French, Brits, Hungarians, and Swiss—all potentially good men but poorly trained and unmotivated.

I hired secretaries and turned the main dining room into a training room, covering its long table with green baize. We put up a large blackboard and propped a velvet-covered board on an easel, where the girls logged each man's output daily, to stimulate a competitive spirit. At the end of my first meeting, my own enthusiasm seemed to infect the group, and I had the pleasure of seeing the men talking excitedly as we toasted to a new beginning.

Hard work lay ahead—not only for the group, but mainly for me. Between individually training each man, accompanying each on client visits, plus giving group training sessions two or three evenings a week—which often lasted until midnight—my days were pretty exhausting, but we did not have to wait long for results. Within six weeks, we celebrated our first $1.2 million month—even outperforming Buenos Aires, to my own personal delight. I should point out that there was never any malicious jealousy if one area produced more than another, as in the end everyone benefited when the company prospered.

Now I had to select a few supervisors and teach them how to recruit and train. As a result, it wasn't long before IOS Peru, with new men in the interior cities—Arequipa and Casa Grande, Chimbote and Chiclayo, Iquitos and Tacna, for example—grew to more than sixty people.

The launch of IOS's Fund of Funds was proving to be an enormous success and considerably boosted sales everywhere. This innovative investment vehicle was the brainchild of Cornfeld and Cowett. The basic idea of a mutual fund was, of course, to pool your money with thousands of other investors to obtain maximum diversification, at the same time enjoying the benefits of top professional management. The IOS Fund of Funds carried this idea one step further: clients invested in a carefully selected portfolio of top performing mutual funds, thus offering unprecedented diversification and a wealth of the best management forces world-wide.

The professional establishment initially laughed at this innovation and predicted failure. Ten years later, most major banks had copied us, and after another twenty years the concept was taken even further by the creation of "Fund of Funds of Funds" and "Fund of Funds of Hedge Funds." IOS thus turned out to be a true pioneer in the investment fund industry.

As business grew in Lima, my new concern was that the competitive spirit within the group was becoming too intense and I realised some fun and games were called for. Jennifer's sister Susan was staying with us, and helped us lighten things up with several garden parties, to which wives or girl friends were invited. At the first party, couples began to dance after dinner and a waltz was called for. Surprised, I dug out a Strauss record, only to find that in South America "*un valsecito*" has absolutely nothing to do with Vienna!

Jennifer organised small dinner parties of six or eight until each and every local IOSer and his wife or partner had been invited. We formed a bowling club, where couples vied happily with each other. Bernard Zutter, a Swiss who had lived in Peru most of his life, organised a car rally for me, as I knew neither the terrain nor the history required to devise clues We were about thirty cars, each with a driver and a navigator. Every car was given the first clue and shot off to the second rallying point, where the next clue was to be found—a motorised treasure hunt, in fact. We zigzagged across the Peruvian desert from small village to hamlet. After hours of planning, Zutter had drawn up a fiendishly difficult course, but fortunately, not all the clues required local knowledge. At one point, participants had to catch a fly. Such is the incipient entrepreneurship of urchins that, after watching silently as cars screeched up outside their small village, the occupants leaping about in search of flies, by the time the last cars arrived, a queue of lads offered jam jars buzzing with annoyed flies for sale to these mad foreigners. Susan was my partner, and to our surprise we came second. A great time was had by all, friendships were formed, and slowly the atmosphere in the office became less cut-throat, and the famous IOS camaraderie reigned.

Another source of pride was the IOS Foundation, a charitable organisation where a percentage of our profits was invested every year. Substantial sums were made available to Africa, Asia, and South America, with emphasis on child welfare. Through direct cash grants and the efforts of IOS personnel and families, support was given to 155 humanitarian projects in fifty-five countries during the first five years of operation.

In 1964 I was invited to the annual Managers' Conference in Geneva, along with my top branch managers. To my dismay, I discovered upon arrival that I was to address hundreds of supervisors and junior managers at four daily sessions held in the Intercontinental, which had been taken over by IOS for the event. I just wished I had been given some time to prepare.

Fortunately, all was not hard work, as every evening social activities were held in Bella Vista, the ex-Colgate mansion on the lake, which was now our entertainment and public relations centre. At the end of the week, regional managers were individually interviewed by Bernie Cornfeld, Allen Cantor, and Ed Cowett—affectionately known as the Three Cs. At my interview I was promoted to general manager and given the additional territories of Chile, Bolivia, Ecuador, and Paraguay. I was now in charge of five countries, four of which in the same sad state that I had found Peru upon my arrival. Of course I was elated, but I was also somewhat daunted by the hard work and travel ahead. As I left the room with all these new responsibilities heavy on my shoulders, Bernie called out, "Courage. Just think of all those stock options you will add to your kitty!"

Back in Lima, before I could get my teeth into my new responsibilities, Peruvians in my group invited Jennifer and me on a trip out to the deserts of Huancayo, where there was an Incan burial ground—not a royal one with gold and emeralds, which would have been guarded even in those relaxed days, just the graves of a small settlement.

We drove for hours and stopped in the middle of sand dunes, where the road suddenly ran out. Here patient Indians squatted on their haunches under the meagre shade of skeletal trees. After long confabulations with our Peruvian friends and much sighing, they hauled themselves to their feet and led us deep into the desert. It would appear that the money they would earn for guiding us was not of much importance, when weighed against the effort involved.

After some trudging over the arid, wind-scraped landscape, they began to thrust long metal rods down into the sand. When a chink sounded as the rod met something hard, we were told to draw back and turn our heads away as otherwise the spirits of the dead would remove the buried bodies from our foreign eyes.

We listened to the sound of digging behind our backs with mounting curiosity, until we were told we could turn around. At the bottom of a hole lay an entire skeleton, complete with hanks of long tangled black hair. Strips of leathery tattooed skin clung to its forearms, and in the ghastly grin of the long dead, a few yellow fang-like teeth remained. It lay curled in a foetal position, just as it had been laid to rest all those centuries ago. Small pots around the bones held beans and red (coral?) bracelets with pieces of cloth, intricately woven, the colours still bright. One of the Indians held up a skull that had clearly been trepanned. Our friends translated that if the hole in the skull was open, the trepanation had caused death, but if the hole appeared to have closed, the patient would have survived. This seemed an extremely unpleasant procedure to us, without anaesthesia or any form of hygiene, probably just a rusty knife. Our friends thought a mixture of coca leaves and alcohol would have been used to dull the pain, but still we shuddered.

Each grave was carefully closed before another was found, and in total we must have seen five or six. As we waited between excavations, we sat on the hard sand, whipped by gritty winds, burnt by the sun, and subdued by the eerie atmosphere, surrounded as we were by skulls and discarded bones where ancient grave robbers had been at work. At one point, as we waited, Jennifer sat cross-legged in the shelter of a small hillock, idly rubbing at a large lump of hard sand. As the sand crumbled away beneath her fingers, she realised it had encased a piece of pottery. With rising excitement, she carefully rubbed until a beautiful little pot emerged, with two curved handles and black-and-white painted designs still clear on the terracotta. It is a simple little pot, one of hundreds of thousands and of no intrinsic value, but it has followed us around the world, a lasting reminder of an unforgettable day.

Immediately upon our return to Lima, we found that a party had been arranged to celebrate my promotion to general manager. During the obligatory speeches, I announced that I was appointing Michel Gantous to be Regional Manager for Peru, to take care of the day-to-day business whilst I was away involved with my new territories. I was nervous about this, but I could not be in two places at once—and, as it turned out, Michel did a good job and IOS Peru continued to thrive.

56

Bolivia

My first trip was to Bolivia. I took the Braniff "Scenic Flight" from Lima to La Paz and was fascinated to fly past the volcanoes with their romantic names remembered from my childhood geography lessons. Our pilot took us so low over Lake Titicaca that Indians in woven reed boats were clearly to be seen, navigating between a myriad of small islands. A seven-course luncheon with as many wines was served during the flight, which ended as we gazed at the stunning beauty of Mt. Illimani's 7,000 metres, with La Paz nestling against it at a mere 4,000. I sat next to a jolly medical doctor whose parting words were, "I hope you have a strong heart, Juan, after this feast. We shall land at the airport at 4,700 metres, which is about the height of Mont Blanc. You will find the air very thin, so don't run!" During my stay this advice was to be repeated by every single person I met.

Waiting for me at the airport were Guy Goulet, Mario Granado, and their team of about fifteen associates, who whisked me off to yet another Hotel Crillon, where a meeting room had been reserved. With no time to even think about the lack of oxygen, I launched into my pitch of the IOS principles and procedures, just as I had done in Lima.

La Paz

The meeting went well, then off we sped through the streets of La Paz, to a typical Bolivian restaurant where an enormous dinner had been ordered which I certainly did not need after the copious lunch on Braniff. Afterwards, trying to hide the altitude-induced fatigue, I sat through speeches from everyone present, all swearing to triple their volume by the end of the year—a good beginning indeed.

As we strolled back to the hotel, I had time to notice the features of the Alti-Plano Indians we passed on the streets, with their Mongolian-like high cheek bones, narrow eyes, very red cheeks and enormous chests. Nature must have given them all these traits to combat the hardships of life in the High Andes. I was beginning to wish I had larger lungs too.

Next morning I felt rather sluggish, and it took me longer than usual to get myself showered and dressed. No headaches however. Guy fetched me after breakfast, and off we went to Potosi, famous for its tin mines, where a large population of foreign mining engineers awaited us—all good prospects with their large salaries and absolutely nothing to spend them on.

I did not envy them their posting. At 4,700 metres, it was a tough place to work. Even the cars had to have special engines to combat the lack of oxygen, and under every hotel bed there was an oxygen bottle for those who woke up with breathing difficulties. One's memory was also affected. Goulet and I visited one of his clients, the manager of a tin mine who gave Guy a cheque for $50,000 to be invested in the IOS Fund of Funds. It was only when we were back in the office that Guy realised the cheque was unsigned. The next morning he drove back to the mine, only to find that the poor manager had died during the night. If only he had remembered to sign, IOS would have honoured his application and his family would have benefited accordingly.

Our next stop was Oruro, another mining camp, this time at a mere 4,000 metres. Here we checked into the Swiss Inn, whose sole connection to Switzerland was its name. We were the only guests, and the Bolivian owner took our dinner order himself, promising to bring us a good red wine. The bottle he brought was undrinkable, and I asked him if he had anything a little older.

At this he grew red in the face with indignation. "How dare you accuse me of selling old wines! All my wines are as fresh as the food!"

In Oruro we managed to close some decent sales and also recruited a promising German engineer. I gave him basic training and Guy promised to keep an eye on him. Subsequently he generated good business for us in this unpromising mountain backwater.

The next day we went down to Cochabamba to meet about six associates, and then continued down to tropical Santa Cruz, where I trained and boosted the spirits of a small group. So all in all I left Bolivia feeling some good groundwork had been laid.

I have to admit that my job was greatly helped by the news printed in the monthly IOS Bulletin, which every Associate read avidly. Our world-wide sales were increasing by leaps and bounds and we were becoming a household name for financial success.

Peron & Stroessner meeting in Asuncíon

57

PARAGUAY

My next stop was Asuncion, the capital of Paraguay. The streets into town from the airport were lined with huge billboards of President Alfredo Stroessner, whose blown-up features and stern gaze loomed over every street, reminding me of the ubiquitous posters of Trujillo in the Dominican Republic.

Stroessner was the son of German immigrants. Born in 1912, at thirty-six he became the youngest General in South America. In 1954 he declared himself President of Paraguay, and was re-elected in eight successive, fraudulent elections. His reign of terror was to last thirty-six years, during which thousands of Paraguayans were tortured and executed. Another South American dictator to be feared and avoided.

One heard Guarani, the local Indian language everywhere, but as Spanish was obligatory in all schools I had no problem. At first glance, the view from my hotel room appeared to be of a vast ocean, but in actual fact turned out to be endless pampas grass, blue and billowing to the horizon. Paraguay, of course, is landlocked.

I met the small group of eight associates and gave them my usual pep talk and training sessions. By now I had it all down pat, but as my own enthusiasm was as infectious as ever, it always seemed to work.

A few days later, Goulet took me into the interior where he had to meet a client. Afterwards we drove for hours through rather monotonous country until we stopped on the shores of a stunning lake, where there was a large settlement of

Mennonites. Grave, bearded men explained that their Christian sect was similar to the Quakers or Amish people. The men wore wide-brimmed hats, the women white bonnets and long cotton dresses, and the children wore identical miniature outfits. Most spoke a weird old German dialect, which I understood only with great difficulty. Their simple life amidst such natural beauty had quite an appeal after my hectic plane-hopping, so it was with some regret that I left them to return to Asuncion.

That night I met Tony Fiddes, the Panamanian Consul General, a most genial character who promised to channel prosperous potential clients Goulet's way. He invited us both to join him on his launch the following day for a jaunt up the Parana.

Just after dawn we met Tony on the banks of the river. He was equipped with a couple of pistols that his diplomatic status permitted him to carry. There was a crew of two, and a captain who could not possibly have had consular dispensation, but nevertheless sported a sidearm. As soon as we were on board, Tony drew our attention to a large Red Cross box that was clamped to the middle of the deck, remarking casually, "You'll never know when you'll need this." And I had thought we were just going fishing!

For the first hour or two we drank coffee, smoked, and chatted as we idled upstream. I remarked on the lack of proportion between the women one saw everywhere and the scarcity of men. Tony nodded. "Most of 'em were wiped out in the Chaco wars." I had never heard of these, so he explained: "Since the nineteenth century, there have been land disputes between Paraguay and Brazil over the huge Chaco region. Skirmishes sometimes turned into full-scale war, and over 100,000 Paraguayans lost their lives. In 1938 there was a peace treaty, but by then fifty percent of the male population of Paraguay had been lost, and so to this day there are still more women than men."

Soon we turned into a small tributary of the Parana and continued chugging along past dense rain forest along both banks. We came to a bend in the stream and saw Indian women dressed only in loin-cloths with white stripes daubed on their cheeks and foreheads, and blue tattoos down their arms. Thick shiny black hair hung to their waists, and many carried babies slung in shawls on their backs. They appeared most welcoming and, siren-like, beckoned us ashore, chattering away amongst themselves in some dialect that had nothing to do with Guarani or Spanish. Our Paraguayan deckhand understood a few words and soon let out a yelp of laughter. We asked him to translate. "The women are willing to remove their loin cloths for photographs in exchange for a few dollars and a cooking pot."

Although they were far from beauties, we were all good sports and the bargain was sealed. We took the money and cooking pot ashore, and the now entirely naked women examined our watches, fingered our shirts, and admired the pistols.

Suddenly there was a sound of crashing through the undergrowth, and onto the small beach stormed what we presumed to be the tribal chief. He wore a short skirt, rather like a tutu, made of white feathers, was enormously fat, and had white and blue paint all over his face giving him a rather disconcerting aspect. He shouted at us and gesticulated wildly, so we imagined it was time to leave—until our deckhand was again reduced to laughter. "He wants one dollar to take off *his* skirt."

So much for the noble savage protecting the virtue of his womenfolk. We declined his kind offer, which simply infuriated him. He shook his fists even when we threw him a few dollars anyway. The deckhand reported that the chieftain was going to call his men to beat us up if we did not depart immediately. However, the women did not agree with this plan and tried to detain us, even attempting to jump in the launch. But we managed to leave with as much dignity as we could muster as we repelled the amorous boarders.

When we finally managed to cast off and were about ten metres from the shore, the chief, now with a bow and arrow, shot at us in his rage. Fortunately he missed us, but several arrows embedded themselves in the deck. The hands examined the arrowheads and told us that most were not poisoned, but one or two were smeared with a substance that, though not deadly, would nevertheless put a man to sleep for ten hours or so.

Half an hour later we passed another settlement up river where six or seven men with blow pipes as well as bows and arrows stood on the river bank and stared at us impassively. We did not make eye contact, and under their expressionless gaze turned the launch around and went back where we had come from, blow pipes being more than we had bargained for.

We knew that we would have to pass the Indian settlement again on our way back to Asuncion, and sure enough we soon saw our chieftain still prancing up and down, still yelling with fury. All the women had disappeared. As we came closer, Tony fired a few shots in the air, which would have scared the pants off him had he been wearing any. Thankfully he shot no more arrows in our direction.

That evening, safe in the arms of the Crillon, we relived our adventures over several bottles of wine, with the women becoming lovelier and our danger greater by the glass.

Now that I had met all our associates, I left for Lima the next day, feeling assured that, with such a basic foundation, Paraguayan business could only grow. I promised to visit three or four times a year.

58

CAJAMARCA - PERU

After having abandoned my small family for awhile, I kept my promise that we should see something more of Peru than just Lima. I had heard a lot about Cajamarca, an ancient city high up in the Andes at over 3,000 metres. We boarded a small DC-3 and flew off with two very excited little boys and one terrified Peruvian nanny, who had never flown before.

We circled a primitive airfield surrounded by snowy peaks, and even from the plane we could see that between the runway and the small airport building there was nothing but a sea of mud. The air hostess encouraged us to disembark, and at the foot of the gangway we found a bare-chested, barefoot Indian giant who insisted on carrying the passengers, one by one, to the small terminal. Fortunately we were only about fifteen people. John and Nick were slung each under an arm, which they thought was tremendous fun, but nanny Flora refused to be touched until she realised that her white shoes and stockings would be ruined if she insisted on wading through on her own. Jennifer and I, and the other adult passengers, found it all most amusing and a new experience. The women were carried like babies, and we men were slung over our ferryman's shoulder in a fireman's lift.

Our hotel was unheated and it was bitterly cold after the mild climate of Lima, so my first task was to find some electric heaters and more blankets. Then we set off to explore.

The city had been built over an old Indian town that had grown up near thermal springs on the ancient overland route to Iquitos, a jungle town on the Amazon. Now there were only a few ruins left of the settlement where Atahualpa, the last ruler of the great Empire of the Incas, had lived and met his death.

In 1533, the Spaniard Pizarro, still on his endless search for El Dorado, entered Cajamarca. The natives had no knowledge of Spanish treachery, and Atahualpa with 4,000 of his unarmed men, greeted the foreigners with courtesy. However, when an interpreter made the Inca king understand that he was to become a Christian and swear allegiance to Carlos V of Spain, Atahualpa threw the bible he had been given to the ground and turned to leave. At a signal from Pizarro, the hidden Spanish troops now surged into the town square and a massacre ensued, decimating the Indians.

Atahualpa was taken prisoner and, despite the fact that sacks of gold were brought by his subjects to appease the Spaniards, they would not release him, always hoping for more. Finally, after months of captivity, Atahualpa gave in and allowed himself to be baptised. Then the perfidious Spaniards half-strangled him and threw him into an airless cell (which still stands today), and told the Indians to fill it to the roof with gold. Somehow they managed to do this, not realising that their king was held there, so in effect he drowned in the very gold his people brought to save him.

We stood in this small stone cell where poor Atahualpa had been crushed to death and marvelled at the cruelty of the avaricious Spaniards. We did not tell the children the grisly details, just that the Indians had filled this room with gold. This did not interest them much. Had we said it had been filled with lollipops, they would have been much more impressed.

On our last day, to save the boys from any more incomprehensible history, we drove into the surrounding countryside. Here in the high valleys were the market gardens that supplied Peru's arid coastal regions with cereals, fruit, and vegetables. Cattle were grazing, and the children were entranced to see their first cows being milked in the middle of green fields by Incan women in voluminous, brightly coloured petticoats and black bowler hats. Apparently whenever a new skirt was acquired, it was worn on top of the old ones, which accounted for the balloon-like effect. Each woman would tie the hind legs of a cow together then squat down to milk it. The women had brown, wrinkled faces and all were chewing and spitting coca leaves as they chattered like magpies and their numerous offspring larked about.

It was hard to drag the boys away, but we lured them with the thought of boarding another plane. Soon we were back in Lima, the children disappointed that no kind giant carried us to customs.

59

Ecuador

Back in Lima I took up the reins from Michel, but because all was flourishing in Peru, I could soon leave for Quito, Guayaquil, and the old interior town of Cuenca with a good conscience.

Quito, the capital of Ecuador (almost as high as La Paz), is set in a deep valley surrounded by high mountains, themselves dominated by the amazingly green Pichincha volcano at 4,000 metres. I was to find Quito's climate most agreeable, with a steady noon temperature of twenty degrees C. It is the oldest of all South American cities, and still bears traces of both its Incan and Spanish colonial past. Pilots hate to land and take off in Quito, as flying around the deep funnel of the valley between the mountains is treacherous, with little space and sudden upsurges of wind currents.

For several days I worked with Bob Brown, the local branch manager, training his group of about twelve before flying down to the coastal town of Guayaquil, infamous for its muggy, humid, mosquito-ridden climate, but also known for what might be the best lobster in the world, thanks to the Humboldt Current.

The IOS Branch Manager of Guayaquil was an ex-captain and pilot of the Rumanian Air Force, and the proud possessor of a gleaming white Beechcraft that flaunted the IOS logo in large gold letters. This charming madman piloted me on a hair-raising trip first to Salinas and then on to Manta. Our final leg was a white-knuckle flight into the high Indian mountain town of Cuenca, during which we swooped down to rivers and flew low over the water before swerving up at the last moment before crashing into a mountain. The Rumanian told me proudly that these were the fighter skills he had acquired whilst bombing Stalingrad when his country had been an ally of the Germans. All I could think of was that he would have to fly me back again.

Finally and reassuringly, on a regular flight back to Lima, I decided that, for the time being, I had had my fill of high Indian mountain towns, however charming they were with their little white churches silhouetted against deep blue skies and dark green volcanoes. I looked forward to my next stop, Chile, the most prosperous country in my area.

60

Bill

Whilst I had been away, Jennifer's father had flown out from England to keep her and the children company. He told me that he had arrived after the boys had gone to sleep, and had woken the next morning to find the two of them, solemn and silent, at the end of his bed. This unknown grandfather was a curiosity. He did not speak Spanish. John and Nick's English was pretty rudimentary, as we had always insisted that the children spoke the language of wherever we were living. This was to stand our sons in good stead later on, but it was disconcerting for Bill and Beth, who were typical English monoglots and not multilingual. However, Bill was great with children, and each taught the other songs and games, to much hilarious laughter.

Bill's attempts to communicate in Spanish were always comical. Armed with his dictionary, he had pointed to an exotic bird in the garden and asked the gardener, "What is that?"

The man had pushed his straw hat to the back of his head, looked pityingly at this slow foreigner, and replied with care, "That is a yellow bird, Señor."

Bill had more luck with Flavio and Aida, however. On going into the kitchen one afternoon, I found the two with handkerchiefs held high over their heads, each with one hand jauntily on a hip, demonstrating La Marinera, a local folk dance, to an entranced audience of two small boys and their grandfather. Unfortunately they stopped with apologies and blushes as soon as they saw me, and nothing would induce them to continue despite my pleas.

During the day, Jennifer took her father to Pachacamac and up some of the many small pyramids until his legs gave out. He was fascinated, but between the heat and his health, he had to give in, much to his disgust. Before he left, as a final treat, some of the chaps who had fallen for his old-fashioned charm thought he ought to see some of Lima's night life. After dinner we took Bill to a club specialising in "exotic dancing." It was late, there had been a lot of wine. and Bill dozed off during the show. At one point, a young mulatto woman wearing a sequinned G-string and nothing else gyrated a couple of inches from the old boy's nose. Everyone thought it a pity he should miss this highlight, and somebody shook Bill awake. He opened his eyes, took one look, said, "Very nice, Dear," and went back to sleep. We often wondered if he thought he had dreamt it all.

On his return to wet and dreary Huntingdon, his Air France plane had engine trouble and the passengers, crew, and plane had to wait in Guadeloupe in the West Indies for spare parts. He cabled us his delight at this extra treat of three days in the island sun, and we could quite believe that he would have sabotaged the plane himself in order to prolong his holiday, had he known how. His descriptions of deserted white beaches and the mixture of French and West Indian cuisine made us decide to take ourselves and the children there at the first opportunity. But first I had to visit my biggest hope—Chile.

61
CHILE

Santiago de Chile was, for me, love at first sight. It seemed to combine the gaiety of South America with European order, all in breathtaking landscapes. Chile has a coastline of some 7,000 kilometres, from the dry deserts bordering Peru and Bolivia, down past rivers, lakes and lush central valleys, to the deep south, where the Antarctic ice regions begin. Like a backbone, the high mountains of the Cordillera run from north to south, where hikers hike and skiers ski. Everywhere good food and music add to the charm of Chile's natural beauty.

Our manager in Santiago was a charming American, Ray Grasty, who lived with his Chilean wife, Martha, and their seven impeccably behaved children in a large, rambling house on an exclusive golf course. The Grastys were golf-mad. Another of Ray's passions was flying, as he had been a fighter pilot in W.W.II and later the chief pilot of Panagra Airways. He left this for his third passion—IOS.

Our meetings always took place in the wood-panelled library of his country club, where I met his group of twenty associates, who were already producing a respectable volume of business. Nevertheless, Ray and I managed to double their sales volume within six months, thus bringing Peru and Chile right on the heels of Brazil.

I made many trips to Chile because of its importance, and once in a while Jennifer came with me, when friends could stay in our house with the children. We especially enjoyed the company of our lawyers, Don Eugenio Perez Cotapos, Chief General Counsel of Kennecott Copper Mines and General Motors, and Don Sergio Diez, then Speaker of the House of the Chilean Parliament, both of whom invited us to many great dinners—although at one (which I thought would be my last) I suffered a terrible reaction to some sea urchins that I was foolhardy enough to eat. I spent that night having my stomach pumped in hospital.

This little contretemps nearly caused us to miss the Italian liner MS Donizetti, which we had chosen for our return to Lima from Valparaiso. When we boarded, I was up and about but still not entirely fit. We stopped at Arica and Antofagasta, and in both ports went on hunts for lavatory paper, as on board only torn-up bits of paper, stapled together, were provided. Unfortunately, all we could find for sale were neatly cut squares of newspaper fastened together with loops of string, but as these did not seem much of an improvement, we politely declined, pretending we were looking for something else entirely so as not to cause offence.

The voyage took five days, and amongst the passengers we found a charming German gentleman who turned out to be Dr. Oetker, the famous industrialist and ship owner who knew my Rickmers and Jebsen & Jessen families well.

Upon our return to Lima, I found a letter from Wolfgang, the twenty-four-year-old stepson of my uncle Peter Rickmers, who had written to ask me for career advice. He kept my reply dated, May 20, 1964, in which I wrote, "If you belong to that category of average European men who dream of security, steady income, and a monotonous life, I do not recommend that you join IOS. If, however, you belong to the small percentage of ambitious young men who are filled with a powerful ambition to achieve success and prosperity before becoming too old to enjoy them, then I definitely suggest that you join us."

At his request, I arranged for him to participate in one of the monthly training classes held at the head office in Geneva. Subsequently he worked under Ray Grasty in Chile, as Santiago and southern Chile have large German-speaking communities where he could flourish, and he did. In 1969 he moved to Spain to work as a resident manager under Marty Seligson, the President of Indevco, our successful IOS Real Estate Division. Indevco was building thousands of apartments ("Playamar") and villas ("El Rosario"), both developments on the Costa del Sol, as well as thousands of luxury apartments in Florida. Indevco also conceived and promoted the New York World Trade Center, with models of the Twin Towers standing in our Geneva HQ as well as in the lobby of "our" hotel, the Intercontinental.

Being part of the IOS family was exciting. We were all making excellent money and our clients were euphoric. New products made selling easier to old clients and enticed new ones. The men who loved IOS were an independent breed who needed to work alone, unhampered by bureaucracy, in places of their own choice. Of course, if a man moved up to management, he had to cope with paper work and stick to his assigned territories. but the normal associate could work at his own pace, leave the boring stuff to us, and have the world as his oyster. Contests and competitions kept everyone on their toes long after all their bills had been paid, and there was constant excitement and fun so that even now, four decades later, IOSers, when they meet, reminisce about the old days and probably bore their wives to tears.

Our flagship products were now the Fund of Funds (FOF); our International Investment Trust (IIT) and our Research Investors Corporation (RIC), the latter then managed by the now famous Sir John Templeton, a member of the IOS Board of Directors. Incorporated within the IOS Investment Program were the Dreyfus and Fidelity Funds. Our in-house International Life Insurance Company (ILI), with insurance companies in the U.K., Luxembourg, Australia, Kenya, and Argentina, offered a wide range of straight as well as term life insurance policies. At the same time, we could open bank accounts for our clients in our own banks, such as the Overseas Development Bank in Geneva or our Orbis Bank in Germany. This facility was especially attractive to clients in overseas territories, and we were fast becoming the most successful, complete financial planning company in the world at that time, with people forming queues to invest or work with us.

Amongst the many who approached me with view to a career in IOS was a Danish-Argentine friend from Buenos Aires, Jorge Andreasen, whom I had known as treasurer and comptroller of a large trading company. I put him under the wings of Ray Grasty in Chile, where he did well, ending up as co-manager/partner of our Argentine insurance company, Neptunia, back in BA.

Once I had visited all my territories, I understood their possibilities better. Apart from my own frequent visits to them, I called all my branch and regional managers to Lima for regular meetings, where they learnt of our future plans and consolidated their knowledge of our wide product range. It was satisfying to watch our constant and dramatic rise in sales volume.

In fact, business in my area grew so rapidly that in 1965 I received a telegram from the Board of Directors in Geneva, naming me IOS Manager of the Year. As there were regional offices in over a hundred countries at that time, this was indeed a gratifying reward for all our hard work. Now seemed a good time for a holiday.

62

GUADELOUPE

We chose the island of Guadeloupe, as not only did we have fond memories of the Caribbean but it made a convenient stopover for the trip I would have to make to Geneva for the annual IOS General Managers Meeting.

We stayed at the northern tip of the island, right on a sugar-white beach, the only hotel in a pretty bay. It was a small paradise. The boys spent their days dashing between the pools and the sea, with four-year-old John falling in love for the first time with an enchanting little French girl called Elisabeth, and Nick learning to swim. Nanny Flora was with us so that we too could enjoy six weeks of *dolce fa niente*—sipping planters' punches under tall palms and relishing the food, which was a tempting blend of Creole and French cooking served in the gardens at night to the sound of steel bands softly puttering in the moonlight.

One morning Jennifer and I lazily watched the arrival of a long, two-masted schooner into our bay. Learning it was available for charter, we took the boys for day trips to Martinique and the tiny island of Marie Louise. Sadly, both Nick and Nanny Flora got seasick, but young John, proudly, was not. We made friends with the young captain, a bearded Frenchman named Jacques, and his girlfriend from Martinique, appropriately called Joséphine. In the long warm nights we would sit on deck as Jacques caught lobsters, which Joséphine then grilled. Under a brilliant canopy of stars, gently rocked by the waves, we listened with rapt attention as Jacques filled us with tales of sunken treasure. His ambition was to discover the *Plata Flota*—the Spanish fleet of seventy-six vessels laden with plundered silver and gold, which had foundered in a hurricane somewhere close by. All ships, men, and cargo had been lost in these relatively shallow waters.

With the help of the moon and hurricane lamps, we pored over old maps, and slowly Jacques' enthusiasm became contagious and an idea was born. I would finance an expedition in which Jacques and several colleagues of his from the islands would try to make the dream come true. The next day I paid for one of his friends, an experienced deep-sea diver, ex-French Navy, to fly over from Fort de France, so that now we were five to plan our treasure hunt.

In order to pin-point the exact location of the *Plata Flota*, telegrams were sent to Jennifer's father, who (in those pre-Google days) was enchanted to spend days in the British Library digging out old maps and manuscripts. Considering the immense wealth this venture could bring, I was willing to finance the search and was only sad not to be a part of the actual fun. Reluctantly, in the middle of all this excitement, I had to fly off to Geneva for ten days, my head full of sunken bullion.

The moment I set foot in the Intercontinental, however, Spanish ships and treasure vanished from my mind as dreams will when confronted with reality. This life, my IOS life, was after all a dream come true in itself.

Above: Lima
Right: Guadeloupe
Below: Our Brazilian Garden/Aubi

63

GENEVA

As usual, the meetings were exhilarating. Managers from around the world told success stories as business soared to new heights. New banks had been created, new insurance companies acquired, and new offices opened across the globe. One of our biggest new markets was Germany, where Ossie Nedoluha, my old friend from our early Mexican days, managed over a hundred IOS offices.

When the next International Sales Contest was held, a new phenomenon occurred as busloads of eager Germans flocked to their closest IOS office, cash in hand, whilst special vehicles ferried their monies to Credit Suisse in Zurich, our depository of cash. Every new German associate was keen to enrol as many clients as possible before the end of the contest, so that each man, each branch, each regional office could be duly credited with this modern gold rush.

During these contests, everyone in the IOS world worked overtime. Additional staff had to be hired to help the secretaries cope with the pre-processing of the deluge of business. Word had spread that our investment program and family of funds gave better returns than banks and bonds, whilst at the same time offering safety and anonymity. Over the moon with all this good news we, the gathered general managers, ended the Geneva meetings as usual with a bash at Bella Vista. This year's theme was Rome, and we all had to come in toga. The gardens sloping down to the lake were lit by flaming torches, and gargantuan buffets were laid out under the trees. The gates were guarded by "centurions," unhappy in those silly skirts, and a bored lion roared intermittently from its cage in the middle of the great lawn.

Bernie strolled around, a genial word for everyone, glamorous film stars Julie Christie on one arm and Victoria Principal on the other, whilst Maria Felix sang to us in the background. At midnight, fireworks were let off from boats on the water, climaxing with the giant letters, I-O-S lighting up the sky. Sedate Geneva had never seen anything like it, and from their initial staid hostility toward anything new, now more and more Genèvois began asking when IOS was to go public and how could they buy shares.

As I so often did, I wished Jennifer were with me, but she was still with the children in Guadeloupe. Most of the European managers had their wives with them, but the chaps from overseas came alone. We formed a "bachelors corner," where Carlos Menendez from Venezuela, George Tregea from Brazil, Bill Masse from Tokyo, Malcolm Fox from Hong Kong, Bob Cameron from Thailand, Ward Griffin from Mexico, José Arechabala from Central America, and many others gathered, cracking jokes and planning mischief.

Before finally slipping off to bed, we serious young executives regressed to schoolboy pranks and ordered elaborate 6 a.m. room-service breakfasts for those friends of ours who had chickened out earlier, but would presumably be fast asleep at that hour. We crept along the corridors of the Intercontinental, switching around the shoes put out earlier in front of bedroom doors by more sober minds, to create havoc and pandemonium in the morning. It is a wonder we did not wake the entire hotel—including the security staff. But we could do no wrong in "our" hotel, and management closed their eyes to this unaccustomed juvenile behaviour. We were, after all, their best clients.

True to tradition, on our last evening we took a swing around Lac Léman aboard *La Suisse*, one of the famous paddle steamers, dancing and drinking before docking at Chateau Coudray. Following the ship's band, we walked through the beautiful park up to the chateau, where a superb dinner was served at midnight before coaches drove us back to Geneva. The next day, exhausted, I flew to Guadeloupe to join my little family and catch my breath.

I found three very brown and happy pumpkins. The minute Jacques caught sight of me, he rowed ashore and bounded over with requests for the promised $20,000 for deep-sea equipment, including a sand-removing vacuum cleaner and anti-shark guns. I was immediately back in treasure mode.

Too soon, however, we were at the airport facing an unexpectedly steep bill for excess baggage. Jennifer swore she had not bought a thing, but as we were late there was nothing for it but to pay up or lose the flight. Back in Lima, the mystery was solved. Nanny Flora, dazzled by the beauty of the fine coral sand, had filled the boys' beach buckets with it, wrapped them in plastic, and stuffed them into her suitcase. She wept when confessing to this, but she had been unable to leave all that white beauty behind, and wanted to show it to her parents—who naturally would never have seen such sand in Peru. All we could do was vow to check her bags in future *before* leaving for the airport.

64

NEW YORK, GENEVA AND RIO

In early 1966 I took Jennifer to New York for a short break. We stayed at the Sherry-Netherland and enjoyed the buzz of the big city, saw "*The Man of La Mancha*," with Richard Kiley, shopped deliriously, danced in the Rainbow Room whilst Eddie Fisher crooned, had dinner in the Four Seasons, lunched in the Russian Tea Room (where we insisted on choosing from the vast menu unaided, ending up with four courses of assorted blinis), and had a fantastic Indian meal at The Pierre. At the end of every evening, we would have a last drink in the Sherry-Netherland's night club, where couples shuffled around the minute dance floor to the soft crooning of a sultry singer and the beat of an excellent trio.

In the middle of all this fun, I received a call from the St. Regis, where Bernie was staying. I was to come over for a chat. I found him together with Ed Cowett, and Bernie greeted me with a bear hug. "Good to see you, Mr. South America!," he said. "We just added Brazil to your territories." I was stunned. "Obviously you will have to relocate to Sao Paulo and run everything from there."

My first thought was that I would be in charge of over 800 associates and managers in six countries. Quite a challenge. At the end of long discussions, Ed told me he was flying back to Geneva that afternoon and that he had given instructions to his driver to be at my disposal with the IOS limousine for as long as Jennifer and I were in New York—a nice touch. As we left together, Bernie beamed benignly at us both.

A few days later I had to fly from New York to Geneva for four days of meetings, during which my added responsibilities were discussed in detail. Jennifer, unused to the autumn weather, had come down with a frightful cold, and I was unhappy to see her fly back to Lima alone, feeling so beastly. Her flight stopped in Quito, and as the passengers trooped over the tarmac she passed out—a combination of her high temperature and the altitude. Perhaps, too, the coming move was more of an upheaval for her than I had realised. Having lived for so long like a nomad, one more country meant nothing to me, but I know Jennifer worried about the children's reactions.

From Geneva I flew to Rio for meetings with George Tregea, the current resident general manager of Brazil. We agreed that my take-over should be in September, when he himself was to become vice president of the South American desk in Geneva.

Back in Lima I wooed Jennifer with tales of our new posting, the beautiful houses I had seen, the *joie de vivre* of the Brazilians. I appointed Michel Gantous as general manager and, leaving Peru in his capable hands, decided to take Jennifer and the boys to Europe for six weeks before moving to Brazil.

65

EUROPE

We flew first to Switzerland to see my grandmother Rickmers in Clarens. She was by now a very old lady, unused to small children, however well-behaved, so we stayed in a hotel. I invited my mother and Dino to join us—they had been living in Florence for some years, and Mother had only seen her grandsons when both were babies. Now aged three and five, they were a constant source of amusement.

Once we took the cable car up Les Diablerets to show the boys their first snow. They were entranced, but so was Flora. Once again she vowed to take some snow back to her family, and my mother watched in disbelief as Flora filled plastic bags.

"Not heavy like sand, Sir," she pleaded. Knowing full well what would happen, I made no objections, and quite soon we all gathered round the poor girl to cheer her up when she found herself clutching dripping bags of water.

Dino and my mother, being tired, took the cable car back down to the lake earlier than we did. Probably the last to leave the mountain, the five of us sat, rather squashed, in a small cabin open to the elements, with only flimsy belts around our waists to stop us from falling out. Down we went, sailing over the tops of giant fir trees laden with snow, over ski trails and gorges. Suddenly, above a deep ravine, we jerked to a halt. Jennifer and I exchanged glances. We pointed out to the children everything there was to see, and for the first five minutes this was fine. Then we sang nursery rhymes and the boys joined in quite happily. After another good fifteen minutes, Flora sighed and said she needed to go to the bathroom. We assured her that just as soon as all the passengers had seen everything, we would continue our descent. She and the boys turned to peer up at the empty cars above us, thus causing the cabin to sway unpleasantly.

"There's nobody else there," little John remarked brightly. His mother and I had noticed this some time ago, and had not dared voice our fears that perhaps the men in charge had thought there were no more passengers and had gone home for the night. The sun was going down and a cold wind began to whip around our ankles causing more swaying. Jennifer and I were becoming increasingly concerned, and Nick began to whimper that he was freezing. One could see that John was too, but he was determined not to say so.

At long last there was a whirr overhead and as we held our breath the cabins began slowly to descend to base station. I was all ready to give the engineers a piece of my mind, but they were so apologetic that there was no need. They had neither forgotten us nor gone home—something mechanical had malfunctioned, and in those pre-cell phone days there was no way of communicating with us. Since that day I have avoided all cable cars and even developed a mild form of vertigo, but fortunately the children suffered no ill effects or traumas.

Our next stop was England—the highlight for Jennifer. Although her mother had come to Buenos Aires and her father to Lima, they had not seen much of each other in five years. She had not seen Elizabeth at all, and Susan only for a short stay in Lima. Bill and Beth were overjoyed to see us and entranced with our two little boys. The only flaw was linguistic—John and Nick's English was far from fluent, and their grandparents could hardly understand them.

"How could you, Jennifer?" Beth cried. "Why didn't you teach them English?"

We hung our heads in shame, but it had not seemed fair to teach them Danish and not English, or vice-versa, so we stuck mainly to the language of the countries they had been living in—Spanish. However, Beth cajoled Jennifer into promising to do something about this. It was going to be difficult, because my mother wanted them to speak German, and Dino insisted on Italian. Bill seemed to think that as long as he spoke slowly and clearly, they could not fail to understand him—a typical Englishman's reaction!

Our European trip was over too soon, and we faced the long flights back with some trepidation because although John and Nick were easy children, endless hours spent confined to a seat was a lot to ask of an active youngster. By the time we got to Panama, we had all had enough, so I decided we needed to spend a night in a proper bed. The next day, before catching our flight back to Lima, there was just enough time to show the boys the Panama Canal, where we were lucky enough to see an enormous atomic submarine glide through. Of course today, neither John nor Nick has a single memory of the entire trip!

66

Brazil

It was time for me to tackle the huge market of Brazil. A good organisation long established by George Tregea was up and running, with about 150 salesmen throughout that vast country. It was producing approximately U.S. $3 million a month—which, compared to the total of my other smaller territories, was really not all that impressive. Over time it was my firm intention to double the amount of associates and to quadruple the monthly volume.

I left alone for Sao Paulo to find a house and staff so that Jennifer and the children could follow directly into a home and avoid yet another long, unsettling hotel stay. I found a lovely place on the outskirts of Sao Paulo in Santo Amaro—Conde Deu number 10. It was a large, sprawling bungalow, with a separate guest house, mature gardens, and a pool. I inherited a chauffeur and cook from Tregea and bought his brand new big Mercedes, which, in those days in Brazil, was considered the height of luxury.

When the final touches had been made to the house, and a nanny had been employed (dear Flora did not want to leave her family), Jennifer arrived with John and Nick and our two Siamese cats—who, when released from their travel box, promptly jumped into the pool. So much for cats hating water.

After a few weeks of almost living in the pool, we enrolled the boys in a school run by Canadian nuns and prepared to settle down properly at last.

Happy days followed, full of satisfying work, trips all over Brazil to Manaus, Salvador de Bahia, Belo Horizonte, Rio, Brasilia, Curitiba, Floreanapolis, Porto Alegre,

Belem, Recife, and Fortaleza, and staying in touch with my old territories.

Socially we gave many parties, and visitors arrived from all over the world to stay in our guest house. We explored beautiful islands, such as Guaruja, off Santos, and often stayed in the elegant Samambaia Beach Club, where we sat on little bridges spanning the sparkling pools, gorging ourselves with small salty oysters, washing them down with icy champagne. We danced at the Tortuga Beach Club, where even my English Jennifer was carried away by the pulsating music and sambaed with me on the tables. The boys' favourite weekend break was the beach resort at Jequitimar, and we took them there as often as we could.

Although my Portuguese was not fluent and more of a mish-mash with Spanish, meetings went extremely well and I managed to kindle fresh enthusiasm from even the most experienced men. Soon volume increased by thirty percent, and when the IOS Winter Contest started, my area was consistently number one world-wide. As the Brazilians kept telling me, "*Brasil nao é um pais, é um continente!*"—Brazil is not a country, it's a continent. Perhaps this accounted for our success, although there were other giant areas too.

Into this satisfying scenario, disaster struck. Humberto de Alencar Castello Branco had been the military dictator of Brazil since 1964. He had abolished all political parties and ruled entirely alone with an iron fist. His word was law, and his spurious benevolence towards his sycophants was well known and ultimately feared.

In November, 1966, in a bolt out of the blue, Castello Branco issued a decree, retroactive for the past *three years,* declaring all foreign investment businesses illegal—to be shut down immediately. Naturally IOS, with its immense success, was the most prominent victim. We had been active in complete compliance with all the local laws for years. Tregea had openly advertised in the most prominent newspapers and serious journals whilst the enormous neon-lit letters, IOS, lit up the sky at the top of our office headquarters in Sao Paulo. Hardly underground activities.

Only in military dictatorships can such decrees be passed, retroactively, cancelling all their own rules and regulations. The execution of this decree was entrusted to the Brazilian Department of War. They immediately ordered the arrest for questioning of all personnel engaged in foreign investment companies. At noon on Nov. 7, the military police arm of the Brazilian Army declared a simultaneous "blitzkrieg" all over Brazil, presumably so that neither lawyers, embassies, nor influential friends could be appealed to.

At the time of this declaration, I was on a plane from Salvador de Bahia to

Recife with Fred Borlin, in charge of Rio and northern Brasil, on a trip through the northern territories to visit our offices. Neither of us had heard or read a word about the decree.

Upon arrival in Recife, we picked up our bags from the carousel and turned to find four military policemen, pistols drawn, standing behind us. To our bewilderment, we were handcuffed, shoved into a military jeep, and driven off to the military police prison in Recife. We were not allowed a single telephone call. We were locked up in solitary cells and kept in the dark, both physically and mentally. Even though I was convinced we would be released within hours, I worried that Jennifer would fret if I failed to call as usual upon arrival anywhere.

At first, both Fred and I thought there must just be some visa hiccup, but peering through the small opening in my cell door I could make out a table where a tripod machine-gun was manned by an alert military policeman. Guards passed to and fro, huge mulattos with submachine guns slung over their shoulders—heavy-duty stuff for consular problems.

Inedible meals were brought in by two guards, one holding the plate, the other pointing a submachine gun in my face. When I asked to speak to the commanding officer, they just laughed. As there was no sanitation at all except a disgusting hole in the ground, no paper, no water, I hardly ate. The temperature must have soared well over thirty-five degrees C., and the cell was infested with mosquitoes and cockroaches. At least the big spiders lurking in all corners ate the mosquitoes. I could handle all this. What I could not was being unable to call Jennifer, who probably thought by now that I was lost in a jungle plane crash.

There was a small hole in the wall at the top of my cell, which let in a little air. If I pushed my filthy pallet up close to it I could see out through the bars to a corner of a large yard. An officer strode by and I shouted, in my poor Portuguese, "I need to call my lawyer, my Embassy, my wife!" But he just laughed.

By the third day I was more than jittery. I had a wife and two children who relied on me, and who could have no idea where I was or what had happened to me. Did the head office in Geneva know? Was the Danish Embassy using diplomatic pressure for my release? Around and around my worries whirled in my overheated brain.

On the fourth day, an execution by firing squad was held on the big yard. I watched, horrified, as a row of men with rifles lined up in silence. A prisoner, blindfolded, was led to the wall. Hardly able to believe what I was seeing, I heard the order to fire, and a volley of shots rang out. The man remained upright! Had they all missed? Then an infuriated officer strode up, pulled off the man's blindfold, and cursed him for not pretending to die!

It had all been a sham, presumably for our benefit. When I say "our," it became apparent that Fred and I were not the only foreign investment managers being held. Even though communication was not allowed, Fred later told me he had heard whispered conversations in the cells on either side of his, between Swiss bankers as well as a pretty hysterical French banker.

A sergeant saw me peering through my bars, he laughed and yelled, "*Amanha é você!* Tomorrow is your turn!" How long were they going to continue with these games? When would the serious stuff begin?

The guards were actually good tempered—it was the officers who were scary. Fred Borlin was about twenty metres down the corridor from my cell, and from time to time we managed to exchange a few words. "How long will they keep us here ?" was a favourite, as well as, "They can't shoot us, can they?"

Each time we were caught talking, a guard would come thundering along in his great boots and slam his truncheon against the bars, screaming, "Silence or no food tonight," although they must have realised by now that I had hardly eaten since our incarceration. There was one decent guard who brought us tap water and sometimes milk as we lay sweltering in our cells.

One day Fred started banging against his door, yelling, "I'm getting out, one way or the other!"

I hissed back that it would be suicidal to try, as the machine gun was manned day and night. I tried to quiet him down, telling him that nobody had ever been shot for marketing mutual funds, but that an escaping prisoner was probably fair game. If we just sat tight, we were sure to be released. I needed my own reassurance, of course, as much as he did.

On the fifth day, an officer in charge of state security came and asked me for a list of all our Brazilian IOS clients. I told him that even had I wanted to, I could not remember any names as I made no personal sales and had no idea at all of the clients over the years under Tregea. He then ordered me to "command" Credit Suisse to release these names. I tried to explain that under no circumstances would a Swiss Bank divulge client names, due to Swiss bank secrecy laws. This concept was beyond him, even though the two Swiss must have tried to explain it to him also.

He came to my cell that afternoon, brandishing an electric cooking plate. "Once you sit on this when it's nice and hot, you will remember." But in actual fact we never were physically tortured or beaten. Fortunately for us, the many threats were empty, and looking back I don't think they quite knew what to do with us.

During those long, anxious days and nights, my main distraction became the planes I could often catch sight of through my hole in the wall. Could one be bringing an IOS lawyer from Geneva or a Danish Consular official flying to my aid? We still had not heard about the retroactive decree, about the nation-wide hunt for all investment counsellors of all foreign banks and investment houses, no idea that it was the Army that had "declared war" on us. I thought constantly of Jennifer and my boys, who had no idea where I was or even if I were alive. Nobody would speak to us.

An Interrogation Officer passed by once and remarked amiably to Fred, "You will stay here until you rot!"

After that Fred began yelling again. "If we are not out in three days I'll attack the guards when they bring us food—even if they kill me!"

By now I only kept hold of myself with difficulty. I had to face it: any government that locks up innocent people incommunicado in single cells with no access to the outside world; allows not a single phone call, stages fake executions, and makes endless threats, seemed capable of anything.

Suddenly, on the seventh day at 4 a.m., two soldiers with rifles and fixed bayonets shining in the corridor light, charged into my cell yelling, "Up, up, it's time!" Obviously I thought the end had come.

Fred and I were shoved into an army jeep with a guard on either side of us. We were driven to the Recife airport, where an old converted B-17 Brazilian Air Force bomber with about twenty passengers already on board waited on the runway. We were pushed into the cockpit with two secret service men to guard us. The captain announced over the intercom that we were going to fly to Rio through a complete eclipse of the sun at 10:30 a.m., and that the flight would take three-and-a-half hours. All we cared about was what our fates would be in Rio. Fred, whose Portuguese was much better than mine, asked our guards if we were to be released there. This caused much hilarity. "Oh, no—you be with us for long, long time."

We landed in Rio at noon and were immediately taken to the airport military police station, where we were each photographed with a number on our chest and the title "*Trafficantes en Dolares*"—black market Dollar traders. Little by little we were learning about Castello Branco's decree, and it seemed that he had now also made it illegal to buy or sell American dollars in the weird wonderland of the Brazilian economy. Presumably we were accused of this too! It is of interest to note that incredibly the black market rate began to be announced on television twice daily and published along with all other financial news in all the major newspapers—together with the source for buying these dollars!

Finally we were taken to the main military police prison on top of a hill, and it was my good fortune that my barred window looked straight onto the Christo, Rio's famous landmark. I found it very comforting. Here I had a hand-wash, if no soap, only another hole in the ground for waste, but paper at least—a luxury! Again I asked a passing officer when we could talk to a lawyer, our embassies (Fred was Swiss), and our families. His reply shot back, "Never."

Because of the rampant robberies on Brazil's streets, I always carried a U.S. hundred-dollar bill in my shoe, which had not been discovered in Recife. I befriended a corporal and offered him the money if he would call my wife in Sao Paulo and tell her that I was alive. He agreed, took the $100, and promised to call when off duty. He never did. However, a sergeant took pity on me and offered to call. I had nothing to give him, but he said, "God will thank me."

He did not let me down, and when Jennifer spoke to him this was the first news she had that I was alive, even if in a Rio prison. Poor girl, as she told me later, one of the worst things was her difficulty in understanding Brazilian Portuguese

After four more days a priest came to bless us, surely a sign that the end was near. Early the next morning we were led through a long dark corridor to two small soundproof underground rooms. Fred and I were again separated. In my room there were two military police guards and an interrogator. Were the long-dreaded torture sessions about to begin?

First came demands repeated over and over again for the IOS client list. Threats were made that if we did not divulge at least the names of a few hundred clients, we would be sent back to the Recife prison to rot forever.

Hours later, or so it seemed, I continued to deny any knowledge of individual client names. This was actually true, as I had only been in Brazil for a few months, and it was my job to lead, not sell. Then I was asked to sign a statement that I was aware of the fact that I had "wilfully damaged the economy of the United States of Brazil." They carefully explained that such a charge entailed long prison sentences, perhaps up to twenty years. With relish they informed me that few people survive more than five or six years in their hard-labour camps, and that escape was impossible as I would be in the middle of a deep jungle that would "eat you up." Still I did not sign, as that would have been an admission of guilt, and I knew that

I had done nothing wrong.

Thirst became a pressing problem, and was also used as a weapon. I was told that Fred had been co-operative, providing some useful names, had been given a cold beer, and would have his sentence shortened. Obviously they told Fred the same thing about me.

Suddenly there was a commotion in the corridor. The door was flung open and a colonel, whom we later knew to be Fiusa, deputy chief of Brazilian National Security, marched in. The guards jumped to their feet and saluted in awe.

Colonel Fiusa sat down, glared at me, and barked in English, "You are free to go, but you are not allowed to leave the *Territorio Nacional.* You will be further investigated, and you will be under constant surveillance. You will report to my office in Rio every week to prove that you are still here. Any attempt to leave Brazil will be severely punished."

Upon this he strode out. The guards saluted him then quick-marched Fred and me out to the street—and there we were, two bearded, dirty, thirsty, and hungry "vagabonds," suddenly breathing in the hot balmy air of Rio, which seemed as exhilarating as champagne to us.

We were so elated that we charged to the first bar (fortunately we were in a poor district or we would never have been served) and, with Fred's last cash, ordered the ice-cold beers we had been dreaming about. I placed a reverse-charges call to Jennifer, and Fred to his girlfriend Maria. After tears of joy and relief, Jennifer told me to immediately contact Ed Coughlin (an IOS lawyer) and Jerry Berkin (head of IOS Security) at the Copacabana Palace Hotel. Elated that help had arrived, we raced there in a taxi with Fred's last cruzeiros. Not surprisingly the door man would not let us in, and only after Ed Coughlin came down and talked to the manager were we allowed to enter this sanctum sanctorum.

In the elevator, Ed told us that stories of "foreign parasites" siphoning "trillions of dollars" out of Brazil "to harm the economy" had been running in the national news for days. Unfortunately, many foreign papers—including the German, Danish, and Italian press—had naively translated verbatim these distorted articles. It was balm to our wounded spirits to talk to men who knew that IOS investments were never politically motivated and purely for individual financial prosperity. Why on earth would we want to harm Brazil? In any case, monies taken out almost always returned, considerably increased.

Before any further talk, we showered, shaved, and borrowed clean clothes, then, tucking into giant room service club sandwiches (never before nor since has one tasted so good), we listened to the weird tale of what had been going on since we had been arrested in Recife.

Ed and Jerry had been in Rio for five days, working with Brazil's most prominent lawyers, politicians, and PR people, so that even the Ministry of War had become nervous at the negative publicity the dictatorship might face. Finally, Colonel Fiusa had been ordered to release us. Until we turned up in the lobby, the two had been unable to find out exactly where we were being held.

Our respective embassies had been totally useless. Only after I was finally back in our house in Santo Amaro did I discover that Jennifer had gone to the Danish Consul General in Sao Paolo, together with my good Swedish friend Johan Streijffert. The Danish consular officials were totally disinterested and offered no help at all. They probably believed the trumped-up stories published by the military regime. The same was true of the Swiss in Fred Borlin's case and the Italians in Mario Venturini's (Sao Paulo divisional manager) . So much for diplomatic assistance.

As I slowly caught up with events, I learnt that most of our local IOS associates had fared better. They were not held for more than a few days, during which they were interrogated and then released. Obviously, as I was the general manager for Brazil and Fred my deputy, we were the "big fish."

Jennifer had gone through hell. She told me that the first sign she had that anything was amiss was when the neighbours' children (with whom John and Nick had played daily in each others' gardens) were suddenly forbidden to play with or even talk to my boys. Then our cook and driver couple walked out after reading their morning newspaper. Unsure of what exactly was going on, she had kept the children home from school and, despite her fears, arranged games in the pool and picnics under the trees to keep up a holiday atmosphere. Apart from a couple of scared reps hiding out in our guest wing, who didn't speak Portuguese either, nobody called, nobody visited.

I found all this so upsetting that there was only one solution—the rental contract would have to be cancelled, we would all move to a hotel, and Jennifer and the boys would have to fly back to Europe as soon as possible. To Jennifer's utter dismay, I told her that I would have to stay behind.

After lengthy interventions by our lawyers, the War Ministry finally declared that "There has been no crime," and all charges were dropped. However, IOS, together with all other financial advisory firms, had to close their offices. With our lawyers' assurances that this would be done and a few top men's promises not to leave the country "for the time being," the entire matter was swept under the carpet. Naturally no disclaimer ever appeared in either the local or foreign press. We had been used as scapegoats for the shaky state of Brazil's finances.

With a sinking heart, I had to arrange for the departure of all our foreign associates, close all the IOS offices, and pay off all our employees. After just a few months and before I had even begun, my dreams of building up Brazil had come crashing down.

Colonel Fiusa summoned me for one last interview. As we concluded, he walked me to the door and, holding me by the shoulders, said, "Please forgive the Brazilian Government for the harsh treatment; please excuse the bad food and poor accommodation, but we are a very poor country. Here is your suitcase. I hope nothing is missing. You are not allowed to leave the *Territorio Nacional*, but maybe I come and visit you one day in Geneva."

How about that for a muddled message! In fact, Colonel Fiusa did visit me in Geneva years later. I gave him a Dunhill lighter and he invested in an IOS fund. That's Brazil—a wonderful country with great people, but as always under military rule, civil liberties go out the window.

I settled our affairs, we packed our belongings, and the last thing I did in Conde Deu was to give our two Siamese cats to an animal-mad friend. We spent a couple of nights in a hotel in Sao Paolo, then as soon as I could arrange it, I took Jennifer and the boys to Rio to put them on board a Swissair flight to Geneva. At the airport, for the first time in front of the children, Jennifer broke down. Once more she was to wait for me, and I couldn't tell her when or where we would be together again. As I kissed them all goodbye, I took little John to one side and said, "Now you must be the man of the family and take care of Mummy and your little brother." Then off they flew.

That evening Colonel Fiusa called me and told me that I had been shadowed all the time by the Brazilian Secret Service, both in Sao Paolo and in the Galeon (Rio) airports, as they were sure I would try to leave with my family. He was pleased that I had obeyed orders.

I could neither sleep nor rest until Jennifer called to say that they had arrived safely in Switzerland. A little light relief from our youngest son cheered me up. After their stop-over in Dakar, all the passengers had to take a crowded bus to re-board the plane. In the crush, John had held his mother's hand whilst Nick sat on her hip. Face-to-face with little blond, blue-eyed Nick stood a very black African. After studying him silently for a few seconds, Nick took the man's face between his chubby hands and said, "You've been too much in the sun, haven't you?" Fortunately the man and all who heard roared with laughter.

They arrived to find Geneva snowbound and went straight to the only hotel Jennifer knew, the small Hotel Eden, where we had stayed during my IOS training. All three curled up in an enormous double bed and slept for twelve hours. They were woken by a phone call from Allen Cantor, president of IOS, insisting that they should move at once to the Hotel Intercontinental, where a large suite had been reserved for them.

So despite the fact that all three would have preferred just to go back to sleep, they moved to their elegant new quarters, where they were to stay for four months. Winter clothes were a top priority, as the boys had none at all. They were immensely proud of their first boots, mittens, and anoraks, and happily scuffed and slid around the snowy parks whilst Jennifer watched over them from a bench, frozen to the bone and miserable.

Allen Cantor managed to bend the rules and have John accepted by the United Nations Kindergarten in Geneva. When he drove Jennifer and the boys there, John allowed himself to be shown around the entire premises, but then refused to stay.

Dictator Castello Branco (died in a plane crash a few years later)

"This is a very nice school, but I cannot stay as I promised my father to look after my mother." And that was that.

These were very difficult and worrisome times for Jennifer, not knowing when she would see me again, nor what the future would hold. She obviously needed some family support. My mother and Dino, having read lurid stories about IOS in the Italian press, would not leave Florence to come to Geneva. They did not wish to be seen with Jennifer, as this might "harm their reputation." An aunt in Montreux, less than an hour away, did not wish to have contact either, for the same reason. The only person who immediately rallied to Jennifer's side was her sister Elizabeth, who flew to Geneva to hold her hand. The Cantors and the Gangels, (Richard Gangel was executive vice president) also came to the rescue. We had all become friendly because they had junketed around the world as we had, and their children were more or less the same age as ours. They took Jennifer to ballets and operas, lunches and dinners whilst the boys were invited over for play dates.. A Swiss nanny was engaged. She would live in the suite and teach the children their first French phrases.

Still in Brazil, now in the middle of December, I waited with the only IOSer left, Mario Venturini. His passport had been confiscated, and the Italian Consulate would not issue a new one, telling him just to wait until his original one was returned. We could not wait that long and concocted a plan.

67

Escape

Mario and I left our luggage with the concierge of the Grand Hotel Ca'd'Oro, together with hefty tips and sufficient funds to have it air-freighted to the Hotel Intercontinental in Geneva. I "sold" my Mercedes back to Herr Wagner, the German car dealer who had sold it just a few months before to Tregea. I was given an official receipt and assured that the money would be transferred to my Swiss bank account in a few days, as the car would be easy to sell. I never saw a penny, of course.

A year later, the man sent me, c/o IOS, a postcard from Australia: "Sorry, but I always wanted to emigrate to Australia, thanks for your help." One never learns.

We contacted a friend of Mario's, who was a travel agent and member of a Flying Club. Yes, for 8,000 American dollars (in those days a lot of money) he would fly Mario and me to Punta del Este in Uruguay.

Of course we now had to evade our "minders." Two days later, at 5 a.m., we were picked up by a small Volkswagen and driven to a Sao Paolo slum quarter. Here we walked for ten minutes and boarded a pickup truck, which drove us to the outskirts of town. There we changed to a minibus, which took us to a small private airport in a deep, funnel-like valley. About thirty minutes later we heard a plane approaching. It circled around and around the valley before landing.

A grey-haired pilot emerged from the cockpit of this single-engine Northrop plane and introduced himself as Captain Borokovski, ex-Polish Air Force and ex-RAF. He demanded a $3,000 advance, which we paid. We then boarded and took off at once.

We circled up through the valley and then low over the hills before descending almost to sea level, skimming over the waves to avoid radar detection by the Brazilian Air Force. We landed first in Laguna and then in Pelotas to refuel, each stop nerve-racking. At this late stage, the pilot asked if we had our passports with us. I told him that I had my Danish passport but that Mario's had been stolen. "No problem," said the pilot, "we will land at the Punta del Este Golf Club airstrip, where many Brazilians land to play golf for the day and return in the evening to Brazil." The police and customs officials were quite lax, and in the worst of cases we might have to bribe them. It was agreed that I should not mention that I had a passport, as otherwise they would expect Mario to show his. At that moment, Mario told the pilot who we were. This would turn out later to have been a mistake.

When we disembarked, a Uruguayan Customs Officer asked for our passports, and we told him that we hadn't brought them with us as we had just come for a round of golf and would depart later that day. He opened my bags and saw in a pouch $12,000 cash. Eyes gleaming, he asked why I would need so much for a day's round of golf, and I told him that I had to pay the pilot and, after the game planned to do some serious gambling in the famous Punta del Este Casino. He then asked for a small "gratification." I gave him $200—and he let us go.

In Borokovski's hotel room, where we had agreed we would pay him the rest of his fee, far from prying eyes, an unpleasant surprise awaited us. He demanded more than the $5,000 still due him. He said that he had no idea he was ferrying the bosses of IOS out of Brazil, and we could surely afford another $2,000. Otherwise he would inform the Brazilian Secret Service, which naturally had agents in Uruguay. He settled for an additional $1,000, so that this little trip cost us $9,000. But we were so elated to be out of Brazil that we would willingly have paid double. We left him immediately after payment, taking a taxi to the Montevideo Victoria Intercontinental Plaza, anxious to leave Uruguay as soon as possible. We obviously could not trust Borokovski even now.

From Montevideo I immediately cabled Jennifer: "Am FREE—back for Christmas !" and once the news was broken, I called her. It was Dec. 21, 1966. The next day Mario got his passport from the Italian Consulate, we booked flights with Air France via Buenos Aires and Dakar to Paris, then Swissair to Geneva. We landed in Geneva at 5 p.m. on Christmas Eve.

The Brazilian nightmare was over.

68

Geneva

Nobody ever checked into the Intercontinental faster than I did that late afternoon. I charged along the corridor, banged on their door like a madman, and when Jennifer opened it we fell into each other's arms, the boys clinging to my knees.

It was Christmas Eve, but naturally I had no presents. However, Jennifer said I was the best gift ever for all three of them. In front of a small tree, John and Nick pounced on all the gifts Father Christmas had secretly deposited, and soon the living room carpets were full of the toy cars, trains, and planes of little boy's dreams. Jennifer gave me a beautiful pair of lapis lazuli cufflinks from Gubelin, and every few minutes we gave each other hugs, hardly able to believe that the nightmare was over.

Once we managed to get the two over-excited little boys to bed, we left them in the care of the nanny and I took Jennifer to the Hotel Richemond for a superb dinner and Christmas Eve celebration, both of us dizzy with relief and happiness.

Once all the holiday excitement was over, I went to see Bernie and Allen for a debriefing. I was praised for having closed down the shop in an orderly fashion and for having organised the evacuation of all foreign IOSers—and, as would a ship's captain, been the last to leave.

The only person who somewhat avoided me, to my great surprise, was my Brazilian predecessor, George Tregea. It was as if he had a bad conscience, which planted the seed in my mind that he might have heard rumours that something like a new law or decree was in the making. He had, after all, been in Brazil for years, knew everyone, and his request to leave had been unexpected and hurried. Now that I thought about it, though, why had he bought a new car just a month before leaving? Perhaps all this was just a fantasy of my "Chinese brain," as Jennifer sometimes teases.

Bernie Cornfeld was as charming as ever. He told me that he had great plans for me. First he suggested I take over Germany, at that time the biggest producer in the world, but I said no. Then I was offered the Far East, another great area, and I was also offered Australia. But I wanted to settle down in tranquil Geneva and give my family the security of Switzerland. When I turned down all the offers and said that I wished to work in the head office, they agreed. Of course I would have to make one last trip to Latin America, where I knew everyone and was trusted. Thanks to the events in Brazil, morale needed boosting, but I could go ahead and settle my family in Geneva.

Jennifer, of course, was delighted. After a meticulous search, she found a charming apartment in a park in one of Geneva's nicest areas, and when I gave her carte blanche to furnish it, she found beautiful pieces in the antique shops of the Vieille Ville. We chose a good school for the boys, and I treated myself to a 4.2 litre Jaguar in British racing green.

In the midst of these preparations, I had to leave on that Latin American swing, so we decided that Jennifer and the boys should stay in the Intercontinental until I returned, and we could all move into our new home together.

69

Central and South America

The Brazilian crackdown on all financial advisory firms had sparked off a contagious, nationalistic, protectionist wave throughout Latin America, where IOS still maintained sixteen offices. Managers were edgy, nervous that a situation would arise on their patch similar to Brazil. It was going to be a hard job to rekindle enthusiasm.

Mexico, my first stop, went well. I was able to boost their not-too-shaky-morale, and by the time I left, their gung-ho spirit was reborn.

I found Guatemala a country riddled with riots, ruled by gangsters, and about to slide into civil war. Indians had named their country *Quauhtlemallan*, or "the place of many trees," but today they would have named it "the place of many deaths." Since 1960, when Julio Cesar Montenegro became president, he and his army had

Guatemalan Highlands

been waging a bitter campaign against his enemies. This quickly became an armed conflict, resulting in the deaths of hundreds of thousands of victims. Some 450,000 farmers fled to Mexico as Guatemala sank into a bloodbath of genocide.

Upon arrival, my taxi was shot at as I was driven into town. A bullet shattered the window and hit the ceiling about twenty centimetres from my head. Quite apart from my feelings, the driver panicked as there was a new law that all cars driving at night must have their interior lights on so that the police could see who was inside. The driver had forgotten this new decree and now feared this might just have been a warning shot from the police. Small consolation for me—a bullet is a bullet.

In my hotel, the IOSers I found waiting for me were demoralised and planning to leave. Business was fifty percent off the previous year, and they only stayed to help those clients in the country who still had money and who were desperate to get it out. As soon as they saw me, several associates asked to be relocated to other Spanish-speaking areas. I did what I could for them and left, discouraged, only to find the situation in my next stop no better.

Since 1931, El Salvador had been in the control of a military dictatorship, where the army controlled the state. Colonels Rivera and Sanchez ruled whilst I was there. Their methods were barbaric, but strangely enough they were supported by the Kennedy administration in an attempt to counter the leftist guerrilla movements inspired by the Cuban revolution. America usually seems to prefer fascism over communism. Corruption and terror ruled the land, and only the fact that many wealthy Salvadorians wanted to have their money safely in Switzerland gave some of the IOS representatives a reason to stay—if only temporarily. I did not even try to persuade them otherwise, as I would not have remained myself.

Next came Nicaragua, where Anastasio Somoza ruled with the heavy hand of yet another military dictator, filling the jails of his country with both the guilty and the innocent. Hundreds of dissidents were thrown into the sewers under the roads, where their anguished cries were said to seep though the manholes. By a systematic repression of his people, Somoza had made enemies of educated Nicaraguans, the Catholic Church—and even the U.S. Government.

I checked into my hotel and prepared to meet a group of fifteen IOSers managed by Bernard Zutter, an ex-Peruvian-Swiss stock broker and old friend from our Lima days. The hotel was the best in Managua, a beautiful colonial building with huge patios and a gigantic lobby with palm trees and parrots. Before meeting the men, I showered and changed, and as I walked to the lift I heard a loud explosion behind me. Rather foolishly, I ran back to my room, only to find that a small grenade, which must have been fired from a tank, had blasted through the bathroom window, turning the shower head into a cauliflower hanging drunkenly from the ceiling—the shower under which I had stood minutes before. I sent a bell hop up for my things, held the meeting, and checked out.

General Somoza

My next stop was San Pedro Sula, the second-largest town in Honduras, where IOS morale was also at a low ebb and our people wanted out. I could not blame them, and promised to help those who wanted to be relocated once I was back in Geneva.

It was a relief to find that in Costa Rica everything was calm and orderly, but the market was very limited and small. All I could do was congratulate them on their successes and reassure them of Geneva's continued support.

The one and only highlight was Panama. I found fine offices and thirty-five bullish IOSers led by José Arechabala—who, over the years, was to become one of my closest friends. I gave a good meeting in the Swiss Club and, after one of my better speeches, enthusiasm soared.

In Colombia and Peru, it appeared that plans were also afoot to curtail foreign investments. South America had certainly changed since my heady days in Buenos Aires and Lima. Now, a toxic mix of nationalism, isolationism, and communism was sweeping through the continent. Che Guevara was the hero of the day, and military dictators reacted with fury to the hordes of his young followers. Foreigners, who had always been welcome, were now generally disliked, certainly by the lower classes. It was a depressing trip, and I knew that I would not be able to repeat it three times a year as had been planned.

Sitting in my hotel room in Buenos Aires, wondering what to do next, I received a call from Bernie. The directors had decided not to waste my "talents" in Latin America. I was to develop the most potentially lucrative area imaginable—the Middle East "and beyond." This turned out to mean that my area would stretch from Libya and Malta through all the Arab countries, Iran, Afghanistan, and Pakistan to India. My headquarters would be in Beirut, where "fantastic" offices were already waiting for me. Thad Lovett, Bernie's current right hand, sent me a letter officially promoting me to executive vice president.

Beirut at that time was called the Paris of the Orient. The Lebanese people were charming, and the educated classes all spoke French. The climate was ideal, excellent restaurants abounded, and there were good schools. One could technically swim in the Med in the morning and ski amongst the cedars in the afternoon. (We were to find that there were actually very few cedars.) Life was inexpensive, and well-trained domestic staff was easily found. Bernie made it sound like paradise.

Of course I accepted—not only for my personal safety, which was becoming a concern, but also for our family life. I picked up the phone to give Jennifer the good news. Major mistake. I should have told her when I was back, but I wanted her to cancel the apartment and schools so we could leave quickly. There were tears and recriminations, and then she declared that she had had enough of this crazy life and was going with the boys to her parents.

I took the next plane from BA to Heathrow and sat in a London taxi until the surprised driver dropped me off outside my in-laws' house in Huntingdon—a hundred miles north of his usual territory. Jennifer was locked in her bedroom and the boys were fast asleep in theirs. Beth was rather icy, but Bill gave me a warm welcome and a whisky, patted me on the shoulder, and promised me that his daughter would soon come around.

When I was finally allowed to speak to her, it took me hours of persuasion, of apologies, of descriptions of our future life in Beirut, before Jennifer relented, but I must not repeat the horrible and indeed dangerous trip I had just taken. After tears and sobs, which I fully understood, she finally said, "If I have to choose between Geneva and us, I choose us."

We would cancel the Swiss apartment and ship all the newly acquired furniture to Beirut—including the almost forgotten crates from Denmark.

Once she had made up her mind, Jennifer rallied to the task of convincing the boys what fun awaited them in Beirut. In the morning we said goodbye to Beth and Bill (who gave me a huge grin, whispering that he knew I could do it) and returned to Geneva from where, within the week, we departed for the Lebanon in that spring of 1967.

70

BEIRUT

Our new Australian nanny, Miss James (pronounced "Jimes," if you please), was as excited as the boys to move to "Ali Baba's country," and all three could hardly wait to see their first camel. The minute John caught sight of the Middle East Airlines Comet sitting on the tarmac at the airport in Geneva, he named it "the Christmas tree airline," as the Lebanese flag it bore was a cedar.

In Beirut we checked into the Phoenicia Intercontinental and started house-hunting the next day. My offices were, as promised, splendid—on the Corniche, over the Rocks of Rausche, on the seventh floor of the Shell Building—700 square meters of air-conditioned luxury, with wonderful views over the harbour. There was a pleasant staff of fifteen people plus about thirty IOS representatives. The local sales manager was a middle-aged Lebanese woman who keenly resented my presence, as she was no longer to be Queen Bee, but this I was not to know until later.

We found a fine house high on a hill in Rabieh, with views over the Mediterranean, the port of Beirut and, behind us, the mountains. It had been built by our neighbour, Shoukri Shammas, for his youngest son's coming of age, but as the boy was about ten it sat empty, as showy a shell as any self-respecting Lebanese could desire. Cool and airy, with marble pillars and high ceilings, it was just the thing to impress local clients.

We found a French-speaking driver, Boutros, a professional cook, Mehran, (ex-chef for Randolph Churchill, with a tall white toque), two maids, and a gardener. Jennifer had her first bit of cultural education with the two girls. In our crates were the Peruvian maids' pretty uniforms, which now had been laid out on the girls' beds. They were told to go and change and then come back for instructions—difficult enough as they only spoke Arabic. An age went by and neither returned.

Thinking they had misunderstood, Jennifer went down to their quarters—only to find the girls sitting on the edge of the beds in tears, still in their own clothes. Mehran arrived to translate, and it transpired that the girls wanted to leave. "But whatever for?"

"They refuse to stay in an indecent house.

Jennifer was aghast. "Indecent? What has happened?"

"It's the uniforms, Madame."

"What's the matter with them?"

"Well, they are short-sleeved, and for a Muslim girl it is indecent to show one's arms."

There was nothing for it but to tell the girls to stay where they were whilst Jennifer shot into town to buy suitably modest garments. Fortunately, sleeves were the only problem. In some countries, much more than arms would have had to be concealed, and in later years hijabs might even have had to be worn.

I bought a Chrysler Imperial and had a Danish flag stuck on the boot, which turned out to be useful. Jennifer happily appropriated the Jaguar. Amongst the people living on "our" hill were the English president of a big construction company with a Labrador called Brandy, soon to become the boys' best playmate; the Lebanese president of Schlumberger M.E.; and the Lebanese Foreign Minister, M. Malik, all charming and hospitable.

As it was summer and very hot, offices were only open from 8 a.m. to 2 p.m. We rented a beach bungalow about twenty minutes away and spent every afternoon there with the boys. When tired of the heat, we all would drive into the cool hills and mountain villages, where little restaurants were to be found serving the delicious mezzes we grew to love. We drove to Byblos, that ancient biblical town where ruins of houses built one on top of the other down through the ages could be seen like a layer cake, and to Baalbeck, where we listened to *Aida*, sung in a setting of ruined Roman temples, flood-lit against a star-studded, midnight blue sky.

The Casino du Liban was justly famous for its fabulous shows, but watching the baccarat tables where sheikhs in desert dress would win or lose immense fortunes without blinking an eyelid was as entertaining as the superb white horses that galloped on stage.

We made new friends, and the children did too, at a Catholic school run by Canadian nuns. This was Nick's first but, as always, he was only too happy to go wherever his big brother went. Boutros was terrified that Nicholas would be kidnapped, and kept telling Jennifer to take care of him. Indignantly she replied that she always took great care of *both* her sons.

"Oh, but Madame does not understand. Nicholas is so blond, so blue are his eyes. There are men who would pay much money for such a boy!"

So a new worry was added to the usual fears a mother always has for her children. Once little four-year old Nicky stomped off alone down the hill to buy some sweets or something, and pandemonium broke loose as the entire staff became hysterical searching for him. When he was found only minutes later, his mother had an old-fashioned attack of the vapours.

As the heat abated a little, I flew to Saudi Arabia, the UAE, Kuwait, Teheran, Kabul and Karachi, Lahore, Rawalpindi, Bombay, and Calcutta. Then to Cairo, Malta, Libya and Cyprus, and on to Israel. When flying to any Arab country after popping in and out of Israel, one had to go via Cyprus using two passports, one in which Israel could stamp your entry and exit, and another where no trace of Israel could be seen. This was due to the Arab boycott of Israel, as no stamps could show that you had set foot there. We were to find this boycott taken to ridiculous extremes. No atlas, map—or indeed any book—could mention the name of Israel. We were learning about carpets and buying quite a few, so we found a book explaining all the details. On the front page was a map and, of course, the name Israel had been inked out. One could only imagine the number of people who must be employed to censor every single book, magazine, or newspaper in this manner.

Another fact which upset us was the amount of squalid Palestinian refugee camps that lined the road from the airport into Beirut. The wretched people could not be moved, we were told, as then the Palestinian problem would be forgotten. The inmates could not be resettled elsewhere in the vast Arab territories as, again, out of sight would be out of mind. Today, forty years later, those camps are still there.

Of all the countries I visited, I found Iran the most fascinating and life in Teheran very civilised. I thoroughly enjoyed gourmet dinners in the French Club or the Persian Room in the Hilton, to which I was often invited. Usually the evenings ended over brandies in the Cheminée next to the Imperial Palace. Our local lawyer, Dr. Aghayan, and our sponsor, His Imperial Highness Prince Sharam, took excellent care of me and introduced me to all the major bankers and local bigwigs. When Jim Roosevelt, then president of the IOS Development Company, came to Teheran, we met the Governors of the Iranian Central Bank and were honoured to meet His Majesty, King of Kings, the Shah of Iran, who charmed our socks off in a few brief minutes.

Trips to Afghanistan and Pakistan seemed like time-travel to the past. Women washed their laundry, vegetables, and the odd chicken along the open sewers of Kabul. One could only hope that hotels and restaurants followed more sanitary practices.

After visiting Kabul, I usually continued on to Karachi and Lahore. Lahore was then a garden city that reminded me of the French settlement of Shanghai I had loved as a boy. My hotel was in the middle of a large park, and my ground-floor room opened onto fine gardens. One evening I returned to find, to my horror, a small cobra enjoying the cool dampness of my bath tub. Two boys with sticks and brooms quickly pushed it out of the French windows—which, despite the lack of air-conditioning, I kept firmly closed thereafter.

After my last experiences in Latin America, it was a joy to find, in all my new areas, bounding enthusiasm from all the IOSers. Not only was business growing steadily, but news that our Foundation was opening children's hospitals and schools meant that IOS was much appreciated.

My best producers were Saudi Arabia, Iran, and Kuwait. In the latter, Jassim Safar, our Kuwaiti sponsor, was extremely helpful, if a bit of a handful. Once he made me promise to bring back twelve bottles of Johnny Walker Black Label on my next trip, for a desert party he planned to give in my honour. It was, of course, forbidden to bring any alcoholic beverages into Kuwait, but I was told to just wrap the bottles in towels or shirts and all would be well.

Nevertheless, upon arrival I quaked as a stern customs officer barked, "Anything to declare?"

My heart pounding, I lied, "Of course not."

The man's fury exploded. "What? You didn't bring the whisky for the party?"

It would take me some time to realise how easy it was to bribe almost anyone to do—or in this case, overlook—almost anything.

That night, four Land Rovers drove a group of us into the desert, where we found two large tents and huge, fragrant spits, where sheep were slowly roasting over open fires. Soft, wailing Arab music drifted from under the palms, interrupted only by an occasional grunt from tethered camels. Enormous desert stars outshone the waning moon, and I felt like Haroun-al-Raschid as I sprawled with the others on layered carpets and stuffed myself with delicious little dishes, all washed down with my whisky.

Toward the end, fire-eating jugglers entertained us, and I was having the time of my life until our sponsor stood up and began a little speech. "My dear John—we wish to thank you for your friendship, and your IOS support. I have a gift for you. Not the usual gold Rolex Oyster, but something infinitely more valuable." As he sat down, beaming at me, a servant brought in a boy of about twelve. My heart sank and I was instantly sober.

"This is Ahmed. He is anxious to give you boundless service. He is yours. Take him with you back to Beirut. You will never regret it!"

What on earth was I to say? A blank refusal would have deeply insulted my host and we would lose his valuable sponsorship. I wracked my brain until fortunately I remembered the desert Arab's reverence for religion, usually his own but perhaps mine also? I had to try.

"My dear friend, I am deeply moved by your generosity in offering me such a fine gift, and I don't know how to thank you. However, although it hurts me deeply, I have to tell you that my faith does not allow me to accept. Not only would God punish me now, but my entire afterlife would be spent in hell."

With my heart in my mouth, I waited for what seemed ages before Jassim spoke. With a frown like thunder, he stood up, snapped his fingers, and declared, "Very well. It is time to leave." With that, the party was over. Although our business relationship continued, our friendship was not the same and he never forgave me.

On his next visit to Beirut, he accepted an invitation to come home for lunch, but hardly touched the exquisite dishes Mehran had so carefully prepared for my eminent guest. Jassim just sat brooding and downing scotch until I fully expected him to disappear under the table. Finally he allowed Boutros to drive him back to his hotel, and that was the last I saw of my car and my driver for a week.

When Boutros sheepishly returned, looking terrible, he told me that Jassim had ordered him to drive to Damascus, where the two spent days drinking and carousing. There was just no point in being annoyed—in Boutros's world, Jassim's word was law.

In order to visit Israel, I flew to Cyprus on my British passport (having been born in Hong Kong I was entitled to one), and then continued to Tel Aviv on my Danish passport, which was duly stamped by the Israelis. The IOS group in Tel Aviv was highly motivated and productive. IOS was held in high esteem in Israel, of course. Egypt was equally productive, as were Malta and Libya. So all in all these were rewarding times, and we enjoyed a pleasant life in Rabieh with our two enchanting little boys and a growing circle of international friends.

Things in the Beirut office, unfortunately, were not as pleasant. Ms. Shaneiaa the divisional manager I had inherited, continued to resent my presence, despite my initial undivided support in all things.

Auditors were regularly sent out from Geneva to check the books in all our offices world-wide, and one day, Roger Ratner, a charming Jewish New Yorker, arrived to check ours. Ms. Shaneiaa, at her most charming, invited Roger and me for drinks in her house, to be followed by lunch in her favourite restaurant.

When we were about to leave, Roger picked up his heavy brief case. "Oh," said Ms. Shaneiaa, all smiles, "just leave that in the drawing room. We'll be back for coffee straight after lunch."

Were we both too naïve or too unaccustomed to the chicanery in Lebanon to suspect anything? Later we were to discover that all Roger's reports and balance sheets from all the countries he had visited were, in our absence, photocopied by the Lebanese Security, as Ms. Shaneiaa hinted that poor Roger was an Israeli spy. She probably just wanted to see all the IOS balance sheets. In any event, nothing even vaguely incriminating was found, and Roger left as peacefully as he had arrived.

It was normal IOS procedure to give new salesmen advances against closed business, as it could take four to six weeks for commissions to arrive from Geneva. Before my arrival, Ms. Shaneiaa had recruited three rather unsavoury salesmen, who I did not approve of, but she was the divisional manager and I was trying hard not to step on her toes. These three characters had never closed a sale, and yet they always received generous advances. As I was ultimately responsible for these advances, I finally said they would have to stop. Violent protests and shrieks were followed by downright refusals. The whole thing was ridiculous, and soon half the office was aware of the situation.

Two sensible and serious associates and friends, Albert Bitar and Christian Aouad, took me aside and explained that these three men were thought to be with the PLO, and, given the unstable state of affairs in the Lebanon, it would be wise to let the whole thing drop.

It was hard for me to keep up with all this cloak and dagger stuff, and I would have dearly loved to get rid of Ms. Shaneiaa and her cronies but she had the highest connections with Muslim leaders, and any action against her could have been disastrous.

I was also warned that she had a contact in the post office, which opened and photocopied every letter I wrote before resealing the envelopes and sending them off. In this way she read all my correspondence about my entire area, which she subsequently sold to our competition!

Quite apart from these shenanigans, black clouds were gathering on the political horizon. Across the Arab Middle East, virulent hate campaigns raged against Israel and America. Once, at the end of my day, as Boutros was about to drive me home, we found the roads around my office swarming with hysterical mobs. Banners declaring "Death to America," "Death to Israel," and "Death to Jewish Interests in the Lebanon" were waved menacingly at me. The car was stopped, and efforts were made to overturn it. Here Boutros came to the rescue. Rolling down his window he yelled (in Arabic, of course), "Look at the flag! The gentleman in the back is the Russian Ambassador—Russe—Ambassadeur Russe!"

The fact that the sticker in the back was the Danish flag was neither here nor there—the crowds let us through and even cheered us on our way. At home I gave Boutros a well-deserved fat tip and myself a stiff whisky.

I was in Baghdad when King Hussein of Jordan sided with Egypt and Syria in declaring war on Israel, so, fearing the worst, I took the first flight back to Beirut to be with my family. Jennifer and I sat at the top of our hill and listened to the French-language Lebanese radio translating orders from the Lebanese government that all car lights should be painted dark blue and a total blackout of all windows after dark was mandatory. As the boys watched Boutros paint out the lights on both cars, four-year-old Nicky asked his six-year-old big brother, "Why is he doing that, John?"

Only Miss James heard John's whispered reply: "It's because there's going to be a war, but don't tell Mummy!"

The Danish and British Embassies advised all their nationals to leave on ships waiting in the harbour to take them to Cyprus. Friends among high-placed Lebanese told us it would be a very short war and would not affect Beirut, so we decided to stick it out, even though many of our Dutch and French friends left.

With incredible speed, the Israeli war machine overcame the three Arab armies, and before we knew it Gaza, the Sinai, the Golan Heights, and Jerusalem were in

Israeli hands. Regarding Beirut, however, our friends had been correct, and only the petroleum depots in the harbour were bombed. At the time, as Jennifer and I watched aghast at the leaping flames far below us, I panicked, thinking that I should have taken my family away, but soon all was quiet again and those families who had left for Cyprus were back within the week.

Nothing was the same afterwards, though. On the Arab streets there was resentment against everything Western, especially American. Anything to do with Israel was, of course, an anathema. We continued to entertain many of the charming Lebanese we had met, most of whom were Christian. They all spoke French, sometimes English, and most came accompanied by their elegant, jewel-laden wives.

If our friends were as warm as ever, the lower Muslim classes hated everybody and everything non-Arab. Not so the Christian community. Boutros was a Maronite Christian, and upon the birth of his twin girls he asked Jennifer to be Godmother. The baptism took place in a quaint little church deep in the Lebanese mountains, and all present had to carry live candles and quick-march three times around the font. My main worry was that my sons, each proudly bearing a candle held at the height of most of the women's veils or long hair, would cause a conflagration. Fortunately, and to their fury, I managed to blow theirs out.

Trips to Jeddah, Riyadh, and Dhahran were tiring and hot, making me dream of an ice-cold Tuborg at the end of the day. On a flight from Dhahran to Jeddah with Sam Welker, one of my general managers, our Saudi Airline Boeing hit a bad sandstorm, forcing us to make an emergency landing in Mecca-Medina.

When the pilot announced this, Sam turned white. He slumped down in his seat and murmured, "It's been nice knowing you, John."

I did not know then that "infidels" intruding on the holy ground of Mecca faced instant decapitation. Sam and I sat low and still. When the captain came into the cabin, he threw a large blanket over us. "Lie still and don't say a word. If any police come on board, I'll say that you are gravely ill Bosnian Muslims."

We sweated, then shivered for an interminable hour, but nobody came near us, and at last the plane took off. Our spirits rose with the aircraft, but what would we have given for a couple of stiff drinks!

When we arrived late in Jeddah, our reserved hotel rooms had been given away and we had to spend the night in the "Red Sea Palace Hotel." If it still exists, avoid it like the plague. Cautious about our bed linen and mattresses, and in an effort to avoid all manner of horrors, we each slept in our rusty bath tubs. The following morning I awoke to find, not the bites I had feared, but a swollen cheek and a raging toothache.

The hotel concierge assured me that Jeddah had an excellent foreign dentist, and he sent me off in a taxi to the clinic on the main square. The dentist turned out to be a frightening 200-kilo, six-foot Prussian woman who announced that I had an abscess and my molar would have to come out.

"Unfortunately, I have no anaesthetic, but sit on that chair and watch the executions. It's Friday, so there will be quite a show. Sharia Law, you know. It's off with heads or arms, and the best bit is when they shove the stumps into hot oil! Oh how they scream—you won't even think about your tooth!

I rapidly removed myself from this woman's tender mercies and sped off to the airport, where I took Middle East Airlines back to the Lebanon. On the plane, at last, I could relax in my seat as a smiling steward served me a double scotch to soothe my aching jaw. Two hours later, a very professional dentist in Beirut saved my molar.

Back in Geneva, a great event was taking place. The IOS Foundation, the humanitarian and philanthropic arm of Investors Overseas Services, with 155 projects in fifty-five countries, embarked on its biggest project ever—to organise the financial and logistical support of PACEM IN TERRIS, a conference to further lasting world peace. Against a background of new crises, the Vietnam conflict and the ever-rumbling Arab-Israel hostilities, over 300 world leaders from seventy-five countries gathered in Geneva.

Bernard Cornfeld

James Roosevelt

The conference was opened by Adlai Stevenson, blessed by Pope Paul VI, and addressed by U Thant, Secretary General of the UN. James Roosevelt, former United States Ambassador to the UN, son of Franklin D. Roosevelt, and now president of the IOS Development Company, presided. The conference was televised world-wide and marked another cornerstone in IOS's endeavours to spread security and peace as well as wealth around the globe.

It was upon my return to Lebanon from Abu Dhabi that I was informed at Beirut airport that my Residence and Work Permits had been cancelled. I was given fourteen days to leave. I raced to our lawyer, a friend of Ms. Shaneiaa, so naturally he told me quite happily that there was absolutely nothing he could do. "After all, Israeli sympathisers and para-spies cannot be tolerated."

I did not object to being called an Israeli sympathiser, but a "para-spy"! What rot. I went to all my influential and powerful friends, but they could not override the law. All they could achieve was a fifteen-day extension, giving me one month to leave.

My protestations that I was a Danish businessman with no ties to politics were to no avail. Alberto Bitar and Christian Auad told me that office gossip had it that I had been denounced as a collaborator of the Mossad (the Israeli Secret Service) by the three PLO agents who still received regular advances from Ms. Shaneiaa—or in actual fact, from me. In other words, I had paid my own denunciators !

We were sorry to leave. The children liked their school and loved the beach life. They had made, as we had, lots of friends. I, however, was not sad to leave such an intrigue-riddled office. To our delight, Jennifer was pregnant again, and it was time to find safer surroundings for us all. I promised her that this time we really would settle down in Geneva, and there would be "no more trouble-spots for us."

Once again we packed up, this time with two enormous pantechnicons of furniture. I booked three adjoining cabins on a Lloyd Triestino liner, one for us, one for the boys and one for their new nanny, Linda. We sailed on the Ausonia via Cyprus, Malta, Syracuse, Naples, and Marseilles to Genoa. This mini-cruise cheered us up, as we all loved to be at sea.

Our first port of call was Cyprus, where we admired Greek Orthodox churches, ate a huge meal under olive trees while listening to zithers, then smashed plates on the floor, to the boys delight—Mummy and Daddy behaving badly!

In Malta, we were all fascinated by a church through which a German bomb had crashed during the war. It hadn't exploded, and there it still lay. I lost my shoe in the yacht harbour basin and had to limp into Valetta on one shoe, another highlight for the children.

Next stop was Syracuse, in Sicily, followed by Naples and a day-long excursion to Pompeii, where the boys were not impressed by the ruins, but stared in horrified fascination at a petrified dog.

The last port of call before we reached Genoa was Marseilles, where Nick saw his first Santa Claus. He soon became very confused, as there were Santas all over town. So John, expressing his seniority, explained that they were just the real Santa's helpers. This infuriated Nick, who said, "Don't you even know that all Santa's helpers are elves?"

We docked in Genoa on a grey foggy morning and left the next day in the Jaguar for France via Switzerland. I had booked us into the Hotel du Golf in Divonne on the Swiss-French border. To our complete lack of comprehension, we were frequently hissed at and booed from passing cars as we drove through Italy. It finally dawned on us that it was the Arab number plates on our car that were causing the trouble. We never seemed to get it right. In Beirut we were booed as westerners, in Europe as Arabs! I made a mental note to get French plates as soon as possible.

71

FRANCE

We had to settle initially in France, as I did not yet have a Swiss residence or work permit. I was to work in the big IOS offices in Ferney Voltaire, just two kilometres from the Swiss border. For the following eight weeks, we lived in the Hotel du Golf in Divonne, which sat in a park where the boys could play to their hearts content in the exciting deep snow with nanny Linda. The hotel was attached to the charming Divonne Casino, where there were no slot machines, and an excellent restaurant served delicious meals to people properly dressed. If you are going to lose money, at least do it in style.

On the grounds was a delightful little theatre where one evening Jennifer and I, together with Beth who had come to visit, enjoyed a moving violin recital by Isaac Stern. Beth became quite girlish and was convinced that Stern had looked into her eyes throughout the concert and played just for her. Obviously, in the heart of this eminently sensible matron beat the heart of the pretty girl she must once have been.

At the beginning of 1968 I was lucky enough to find, outside Gex, a small village at the foot of the Jura, a charming old farmhouse belonging to a Dutch count who worked for the ILO and had to spend a couple of years in New York. The house was on the road up to the Col de la Faucille. It had practically no furniture (which was just as well), but had been completely renovated. There were sufficient bedrooms for all of us, as well as magnificent views from an enormous drawing room with high, soaring windows at the centre of which, on clear days, the Mont Blanc rose majestically.

Covered with juniper (hence its name Les Genévriers), the house had cobbled courtyards and a trough into which water splashed soothingly. There was a small manicured garden that gave onto orchards, then thirty-three hectares of land, which was let out to local farmers for pasture. A paradise of the promised tranquillity.

All the barns were empty now except for one, where the owner had installed an authentic fairground carousel, with scarlet, gold, green, and blue elephants, giraffes, and horses—all rising and falling to the strains of an original barrel organ. It was a collector's piece and we treated it with respect, using it rarely, but every children's party seemed to end there—as did almost every grownups'.

With the property came an eighty-year-old gardener, who took care of the orchards and cut the grass along the drive with a scythe. In the summer, a few local lads would help him, scoffing at the old man, but slowly and effortlessly he always out-scythed them all. He was as silent as a clam to begin with, but the children's efforts to speak French soon had him laughing silently behind his pipe. One day he told Jennifer that he had lived his whole life in Gex and had never been to Geneva, eighteen km away. When she asked him why not he simply said, "Je ne suis pas curieux"—which was taking a lack of vulgar curiosity too far, in our opinion.

Clockwise: Our house in Beirut; Our farmhouse in France; Our house in Geneva

Above Left: Our cows; Above Right: Beth; Below Left: Family gathering;
Below right: Tea in our garden: mother, 3 boys, Nanny and Jennifer

He taught us a lot about the traditions of the Jura, and we were all enchanted at the end of each summer to see the herd of cows that had been taken from our fields in spring up to the high mountain pastures now returning to us again. Each cow had a heavy bell around its neck, of course, but now, at the head of the herd, the best milkers wore crowns of wildflowers as they ambled proudly past.

Installed in the Ferney Voltaire offices until my Swiss permits came through, I was entrusted with the marketing co-ordination of Latin America, North Africa, and the Middle East, including Pakistan and India. This involved frequent travel. I flew to Buenos Aires for the inauguration of a newly acquired insurance company; to Karachi for a regional meeting; to Teheran to plan an Iranian mutual fund; to Spain and Portugal to plan Spanish and Portuguese mutual funds. I held meetings with the Spanish arm of our operation in Germany, and addressed 400 British insurance salesmen at the ILI/IOS offices in Wembley and later was one of the main speakers at an enormous IOS meeting in Albert Hall.

After the disagreeable days in Brazil and Beirut, it was a relief to be involved in constructive work for a company in which I was by now an important shareholder.

Not only had I made a great deal of money, but as well as senior vice-president I was also a board director.

However, the main event of 1968 was, of course, the arrival of our son Mark Christopher on April 17, and now we were five! Unfortunately, Mark had a tricky start, with jaundice and projectile vomiting, so that in June we decided to take him up into the Swiss mountains, where we hoped the alpine air would do him a world of good. Gex, after all, was only at 600 metres. I remembered how I had enjoyed the Rickmers family holidays in Flims every summer, so I booked us into the Park Hotel Waldhaus, where we had always stayed.

From Gex I drove one car, and Åke, our Swedish driver, the other, up to the canton Grisons and Flims. We had decided to have Mark's christening there during our holiday. My mother's sister Moni would be Godmother; whilst Wolfgang and my manager for the Middle East, Samuel Welker, would be Godfathers. My sweet old grandmother, Mai Rickmers, accompanied Moni and, frail at 82, was very much the honoured centre of the gathering for her great-grandson.

Jennifer and I found a picturesque little village church in Fiduz, and a retired Anglican vicar who lived in Davos agreed to come and officiate. It had taken us a full day to organise all this, and when we returned to the hotel it was to find young John with a nasty gash at the back of his head and stitches. Once we had assured ourselves that there was nothing seriously wrong, Jennifer and I gave vent to our anger that the poor child had come bleeding out of the hotel swimming pool, only to find that nanny said she had to stay with Nick and Mark and the concierge could find nobody to take John to the doctor. Our not-yet-seven-year-old had been told to walk by himself to the doctor, get himself stitched up, and walk back. Admittedly the clinic was only a few hundred yards or so away, but our son was bleeding! Had it not been for the people arriving and all the christening arrangements, we would have immediately marched out of that hotel and fired the nanny.

The next day, John had not forgotten nor forgiven us for having left him behind with "the babies." He decided to leave us and go to Africa. Into his rucksack he packed his sweets, a leftover breakfast bun, his pyjamas, and his metal camping bottle filled with water. Without a farewell, frowning with determination, he set off. His mother and I watched from our bedroom balcony as he stomped through the hotel gardens. He took his first break after five minutes and drank from his bottle, then wandered slowly on for another few minutes before he sat down under a tree and sadly munched his bun. Jennifer could stand it no longer and sent me down to negotiate. I shared his sweets and persuaded him to go to Africa another day. Not to be outdone, Nick tried the same trick that afternoon, but John said that was not fair as he had no stitches in his head, and therefore no cause for complaint.

A few days later was Mark's big day, and when we arrived at the little church it was to find that the villagers had decorated every pew with posies of white and yellow spring flowers—pure and fresh against the simple whitewashed walls. The ceremony was short and simple, but the celebratory dinner that followed back in Flims was a big success. In fact, the old English vicar fell asleep half way through the toasts and had it not been for my presence of mind he would have slipped under the table, unaccustomed as he was to "so much fun."

Three weeks in the mountains did us all a world of good, and Mark especially simply blossomed, with renewed appetite and every sign of good health. In fact, when we got home, his paediatrician was so delighted with Mark's improvement that he pronounced him fit for military service. As he had been born in Switzerland, he would qualify for the Swiss Army. Nick, of course, had to be ready to be *un soldado Argentino,* and John presumably would be called up by the Danish military. We could only hope that their countries would be allies.

Back in Gex, I surprised Jennifer with a V-8 Mustang, long her dream, to congratulate her for Mark's birth. Åke taught her how to do racing gear shifts and, finding the car too light for the speed she could do, put concrete slabs in the boot so that Jennifer did not actually take off in her enthusiasm. It was scarlet, and had one of the first electric roofs so she could wow passers by at traffic lights by nonchalantly raising or lowering it.

I returned to the office to find great excitement reigning about the forthcoming IPO of our IOS Management Company. The now-eager Genèvois, the German public, international brokers and bankers were all desperate to secure shares in this underwriting. I was content with the shares I had, and knew I would quadruple my money. Some were greedy, and margin loans were extended freely and accepted. I myself was approached by the IOS Overseas Development Bank and Merrill Lynch. Had I taken them up on their offers I would have been able to amass a major "bundle" of IOS management shares. Unfortunately, I was too conservative to accept these offers, despite the fact that I would have made another $10 million or so. I told myself that I would wait for the IPO of IOS Ltd., the parent company, and then go in with all I had and make a real killing.

Through all the excitement, IOS continued to prosper and grow. I was constantly on the move, meeting top government officials and central bankers. Together with Jim Roosevelt, Senator Wilson Wyatt, Sir Wyndham White (architect of the General Agreement on Tariffs and Trade—GATT), Colonel Gordon West, and several top IOS lawyers, we worked on the creation of National Investment Trusts in South America, Iran, Spain, and Portugal.

Sales of mutual funds were exploding world-wide, our insurance companies and banks were euphoric. The real estate division built thousands of apartments and houses in Spain and Florida, which were snatched up before they were off the drawing boards.

IOS was instrumental in the creation of the Twin Towers of the World Trade Center in New York. Major fund products from companies such as Fidelity, Dreyfus, and RIC were incorporated into the IOS Investment Program, further enhancing our fund and insurance inventory. Huge tracts of highly promising oil land were bought in the Arctic. Today, forty years later, this land is priceless, another sign of Bernie's vision. There was no stopping us. We were becoming a world-class financial power house.

We celebrated my thirty-seventh birthday in November, 1968, at our house in Gex. The long drive down to the farmhouse was lit by flaming torches, and the local police managed the traffic. The Golf Hotel in Divonne catered the whole affair, with cooks and waiters swarming all over our ground floor as tables were arranged and mikes set up for the small band. When all the guests had arrived in full evening dress, the main table groaned under the elaborate supper buffet with its centrepiece of a mountain of grey Iranian caviar piled high on a silver platter. Therein lay a tale: I had flown back from Teheran a few days before with a hundred tins of the stuff. Unfortunately, in the baggage retrieval hall at Geneva's airport, the refrigerated cartons in which the tins had been carefully packed burst open. As they rolled between the bags on the carousel, word flew around—"Caviar!"—and there was a mad dash for it. Had it not been for the efficiency of the Swiss police, I would have lost most of it, but finally was happy to retrieve about ninety percent.

During my birthday supper, a few guests greedily attacked the glistening mound of caviar with large serving spoons, but ended up feeling decidedly queasy. Apart from this, the party was a triumph—ending, of course, with hilarious rides as we rode on the animals of the fantastic merry-go-round. The barn was icy, but brandy kept us warm—our glasses were topped up when we held them out from our mounts as we jubilantly circled around.

But in the wings, as yet unknown to us, jealousy was brewing. Anxious European bankers, especially in Germany, were alarmed by the amount of savings that were being withdrawn from them and invested with us. Germany was far and away our best European market, and our reputation amongst investors was enhanced when Dr. Erich Mende (ex-*Vizekanzler* and *Ritterkreuztraeger*) became our German chairman, with Dr. Preussker the head of our own Orbis Bank. But still the bankers' polemic rumbled on.

Obviously unaware of, or impervious to, any criticism, IOS Germany gave bombastic parties in Hamburg, Munich, Duesseldorf, Cologne, Frankfurt, and Stuttgart. Every economics student silently dreamt of joining us. Leading newspapers carried daily full-page IOS advertisements, and money magazines were full of praise and admiration of this growing financial empire.

But Nemesis lay waiting. The mounting jealousy was not only prompted by our success, but also by the unfortunate attitude of many German IOS managers. Swimming in new money, eager to flaunt their wealth with the biggest houses; indoor swimming pools; gold flashing everywhere from bathroom taps to wine goblets, garages crammed with flashy cars, their greatest delight was to have their possessions fill the pages of *Stern and Quick*.

Resentment, simmering at first, grew alarmingly, until finally we could ignore it no longer. Bernie, unfortunately, did not help matters. His "baby" up and running, he spent more and more time surrounded by beautiful actresses, singers, and film stars, so that hardly a week went by that he was not in the gossip columns himself. At Bella Vista, on his yacht, the cameras were everywhere. He flew in his private jet to walk barefoot along Via Venito with the best of the swinging sixties' celebrities. Harmless enough, but the public, especially the Calvinistic Swiss, judged this life style to be entirely inappropriate for a financial powerhouse. The fact that practically every fund manager, director, sales manager, and associate worked as hard as ever (otherwise we could not have continued to go from strength to strength) interested no one.

72

SWITZERLAND

My own confidence unshaken, I rejoiced when my Swiss Resident Permit finally came through and we moved to Conches, Chemin Calendrini number 4, in the outskirts of Geneva. We enrolled John and Nick in the nearby *école communale*, where their French improved by leaps and bounds so that soon it was all they would speak. I bought myself a thirty-six-foot twin-engine cabin cruiser and named her *Ding How*—"very good" in Chinese.

I had to pass a Swiss water-police test to be able to take her out, and the warnings that Lac Léman could be treacherous were soon proven to be correct. Jennifer and I took *Ding How* up to the top of the lake, above Evian. On our way back a storm blew up out of nowhere, and I made for the small port of Clarens, where I had fished as a boy.

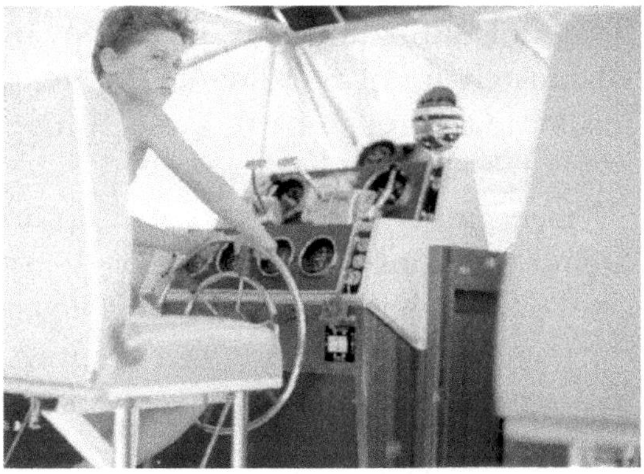

Our boat on the lake ; Capt. John Jr.

Petit Crêt with mother

Through the wild wind and lashing rain, an ancient mariner—Monsieur Chevalier, who years ago had taught me to swim—in yellow oil-skins and sou'wester rowed out to us and yelled for a rope. I was the captain, of course, and Jennifer my deckhand, so she threw him a rope and away he rowed, only to find our end flopping in the water.

"You never told me to tie it *to* anything!" Jennifer wailed and retired to the galley in high dudgeon.

John and Nick, wearing life jackets, were highly excited by the noise and sudden slamming of the hull into the choppy waves, very cross to be ordered to stay below. Fortunately we had left Mark at home with nanny, as even on calm days it was no fun for him or us to have to watch his every move.

Later in the year the weather improved and there came many happy days sailing to and exploring the old ports of the small Swiss and French lakeside towns; days on the water when the boys were allowed to invite a chum or suppers on deck with our own friends in the summer evenings when lights from the shore glittered on the dark water and our laughter echoed from the surrounding hills.

Now the long-awaited day of our parent company's IPO drew closer. Major European banks were engaged as underwriters, and all current IOS shareholders were asked to sell ten percent of their stock at the to-be-established offering price to create a market. Auditors from Arthur Andersen practically camped out in our offices throughout the world, in order to establish a realistic offering price based on IOS's assets, such as our banks, insurance companies, real estate holdings—including enormous tracts of Alaskan land—and above all, our mutual fund empire. The final judgement was that the IOS IPO should open at U.S. $10 per share.

This was the price all IOSers received when selling the mandatory ten percent of their stock, thus converting a "paper fortune" to cash. Of the remaining ninety percent, we would be allowed to sell ten percent a year until one was vested with the company, at which time all remaining stock could be sold.

With the IPO, it was open season for outside investors to approach the underwriters and buy as many shares at U.S. $10 as they could lay their hands on. Everyone was confident that these shares would soar by ten-fold or more, just as had been the case with the IPO of IOS Management.

Caught up in the excitement, I contacted my bankers in order to scoop up as many shares as I could at the opening price. I managed to get my hands on a sizeable amount, and then pledged them as collateral in order to buy additional shares on margin ranging between $12-$20 per share. The prudent investor I had been at the time of our last IPO, when I had missed out on the opportunity to make millions, was not going to be repeated! I sold all my IOS investment programs and put the proceeds together with all my cash into the underwriting. This time, when bankers approached me, offering me more money to buy more shares—which again were used as collateral—I accepted, and thus gathered an impressive war chest.

Although wiser heads would frown because I was putting all my eggs in one basket—something we had preached against for years—I can only point out that the aura surrounding our success coloured all our lives. IOS was our religion; we were her missionaries spreading wealth in our paths—how could anything go wrong?

IOS stock doubled overnight to $20. Bankers called, advising me to sell and pocket a tidy profit. But we, the believers, laughed. We were waiting for the stock to hit at least $100. Carefree and exhilarated, Jennifer and I flew to London to celebrate our tenth wedding anniversary. We stayed in the bridal suite at The Dorchester, and went to Dick and Roni Gangel's house-warming party at their new abode in Rutland Gate, previously the home of English aristocrats who would have been surprised to see it now, with a swimming pool in the basement and a whole host of trans-Atlantic must-haves. But the Gangels were a very special and dear couple—they could do no wrong in our eyes.

That Christmas we spent in Zermatt with Johan and Zoila Streijffert, where our children played with theirs in the snow. John, Nick, and little Mark never knew that the sea-trunk out on our bedroom balcony was full of gifts. Late on Christmas Eve, we found the locks frozen solid with Santa's loot locked inside. It took over an hour of careful defrosting with tooth mugs full of hot water before the toys could be scattered around the small tree in our salon.

In March we drove to Genoa, where we boarded the Michelangelo, a 47,000-ton Italian cruise ship, stopping at Malta, Athens, and Istanbul, then through the Bosphorus and into the Black Sea (where we were excited to see the Russian Fleet) and back to Sicily, Barcelona, and Genoa. In Istanbul, Jennifer and I visited the Blue Mosque and the Topkapi Museum, where my wife fell in love with a small cup made of emeralds which were held together by veins of gold. She advised me that if I was thinking of filching anything for her this was all she wanted.

The children's highlight was leaping back and forth over the white line that divided Europe and Asia on the bridge over the Bosphorus, thus creating a world record of having crossed from one continent to another twenty times in five minutes. Mark managed it twice.

Once we found John and Nick sitting at our table in the ship's dining room waiting for us. They had taken quick advantage of this unusual situation by ordering ten forbidden Cokes and a lurid variety of ice creams, to the amusement of a group of indulgent waiters. Mark, too young for such hijinks, spent happy hours in the well-equipped ship's playroom with Nanny and other toddlers, so each enjoyed the cruise after his own fashion.

Our cruise ship - T/S Michelangelo – Italian Line (which I represented in the Dominican Republic.)

73

The Beginning of the End

Although I returned to head office in Geneva to find the IOS story still being extolled in every newspaper, for some reason our sure touch seemed to be faltering—even though we were at the peak of our success—and unfortunate decisions began to be made. Personally I put a lot of the blame on the dozens of freshly graduated American MBAs from Ivy League universities, who arrived at the head office wasting everyone's time and energy with endless charts and statistics.

When a group of German managers demanded increased overrides for a newly invented breed of super-super general managers, these inexperienced young guys thought this was a great idea and pushed for it. At a board meeting, I said I thought it would be counter-productive, ill-advised, and cause trouble in the field. How would we cover our huge overheads, which were partially paid from up-front commissions? I voted against it. Unfortunately it went through.

Then our eager MBAs kept coming up with new, unprofitable product lines, leaving me, at least, with the impression that they felt honour-bound to pay for their keep by presenting us with almost anything rather than leaving our extraordinary achievements alone.

To add to the confusion, the stock market began to fall, reducing our assets under management and, of course, our stock value. Now the newly increased commissions meant that the more we sold the less the company made. As I had foreseen, the greed of the German managers was dangerously rocking the boat.

And so one thing led to another as an accumulation of unnecessary decisions caused circumstances that slowly but surely pulled us down. Our "friends" at the press, who had heralded our success story for years, now turned against us, as is their wont. A smear campaign began with the gutter press, delving into Bernie's private escapades and the personal lives of men at the top of IOS Development Company. Whether what they reported was true or invented, I wouldn't know. Then the lavish parties, the extravagant gifts, and the celebrity life styles of the top men in Germany and Italy were splashed across the tabloids.

Everyone in the company was aware of the falling share price and shrinking assets, and a general feeling of gloom and discontent spread like influenza as the swarms of MBAs, who had no loyalty to the firm, now wanted to distance themselves from us.

In spite of endless PR efforts and press conferences, the beginnings of real trouble were watched with glee by the banking community, which had waited for years to wrest their customers back from us. This was the moment they had longed for, and their damaging and highly speculative remarks about the state of IOS's affairs dragged us down with an unstoppable undertow of malice.

A great blow to the marketing division was the cancellation of our traditional yearly supervisors and managers meeting in that summer of 1970. Triggered by the insupportable increase in commissions and overrides and the resulting reduced cash flow, this ill-considered decision was an enormous mistake. Immediately the morale of our thousand supervisors in the field was undermined, prompting panic and insecurity in the sales force and resulting in mass desertions to our competitors. At times I despaired that the head office did not understand how vital our sales force was to our very existence.

The cash flow problem could have been easily and quickly solved by the sale of some of our massive real estate holdings, or by divesting ourselves of some of our banks and insurance companies. Instead, negotiations began to raise cash from unknown entities in Texas and New York, rich men who ultimately were eager simply to raid IOS of its world-wide assets.

We were brilliant builders, but we panicked when unforeseen problems arose. Suddenly we were attacked in the press for "over-valuing" our Alaskan oil land to Arthur Andersen, thus encouraging them to inflate the underwriting price. Actually this Alaskan oil land was one of the best investments IOS ever made and is worth many billions of dollars today.

Unbelievably, in the summer of 1970, the founders of this amazing company were asked to stand down by the newly created crisis committee. Our famous three

Cs—Cornfeld, Cowett and Cantor—all agreed to resign for the sake of the company they had worked so hard to build. John King, a potential buyer from Texas brought in by Bernie, had insisted upon this.

In Allen's place, Harvey Felberbaum, the general manager of Italy, was made president of the sales company, and Sir Eric Wyndham White became president of the IOS parent company. Crisis meeting after crisis meeting was held until the "Executive Crisis Committee" ran around in circles like a chicken with its head chopped off. Their final conclusion was that IOS was no longer a "viable" company.

Even now there remained one great ray of hope. The Rothschild Group in France had been our partner for years in the form of IOS-Rothschild Expansion, France, and they offered us a lifeline. They would buy the majority of IOS stock and take over the management. I pleaded at a directors' meeting that we should grab this straw. It would reduce our company's size, but would give us the credibility to start building again on a solid base, making IOS-Rothschild as big or bigger than we ever were. It might take five to seven years, but we would survive and rise again like the Phoenix.

Unfortunately, this lifeline was rejected due to a mixture of vanity, greed, stubbornness, and myopia. Many members of the new management apparently feared that an acceptance of the Rothschild offer would result in their own dismissal—which, in some cases, might have been a very good thing. In my opinion, it was an egregious blunder.

Now nobody was happier than the banks, especially the German banks, which gleefully watched the decline they had contrived. They began by massively selling IOS stock short, thus causing it to collapse. Anxious investors then rushed to get rid of their stock as well as IOS investment funds, returning their money into the open arms of the very banks whose discontented customers they had originally been.

Daily thousands of clients, first from Germany and then from all sides, redeemed their investments. It was like a run on a bank. But instead of closing their doors, as many banks have done in the past, the "original" IOS (prior to "new management") honoured all redemption requests, transferring additional staff from other administrative divisions to the liquidations department (which previously had been insignificant) in order to comply swiftly with clients' redemption orders.

By August, the flying rumours of succession coalesced on a Mr. Robert Vesco from New York as our saviour. Banking friends immediately called me to point out that this was a very unwise choice. Vesco had a rotten reputation. As it turned out they were right—the only "rescue" Vesco undertook was to cover IOS's payroll for the month of September, 1970. After that, safely installed in 119 rue de Lausanne, he methodically looted the till.

I decided it was time to go. This was not my IOS. I wanted no part of the insane management decision that had played right into the hands of a notorious financial crook. So far the old company had a clean shirt, having paid out all clients in a correct and efficient manner. Who knew what Vesco would do. I had lost my fortune, but not my reputation, and I refused to be associated with some underworld con-man. How could the new management hand the whole company over to such a character, rather than join the prestigious Rothschild Group?

Our world was collapsing around us. Lives were ruined, there were suicides, divorces, and bankruptcies. I sold my beloved boat (the last thing you buy is usually the first to go) and all the lovely cars except our Volvo station wagon, and let go most of our staff.

Occasionally there were moments of light relief. We gave a few last dinners in Conches without the help of Åke, who had always doubled as an impeccable butler when we needed to put on the Ritz.

As a last-minute stop-gap, Jennifer tried to train Hilaria, our unpredictable, Portuguese maid, to stand at the library door and say, "*Madame, le diner est servi.*" When the time came to go into dinner, Hilaria stood in her uniform before the assembled guests, frozen with stage fright. After a few seconds, she raised her hands to her mouth and said simply, "*Mangez, le mangez,*" which turned a stiff affair into a riot, as everyone remembered their own similar disasters, and the evening was a great success. But such moments were few. The very worst part for me was having to face family and friends who had trusted me and invested in IOS. I had lost my own money too, but that was small comfort to them. Never again.

I was contacted by a number of competitive companies, finally accepting the position of Executive Vice-President of the PAR Fund, a subsidiary of Gulf American, in 1970 a $950-million company. I was put in charge of their real estate orientated fund, just the right thing after IOS. My headquarters were in Frankfurt, with thirty-six offices throughout Germany and Austria. I was given a Mercedes 600 with chauffeur and a royal salary. The *Geschaeftsfuehrer* working with me was Prince Michael von Preussen, Grandson of Emperor Wilhelm II, a very charming young man—and, of course, excellent "window dressing" for the German public.

Most of my 400 salesmen were ex-IOS, and sales picked up rapidly. Jennifer and I planned to move lock, stock, and barrel to Frankfurt, and got as far as checking out the Frankfurt International School.

Now all of IOS's competitors rushed to flood the market with new investment vehicles. Gramco in particular, long a bitter and ruthless rival of IOS, pushed too hard in its desperate efforts to capitalise on IOS's demise, ran into difficulties, and stopped paying redemptions. A short time before he stepped down, Allen Cantor had said to me, " If we go under, all the others will follow shortly, mark my words." And so it happened. With the collapse of IOS and now Gramco, the whole industry was shaky.

In such a climate, the chairman of the Par Fund decided to close down Germany. He asked me to come to California to develop and market the casino/hotel/golf Calvada Valley complex he intended to build there. He offered me the position of Executive Vice President in charge of U.S. marketing, but by now I was shattered and momentarily incapable of tackling another product or another continent.

I was never to meet Vesco personally but, adrift in Geneva, I listened helplessly to horror tales from those insiders who had stayed on board. All they could do was watch Vesco rob IOS and our clients blind. He literally raped the funds of their remaining assets, sold the insurance companies, banks, and real estate holdings before disappearing off the radar with the proceeds. Almost his last act had been to pilfer more than a thousand Patek Philippe gold watches—the traditional reward to outstanding IOS managers—before boarding a plane with the Swiss police hot on his tail. The U.S. Securities and Exchange Commission charged that he had stolen more than U.S. $224 million.

Later we were to discover that his flight took him first to Costa Rica, but even there he was declared persona non grata after a year. Next the Bahamas were happy to accommodate his riches, but he also outstayed his welcome there and had to leave. He had only one "buddy" left—Fidel Castro, who initially received him with open arms. Vesco returned this hospitality by producing fraudulent patent medicines in Cuba and was ultimately jailed there.

Vesco

His death has been reported many times over the years, the last being a few months ago in 2008. If true, the world is well rid of the man, but I will not be surprised if he pops up again one day.

And so ended an honest and idealistic company that had simply grown too fast. Had we joined the Rothschild Group, we could have regained our position as a major financial player within five years, but greed, panic, and a complete lack of professionalism displayed by the new "management" was the greatest contributor to our totally unnecessary downfall. Most of us lost fortunes, but some, willing to sell short, came out of the debacle with theirs intact. Fear not—I shall not name names.

And what of Bernie himself? Distraught by the collapse of the empire he had built up and then so woefully neglected, he now suffered the humiliation of arrest. The Swiss system allows the imprisonment of suspects before any trial takes place. Once Cornfeld was under lock and key, *then* investigations and interrogations began.

One of the main accusations against him was that the Arctic oil fields were a fraud and had merely served to establish an artificially inflated underwriting price before the IPO. These "worthless" oil fields today represent a value of more than 200 times the value that IOS and its auditors had established. It was also easy to prove that major auditing firms had spent six months analysing all of IOS's assets before reaching the conclusion that U.S. $10 per share was a fair price.

Next the Swiss tried to prove that IOS had "put its fingers in the cookie jar,"—i.e., used clients' deposits to finance its spectacular growth. Here again the accusations did not stick. Assets belonging to IOS investors were always immediately redeemable upon request. Client monies went immediately and directly to our depository bank, Credit Suisse Zurich. Neither Bernie nor any of the old guard could be held responsible for what happened once Vesco and his new management team came on board and looted everything not nailed down.

After a few agonising months in a Swiss jail, Bernie was released and declared "not guilty" of all the charges levied against him. He was, however, a broken man. He died in poverty in a London hospital some years later. Many of us chipped in to pay his hospital bills.

To this day I remember him with affection, and still see him as an idealistic, caring man whose too-rapid rise to great success and riches was totally destabilising. He became bored by the day-to-day running of his empire and lost himself in *la dolce vita*. When he saw what was happening to IOS, he came to his senses—but, by then, it was too late.

Curiously enough, after years of ridiculing our investment funds, all the banks involved in the collapse of IOS launched their own funds—not only copying our fund programmes to the letter, but also building up marketing systems identical to ours. How does that saying go? Imitation is the highest form of compliment.

74

SPAIN

Now that all my ties with the new IOS had been severed, I felt completely and utterly rudderless. For ten exciting years I had delighted in my work, and now everything was over, all was flat. As my Swiss work permit and residence were linked to IOS, our dreams of permanent residence in Switzerland collapsed along with everything else.

Thanks to Jennifer's encouragement, I decided to leave Geneva behind. Spain beckoned. When all seems drab and hopeless, there is nothing like the sun to cheer you up. We had stayed in Andalucia before on holiday, and I had a few contacts there from Indevco, the old IOS Real Estate Division. Wolfgang, my young cousin, had been there for years, and promised to find us somewhere to live.

He came up trumps with a big old rambling house in the empty hills behind Benalmadena, where only rabbits and goats, rosemary and thyme flourished. In those days, the southern coast of Andalucia was still Spain.

Our new home was called San Miguel del Pinillo and sat in a large garden surrounded by tall pines. In the middle there was a big pool fed by a natural spring, to the south was the sea with clear views of Gibraltar and the coast of Africa, whilst to the east the snow-covered Sierra Nevada loomed in the distance and Monte Aguila rose immediately behind us.

The house sat amidst ancient olive groves, and in the early mornings men ambled past on donkeys selling bread, vegetables, or eggs. On Fridays there was fish, fresh from the boats, sloshing around in rather mucky buckets. There was a man on a bicycle who kept our kitchen knives razor sharp as he pedalled furiously away, keeping his whetstone whizzing, chatting to our entranced boys in the broad Andaluz they were so quick to learn.

I rented offices, found a Swedish secretary who spoke all the necessary languages, and started selling a wide range of real estate products through my remaining salesmen. I made enough for us to have a pleasant life in the sun. We found an excellent cook, proud Amparo from Madrid, who made the hottest patatas bravas we were ever to eat. There was good-natured Paca, una Andaluza de pura cepa (of pure Andalucian stock) who cleaned and ironed and told Jennifer lurid tales of life during the Civil War, when for years her family had lived on bread, garlic, and oil because even the catch her fisherman father brought in was confiscated by the feared Guardia Civil. Our gardener, Juan, blithely watered everything every evening—including the non-insulated electric cables for the garden and pool lights. The switches for the rather primitive filter system of the latter were under water in the well, and only Juan ever dared touch them. We called the local electrician to make things safer, but he just shrugged his shoulders and could see nothing wrong.

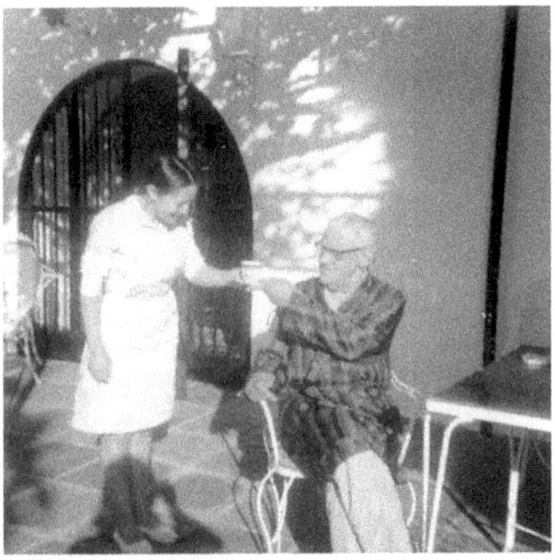

Top left: Our pool;
Top right: Bill`s early morning coffee + Amparo;
Left: Sportsday at Sandle Manor Prep School, England

Once a small rodent fell into the pool, and Jennifer declared that nobody was going to swim in "mouse soup," so all the water had to be drained out, then slowly refilled from the spring like a large bath tub. Once in a while Juan would toss in a few litres of chlorine, and certainly none of us ever got sick.

Into Jennifer's life at this time came a tiny Godchild named Nicola, who was to become the daughter she never had—and who, to this day, is her dear friend and confidante despite the great age difference.

We were to spend four happy years here—including 1972, with the exciting Summer Olympics. John and Nick, already mad about tennis and swimming, watched every event. Their excitement was contagious, and soon the whole family would have knowing discussions about the relative merits of the athletes during every lunch. Mark Spitz was everyone's hero, and it was Mark Spitz this and Mark Spitz that, until one day little Mark jumped off his chair, stood with hands on hips, face red with fury, shouting, "It's not true. I do not spit!"

The only flaw was the schooling. It did not matter yet so much for Nick or Mark, but John was falling far behind in the best school available at that time. The day the young basketball coach became head was too much, and another solution had to be found.

Jennifer scoured the English-speaking schools in Malaga and Madrid, but in those days they were not much better than our local one, so we began, very reluctantly, to think of prep schools in England. Finally we chose Sandle Manor, close to the boys' Aunt Liz, in Fordingbridge.

For John this was a terrible shock. Tossed around the world as we all had been, family had become the only rock when everything and everybody was constantly changing. He loved the open-air life in Spain, and he would sit with a group of his friends for hours under our spreading rubber tree in the late afternoons, strumming guitars and singing folk songs. He showed so much talent that his music master wanted us to send him to a flamenco guitar school in Malaga. It is one of our biggest regrets that we told him he could not go, as the classes were, Spanish style, from nine to eleven in the evening. He would not have been home until after midnight, and we foolishly denied him this unique opportunity. Sorry, John.

For Jennifer too this was a heart-wrenching time, exacerbated by the unexpected death of her mother. The following year, Nick joined his brother, and so we missed our two big boys immensely. Poor Mark began to feel like an only child, and Jennifer lost her *joie de vivre.*

I was distracted by an exciting new venture. Tennis was the ideal sport for southern Spain, but Marbella (a forty-minutes drive to the west) had no tennis facilities to speak of. Arthur Scampa, an American friend in the real estate business, had met with Prince Alfonso Hohenlohe, the founder of the legendary Marbella Club, and told him of our plans. Alfonso was delighted with the idea and encouraged us to call the planned tennis village the "Tennis del Marbella Club," thus giving us instant prestige and credibility.

With Alfonso on board, we contacted the son of the famous tennis champion of the 1930s, Fred Perry, who won three times at Wimbledon; the US Open three times plus the French and Australian once each. His son David, from Beverley Hills, was eager to endorse our project. So under the lions and crown of the Hohenlohe crest, we put Fred Perry's crossed olive branches and created a fine logo. Another celebrity in the tennis world, Jimmy Connors, agreed to become our head pro.

The plans called for a multi-million dollar clubhouse, fourteen courts plus the centre court, Olympic swimming pool, all to be surrounded by 350 tennis villas. We had found an ideal piece of land in a green valley overlooking the sea and reasonably close to the Marbella Club. Alfonso arranged for us to work out of an office next to the hotel's front entrance and agreed to allow us to place our large architects' model of the village in the main hall close to the reception area. It just could not be missed.

With all systems now go, we had a luxurious sales brochure printed, and thanks to all the marketing tools, local sales took off like a rocket. Soon salesmen in Germany, Austria, Italy, Spain, and the U.K. were pleading for inventory, which we had to ration. It was a salesman's dream.

As I was in Marbella every day and John and Nick were now both at Canford, a public school in Dorset, Jennifer asked if we could move down the coast to be closer to my new office. We found a house with a garden and pool in El Rosario, which delighted all three boys as there was a lively club with excellent tennis courts, where they practically lived during school holidays. There were lots of pretty girls for John and Nick, whilst Mark lost his heart for the first time to a little Swedish beauty who went to Ecos, his new school in the hills above Elviria.

I was utterly focused on our tennis village, listening to our very experienced architects and engineers estimate their construction and material costs, based on 1972-73 prices. According to our accountants, a handsome final net profit could be anticipated, of which my own share, based on my investment of forty percent, would be in excess of $4 million (1970 dollars). We rubbed our hands as sales rushed in, and construction had barely begun when the tennis villas were almost sold out.

Unfortunately, it's seldom possible to factor in politics. With no declaration of war, Israel was attacked in 1973 on Yom Kippur. An oil embargo was immediately implemented by the Arab nations, forcing gasoline and diesel to stratospheric heights. Cement prices increased by forty percent, the cost of construction materials in general rose in tandem, inflation soared, and southern Spain slid rapidly into recession. At the prices we had sold the village, there was no way we could build it with a profit now.

Top: John & Nick in our Rosario garden
Right: Jennifer and Mark in San Luis Obispo, California
Below: Mark´s Rosario birthday party, Nick in background

So what to do? What to tell 350 eager villa owners and tennis players? Fortunately, through our architect, we established contact with a group of wealthy Moroccans with close ties to the Royal Moroccan family and very deep pockets. They gladly agreed to take over the whole project. My partners and I gave a sigh of relief. We recovered our investment, but naturally no profits nor the enormous fun our dream tennis village promised, could now be realised.

So it was back to selling real estate from a new office in downtown Marbella. We began to concentrate on farms in California, as anything Spanish was dead for the time being. Thus began a period of frequent trips to California to check out the properties, most of which were easily saleable in Europe, if not to Spaniards, who were not willing to hear about any land investments for some time to come.

75

GERMANY

As Spain remained stuck in the doldrums, we moved to Germany, where demand was brisk for U.S. real estate. We found a house almost in the woods between Pöcking and Possenhofen, above the Starnberg Lake. It stood in a park with five or six other houses, and we were to discover that our nearest neighbour was Leni Riefenstahl, once a renowned film director and actress but by then a reclusive old lady. The wives in the other houses were kind to Jennifer, and set about teaching her to make delicious Bavarian cakes. To this day in her cookbook, she has Frau Goerdel's marble cake; Frau Schmidt's nut cake, and Frau Heidinger's lemon cake, together with instructions on baking in the correct Bavarian way.

Mark was enrolled in the Munich International School, John was taking his Handel's Exam in Hamburg, and Nick was supposedly learning Italian in Florence, but soon came home to join us. John came back to us regularly as Jennifer strove to keep the family together come what may.

Before long it became apparent that demand for U.S. real estate was at its most buoyant in the Arab countries. I was approached by Allen Cantor and George Tregea (both ex-IOSers), who persuaded me to spend seventy-five percent of my time in their offices in Sharjah, Dubai, Kuwait, and Doha from 1983-1985.

I was the lonely one in my Middle Eastern hotels, as Jennifer had two sons at home—Mark, who was studying for his O levels at MIS, and Nick, who didn't really have any ambitions at that time. John was doing his apprenticeship with Jebsen & Jessen in Hamburg. The long separations were tough. Sometimes I was away for a six weeks at a time, and those two years were unhappy ones. Quite apart from missing my family, life in the UAE, as well as in Kuwait and Doha, was not pleasant.

Fortunately relief was at hand. I received a call from Allen's partner, Augusto Menendez, asking me if I would like to take charge of the marketing of a major real estate development on the coast north of Caracas. Would I!

76

VENEZUELA

I flew to Caracas with Jennifer to see what she thought of the move, but it was a foregone conclusion that she would agree as we both had had enough of being separated. I stayed there whilst Jennifer returned to Germany to wait until Mark's exams were over, then close up the house. Mark was to do his A levels at Exeter, a boarding school in England, this time close to his grandfather and Jennifer's younger sister Susan.

Jennifer stayed in England with Mark for some months, but we had decided that Nick should join me in Caracas. He was going through a difficult period, and I wanted to show him that getting up every morning, wearing a suit, and making a living could be fun. Of course, being in Caracas made this easier than if I had tried to convince him of this in, say, Birmingham. He took to selling real estate like a duck to water, and was happier than he had been for years.

Finally Jennifer joined us. She didn't think much of Nick's and my bachelor pad, and quickly found a pretty house at the top of some hills so that we could look down at Caracas glittering at our feet at night, but not have to listen to the city racket or breathe the polluted air.

Our air was so pure that one evening we were visited by a sloth! I had been standing, smoking a last cigarette, when a strange smell overwhelmed me and I felt the warmth of some large animal a few inches away. I don't know which of us was more scared, but I stepped back quickly as the terrified creature fled—and being a sloth, it took almost half an hour for it to climb down from the tree and disappear into the darkness. I felt strangely blessed by such a close encounter with this wild creature.

We loved the climate, the people, the language, and the life style. Mark had to finish his A-levels at Exeter, whilst John was at the European Business School in London, but both flew out three times a year and had wonderful holidays with Nick as their guide to the high life of Caracas. As a family, we made frequent excursions to the various beach and mountain resorts of beautiful Venezuela—including Puerto de la Cruz, where the snorkelling was unbelievable. Everything looked rosy once again.

Early on I was approached by the Metropolitan Rotary Club, became a member, and a year later, in 1986, was elected president whilst Jennifer became the "*Presidenta del comité de Damas*," as the inner wheel was called in Venezuela. I gave many speeches, and we raised money in as many ways as we could imagine. Jennifer also organised successful fundraising events, such as *Una Noche en Paris*, with Can-Can girls and a French menu for well over 800 guests.

So much money was raised that our club could finance the complete renovation of a dilapidated old people's home on the outskirts of Caracas, where the elderly residents slept on bare metal bed-frames whilst water ran down the slimy green walls behind their heads. In South America, charity has to take the place of most governments, and Jennifer became known as *el angel blanco* by the destitute of Charallave, to her great embarrassment. This prompted her to stop wearing her customary white for a while. On the day when the entire club came out to see the renovated home, everyone admired the rebuilt and painted walls, proper beds with sheets, pillows and mattresses, waterproofed ceilings, adequate sanitation, and well-stocked kitchen cupboards. The Rotarians were as delighted as the residents, and a promise was made that each *presidenta* would remember Charallave during her year in office.

One of the most exciting trips we made with our three sons was an excursion to Canaima, deep in the Orinoco basin. We flew first to Puerto Ordaz, changed flights, and flew on through deep valleys and gorges with the wing tips of our 737 almost

Jennifer in Charallave

Above: John's 25th at the Caracas Hilton
Left: Jennifer addressing a United Nations Association meeting in Cambridge Mass.

touching the rocks on each side as we marvelled at El Angel, or Angel Falls, the tallest waterfall in the world, its cascading waters falling a thousand metres down into the valley.

When we landed in Canaima, we were driven in jeeps to a small settlement, where we were shown to straw thatched huts, fortunately with primitive sanitation. At dawn the following day, Indian guides took us in dugouts down the river through dense jungle, where toucans and large, brilliant green parrots flew screeching through the trees, adding their raucous racket to the piercing shrieks of families of monkeys.

Whenever we reached white water, we all had to get out and follow the Indians over the rocks as they strode ahead, carrying the dugouts on their heads, until we reached a navigable stretch of the river again. We stopped beneath giant trees laden with small violet orchids, where my sons and I, plus one or two other brave souls, splashed about in an icy pool created by stunning waterfalls, where huge blue butterflies flew in and out of the spray.

We walked back to the river where the guides built a fire on the sand, pulled some chicken out of a bag, pierced them with bamboo sticks, and balanced them like a tepee-frame over the flames to roast. Either we were ravenous, or this is the ideal way to cook birds. Whichever the case, they were delicious.

Now Mark began two years at Berry College in Georgia, John continued his EBS studies in Frankfurt and Paris, but both continued to fly out to us at every possible break. Nick was at last settling down, and he and I became very close. These were good days all around.

77

Florida-USA

After two-and-a-half happy years in Venezuela, Carlos Menendez called me over to Florida to begin marketing his real estate project close to Fort Myers on the Gulf of Mexico. I went ahead and left Jennifer, good trouper that she was, to close up our house, then fly together with Nick to join me.

At long last they arrived in Miami one evening, and we set out by car to yet another new home. It was a long drive on the Tamiami Trail from one coast to the other, and as we drove through the Everglades in the dark, we saw warnings of crossing alligators and panthers, making both my son and wife wonder what on earth I was dragging them into this time.

Their fears vanished as they raced through the house I had found. It was a large bungalow, every room opening onto a big indoor pool, with a garden leading down to a creek. Jennifer said she loved it, but the netting around and over the pool would have to go as it was ugly.

The agent who had brought the keys roared with laughter. "You take that netting down, Ma'am, an' you'll share your mornin' swim with critters from that thar creek."

Nick was intrigued. "Like what?"

The man gave him a huge grin. "Only 'gators n' rattlers!"

So the netting stayed, and we ended up not noticing it. Indeed, when the lawn man showed us the snakes he had caught in the garden and the local newspaper ran articles about alligators getting into pools, we became quite fond of it.

Life in Florida was pleasant but boring. The heat, only bearable with air-conditioning, seemed to dull the brain with lethargy. We missed the cool mountain air of our house over Caracas and our lively Latin friends. I joined the small, local Rotary Club, but it couldn't hold a candle to the one in Caracas. We were surrounded by golf courses, but we did not play golf. The people around us were mostly retired "snowbirds" from the North, and not really on our wavelength. But I was busy setting up a marketing network of overseas brokers, and sales started to go well.

Nick was beginning to realise that if he did not finish his education, his two brothers would leave him far behind. He agreed to go to college, and I managed to get him enrolled into Fort Myers Edison College, which filled our hearts with pleasure. Mark visited us for many a weekend, as he was only a ninety-minute flight away, and John came from England for every possible holiday to sample the American way of life, which was so new to us all.

Sales went so well that soon we were sold out, but Menendez, who had promised me a continuous flow of product, decided not to go ahead with more real estate ventures for the time being. Now what?

Thanks to IOS, I still had many close friends who were living in the U.S., and once again they helped me out. In this instance, it was Bob Sutner, my first manager in Mexico City, and Dick Gangel from Geneva, who came to my rescue. Both lived in New York now, and within a few weeks, thanks mainly to Bob, I landed an excellent job as International Marketing Director and Managing Director of Liberty Financial International, based in Boston.

This of course entailed a move to their Boston headquarters, and there would be lots of international travel. We decided that Jennifer and Nick should remain in Florida so that Nick could finish his school year, and I flew down from Boston every weekend. I wanted time to judge whether or not this job was really what I wanted. I was then fifty-six years old, in reasonably good shape, certainly happy to face hard work, but concerned about the intensive international travel around the world, sometimes covering thirty countries in forty-five days. Quite apart from its effect on me, I worried about leaving Jennifer so much.

My office building in Boston, called "washboard" by the Bostonians

78
Boston

We took an apartment in Boston, and Nick was accepted by Northeastern University to their Business Administration course. Mark began his master's at the Georgia Institute of Technology in Atlanta, affectionately known as Georgia Tech. One always had to explain to non-Americans that this meant an institute like MIT, and not a technical school for carpenters and plumbers! John was soon to graduate from EBS, and afterwards would join the family company in Hong Kong.

Although everyone came "home" as often as possible, Jennifer, left alone a lot, began voluntary work for the United Nations Association under Mylo Housen. She was thrown in at the deep end by Mylo who, on her first day, told Jennifer to organise a reception at the Boston State House for UN Day. She gave Jennifer a list of ambassadors and their wives, as well as all the local politicians and bigwigs to whom she was to send invitations. Mike Dukakis was then governor of Massachusetts, and on the big day Jennifer was a bundle of nerves, but there was not a hitch, and Nick and I, standing at the very back of the hall, were proud of her.

Most of the Boston UNA's work involved setting up discussion groups, where diplomats and others involved in foreign affairs would talk to undergraduates in order to encourage them to take up similar careers. With so many top universities in the area, there was a lot to do to cover them all once a year. Mylo always had Jennifer make the difficult calls to see if very busy men would give the UNA an hour or two of their time. A staunch anglophile, Mylo was convinced that an English accent would impress. Had Jennifer known the importance of the people she was telephoning, she might have been nervous, but in her ignorance she was able to chat easily with Negroponte and Eagleburger as their names sounded to her like Indian chieftains. She was unaware of their eminence and thus unabashed.

Meanwhile I was travelling more than IATA—International Air Transport Association—rules would allow their pilots. My job entailed visits to all major Merrill Lynch and Nomura offices throughout the world as they were our main distributors selling hundreds of millions of Liberty Financial Funds to their international clients. I usually flew from Miami and then Dallas to Tokyo, Nagoya, Osaka, Hong Kong, Singapore, Bahrain, Dubai, Doha, Kuwait, Cairo, Athens, Rome, plus another eight or nine European capitals before heading back to Boston.

Then it would be down to Central and South America. These trips usually lasted thirty days. Although I flew first class and stayed in the suites of the worlds best hotels, it was nevertheless exhausting.

With my cousin Michael Jebsen in front of Villa Lensnack - Denmark

Occasionally I only did twelve major European cities, when I would take Jennifer along as my "carefree companion." Those trips were obviously much more fun. Another highlight we both enjoyed were the Liberty Financial Directors' meetings in the Bahamas, where we all usually stayed in the rather exclusive Lyford Cay Club. Sometimes, though, the venue was Bermuda or Paris—and once, on my suggestion, everyone flew to Switzerland and we stayed in the Montreux Palace. I had waxed enthusiastic about the fantastic Alpine scenery, but it rained every wretched day. Not surprisingly, it was back to the West Indies the following year.

I brought brokerage firms other than Merrill Lynch and Nomura on board, and was now asked to develop new products—such as insurance "wrappers" around our funds. This entailed visits to French, German, and Belgian central banks—plus the Bank of Japan—and their respective law firms. Once these new products were ready, I organised a retail distribution network and found myself giving speeches to major sales groups, sometimes 1,000 strong. In Germany I spoke to 2,000 people at a time, and was thus back in my old IOS element.

In 1991, Jennifer and I spent a few days with John, who was working in Hong Kong, and then we three travelled through China for two weeks on a trip wonderfully organised by our son. It was the first time I had been back to Shanghai since I was a boy and the memories were bittersweet.

Much had changed, but with the help of a 1940's map, we found our old street, Tung-Ping-Lu, and there stood my father's house. Several apartment blocks had been built on the grounds, but the house itself was unchanged. I began to film it from the road, but Chinese guards came out to stop me. Our driver warned us that this house was now used by top Chinese Army officers. After much persuasion, we were allowed through the gates, minus all cameras. As I was pointing out my bedroom, the room where my father had died, et cetera, an irritated general decked out with gold braid and medals appeared at an upstairs balcony and began to yell at us. My intrepid wife called back, "You are standing in my mother-in-law's boudoir!"

He cannot have understood her but, hands on hips, he threw back his head and roared with laughter. "People's property now—ha, ha!"

Indubitably.

From Shanghai we flew to Beijing to wander, frozen, around Tiananmen Square, then into the once-Forbidden City, empty now of all ghosts. In Xian we saw the Terracotta Army—which, even though still not fully unearthed, amazed us with its endless lines of statues, the men in strange costumes, each with a different facial expression. They were accompanied by their animals, by artisans, by obviously eminent personalities—and as dead as the last emperor's palaces seemed, so was this army about to jerk into life and march off to fresh glory.

Our driver and interpreter drove us into remote villages, where we caused great hilarity to all—especially the children. Probably they had never seen such odd foreign devils before. We were invited into one small cottage, where a toothless old woman took Jennifer's hand and dragged her into her back room to see a washing machine, still in its plastic wrappings, waiting for the arrival of electricity—not to mention running water. We were more impressed by her high brick bed atop a stove, to keep her from freezing to death in winter.

Back in Boston, where we had been for four years, Liberty asked me to relocate to Europe to open offices as Managing Director of Liberty Financial International. They asked me to pick a town, but this was not easy. Obviously London, Paris, Rome, or Madrid would have been great, but I chose Brussels because of its proximity to major European capitals.

In the midst of this relocation, Credit Suisse approached me through some head-hunters. Three marathon interviews in Zurich followed, ending with Credit Suisse asking me to move to Hong Kong and be in charge of promoting their funds throughout South East Asia. My experience in this particular financial sector, plus the fact that I had a Hong Kong residence permit due to my birth in Hong Kong, persuaded them that I was "their man." Although the offer was excellent, Jennifer and I decided it would be good to be back in Europe—and after all, I was quite happy with Liberty Financial.

79

BELGIUM

In May, 1992, we moved into a duplex penthouse with a large roof garden overlooking le rond-point Montgomery on the boulevard Saint Michel in Brussels. Finally we unpacked all our furniture, carpets, and pictures, which had been stored in Munich for the past eight years. We had quite forgotten how much we had.

That summer, Nick and Mark both graduated—Nick with a bachelor's degree from Northeastern University, and Mark with a master's from Georgia Tech. Now their U.S. student visas had expired, and they both flew to Brussels, where their mother and I were delighted to have them live with us whilst they looked for jobs. John had graduated from the European Business School in London some time ago, and had worked first in Hong Kong and now in Shanghai for Jebsen & Co. He joined us during his home leaves to make our lives complete, then Jennifer's cup ran over. In the Brussels Rotary Club, we made new friends, I found a good gym, and Jennifer joined French and English book clubs plus a Mah-jongg circle, thanks to Lori Jessen, who had lived in Brussels for many years and became her great friend.

The Eurostar high-speed railway meant that we could pop over to London for the weekend, to Paris for the day if one felt like it. Le Hague, with its marvellous art galleries, was only a couple of hours away also.

My cousin Bertram Rickmers invited Jennifer and me to Antwerp for the launch of the *Rickmers Antwerp*, and when his mother, Christa, learnt that I was writing a family memoir, she had long chats with Jennifer about the early days of her marriage.

Left: Elizabeth in hall; Above: Susan on roof garden

Her first home had been in the middle of the almost bomb-flattened shipyard in Bremerhaven. With fond remembrance, she had called her little home "the barracks." By the time my cousins Etha and Bertram arrived, Christa had created a garden, and when the children were out on the grass in their prams, they would watch the swaying cranes overhead as if they were giant nursery mobiles, and the endless racket of hammering in the shipyard would rock them to sleep better than any lullaby. Today both Bertram and his brother Erck run successful shipping companies, with enormous vessels sailing the oceans of the world. Their grandfather would be proud.

In 2004, in the Hanjin Shipyards in South Korea, Jennifer became the godmother of the *Jennifer Rickmers*, a 70,000-ton containership (now sailing under the charter name *Maersk Durban*), a source of great pride for her.

She carried her ceremonial axe (used to cut the rope and release the christening champagne) through several airports on our way home and, although my nail scissors were confiscated, no security check noticed it!

In Brussels, from 1993-99, my business travel was still pretty heavy, but more or less limited to Europe, the Middle East, and Boston. We did, however, have a fascinating drive through Malaysia by car with John, from Singapore to Malacca, Kuala Lumpur, the Boh tea plantations in the Cameron Highlands, and on to Penang, where we stayed in the Eastern and Oriental Hotel, where Somerset Maugham wrote some of his tales.

Once I broke a business trip to stay with John in Thailand, and once Jennifer and her sister Elizabeth stayed with him. As usual he organised great itineraries for us. He took *me* to Phuket, but Elizabeth and Jennifer had a more cultural tour—the hill villages in the Golden Triangle, Chiang Mai and Sukhothai, celadon potters, monasteries, and silk farms. I rode on an elephant.

Flower carpet on the Grand Place in Brussels

Mark was now based in Munich, working for Philip Morris, where we visited him. Once he invited us to Orléans, which we used as a base to visit those wonderful chateaux on the Loire.

Nick left Brussels for London to work for a major head-hunter and met a lovely Brazilian girl, Silvana, whom we also immediately fell for. After all the somewhat unusual girls he had brought home, he astonished us by saying, "It's so nice to go out with a girl who knows how to use a knife and fork properly." This from our rebel Nick! Wonders will never cease.

In 1995, Nick and Silvana were married in a London Registry Office, but in August of the following year, he went to Brazil with Silvana for her sister's wedding in the cathedral of Salvador de Bahia, and was so carried away by the ceremony that he wanted one too. Silvana's mother, exhausted by this wedding, begged them to wait a year.

But by the end of the summer of 1996, Nick started to feel ill. He lost all his energy and *joie de vivre* and a great deal of weight. Having been examined by several British doctors, all of whom confirmed that there was nothing wrong with him, Nick finally decided, just before Christmas, to consult a renowned Harley Street specialist.

This famous doctor was about to leave for Scotland and obviously in a hurry. "Bit of a hypochondriac, are we?" was his diagnosis. He gave Nick a bottle of heavy codeine-morphine tablets for his pain and told him to come back after the holidays.

Unfortunately, these holidays were to be Nick's last.

When he arrived from London with Silvana, we were shocked to see how very pale and thin he was, but he put on a brave front and we had a traditional, if rather low-key, Christmas. By Dec. 30, Nick complained of a strange tingling in his legs, by late afternoon he had no more feeling in them, and the following morning he was paralysed from the waist down.

Top: Jennifer's 60th;
Left: Nick's Silvana;
Right: Nick in Denmark

Family Rickmers, 1967

Left: Jennifer with Elisabeth Prinzessin von Sachsen, Bertram, and other guests; Above: christening the Jennifer Rickmers.

Rushed to Saint Luc, Brussels' university hospital, Nick was given an MRI. He was admitted to the Hôpital Saint Jean, where he underwent a three-hour spinal operation on New Year's Eve. The magnetic images had shown that there was a tumour on his spine. It was cancerous. Subsequently his whole body was found to be riddled with an extremely aggressive non-Hodgkin's Lymphoma.

Alerted to the crisis, John arrived from China early in the morning of Jan. 1. Silvana and Jennifer had spent the night with Nick in the intensive care unit, and were sitting, stunned, in the hospital lobby when I arrived from the airport with Mark and John. Now a calvary began for the whole family (including faithful Elizabeth—who, as always, came to her sister's rescue), which was to continue at Nick's bedside through all the months to come.

There were months when John flew in from Asia every few weeks and Mark came home every weekend, months full of wild hopes which turned out to be false,

Maersk Line photo archives

Left: Dinner at Michael and Désirée's in Hong Kong; Rigtht with Désirée in Hong Kong

months when we fought against despair, months of radio therapy, more operations and chemotherapy—until Nick's poor wasted body could take no more.

He was to battle in that clinic for over six months, never to leave it. His optimism stayed with him, and he refused to talk with us about any outcome other than recovery. His long, lonely nights of darkness he preferred to keep to himself—even when both religious and secular counsellors, came to his aid. As his brother John said: "Doubt is acceptable; certainty is not."

Despite the dedicated care of a fantastic team of oncologists, surgeons, and nurses, Nick died in our arms exactly one month before his thirty-fourth birthday. With the whole world seeming empty, we scattered his ashes in the woods he loved.

To Nick—
The part of you that travels on,
I'll not hold back, with tears, with grief.
I will not call out through the dark,
"Come back!" to make my life complete.
But all the years I shared with you,
the good, the happy, sad, the true,
all these are mine and these I'll keep.
This part of you is part of me
and so won't go before I do.

80

WE LEARN HOW TO GO ON

The horror of watching a cherished son die cannot be described. It goes against nature. Parents are meant to die before their children. Life for Jennifer and me has never been the same—and never will be—but we have to remember that John and Mark lost their beloved brother and Silvana her Prince Charming.

Everyone tried to pick up where his life had been put on hold.

Silvana returned to her family in Brazil and went back to University. She continues to turn down all suitors, unable to forget Nick.

Liberty Financial was acquired by Fleet Bank, Boston, which subsequently was bought by Bank of America. The European office was closed and thus I more or less retired.

Ultimately Jennifer and I found escape from our grief through John and Mark and their families.

In November, 1999, John married Karen in New York in the Central Park Boat House. She is the ideal partner for him and a wonderful mother. She gave up a glamorous and successful career with Creative Artists Agency, one of the biggest casting agencies in Los Angeles, when she left to join John in rainy Frankfurt. Karen and John have given us three beautiful grandchildren—Sophie, Oliver, and Antonio. They live in Singapore, where John is building the Asian arm to the already successful company he and his partner created in Germany. They have offices in Europe and Asia. He knows how proud we are of him.

Top left: John and Karen's wedding in New York; with Billy Crudup; Top right: Nick and Silvana's wedding in London; Right: Mark and Gitte's wedding in Denmark

In 2002, Mark married Gitte on her Danish island home of Falster. They now live in Farnham with their three lovely children, Emma, Sebastian, and little Millie. Gitte makes Mark very happy and is an excellent, loving mother and wife. Mark is Symantec's Head of Audit for Europe, the Middle East, and Africa. He too knows how proud we are of him.

It may be a cliché, but children and grandchildren are the essence of life. Soon Jennifer and I will have been married for fifty years, and to be surrounded by our two sons, three daughters-in-law, and six grandchildren is the only gift we want for our Golden Wedding Anniversary. It goes without saying that Nick will be there with us too, as he always is.

Jennifer and I now live in southern Spain, enjoying the sun and the slow pace of life. Spain has changed, but in Andalucia, *mañana* is still *mañana*. Each year we visit our children and count the days until they all come to us. After so many moves, we hope not to have to do so again, but we have learnt never to make plans. Who knows where our caravan will travel next—but for as long as we are together, it doesn't really matter.

Above: Our Singapore family: Oliver, Karen, Sophie, John, and Antonio;
Right: Emma and Sebastian

Above: Millie's Christening—Danish Church London, 2008; Below: Gitte and little Millie

The four Jessens—clockwise: John, me, Nick, Mark

New Year's Eve 2006 in Singapore

EPILOGUE

Many years ago, my son John told me a tale. Two Asian monks had been walking for weeks towards a shrine. On their way, they came to a river where a woman waited, unable to cross. The younger monk offered to carry her, whilst his companion hissed in his ear that it was a sin to touch a woman. The young monk, disregarding this, carried the woman to the other bank, where she thanked him and went on her way. The two men continued in silence until nightfall, when they lay down to rest.

"You have committed a grave sin," grumbled the elder as he stared crossly up at the night sky.

The younger smiled quietly. "I set that woman down hours ago. You are still carrying her."

As an analogy of how one can carry old resentments throughout one's life, this is a fine example. If writing these memoirs began as an effort to make some sense for my sons of my rather eventful life, they have had the unexpected benefit of allowing me to set down the burden of many disappointments, which I have carried for far too long. Now I can see how little they matter.

At the end of my seventies, the ups and downs of my business life have lost their importance, allowing me to realise at last that the essentials without which I could not live are, and have always been, my Jennifer and my sons. On these four pillars I rely for all that is important to me, and I thank them for their loyalty, understanding and love.

I cannot wish more for John and Mark than that they, in turn, will understand that their family matters above all else. May they be as blessed as I have been.

Andalucia, 2008

JENNIFER'S CODA

John ended his book with two old dears walking hand-in-hand toward the sunset to the sound of celestial choirs; pure 1950s' Hollywood. There has, however, been a slight hiccup in this moving scenario.

On Aug. 13, 2008, after another wonderful holiday in Singapore (our third in eighteen months), John and I flew to Frankfurt to spend the night before continuing down to Malaga. That one night in Germany was to stretch to seventy-one.

In the airport hotel, John became ill. He was in great pain and his abdomen ballooned up alarmingly. Despite his protests, I called for an ambulance, and with frightening speed we were whisked to the Städtische Kliniken Frankfurt Höchst. He was wheeled away from me into the x-ray department, and I was told to sit and wait. After half an hour I became increasingly anxious and returned to a now-deserted area. I ran up and down the night corridors calling for help in my atrocious German. Eventually a junior nurse appeared, and when I asked her if my husband was dead, my worst nightmare, she replied laconically: "*Noch nicht*"—not yet.

I hardly dared to hope but I knew I had to call our sons. To add to my distress, I had left my wallet and cell phone in the hotel, the name of which I could not even remember. Only thanks to a lonely night telephonist was I able to ring my sister Elizabeth, whose number I knew by heart. She promised to contact John and Mark and rang off with both of us in tears.

Someone took me up to the visitors' waiting room in the intensive care unit, where a couple of nurses bundled me up in blankets and gave me sweet tea to drink. Eventually a doctor arrived to give me some explanations.

John was still talking when he left the MRI unit, but almost immediately his torn abdominal aorta ruptured, causing him to "crash" and his heart to stop. A senior anaesthetist happened to be passing by and immediately resuscitated John. Miracle number one.

He was rushed to theatre, where the chief surgeon and specialist in aneurysms was still in scrubs at 10 p.m. Miracle number two.

Chefarzt (head physician) Professor Dr. Ernst and his team worked on John for over five hours, their task of stopping the stream of blood from his ruptured aorta complicated by the fact that the haemorrhaging was so violent, nine litres of blood had to be transfused. John was now in intensive care, and I would be able to see him in the morning. The prognosis was very poor.

I spent the rest of that agonising night in a chair, and in the early morning was taken to see John. He was in an induced coma, on full life support, and connected to three tall banks of drips and machines. A terrifying sight. A nurse came to tell me that someone was waiting to see me. Who on earth could it be? I nearly did not leave John, but the nurse insisted. What a joy it was to see Hanna, a friend alerted by my daughter-in-law Karen in Singapore, who had come to see if I needed anything. I hugged her for her kindness and returned to John feeling a little less abandoned.

Within hours, Mark flew in from London, and that afternoon John arrived. He had been contacted in the airport in Hong Kong, about to fly home to Singapore. He immediately changed his flight and arrived, frozen like me, in tropical clothes. Fortunately both sons are fluent in German and one of the doctors was Chilean, so we could all follow in shocked silence as grave, white-coated men explained the seriousness of the situation to us. They gave John a one-percent chance of survival—and probably not even that, given his age. As they left us, we three sat around John's bed, stunned. There was nothing we could do but pray. Including the flight from Singapore, I was to stay awake for three days and two nights—but sleep, naturally, was the last thing on my mind.

All the time John was kept in a coma, his nurses washed and shaved him daily, combed his hair and even his eyebrows. We shared their vigil and tried to understand what all the machines were telling us. We held his hands and knees and rubbed his feet. We talked to him in relays, and once in a while I would sing softly in his ear. This, incidentally, is the only thing he remembers. His situation fluctuated daily, and with it our hopes and fears. He was to have a total of five operations as complications arose, and it remained impossible to close his eleven-inch open wound. Eventually, after nine days, he was awake enough to recognise us. For short periods he was taken off the hated respirator and began to talk. Most of it was pretty wild, as during his days and nights of coma he had vivid dreams which he could not distinguish from reality. He was convinced that the nurses' office was a bar where "Guys queue up for Jack Daniels. Give me my credit cards. I want some too." He thought he was on a cruise and asked the doctors if they liked life at sea. Then the liner became a prison ship, probably because he had to have restraints on his arms to stop him from pulling out all his wires and tubes. Nevertheless, he recognised us, which gave Mark the confidence to return to his young family and job.

When John developed pneumonia, John Jr. and I again feared the worst, but then came an improvement, and John felt he could return to Singapore, having been at his father's side for two weeks. I do not know what I should have done without our sons. Apart from keeping my spirits up and never allowing me to despair, they sorted out practicalities, such as finding a hotel close by, having our bags traced and sent there, taking me to buy warm clothes, arranging for money transfers, and dealing with the health insurance people—all this whilst coping with the depths of their own grief. I shall be forever grateful to them.

When both had to leave, my sister Elizabeth came to support me. She arrived to find John in a very bad way, as his pneumonia had returned, this time a particularly nasty atypical case which responded to nothing. He was again unconscious and on life support. Weird-looking mad scientist types arrived, took swabs, and came back with an anti-mycotic, which eventually killed the fungus in the lung—and another crisis was overcome. Elizabeth stayed for two weeks and then was relayed by my sister Susan. Thank heavens for family. When Susan had to leave, Mark came back, and so I was hardly alone.

Finally, after seventy long days, John was discharged. He has no memory of those dreadful first weeks—and indeed is rather upset to have missed out on his starring role. He was to become known throughout that huge hospital as "das Wunderkind," and was interviewed in the local papers as a phenomenon. I cannot praise highly enough the dedicated care, expertise, and compassion shown by the incredible ICU team. Against all odds, they pulled John through and our special thanks go to Professor Ernst as well as Chef and Oberärzte Drs. Sierra and Lindenberger, who never gave up hope even in the darkest days. All three were John's guardian angels. Indeed Désirée Jebsen wrote, "*Es muss ja nur von Schutzengeln gewimmelt haben*"—There must have been a swarm of guardian angels. How right she was. Miracle number three.

Now in November, 2008, John and I are back in Andalucia. John improves daily. His main drawback is his left foot, which is paralysed after so many months in bed. He is having therapy and hopes to be able to throw his stick and leg-brace away just as soon as I stop looking. He is rather sad that his days of victory in Abdominal Beauty Contests are over, but that is a small price to pay. A few days ago, John Jr. flew out from Singapore to see how his father is getting along, so we continue to be surrounded by love—the best medicine in the world.

We fully intend to have many more happy years watching our grandchildren grow up, and John has promised not to give me any more reasons to mutter,

Whatever next?

Ingram Content Group UK Ltd.
Milton Keynes UK
UKHW050839140623
423332UK00007B/222

9 781608 602827